W9-DCF-773

JOURNAL FOR THE STUDY OF THE NEW TESTAMENT
SUPPLEMENT SERIES
280

Editor
Mark Goodacre

Cohesion and Structure in the Pastoral Epistles

Ray Van Neste

T & T CLARK INTERNATIONAL
A Continuum imprint
LONDON • NEW YORK

Copyright © 2004 T&T Clark International
A Continuum imprint

Published by T&T Clark International
an imprint of Continuum

The Tower Building,
11 York Road,
London SE1 7NX

15 East 26th Street,
Suite 1703,
New York, NY 10010

www.tandtclark.com

British Library Cataloguing-in-Publication Data
A catalogue record for this book is available from the British Library

Typeset by Tradespools, Frome, Somerset
Printed on acid-free paper in Great Britain by Antony Rowe Ltd, Chippenham, Wilts.

ISBN 0-567-08337-3

To Tammie,
whose frugality, strength, love, and spirit of adventure
ensured that this was not simply a time to endure
but an experience to cherish.

CONTENTS

ACKNOWLEDGMENTS

To acknowledge adequately my indebtedness to others and to record the many ways I have been aided in this project would require an even lengthier tome than the current one. All that can be done here is to list some of those who have made this effort possible. Financial support came from the Southern Baptist Foundation and Ola Mae Van Neste, my grandmother, who paid for our second year in Aberdeen. Maxine Thornton, my mother-in-law, also provided financial support. Our third year was graciously financed by friends in the local churches including Paul Mitchell (who initially broached the idea of provision for the third year), Chris and Anne Gault, Foster and Fiona Gault, Dr. Mark and Norma Donaldson, Mr. and Mrs. James Stephen, Robert and Hazel Bruce, Scobere Company, David and Katrina Logan, Lionel and Hazel Craze, and several others including anonymous gifts. Gene and Lynda Kay Wilson also helped with the third year and provided us with a car for our three years and much more. We received so much from the friendships and opportunities to minister among several local churches especially International Baptist Church, Peterhead Baptist Church, Gerard Street Baptist Church, Stonehaven Baptist Church, and Hebron Evangelical Fellowship. In addition to those individuals just mentioned, others from these churches need to be specifically mentioned including Thomas and Suzanne Stephens and girls, Mr. and Mrs. Ernest Buchan, Roy and Anne Bollerwell, Donald and Carol Campbell, James and Linda Strachan, Bruce and Arlene McLeod, Bruce and Paula Leggett, Ian and Jane McDonald, Willie and Kinsey Taylor, Jack and Mabel Girdwood, Steve and Jane Williams, and Matthew (our pastor) and Anne Henderson. Fellowship Baptist Church, Kenosha, WI, also encouraged and helped us. The generous Terminal Degree Grant from Union University covered the final costs for finishing up the thesis and traveling back for the viva. Cornerstone Community Church and my fellow elders, Lee Tankersley and Nathan Young have provided much prayer and encouragement.

My supervisor, Prof. Howard Marshall, deserves much gratitude for his careful, patient help throughout this research. The opportunity to have worked with him is a reward in itself.

I am also deeply indebted to the camaraderie, fellowship, and encouragement found among several of my fellow students at the University of Aberdeen and their families including: Dr. James and Kerstin Hering, Dr. Steve and Lisa Chang, David Riker, Alec Warren, Ashish Naidu, John Heglie, Dr. Jason and Kimberly Lee, Drs. Keith and Coreen Bodner, Dr. David Hoffeditz, Brian Johnson, Brian and Valerie Abasciano. James Hering has been to me the friend closer than a brother.

Student workers Jimmy Duke, Andy McNutt, Adam McCollum, and Matt Crawford have helped greatly with tracking down references and helping me reset Greek fonts. My colleague, Brian Denker, also gave invaluable assistance in compiling the indices.

Lastly, my family deserves the most profound gratitude. My four young boys, Nathan, Matthew, Jonathan, and Benjamin, have provided much enjoyment and balance in the process. Finally, my wife, Tammie, has been my co-laborer working *at least* as hard at home as I was at the university in order to make this work. In so doing, her frugality, strength, love, and spirit of adventure ensured that this was not simply a time to endure but an experience to cherish. It is to her that this work is dedicated.

'O to grace how great a debtor, daily I'm constrained to be'

Conventions and Abbreviations

ABD	David Noel Freedman (ed.), *The Anchor Bible Dictionary* (New York: Doubleday, 1992)
AnBib	Analecta biblica
ANRW	Hildegard Temporini and Wolfgang Haase (eds.), *Aufstieg und Niedergang der römischen Welt: Geschichte und Kultur Roms im Spiegel der neueren Forschung* (Berlin: W. de Gruyter, 1972–)
ATR	*Anglican Theological Review*
AUSS	*Andrews University Seminary Studies*
BAGD	Walter Bauer, William F. Arndt, F. William Gingrich, and Frederick W. Danker, *A Greek–English Lexicon of the New Testament and Other Early Christian Literature* (Chicago: University of Chicago Press; 2nd edn, 1958)
BDF	Friedrich Blass, A. Debrunner and Robert W. Funk, *A Greek Grammar of the New Testament and Other Early Christian Literature* (Cambridge: Cambridge University Press, 1961)
BJRL	*Bulletin of the John Rylands University Library of Manchester*
BSac	*Bibliotheca Sacra*
BT	*The Bible Translator*
BTB	*Biblical Theology Bulletin*
BZ	Biblische Zeitschrift
BZNW	Beihefte zur Zeitscrift für die Neutestamentliche Wissenschaft
CBQ	*Catholic Biblical Quarterly*
ClQ	*Classical Quarterly*
ConBNT	Coniectanea biblica, New Testament
CTR	*Criswell Theological Review*
EBib	Etudes bibliques
EDNT	Horst Balz and Gerhard Sneider (eds.), *Exegetical Dictionary of the New Testament* (Grand Rapids: Eerdmans 1990–93)

EKKNT	Evangelisch-Katholischer Kommentar zum Neuen Testament
EvQ	*Evangelical Quarterly*
EvT	*Evangelische Theologie*
ExpTim	*Expository Times*
FN	*Filología neotestamentaria*
FOTL	The Forms of the Old Testament Literature
FRLANT	Forschungen zur Religion und Literatur des Alten und Neuen Testaments
GEP	Gordon Fee, *God's Empowering Presence: The Holy Spirit in the Letters of Paul* (Peabody, MA: Hendrickson, 1994).
HTR	*Harvard Theological Review*
HUT	Hermeneutische Untersuchungen zur Theologie
ICC	International Critical Commentary
JBL	*Journal of Biblical Literature*
JETS	*Journal of the Evangelical Theological Society*
JR	*Journal of Religion*
JSNT	*Journal for the Study of the New Testament*
JSNTSup	*Journal for the Study of the New Testament*, Supplement Series
JSOT	*Journal for the Study of the Old Testament*
JSOTSup	*Journal for the Study of the Old Testament*, Supplement Series
JTS	*Journal of Theological Studies*
LCC	Library of Christian Classics
LCL	Loeb Classical Library
LSJ	H.G. Liddell, Robert Scott and H. Stuart Jones, *Greek–English Lexicon* (Oxford: Clarendon Press; 9th edn, 1968)
LTP	*Laval théologique et philosophique*
NICNT	New International Commentary on the New Testament
NICOT	New International Commentary on the Old Testament
NIDOTE	Willem A. VanGemeren (ed.), *New International Dictionary of Old Testament Theology and Exegesis* (5 vols.; Grand Rapids: Zondervan, 1997)
NIDNTT	Colin Brown (ed.), *The New International Dictionary of New Testament Theology* (3 vols.; Exeter: Paternoster Press, 1975)
NIGTC	The New International Greek Testament Commentary
NovT	*Novum Testamentum*
NovTSup	*Novum Testamentum*, Supplements
NTG	New Testament Guides
NTL	New Testament Library
NTS	*New Testament Studies*
NTTS	New Testament Tools and Studies
OCD	*Oxford Classical Dictionary*

RNT	Regensburger Neues Testament
RSR	Recherches de science religieuse
RTR	*Reformed Theological Review*
SBL	Society of Biblical Literature
SBLASP	SBL Abstracts and Seminar Papers
SBLDS	SBL Dissertation Series
SBLSBS	SBL Sources for Biblical Study
SBT	Studies in Biblical Theology
SJT	*Scottish Journal of Theology*
SNTG	Studies in New Testament Greek
SNTSMS	Society for New Testament Studies Monograph Series
SNTU	Studien zum Neuen Testament und seiner Umwelt
SUNT	Studien zur Umwelt des Neuen Testaments
TDNT	Gerhard Kittel and Gerhard Friedrich (eds.), *Theological Dictionary of the New Testament* (trans. Geoffrey W. Bromiley; 10 vols.; Grand Rapids: Eerdmans, 1964–)
TNTC	Tyndale New Testament Commentaries
TOTC	Tyndale Old Testament Commentaries
TrinJ	*Trinidad Journal of New Testament Studies*
TynBul	*Tyndale Bulletin*
TZ	*Theologische Zeitschrift*
UBS	*The Greek New Testament* (Stuttgart: United Bible Society, 1993)
WBC	Word Biblical Commentary
WTJ	*Westminster Theological Journal*
WUNT	Wissenschaftliche Untersuchungen zum Neuen Testament
ZNW	*Zeitschrift für die neutestamentliche Wissenschaft*
ZWT	*Zeitschrift für wissenschaftliche Theologie*

INTRODUCTION

Until recently one of the widely accepted tenets of modern scholarship regarding the Pastoral Epistles was that they lacked any significant, careful order or structure. Rather, it was held, these letters are composed of various different literary forms which have been combined in a less than artistic form. This can be illustrated by a few representative quotations from the commentaries:

> 'There is no sustained thought beyond the limits of the separate paragraphs; from paragraph to paragraph – and sometimes even within paragraphs (e.g., 1 Tim 2:8ff) – the topic changes without preparation and sometimes apparently without motive.'[1]
> 'There is a lack of studied order, some subjects being treated more than once in the same letter without apparent premeditation ... These letters are, therefore, far removed from literary exercises.'[2]
> 'The Pastorals are made up of a miscellaneous collection of material. They have no unifying theme; there is no development of thought.'[3]

Indeed, Lewis Donelson, writing in 1986, could even state, 'Commentators on the Pastorals simply do not detect any logical interplay among the types of literary material,'[4] and Jeffrey Reed, writing even more recently, refers to the 'abusive estimation that the PE are, to put it bluntly, incoherent.'[5] Furthermore, as the quotations above show, this negative view of the Pastorals was found among supporters of Pauline authorship (e.g. Guthrie) as well as those who argue against Pauline authorship (e.g. Hanson). It was, in fact, this perceived lack of connection between various portions of the letters which provided grounds for the suggestion that the

---

1. Easton 1947: 14.
2. Guthrie 1990: 18.
3. Hanson 1982: 42.
4. Donelson 1986: 67. This was probably overstated but does illustrate the general situation in the study of the Pastoral Epistles.
5. Reed 1993b: 91.

letters were built on short genuine notes from Paul.[6] Thus, while opinions varied concerning how severe was this lack of order, that there was such a lack was hardly questioned.

However, this consensus began to be challenged in the 1970s with Jukka Thurén's article which argued for a coherent structure in 1 Timothy 6.3–21 and Robert Karris' unpublished (though often cited) dissertation which examined possible relations between the various traditional materials within the Pastoral Epistles.[7] The floodgates opened in the 1980s with the appearance of four monographs which dealt with the coherence of the Pastorals.[8] D. C. Verner argued that the use of household codes in the Pastorals revealed a clear and consistent social setting for all three letters and that the letters united around the purpose statement of 1 Timothy 3.14–16.[9] L. R. Donelson argued that Aristotelian ethical logic provided the way to understand the connections between the various units within the Pastorals.[10] B. Fiore found coherence in the use of personal example in the Pastorals on parallel with their use in the Socratic epistles.[11] P. H. Towner demonstrated the coherence of the theological message of the letters, with the message of salvation at its core.[12] While these studies differed from each other and received their critiques, the overall coherence of the Pastorals was largely accepted. Indeed, writing after the completion of his monograph, Donelson stated,

> There is a change of mood in scholarship on the Pastoral Epistles. No longer do scholars simply assume, as they did for several generations, that these letters are awkward combinations of diverse literary forms.[13]

Towner, in 1995, could write of a new consensus marked by, among other things, the fact that 'the PE are recognised as presenting a coherent theological and ethical argument to a real church or churches somewhere in time.'[14] This consensus has been affirmed and furthered by articles by

---

6. Cf. James Moffatt, 'The more or less loose connection of the three epistles and the frequent abruptness or awkwardness of transition between successive passages, naturally suggest a recourse in the first instance to the hypothesis of transposition or redaction' (Moffatt 1918: 402). Also Harrison 1921; Falconer 1937: 13–17.

7. Thurén 1970; Karris 1971.

8. Gordon Fee's commentary (1988) should also probably be mentioned as he devoted significant space to arguing for a a real-life situation which pulled together the different parts of each letter.

9. Verner 1983.

10. Donelson 1986.

11. Fiore 1986.

12. Towner 1989.

13. Donelson 1988: 108.

14. Towner 1995: 288.

P. Bush, J. T. Reed, and R. J. Gibson on the structure of 1 Timothy,[15] articles by C. J. Classen and E. Wendland on the structure of Titus,[16] and the significant interest in the structure of the letters in the commentaries by Roloff,[17] Quinn,[18] Mounce,[19] and especially Marshall, who gives more attention specifically to structure than any other commentary.[20] Also, more recent theses and monographs have further pursued theological coherence in the Pastoral Epistles.[21] Thus, Marshall can state:

> There is a growing body of evidence that the Pastoral Epistles are not a conglomerate of miscellaneous ideas roughly thrown together with no clear plan, purpose or structure. On the contrary, they demonstrate signs of a coherent structure and of theological competence.[22]

While this more positive opinion of the Pastorals advances, however, not all have been convinced. Indeed, in a recent review of Marshall's commentary, C. K. Barrett indicated that he remains unconvinced of the level of coherence which Marshall argues.[23] Furthermore, in 1997 Cambridge University Press published James D. Miller's *The Pastoral Letters as Composite Documents*, probably the most thoroughgoing argument to date for incoherence in the Pastorals.[24] Miller argues that Hanson (just quoted above) allowed for too much coherence because he allowed for a single author. Miller states, 'Organization and development of thought are expected from an author, but the Pastorals are characterized by a remarkable lack of both.'[25] Thus, Miller argues that the connections between paragraphs, and even sentences and phrases, are so poor that no single mind could be responsible for such a 'disorganized collage.' Rather, the Pastorals are composite documents which began as short genuine notes from Paul but were enlarged over time by the addition of other, disparate materials from Christian, Jewish and pagan sources.

---

15. Bush 1990; Reed 1992; 1993a; 1993b; Gibson 1996.
16. Classen 1997; Wendland 1999.
17. Roloff 1988.
18. Quinn 1990; Quinn and Wacker 2000.
19. Mounce 2000.
20. Marshall 1999. In his review of Marshall's commentary (*JTS* 52.2 [2001]), C. K. Barrett says Marshall's section on genre and structure 'may well be regarded as the most original part of the commentary' (825).
21. E.g. Lau 1996; Stettler 1998; Couser 1992.
22. Marshall 1994: 171.
23. Barrett, review of I. H. Marshall, *A Critical and Exegetical Commentary on the Pastoral Epistles*, in *JTS* 52.2 (2001): 825. Barrett writes, 'It may be that he is sometimes too ready to defend the logical argument of the epistles.' This is not a stark criticism but is evidence that the opinion of cohesiveness has not yet gained full acceptance.
24. Miller 1997.
25. Miller 1997: 139.

This hypothesis, according to Miller, accounts for the impression that 'the letters have no driving concern, no consistent focus of interest; instead they read like an anthology of traditions, many arranged mechanically together by topic, some simply juxtaposed.'[26] Therefore, Miller's method is to examine each letter unit by unit and even sentence by sentence demonstrating the lack of connection between units and sentences.

Some of Miller's complaints against the Pastorals have been answered by the works just mentioned, as he acknowledges in his appendix.[27] However, Miller's challenge shows there is more work to be done. Miller works straight through each of the letters arguing paragraph by paragraph (and in some places phrase by phrase) for discontinuity and incoherence. The arguments for coherence so far have focused on the 'big picture', i.e. the theology behind the letters or the social setting behind the letters. These studies are important and begin to form the basis for a coherent view of the Pastorals. However, none of them actually traces the movement of the language through each letter asking how each sentence or paragraph connects to the next or how the whole letter holds together linguistically. Indeed, they all focus on certain portions of the letters (conceived of as a group), rather than on the entirety of each individual letter. What is needed is a literary or linguistic approach which analyzes the devices of language that create links between units of a discourse. This would be an analysis of what Jeffrey Reed calls 'linguistic cohesiveness,' a term he has chosen to emphasize that what is being examined is the way in which language is used to create cohesiveness.[28]

Donelson comes close to this in his effort to demonstrate the logic of the argumentation in the Pastorals. However, he actually focuses on the logic within paragraphs and says very little about how the different paragraphs relate.[29] He also only deals with a few selected portions of the Pastorals. Towner and Lau give significant attention to cohesion arguing strongly for the coherence of certain paragraphs.[30] However, the cohesion of the paragraphs into larger sections does not fall within the scope of their work. Thus, the tasks of tracing the connections both within and between

26. Miller 1997: 138. See similar statements, pp. 9, 11, 13, 17, 59–60, 80, 82, 86, 91, 100, 101, 129, 130, 132, 135, 139.

27. Cf. Miller 1997: 167. Miller refers to Verner, Fiore and Donelson.

28. Reed 1999a: 29.

29. David L. Balch, review of *Pseudepigraphy and Ethical Argument in the Pastoral Epistles*, by Donelson, in *JR* 69 (April 1989): 236, 'Donelson uses much less space (pp. 109–13) arguing his thesis that a similar coherence exists among the larger sections of the argument in the Pastorals, and he is correspondingly less persuasive.'

30. The arguments of Lau and Towner and other articles will be taken up in the sections of the following chapters that deal with these specific portions of the letters.

paragraphs in each letter and of noting the overarching coherence of each letter remain to be done.[31]

This thesis, then, will seek to analyze the way in which language is used to create connections within 1 Timothy, 2 Timothy, and Titus. In doing so, it is expected that this work will add to the previous work done on the coherence of the Pastorals. The work will respond to Miller, but move beyond his challenges to an attempt to see what sort of literary structure might be present. Indeed, little work has been done specifically on the structure of these letters. G. Couser in a recent article, speaking specifically of 1 Timothy, states, 'Little direct work has been done on the structure of the book [1 Timothy] as a whole ... '[32] The same could be said of 2 Timothy and Titus. Furthermore, Howard Marshall has written, 'A comparative study of commentaries on the PE will quickly reveal that there is a remarkable lack of unanimity on the question of the structure of the letters.'[33]

If significant levels of coherence are found at the linguistic level, this will provide further and significant support for the previous arguments for coherence. This investigation will also provide further insight on how each letter as a whole 'works,' i.e. how each paragraph connects to others and how these paragraphs unite to form a discourse. This will be the most thorough analysis of the structure of these letters to date. Therefore, the analysis should help to arbitrate between the different analyses of the letters offered in briefer format by some commentaries and monographs. If there is coherence at this level, this study should provide a basis for further exploration of the meaning of these letters as the different sections are seen in light of the whole.

31.   Davies' assessment of Donelson's work is simply overstated: 'The study is successful in elucidating the coherence of the final form of each of the Pastoral epistles' (Davies 1996: 37).

32.   Couser 2000: 272.

33.   Marshall 1997: 18.

Chapter 1

Methodology

Approach

In order to examine the cohesiveness of the Pastoral Epistles, this study will examine each letter individually. The primary interest will not be the interrelation of the letters with each other or with other letters attributed to Paul but how each letter as a distinct discourse coheres or fails to cohere. As mentioned in the introduction, this will be an advance in the analysis of the coherence of the Pastorals since the previous monographs which argued for coherence dealt with the Pastoral Epistles as a corpus.

This will, then, be a detailed analysis of the use of language within each letter to bind together the various statements which make up the discourse. Following James Muilenberg, widely hailed as the initiator of modern rhetorical and literary analysis,[1] we will first seek to determine the boundaries of each literary unit and then examine the ways in which the different units relate to each other.[2] The analysis will take up each letter in turn, and in the analysis of each letter three basic steps will be involved: (1) identification of the boundaries of the basic communicative units (paragraphs), (2) examination of the cohesion within each unit, (3) examination of cohesion between units. Steps 1 and 2 will be found in the first chapter dealing with each letter and step 3 will be found in the second chapter dealing with each letter.

A further note on terminology may be helpful. Throughout this work, the word 'unit' will be used to refer to the basic unit of a discourse, i.e. a paragraph. The word 'section' will be used to refer to a larger section of discourse made up of two or more 'units.' In other works these terms can

---

1. Cf. Kern 1998: 44; Kennedy 1984: 4; Wuellner 1987: 448–63; Robbins and Patton 1980: 327. Muilenberg's rhetorical analysis was not concerned with the categories of classical rhetoric (see the article in note 2).

2. Muilenburg 1969: 1–18; repr. in *Beyond Form Criticism: Essays in Old Testament Literary Criticism*, ed. Paul R. House (Winona Lake, IN: Eisenbrauns, 1992), 46–69. For a recent work following this approach and expounding similar methodology, see Dorsey 1999.

be found used interchangeably, so for the sake of clarity they will be used as technical terms.

No position on the authorship of the Pastorals is taken in this study. The concern here is strictly how the text operates. Thus the names 'Paul,' 'Timothy,' and 'Titus' will be used to refer to the people portrayed in the text without assuming any conclusion on the authorship issue.

Method and Theoretical Foundation

For tools to use in determining unit boundaries and coherence both within and between units, there are three primary disciplines to which to turn, and all three will be used. The first discipline is discourse analysis, a subset of modern linguistics. Since the analysis of boundaries and coherence are central concerns of this discipline,[3] it will form the basis of the method employed here. Second, rhetorical analysis provides more limited help. Since the question posed in this study is connection between units, the classifications of speeches in classical rhetoric are not of much use.[4] What is of more interest here is the area of rhetoric referred to as 'Style,' which incorporates rhetorical devices such as repetition, chiasm, parallelism etc. The propriety of the use of this category of rhetoric is underscored by J. T. Reed in his thorough analysis of the use of rhetoric by ancient letter writers in which he states, 'epistolary theorists and letter writers show signs of rhetorical influence mostly in the area of style.'[5] These devices are easily subsumed under discourse analysis (as many works on discourse analysis show).[6] Third, since the Pastoral Epistles purport to be letters (and strong evidence suggests they should be accepted as such),[7] ancient epistolography

3. For example, J. T Reed writes, 'One traditional task of discourse analysis has been to determine the coherence and incoherence of discourse' (1997b: 59).

4. For significant critiques of the use of the canons of classical rhetoric in the analysis of NT letters see: Kern 1998; Porter 1993a; 1997a; Reed 1993c; 1997b: 156–68, 442–54. Note also the similar reservations expressed in Stamps 1997: 233.

5. Reed 1997b, Appendix B, 'The Influence of Rhetorical Theory on Graeco-Roman Letter Writing', 450–51. Galen O. Rowe, noting the 'especially pervasive and lasting influence' of the categories of style, states, 'the ancient precepts on style apply to any verbal expression and not simply to that which is used to persuade. These precepts inform poetry as well as prose, historical writings, philosophical essays, and *letters* as well as political and forensic speeches' (1997: 121; italics added). Cf. also the statement by Porter 1993a: 115: 'One can be certain from the evidence of the ancient rhetorical handbooks themselves of only one thing: with regard to epistles only matters of style were discussed in any significant way, virtually always with epistles mentioned in contrast to oratory.'

6. E.g. Nida, *et al.* 1983.

7. Cf. Wolter 1988; Johnson 2001: 96–97; Marshall 1999: 12–13. However, for a recent critique of some of this work (esp. Johnson) see Mitchell 2001.

should be consulted.[8] While epistolary analysis has not yielded as much fruit as some had hoped, it has provided much useful information in understanding ancient letters, including common transitions and literary forms. Indeed, S. E. Porter writes, 'The major importance of the study of the ancient Greek letter form for exegesis is seen in relation to the structure of the letter.'[9] Thus, the insights of epistolary analysis will be used to supplement the tools of discourse analysis.[10] The way in which these disciplines will be utilized will be discussed below as they relate to the three steps outlined above: delimitation of units, cohesion within the units, and cohesion between units.

Cohesion

As used in this study, the terms 'cohesion' and 'coherence' are somewhat synonymous.[11] These terms refer to the quality of a text which creates a sense that it 'hangs together,' and makes sense. This happens in a text when material in a text has links to other material in the text. Halliday and Hasan, in the standard work on cohesion, define cohesion in the following way:

> Cohesion occurs where the INTERPRETATION of some element in the discourse is dependent on that of another. The one PRESUPPOSES the other, in the sense that it cannot be effectively decoded except by recourse to it. When this happens, a relation of cohesion is set up, and the two elements, the presupposing and the presupposed, are thereby at least potentially integrated into a text.[12]

In other words, cohesion occurs when an understanding of one element requires an understanding of other elements in the text. The interdependency of various elements creates links which provide cohesion. Thus, this study will follow a theory of similarity in texts which Reed describes as 'the view that, with respect to textual cohesiveness, the main basis for coherence lies in similarity ... that cohesiveness is created by speakers

---

8.   Reed 1996: 89, writes, 'despite the continuing enigma regarding the precise genre of Paul's letters, various epistolary traditions should play a key role in how we understand not only the generic macrostructure of his writings but also the microstructural formulas occurring in them.' He is expressing agreement with Arzt 1994.

9.   Porter 1997b: 543.

10.   It is often suggested that the weaknesses of epistolary analysis can be overcome when it is supplemented with another method. Cf. Reed 1997b: 175–76; Watson 1997a: 406–409; White 1993; Stowers 1986: 17–27.

11.   Some scholars have distinguished between these two terms. Cf. the discussion in Guthrie 1994: 49, n. 9.

12.   Halliday and Hasan 1976: 4.

saying similar kinds of things ... about similar kinds of phenomena.'[13] Various means of creating such connections will be discussed below.

Reed also helpfully notes that the cohesiveness of a given text must be viewed as a continuum.[14] At one pole are texts with a high degree of unity and at the other are texts which are instantly recognizable as a jumble of words and sentences with little meaning. 'Somewhere between these poles lie most texts – neither altogether cohesive nor altogether incohesive.'[15] Many scholars have suggested the Pastorals are located on the incohesive side of the continuum, and Miller has argued that they belong at the extreme pole of incohesiveness. This study will attempt a further analysis of where in this continuum the Pastoral Epistles fit.

Delimitation of Units

Linguists Brown and Yule, in one of the standard works on discourse analysis, write, 'Between two contiguous pieces of discourse which are intuitively considered to have two different "topics", there should be a point at which the shift from one topic to the next is marked.'[16] Thus, they suggest that there should be some markers to indicate the transition from one unit to the next, thereby indicating the boundaries of the units. G. H. Guthrie has developed a method of 'cohesion shift analysis' which suggests that such transitions between 'contiguous pieces of discourse' are typically marked by significant shifts in 'cohesion fields.'[17]

'Cohesion fields' as used in this study refers to literary form (or subgenre), topic, subject, participants, verb tense, person, and number, as well as temporal and local frames of reference. Linguists within and without NT studies are in large agreement that continuity in these fields is a significant contributor to cohesion within a discourse – thus, the term cohesion fields.[18] This point is basically clear and is primarily a classification of something often realized intuitively. For example, statements in a certain subgenre or literary form hang together. These forms can be recognized because they exhibit certain consistent character-istics and these characteristics provide cohesion. For example, items in a vice list or elements of a diatribe cohere because they function together. Also, the consistent use of the same subject, the same verb tense, person, and number adds cohesion to a unit of material as it creates the sense that

13.   Reed 1999a: 44–45. See also Reed 1997b: 101.
14.   Reed 1997b: 89.
15.   Reed 1997b: 89.
16.   Brown and Yule 1983: 94–95.
17.   Guthrie 1994: 73; 1995: 36–59.
18.   Dorsey 1999: 23–24, lists very similar items as 'techniques for creating internal cohesion.'

the author is on about the same thing. The 'Participants' field refers to those involved in any given action. This field is useful because the participants in a discourse may be grammaticalized in different ways or not at all. For instance, the actor in a sentence is not the grammatical subject if a passive verb is used. Or, in the imperative in Titus 2.1, 'You teach,' 'you' obviously refers to Titus, but there is another very significant participant who is not grammaticalized at all – the one giving the command, Paul. When the same participants are regularly in view, this creates a sense of cohesion. Lastly, 'topic' refers to the basic idea, or theme of a unit. Continuity in topic is often seen in the use of words from the same semantic field.[19] Kathleen Callow writes, 'Selection of vocabulary items from a common semantic area contributes greatly to discourse cohesion.'[20] While each of these fields is important, specific weight is given to continuity (or lack of) in topic and genre.

A coherent paragraph will usually demonstrate a significant continuity in these cohesion fields. Though some shifts will occur in even the most cohesive paragraph, where there is a significantly high number of shifts then there is likely to be a shift from one paragraph to another.[21] This would then mark the beginning of a new unit within the text.[22] Noticing such points of high level 'turbulence' in cohesion fields then will provide a *starting point* for determining the individual units of a text. Sometimes the precise boundary is not entirely clear and the possibilities have to be debated using other exegetical tools.

These cohesion fields will be traced through each of the Pastoral Epistles and the points of 'turbulence' will be taken as starting points for marking the end of one unit and the beginning of another.

Another helpful tool in determining unit boundaries will be the work done in epistolary analysis which has isolated various devices which often marked the transition to a new point.[23] For instance, J. L. White has shown that the vocative was often used to effect a transition to a new topic.[24] Also it has been shown that sentences beginning with the verb παρακαλέω often

19.   Brown and Yule 1983: 71–75 note the difficulty with the use of topic.
20.   Callow 1974: 31.
21.   Guthrie 1995: 39. Cf. also Snyman 1991: 90; Callow 1974: 22.
22.   Holmstrand 1997 notes the same thing stating, 'To be regarded as a unit of meaning, a text sequence must have a certain coherence as regards its content ... and it must be delimited by certain breaks in terms of content. In other words, it should be possible to distinguish such units of meaning by observing links and breaks in the content of the text' (19).
23.   While there has been some debate over whether certain devices signal major or minor transitions, this is not of concern here. All that is important is that these devices can be indicators of a shift of some sort. Cf. Watson 1997a: 400.
24.   White 1972a: 29.

'have a traditional function indicating a change in subject...'[25] Lastly, White also showed the use of 'disclosure formulas' to introduce a new unit.[26] These disclosure formulas consist of a verb of cognition (typically οἶδα or γινώσκω) expressing the author's desire for the recipient to 'know' something often followed by ὅτι introducing the content of what is to be known.[27] Other devices have been found in the study of ancient epistolography, but these appear to be the most germane to this study.

These tools will be used to define boundaries of the units of each of the Pastorals. If the boundary is in significant disagreement with the boundaries noted by other scholars, their arguments will be treated and other potential indicators of cohesion (see below) will be examined.

Cohesion Within and Between Units

Indicators of cohesion within and between units overlap enough that in places it is difficult to separate them. Therefore, a number of devices which can function within or between units will be discussed first. Possible cohesive devices are numerous so the intention here will not be to list all possible devices but to mention, explain, and justify key devices for this study. Following these devices some devices will be discussed that function especially to unite distinct units (transitional devices and semantic chains).

Cohesion Fields

One indicator of unity within a unit is a high level of continuity in cohesion fields as just mentioned. Shifts in these fields mark boundaries of units, but continuity in these fields suggest cohesion. In the analysis of cohesion within units, the discussion of literary forms may be especially useful. The results of epistolary analysis will be used in identifying, for example, thanksgivings. Since this is a recognized literary form in letters, any items which are identified as part of a thanksgiving will cohere with each other.

Other Devices

Repetition of key words, phrases or concepts is one of the most common and multifaceted means of creating cohesion.[28] It can occur without artistic intent

---

25. Aune 1987: 188. Aune is drawing from the work of C. J. Bjerkelund, *Parakalô, Form, Funktion und Sinn der parakalô-Sätze in den paulinischen Briefe* (Oslo: Universitetsforlaget, 1967).

26. White 1972a: 11–15.

27. White gives various examples and specific variations of the formula which he found in the papyri.

28. Berger 1977: 13, 'Das wichtigste und vielseitigste Mittel der Textverknüpfung ist die *Wiederholung*.' E. Wendland has even suggested a form of structural analysis based on repetition alone in 1992: 28–62.

simply as the result of the continued discussion of a common theme, or can occur as a deliberate device. In either case the subsequent occurrence of a word naturally connects back to the previous occurrence(s) thus creating cohesion. Linguists note that this is common in a variety of communication forms.[29] In fact repetition could serve as an umbrella category for many of the other devices which will be mentioned since many involve the repetition of words or phrases. However, here we will simply refer to the repeated use of words or phrases which bind together a unit or create connections between units simply because of their frequent occurrence.

Several cohesive devices involve symmetrical repetition and are identified as rhetorical stylistic devices. These include chiasmus, parallelism, and inclusio.[30] Each of these is well-known in New Testament studies and has been analyzed extensively, most recently by J. D. Harvey.[31] There is no need to repeat all of the theoretical evaluation of these devices, but it will be useful to provide some definition and criteria for evaluation. In this study chiasm will refer to 'a symmetrical structure involving an inverted order of corresponding elements.'[32] Following Harvey, a pattern need not have a central element in order to be considered a chiasm.[33] 'Chiasm' will then refer to items in both of the following patterns: ABCB'A' and ABB'A'. Parallelism will refer to items following an ABA'B' pattern. While there is debate concerning the terminology it is difficult to determine which is necessarily best.[34] Therefore, it has been decided simply to state clearly the ways in which the terms will be used in this study.

Inclusio, or inclusion, is more uniformly understood and refers to the repetition of words or phrases at the beginning and the closing of a grouping of text (sentence, unit, or section).[35] In each of these devices exact repetition is desired. The repetition of close synonyms or antonyms is also possible.[36] The more exact the repetition (or the more direct the contrast) the stronger the device. Conceptual patterns may also be noted tentatively.

---

29.   Cf. Halliday and Hasan 1976: 319; De Beaugrande 1980: 133; Grimes 1975a: 259; Nida *et al.* 1983: 46.

30.   Marrou 1956 states that basic education in Roman times included learning the alphabet not only backward and forward but also 'both ways at once, ΑΩ, ΒΨ, ΓΧ … ΜΝ' (151; cf. also 269–70). This supports the suggestion that people in that time could naturally think in chiastic patterns (cf. Stock 1984).

31.   Harvey 1998. Other analyses of these devices include the following: Bailey 1996: 14–30; Bar-Efrat 1980; Blomberg 1989; Breck 1987; Collins 1961; Clark 1975; DiMarco 1975, 1976a, 1976b, 1993; 1976; Garland 1985; Lund 1942; Steele 1902; Stock 1984; Thomson 1995.

32.   Harvey 1998: 99.

33.   Harvey 1998: 98–100.

34.   For the most recent evaluation and suggestions see Harvey 1998, esp. pp. 97–118.

35.   At the sentence level at least this device was noted in classical rhetoric as 'prosapodosis' (Rowe 1997: 130).

36.   Cf. Harvey 1998: 98–100, 283.

These devices produce cohesion by the repetition of words and concepts as well as by revealing ordered thought and perhaps artistic intention. When the connections are clear and strong (exact repetitions, several items or a phrase, etc.) there is significant indication of the intentionality of an author. These repetitions, especially due to their symmetrical arrangement, cause the reader/hearer to make connections to the previous material. These devices may then be used to create cohesion within a unit or be used to create connection between units. While the identification of symmetrical arrangements may be abused at times, it is clear that these were devices that were taught and used in the ancient world.[37] Therefore, it is reasonable to look for such devices in ancient letters such as the Pastoral Epistles.

Other cohesive devices include plays on words and ellipsis. The use of one word which sounds quite similar to a previous word but has a different meaning naturally causes the reader/hearer to make a connection to the similar sounding previous word. This connection is of course what is intended by the author and thus it creates cohesion. This device was known in classical rhetoric as paronomasia (παρονομασία, παρήχησις, *annomina-tio*).[38] Similarly, the omission of material in one line, sentence or phrase which must be supplied from previous text naturally produces cohesion since, as stated in the discussion of cohesion above, 'the INTERPRETA-TION of some element in the discourse is dependent on that of another.'[39] The statement which is missing essential material must depend on previous text and thus connection, or cohesion, is created.[40] This too was a classical rhetorical device.[41]

A common device for creating links between words, clauses, sentences, or units is the use of conjunctions. This is by no means a novel idea, but it will be essential to consider the use of these words when analyzing connections both within and between units.[42] Also the lack of conjunctions (asyndeton) can be significant and the various possibilities for interpreting

---

37. Harvey 1998: 61–96 provides examples from Greco-Roman literature and the Septuagint (see also pp. 97–118).

38. Rowe 1997: 132.

39. Halliday and Hasan 1976: 4.

40. J. T. Reed substantiates this in part of a more technical discussion in 'The Cohesiveness of Discourse: Towards a Model of Linguistic Criteria for Analyzing New Testament Discourse,' (1999a: 40–41). He states, 'The simple act of elision invokes a cohesive interpretation by the reader' (41).

41. This device could be classified as 'ellipsis' or 'zeugma.' See Rowe 1997: 135–36.

42. Reed 1999a refers to conjunctions and particles as 'organic ties' and states, 'organic ties provide a vital means of creating and interpreting cohesiveness in Greek discourse. A thorough discourse analysis of any New Testament text should include a serious study of organic ties' (36).

asyndeton have to be considered.[43] Recent work on conjunctions and particles in the Pastorals may be especially helpful here.[44]

Transitional Devices

The next device is not mentioned as often as the previous ones though it might be more common and more basic to regular discourse. These are actually a number of devices commonly referred to as 'transitional devices,' and they emerge from the fact that, 'Linkage, or repetition of what was just said as a means of getting started on the next part, provides cohesion within paragraphs in some languages and between paragraphs in others.'[45] In other words it is common in a new unit (or sentence) to repeat, or in some way to link back to, information from a previous unit (or sentence). Albert Vanhoye pioneered the work in differentiating devices of such linkage in his work on Hebrews.[46] Vanhoye discussed 'hook words,' referring to a pattern in which an expression or word inserted at the end of one unit (but not common earlier in the unit) is taken up again at the beginning of the next unit (but is not common in the rest of the unit). It is important that words that serve as 'hooks' are not common elsewhere in the units connected. This suggests the author has intentionally placed them at the end of one unit to prepare for the next one. Vanhoye's work was subsequently developed by H. V. D. Parunak[47] and, more recently, G. H. Guthrie.[48] From these works we can glean several potentially useful devices, in addition to the 'hook word' already mentioned.

First, Guthrie argued that the author of Hebrews employed 'distant hook words,' in which a word at the close of one unit links to the beginning not of the immediately following unit but of a later unit.[49] In other words, between the two 'hooks' there is an intervening unit (or, perhaps, units). Second, there may be 'hooked keywords.'[50] This could occur when a term which is prominent in one unit (hence 'keyword') is repeated at the beginning of the next unit (but is not a keyword in the second unit) or when a hook word occurs at the end of one unit and then becomes a keyword in the following unit.[51] Third, there is the

43. Cf. esp. Denniston 1953; Grimes 1975b: 151; Güting and Mealand 1998.
44. Heckert 1996; Levinsohn 1999.
45. Grimes 1975: 259.
46. Vanhoye 1976; 1989.
47. Parunak 1983.
48. Guthrie 1994; 1995.
49. Guthrie 1994: 96–97.
50. Guthrie 1994: 100–102; Parunak 1983: 532–40. Parunak calls this device 'linked keyword.'
51. Guthrie also refers to the possibility of a combination of these two sorts of hooked keywords (1994: 100–102).

'hinge,'[52] in which one unit of text serves as a transitional element between the units on either side of it. The preceding unit connects to the hinge which then connects to the following unit. It may be difficult to determine whether the 'hinge' should be considered part of the preceding or following unit since it connects strongly to both and thus creates a transition. Similarly, Guthrie identified the transitional effect of 'overlapping constituents' in which a passage is used simultaneously as the conclusion of one unit and the introduction to the following unit.[53]

What is common in these transitional devices is the intermingling of prominent words or phrases at the extremities of two units in order to create a connection. Recently B. W. Longenecker has provided some historical basis for these linguistic ideas when he demonstrated that creating this sort of connection between units was encouraged at least by Lucian of Samosata, the second-century rhetorician (c. AD 125–80).[54] As Longenecker notes, Lucian in his *How to Write History* encourages the achieving of 'clarity ... by the interweaving of subjects' (τὸ σαφές ... τῇ συμπεριπλοκῇ τῶν πραγμάτων). This sounds quite similar to several of the transition devices just mentioned. This is even clearer in the advice Lucian gives about linking separate sections in a narrative:

> [T]hough all parts must be independently perfected, when the first is complete the second will be brought into essential connection with it, and attached like one link of a chain to another; there must be no possibility of separating them; no mere bundle of parallel threads; the first is not simply to be next to the second, but part of it, *their extremities intermingling*.[55]

As Longenecker notes, there is no indication that Lucian thought of his advice as novel; rather he sets out what seems to him to be normal practice. This combined with the occurrences deduced by Guthrie in Hebrews and by Parunak in various portions of the Bible suggest that this was a common technique in the ancient world.[56]

---

52. Parunak 1983: 540–46; Guthrie 1994: 105–11. Guthrie refers to this device as a 'intermediary transition.' Guthrie's term is more precise, but Parunak's term will be used since it is probably recognizable to most and is more manageable.

53. Guthrie 1994: 102–104.

54. Longenecker 2001.

55. Translation by Fowler and Fowler, *The Works of Lucian* (vol. 2, 1905): 133 (italics added). The Greek text reads: καὶ τὸ πρῶτον ἐξεργασάμενος ἐπάξει τὸ δεύτερον ἐχόμενον αὐτοῦ καὶ ἁλύσεως τρόπον συνηρμοσμένον ὡς μὴ διακεκόφαι μηδὲ διηγήσεις πολλὰς εἶναι ἀλλήλαις παρακειμένας ἀλλ' ἀεὶ τῷ πρώτῳ τὸ δεύτερον μὴ γειτνιᾶν μόνον, ἀλλὰ καὶ κοινωνεῖν καὶ ἀνακεκρᾶσθαι κατὰ τὰ ἄκρα.

56. Longenecker also cites Quintilian (*Quintilian*, vol. 3, trans. H.E. Butler; Loeb 126 [London: Heinemann, 1986]: 579–81) but Quintilian's statements are not as clear.

Two other devices require notice. Guthrie mentions 'parallel introductions,' in which roughly parallel statements are used at the beginning of two successive units.[57] This would naturally create a connection between the two units. By analogy, then, successive units could also be connected by 'parallel closings.'[58]

Semantic Chains

The last tool that will be used is the concept of 'Semantic Chains' which has been developed by Halliday and Hasan[59] and applied to NT studies by J. T. Reed.[60] A 'semantic chain' is basically a set of words in a discourse which are related to each other semantically because they refer to the same person/concept or to the same general class of people/concepts.[61] For example, in a certain discourse the words 'grace,' 'Savior,' 'life,' and 'redeem' may all relate to the idea of 'salvation.' These words then connect with each other because of their semantic relationship, thus creating a 'chain' of related words running through a discourse. The occurrence of such a chain throughout a discourse creates some cohesion between the different units in which it occurs, uniting the units by the repetition of a common idea. However, significant cohesion is created when prominent semantic chains which run through the discourse connect with each other.[62] For example, there may be a semantic chain referring to 'good works' in a discourse in addition to a chain referring to 'salvation,' as mentioned earlier. If these two chains are prominent in the discourse and they do not simply exist independently of each other but intermingle in specific ways, this creates significant cohesion. Thus, a cohesive discourse is not merely a group of strings laid alongside each other, but a collection of strings which are interwoven with each other at various places and in multifaceted ways and are, thus, inextricably bound together.

57.   Guthrie 1994: 104. This would appear to be the rhetorical device 'anaphora' (Rowe 1997: 131) exercised at the paragraph level.

58.   This would appear to be the rhetorical device 'antistrophe' (Rowe 1997: 131) exercised at the paragraph level.

59.   Halliday and Hasan 1980: 4–90.

60.   Reed 1992: 133–38; 1997b: 100–101; 1999a: 43–45; 1997a: 205–12.

61.   Reed 1999a: 43 defines semantic chains as 'a set of discourse lexemes each of which is related to the others by the semantic relation of co-reference, co-classification and/or co-extension.' (The same definition is found in Reed 1997b: 100). The three semantic relations are described in the preceding pages. The definition in the text above collapses co-classification and co-extension since they are so similar and Reed notes that co-classification is a subtype of co-extension (41, n. 26).

62.   Reed refers to the linguistic items in different chains which connect with each other 'Central Tokens' (1999a: 44; 1997b: 100; 1997a: 211–12). Reed states, *'Textual cohesiveness is primarily occasioned by central tokens'* (1997a: 211–12).

Therefore, the goal in the analysis of semantic chains will be to identify significant semantic chains in each letter and then to identify ways in which these chains interrelate. If there is little connection between the chains, the letter is not very cohesive. If there is significant connection between the chains, the letter is significantly cohesive.

Conclusion

The analysis of cohesion is a prominent topic in modern linguistics and the discussion is broad. The method used here is based on modern linguistic study of cohesiveness, following the theory of similarity, that cohesion is created by the use of similar terms discussing similar things. The method also incorporates insights from ancient epistolography and rhetorical stylistic elements. Chapters 2, 4, and 6 will seek to determine the boundaries of the basic units of 1 Timothy, 2 Timothy and Titus, respectively, and the level of cohesion within each unit. Chapters 3, 5, and 7 will trace connections between the units of each letter – connections between specific units (e.g. transitional devices) and connections across the entire discourse (e.g. semantic chains). The results will suggest where each letter falls on the continuum of cohesiveness and whether or not any clear macrostructure of the letter emerges.

Chapter 2

THE TEXTUAL UNITS OF 1 TIMOTHY

The goal of this chapter will be to divide 1 Timothy into discrete units of thought (paragraphs) and to examine the cohesiveness of each unit. The following chapter will examine connections between these distinct units. In order to delineate the separate units, attention will be paid to shifts in cohesion fields and common epistolary transitional devices. The distinction between units is often clear, but it is not always precise. In some places where it has been argued that a group of verses is one unit comprised of a couple of interrelated pieces, one might also argue that these are distinct units which then have connections. At the end of the day this is not problematic for the current study since it is argued that a high degree of cohesion is found throughout the letter. However, in order to discuss the cohesion of the entire letter it will be important to be able to refer to individual units.

Once a unit is delineated, arguments of scholars concerning its cohesiveness are noted. Since Miller mounts the most thoroughgoing attack on coherence, his views will often provide the framework for the discussion. Then cohesive elements within the units will be noted.

1.1–2

1.1–2 are clearly identified as the epistolary prescript and salutation in a form clearly recognizable for ancient Greek letters. The end of the salutation at v. 2 marks the close of this form and therefore the close of this unit. The cohesion of this unit is not seriously challenged since it follows a clearly established form for ancient letters, a form which was in fact fairly flexible.

1.3–7

Boundaries
There is widespread agreement among commentators that 1 Timothy 1.3–7 forms the first textual unit after the epistolary opening. The beginning of the textual unit is marked by the close of the epistolary opening in v. 2.

Also, the use of an introductory adverb like καθώς with a verb of instruction (παρακαλέω) was a fairly common way to begin the body of an ancient letter.[1]

Since a number of shifts in cohesion fields occur at 1.8 (discussed below), 1.7 is considered the final boundary of this unit.

Cohesion

Concerning the internal coherence of this unit, Miller states 'The paragraph as a whole reflects little sequence of thought, and is characterized throughout by abrupt and puzzling transitions.'[2] However, he provides no real examples or argumentation on this point. He and others point to the awkward syntax arising from the anacolouthon in v. 3. However, despite this awkwardness most have understood the 'sequence of thought' to be clear. Indeed, a number of arguments have been proposed which suggest the author deliberately created the anacolouthon either to create a sense of urgency, or as a means of indicating the original command is still in force.[3] Lastly, the anacolouthon, though awkward, is no real basis for arguing incoherence since it is a phenomenon which occurs in other Greek letters (including accepted Paulines) whose coherence is not suspect.[4]

Other elements in the unit suggest cohesion. For example, the topic throughout is opponents. Verse 3 involves three actors: Paul exhorting Timothy about 'certain ones' (τισίν) who are teaching falsely. Paul and Timothy, already introduced in the epistolary opening, remain in view since this is framed as correspondence between them. The focus, however, is on the new participants introduced in this section, the false teachers. Their habits are described in v. 4a, contrasted in 4b–5, and they are described again in vv. 6–7 (τινές, v. 6). The concern is with the content of this group's teaching (myths, genealogies, and law), and with the results of the teaching – speculation (v. 4), and verbal disputes (v. 6) – especially as contrasted with the result of Pauline teaching (vv. 4b–5). Thus, there is cohesion of topic and subject in 1.3–7.[5]

---

1. White 1972a: 41–42. He lists some papyri examples. This fact makes very unlikely Hanson's suggestion that the author stuck καθώς at the beginning of the sentence simply because it was a favorite of Paul's and would add a note of solemnity (1982: 56).

2. Miller 1997: 59–60.

3. As representatives of these views Marshall 1999: 363, cites the following: for the former, E. Schlarb 1990: 17, and Holtz 1972: 34; for the latter, Roloff 1988: 62f., and Oberlinner 1994: 11.

4. Quinn and Wacker 2000: 69, 'This phenomenon is by no means unheard of in the openings of Greek letters ... The rest of the Paulines too on occasion offer impenetrable anacolutha.' They cite Gal. 2.4–6.

5. Blight 1977: 38 argues similarly.

There are two sentences in this unit: vv. 3–4 and vv. 5–7. These two sentences are connected in a couple of ways. First, lexical cohesion occurs because a cognate of the verb stating the task of Timothy in v. 3 (παραγγέλλω) is repeated in v. 5 (παραγγελία). Timothy is left in Ephesus to **command** ..., and the goal of this **command** is ....

Secondly, the unit begins and ends with discussion of false teaching. 1.3 introduces certain people who teach falsely (ἑτεροδιδασκαλεῖν) and 1.7 closes with the mention of opponents who desire to be teachers of the Law (νομοδιδάσκολοι). After the introduction of false teachers in v. 3, v. 4 goes on to mention the unprofitable results of their teaching – it gives rise to meaningless disputes (ἐκζήτησις). The mention of those who desire to be teachers of the Law in v. 7 is preceded by a mention of the bad results of these opponents – they reject things associated with proper instruction and turn aside to meaningless discussions (ματαιολογία). Thus, 1.3–4 and 1.6–7 both discuss the opponents, taking up their teaching (using words with the same root) and its results (using words in the same semantic domain)[6] in inverted order. Between these discussions of opponents comes v. 5, which stands out from the rest of the unit on several accounts. First, after τίς is introduced in v. 3, every verb in the unit refers to them except ἐστίν in v. 5. Similarly, every verb from the end of v. 3 onward is plural (every finite form is third person as well) except ἐστίν in v. 5. Accordingly, v. 5 stands out since the subject is proper teaching rather than opponents. More specifically there is a contrast (δέ) between the results of the two different teachings. Whereas the false teaching leads to futile results, the proper teaching leads to love. Thus there is a chiastic development in this unit:

A Improper teaching – ἑτεροδιδασκαλεῖν
  B Negative results of improper teaching – **meaningless** speculations
    C (δέ) Positive results of proper teaching – love
  B' Negative results of improper teaching – **meaningless** talk
A' Improper teaching – νομοδιδάσκολοι

The central contrast between the results of the two ministries (BCB') is strengthened by the two occurrences of πίστις in the unit. In v. 4 the result of false teaching is contrasted (μᾶλλον ἤ) with the work of God which is characterized by faith (τήν ἐν πίστει). Verse 5 then seems to explain further what the work of God is, and it is characterized by 'sincere faith' (πίστεως ἀνυποκρίτου). However, this has been rejected by the opponents (v. 6, ὧν τινες ἀστοχήσαντες). Thus, the opponents are at odds with the faith and have rejected God's work. The logical development could be represented as follows:

---

6. Louw and Nida (1989) classify both words in Domain 33, both having a negative connotation and suggesting meaninglessness.

v. 4 – rather than the work of God
    v. 5 – explanation of the work of God
v. 6 – rejection of the work of God

These lexical and semantic connections, as well as the logical development, provide a strong argument for cohesion in this unit in direct contradiction to Miller's assertion that there is 'little sequence of thought.'[7] The chiastic arrangement does not explain all that is going on in these verses but demonstrates the flow of thought and the unity of these verses. The evident concern is to contrast the teaching of Paul and the opponents, with special attention to the results of the teaching.

1.8–11

Boundaries
Many commentators have understood 1.8 to mark the beginning of a new unit, and this is confirmed by a number of shifts in cohesion fields. Most obviously, the fronted verb of 1.8 is first person plural (first occurrence of such in the letter) in contrast to the predominately third person plural verbs in the previous unit. Accordingly the subject shifts from 'certain ones' to 'we' and the topic moves from discussion of false teachers to a statement of acknowledged Christian belief. Whereas the opponents were the key participants in 1.3–7, they are no longer explicitly in view in 1.8–11.[8] The topic has shifted to the use of the Law. Thus, 1.8 clearly begins a new unit. The appearance of a thanksgiving at 1.12 confirms 1.11 as the final boundary of this unit.

Cohesion
Scholars have pointed to a few places within this unit which could suggest incoherence or disconnectedness. Miller sums up his view of this unit when he refers to the 'patchwork nature of this collection of disparate materials.'[9] There are three major points at issue: (1) the connection between v. 8 and v. 9, (2) the connection of v. 10b to what precedes, and (3) the connection of v. 11 with what precedes.

First, Miller says there is no logical connection between v. 8 and v. 9, and says this suggests the two verses originally existed independently.[10] Dibelius and Conzelmann seem to agree saying that v. 9 'implies something entirely different from the preceding clause.'[11] However, such a radical

---

7. Miller 1997: 59.
8. The vice list in vv. 9–10 may have the opponents in view, but this is not stated explicitly.
9. Miller 1997: 63.
10. Miller 1997: 61–62.
11. Dibelius and Conzelmann 1972: 22. Cf. also Wilson 1979: 91–92.

stance is not necessary. It is completely logical to understand εἰδώς in v. 9 as qualifying τις in v. 8 stating that the way to use the law properly is to know the truth which follows in the ὅτι clause.[12] Thus, v. 9 does not say something entirely different, and the 'further exposition on the meaning of "lawful" use of the law' which Miller expected is given.[13] Additionally, structural parallels suggest vv. 8–9 belong together. They both begin with a form of οἶδα, followed by a ὅτι clause which has νόμος as its subject and gives the content of that which is known. A second use of the νομ- root occurs in both sentences.

1.8 – Οἴδαμεν ... ὅτι ... ὁ νόμος ... νομίμως
1.9 – εἰδὼς ... ὅτι ... νόμος ... ἀνόμοις

Both sentences make statements about the law with a further clarifying statement:

The Law is good, **if** used properly
The Law is not for the just, **but** for sinners

Lastly, both sentences have two occurrences of words with the νομ-root in what appears to be a deliberate wordplay. This creates significant lexical cohesion as this root appears four times within just two sentences: νόμος (v. 8), νομίμως (v. 8), νόμος (v. 9), ἀνόμοις (v. 9). These factors along with a justifiable logical connection negate Miller's criticisms and suggest vv. 8–9 go together. This then unites vv. 8–10a since 9b–10a cohere as a vice list as all agree.[14]

The next potentially incohesive point is the general proviso which concludes the vice list in v. 10b (καὶ εἴ τι ἕτερον τῇ ὑγιαινούσῃ διδασκαλίᾳ ἀντίκειται). Miller and Hanson both criticize this proviso as out of place following a list of such serious offenses, with Hanson dubbing it 'a rather lame ending.'[15] However, similar clauses are used to conclude such lists in the accepted Paulines (e.g., Rom. 13.9; Gal. 5.21).[16] More importantly, Fitzgerald, in a study of catalogues or lists in the ancient world, found that 'many end with a formula of abbreviation ("and the like") or a collective reference ("and all the others").'[17] Thus, even if the proviso may seem

---

12. So Marshall 1999: 376; Knight 1992: 82; Bernard 1906: 27.
13. Miller 1997: 62.
14. Quinn and Wacker 2000: 95 also note the assonance created in the vice list since eight words have an initial alpha. Since they are not all privative, they suggest this shows the words were chosen for aural effect. They also note a rhyming scheme created the ending οις/αις in 13 of the items. Cf. also Mounce 2000: 30.
15. Miller 1997: 63; Hanson 1982: 59.
16. So also Bernard 1906: 28; Knight 1992: 88; Quinn and Wacker 2000: 102. Hanson concedes this.
17. Fitzgerald 1997: 288.

'lame' to modern readers, there is no basis for seeing here a shift to a different disparate source because this was a common way to end such lists in the ancient world. Lastly, the choice of the verb ἀντίκειται in v. 10b provides a link back to κεῖται in v. 9a, suggesting this last proviso has been composed with v. 9 in view.

The third point of contention concerning the cohesion of this unit is v. 11. Miller and Barrett both note that the connection is unclear, with the use of κατά being imprecise. It is true that v. 11 appears somewhat as a tag.[18] It also contains some shifts in cohesion fields. The verb shifts to aorist tense from the predominant present tense, and to first person singular from the third person singular which was common since Οἴδαμεν. Paul also returns more explicitly as a participant (though he would have been involved in the 'we' of 1.8). God and the gospel appear here for the first time in this unit.[19] For these reasons, it is understandable that interpreters might wonder about the connection of v. 11 to vv. 8–10. However, v. 11 is still syntactically connected as part of the same sentence and κατά can be used to denote the standard by which something is judged (BAGD, s.v. κατά 5). The introduction of such a standard is understandable since v. 10 closed with the first reference to 'sound doctrine' in the letter. 1.11 can then serve as a further explanation of a term which will be important in the letter. The new items introduced in 1.11 are more fully developed in the following unit, suggesting not that 1.11 lacks connection with surrounding material but that it is providing the basis for the following unit in a common transitional device. This will be discussed more fully in the next chapter.

Thus, 1.8–11 form a coherent unit. The flow of thought is basically straightforward. Verse 8 gives the thesis statement of the unit (the Law is good when used properly), followed by explanation (vv. 9–11). The explanation includes for whom the Law is not intended ('the just,' v. 9a) and for whom it is intended (the vice list in vv. 9b–10a). Then, verses 10b–11 provide the standard by which the qualities in 9b–10a are considered vices.

1.12–17

Boundaries
1.12–17 shifts to the genre of thanksgiving,[20] and practically every commentator has recognized 1.12–17 as a self-contained unit. Other shifts

---

18. E.g., Marshall 1999: 381 says the phrase is 'added loosely *ad sensum*.'
19. Indeed, this is the only time εὐαγγέλιον occurs in the letter.
20. Blight 1977: 41 says the placement of χάριν at the beginning of the sentence signals a shift in theme.

confirm this. The topic in 1.12ff. is no longer the Law, but Paul's personal conversion. Whereas in 1.8–11 the subject was the collective 'we', virtually no one is in view in 1.12–17 but Paul and Jesus Christ, with God in view in the closing doxology.[21] This is the first time in the body of the letter that Jesus has been a participant. The first person pronoun occurs four times and there are five verbs in the first person singular. The subject of every verb (stated or implied by the verb ending) is either Paul or Jesus Christ, except ὑπερεπλεόνασεν in v. 14 whose subject is 'the grace of our Lord.'[22] This section is devoted to the interaction between Jesus and Paul, himself.[23]

The doxology in 1.17 marks it as the closing of this unit. This is confirmed by significant shifts in cohesion fields at 1.18.

Cohesion

Miller concedes that in the present form 1.12–17 form a unit. However, he suggests that literary 'seams' in the passage show that the unit does not really cohere. The two 'seams' he mentions are the faithful saying in 1.15 and the doxology in 1.17. Miller notes that most scholars understand the faithful saying to be introducing traditional material. It is not clear, however, why this must suggest a seam. Surely an author can use a quotation in the midst of an argument or discussion without vitiating the coherence of his argument. The introduction of the faithful saying would be a problem only if the faithful saying did not cohere with the previous discussion. Yet, several points suggest the faithful saying does cohere with the previous discussion. Note the symmetry between the discussion of Paul before and after the faithful saying. In 1.13, the previous sinfulness of Paul is introduced using a participial form of εἰμί. This is then contrasted with the fact that Paul received mercy (ἀλλ' ἠλεήθην). After the faithful saying, a participial form of εἰμί introduces Paul's sinfulness, thus connecting Paul to the 'sinners' of the faithful saying. This is then contrasted with the fact that Paul received mercy (ἀλλὰ ... ἠλεήθην). The significance of the word use here is heightened by the fact that these are the only occurrences of the verb ἐλεάω in the letter.[24] Thus, both sections are concerned with Paul's

---

21. 'Those who will believe' do appear in v. 16, but then as those to whom Paul will be an example.

22. Bassler (1996) in a similar sentiment states, 'The entire passage (vv. 12–16) has a strong christological emphasis' (44). The doxology which, as most agree, refers to God does not have an expressed verb.

23. Dibelius and Conzelmann 1972: 26 take 1.12 with 1.8–11 but provide no argumentation for doing so. In fact, they note the connection between 1.12 and the following material. The facts that Χάριν ἔχω introduces an epistolary convention and that 1.13 is grammatically connected to 1.12 simply will not allow for Dibelius and Conzelmann's position. No other commentators agree with Dibelius and Conzelmann.

24. Also, according to Heckert (1996: 24), these are the only two occurrences in the Pastoral Epistles of ἀλλά without a negative marker.

reception of mercy in spite of his sinfulness. Also, the faithful saying has a logical function in the argument of the section. Verses 12–14 state that Christ Jesus saved Paul in spite of his sinfulness.[25] The faithful saying (vv. 15a–b), then says, indeed the reason Christ Jesus came was to save sinners. Verses 15c–16 then hold up Paul as the representative of such sinners who will be saved. Thus, the faithful saying links vv. 12–14 with 15b–16 by raising the discussion of Paul's conversion to the paradigmatic level. Indeed, Andrew Lau, after his discussion of the contextual function of the 'faithful saying' in this unit, concludes that the saying is 'intentionally integrated into the presentation' and 'serves as the linchpin of the entire section.'[26] There is therefore no need to posit an incohesive seam at 1.15.

There are other observations from the analysis of cohesion fields that suggest cohesion in vv. 12–16. The previously mentioned focus on Christ Jesus and Paul is indicative of a strong continuity in the participant field. The participants throughout are Paul and Jesus, and there is no other unit in the entire letter so focused on these two participants.[27] This naturally leads to significant lexical cohesion as well since Χριστὸς Ἰησοῦς occurs four times (vv. 12, 14, 15, 16), 'our Lord' occurs twice (vv. 12, 14), and there are nine references to 'I/me.'[28] There are also other significant instances of lexical cohesion.[29] Πιστός and its cognates occur five times in this unit (vv. 12, 13, 14, 15, 16), occurring in every verse but 1.17. No other unit in the letter contains as many occurrences of this word group.[30] Verse 17 is then connected to v. 16 by a device similar to the hooked keyword used between units. Verse 16 closes with a reference to 'eternal life,' the first occurrence of αἰώνιος (or its cognates) in the letter. The noun, αἰών, then occurs three times in v. 17 as it opens with a reference to the 'King eternal' and closes with 'forever and ever.'

This begins to take up the second seam suggested by Miller, namely the doxology of v. 17. The inclusion of 1.17 in this unit could, however, be contested since the genre of 1.17 shifts to that of a doxology. Doxologies were not an epistolary convention of ancient Greco-Roman or Semitic

---

25. Mounce 2000: 53 also notes a significant parallel between v. 13b and v. 14a.

26. Lau 1996: 71.

27. The first person singular pronoun occurs 5 times in the letter, and 3 of those are in this unit.

28. There are 4 occurrences of the pronoun (1.12 [2x], 15, 16) and 5 occurrences of first person verbs (1.12, 13 [2x], 15, 16). Mounce 2000: 47 also notes this repetition as part of the author's literary technique.

29. Lau 1996: 67 also notes several of these cohesive elements which led him to refer to the 'literary and thematic coherence of this tightly structured digression.'

30. 'By his use of the faith theme (the root *pist-*), the author of the passage clearly demonstrates that he considers that the entire passage constitutes a single unit of literary material' (Collins 1975: 166). Mounce 2000: 47 also notes this briefly.

letters in general[31] but are common in New Testament letters. There are four basic components of New Testament doxologies: the object of praise in dative case, the element of praise (commonly δόξα, though other elements may be added), the indication of time using a form of αἰών, and the confirmatory response (ἀμήν).[32] 1 Timothy 1.17 fits this pattern exactly, and is therefore considered a doxology. However, before deciding on these grounds that 1.17 should be removed from the previous material, the function of doxologies in the New Testament should be considered. There are at least 16 doxologies in New Testament documents,[33] and each one occurs at the close of a unit or section. For this reason, doxologies are commonly believed to serve a concluding function.[34] Additionally, the only time doxologies exist as independent units is when they occur at the end of a letter functioning to close the letter (Rom. 16.25–27; Jude 24–25). Such doxologies are also considerably longer than other doxologies. Since 1 Timothy 1.17 neither occurs at the end of the letter nor is as long as such 'letter-ending' doxologies, it seems that the function of the doxology genre would argue for the inclusion of 1 Timothy 1.17 with the preceding material as a concluding device.[35]

However, Miller claims a significant lack of cohesion between 1.17 and the preceding material, suggesting 1.17 is not a part of 1.12–16. Miller adduces two reasons: (1) verse 17 has 'little connection with the immediate context' and (2) 'The doxology contains no specifically Christian elements and most likely had its origins within the Jewish synagogue.'[36] Neither of these are viable criticisms because both statements are common characteristics of New Testament doxologies in general. Regarding the issue of connection with preceding context, L. G. Champion in his seminal work on New Testament doxologies writes, 'often they [benedictions and doxologies] do not seem to have any particular connection with, or to have grown out of the preceding section.'[37] Later he again states that their

---

31. Weima 1994: 140.

32. See Weima 1994: 136; Aune 1987: 195.

33. Weima 1994: 137 includes 15 examples in his table which is presented as exhaustive. However, 2 Pet. 3.18 fits the criteria as well.

34. Cf. Weima 1994: 141; Aune 1987: 193; O'Brien 1991: 549. Aune also lists three examples of doxologies from the Apocrypha (4 Macc. 18.24; 1 Esd. 4.40, 59) which serve to conclude a section. In each of these cases it is a speech which is concluded with a doxology. Quinn and Wacker 2000: 124 also note the work of Audet who found a development in the form of the Jewish thanksgiving in which a doxology was used as a conclusion, returning to the note of praise with which the thanksgiving began (Audet 1958: 371–99).

35. According to Sanders, Schubert defined the thanksgiving unit in 1 Tim. as 1.12–16 with a doxology at 17 which 'provides a definite end to the period' (1962: 355). Achtemeier 1990: 24 also discusses the concluding function of benedictions.

36. Miller 1997: 65.

37. Champion 1934: 17.

'completeness of form separates them largely from their context, with which they sometimes have little to do as regards the development of thought.'[38] Thus, the somewhat independent nature of 1 Timothy 1.17 is simply typical of New Testament doxologies.

The connection between doxologies and the material they follow is not necessarily linguistic or thematic but logical. When doxologies occur within the body of a New Testament document (i.e., not in the closing),[39] they follow discussions of God's wisdom (Rom. 11.36), or God's salvation (Gal. 1.5), or God's provision (Phil. 4.20), or God's work in maturing believers (Eph. 3.20–21; Heb. 13.21; 1 Pet. 5.11). Discussions of such gracious activity from God on behalf of people regularly led New Testament authors to express praise to God in a doxological form. The appearance, then, of a doxology following the discussion of God's graciousness in saving sinners, even the 'chief of sinners,' is in line with the general New Testament pattern regarding context for a doxology.[40]

Regarding the second of Miller's criticisms, that there are no specifically Christian elements in 1 Timothy 1.17, Champion's analysis is once again helpful. Champion writes,

> Now the remarkable feature of the doxologies and benedictions both in the epistles of Paul and in other early Christian literature, is that they contain very few definitely Christian elements ... All the forms which we have examined above are familiar to us from our study of the Old Testament and Judaism.[41]

Later, he states again, 'the distinctly Christian elements in the benedictions and doxologies are very few, and ... the characteristic expressions were taken chiefly from the Septuagint, or to a lesser extent from the synagogue prayers.'[42] The Jewish nature of New Testament doxologies is a commonplace, and is therefore no basis for criticism of 1 Timothy 1.17.[43] It is true, however, that Champion says the distinctly Christian elements are 'few,' and he mentions the insertion of the name of Jesus as one such characteristic, but in 1 Timothy 1.17 there are no distinctly Christian elements at all. A closer look at New Testament doxologies is in order then

38. Champion 1934: 17.
39. Since doxologies were not an epistolary convention in Greco-Roman or Semitic letters, the proper source for comparison is other NT examples. However, other examples from the Pastoral Epistles are not included here since they are suspect in Miller's view.
40. Cf. Guthrie's statement, 'A typical Pauline doxology results from these moving reflections on the mercies of God' (1976: 76).
41. Champion 1934: 108.
42. Champion 1934: 116.
43. A clear, compelling case for the Jewish background of NT doxologies is made by Weima 1994: 140, where he demonstrates a Jewish source for each of the four components of doxologies.

to see if 1 Timothy 1.17 is odd in its total lack of explicit Christian references.

Doxologies in the New Testament, though they share the same basic structure, can be divided into two basic structural groups. One group consists of those examples where the doxology is actually a continuation of the previous sentence. In these cases the doxology begins with a pronoun whose antecedent is in the previous material.[44] The second group includes those examples where the doxology is effectively a new and separate sentence. These examples begin with a noun or substantival participle and often a postpositive δέ.[45] One might not be surprised if examples from the first group lacked any explicit Christian reference since such reference could be supplied by the antecedent of the pronoun or by the antecedent's modifiers.[46] It is interesting to note, however, that in Romans 11.36, not only does the doxology lack any explicit Christian reference, but the preceding context (vv. 33–36) does not have any explicit Christian reference either. Indeed, the material directly preceding the doxology is an OT quotation. This presents at least one Pauline precedent for 1 Timothy 1.17. Regarding the second type of doxology, it might be considered more necessary for Christian reference to be made explicit since it is a new sentence and since these examples generally involve a more expanded description of the one being blessed (God). 1 Timothy 1.17 falls in this category and that may explain Miller's criticism. However, Philippians 4.20 also falls in this category,[47] but it contains no explicit Christian references.[48] Therefore, the lack of any explicit Christian reference in 1 Timothy 1.17 provides no basis for criticizing its place in the flow of this unit. Indeed, it appears to be in harmony with doxologies found elsewhere in the New Testament and in Pauline letters specifically. These statements apparently were expected to be read in light of their context which provides a Christian coloring of their elements.

Thus, 1 Timothy 1.12–17 should be considered an individual coherent unit. Its beginning is marked by the initiation of a thanksgiving and it is

---

44. For e.g., Rom. 11.36; Gal. 1.5; 1 Tim. 6.16; 2 Tim. 4.18; Heb. 13.21; 1 Pet. 4.11; 5:11; 2 Pet. 3.18.

45. For e.g., Rom. 16.25–27; Phil. 4.20; Eph. 3.20–21; Jude 24–25; Rev. 1.5–6; 5.13; 7.12. The only examples from this group which do not have the postpositive δέ are the examples from Revelation (1.5b-6; 5.13b; 7.12).

46. The doxology in Gal. 1.5, an example from this group, contains no explicit Christian reference, but it is provided by the preceding material.

47. The partition theories for the letter of Philippians do not affect the argument here because 4.10–20 are still usually regarded as a unit.

48. One might suggest the reference to God as 'Father' in Phil. 4.20 is an explicit Christian reference. However, God is referred to as the Father of his people in the OT (Isa. 9.6; Jer. 3.4, 19; Mal. 1.6; 2:10). God is even called 'our Father' (Isa. 63.16 [twice]) as in Phil. 4:20. Thus, while the reference to God as Father may be due to Christian influence, it need not be.

concluded by a doxology.[49] The unit is held together is by its continuity in genre and participants, as well as by significant lexical cohesion. Miller's supposed 'seams' provide no basis for postulating incoherence in this unit.

1.18–20

Boundaries

A widespread consensus considers 1 Timothy 1.18–20 a new unit. This is logical since the doxology in v. 17 closes the preceding section. This is also confirmed by several notable shifts in the cohesion fields. Perhaps the greatest shift is in the participants. Whereas the previous unit focused exclusively on Christ Jesus and Paul, Jesus is not mentioned at all in 1.18–20. The participants now are Timothy in vv. 18–19a (reintroduced with the vocative address and the first occurrence of the second person singular pronoun since it was used in 1.3) and 'certain ones,' τινες from vv. 19b–20. Thus, the viewpoint has returned to Paul specifically addressing Timothy concerning opponents. This corresponds to the fact that in this unit the genre shifts from thanksgiving to exhortation, and the topic is no longer Paul's conversion or even salvation in general but endurance in faithfulness to the 'command.' The time frame also shifts, with 1.18–20 envisioning a current exhortation rather than a remembrance of the past or even a timeless consideration of salvation in general. Thus, 1.18 begins a new unit.

Cohesion

The cohesiveness of this unit does not appear to be contested, and there are several indicators that 1.18–20 cohere as a unit. First, these verses are grammatically and syntactically connected as one sentence. Second, there is a deliberate contrast of the two main subjects of the discussion in 1.18–20. The subjects in this section are Timothy (vv. 18–19a) and the opponents (τινες, vv. 19b–20) who are addressed in turn and are directly contrasted. Whereas in v. 18 Paul has entrusted Timothy (παρατίθεμαι) with a command, with the result that he should fight the good fight (ἵνα στρατεύῃ ... τὴν καλὴν στρατείαν), in v. 20 Paul has handed over (παρέδωκα) Hymenaeus and Alexander so that they might be taught not to blaspheme (ἵνα παιδευθῶσι). The key contrast comes in the middle verse as the focus

---

49. Collins 1975: 166 says the thanksgiving in v. 12 and the doxology in v. 17 create 'a sort of inclusio.' However, he does not explain why this might be so. The general similarity in idea between thanks and praise is not firm enough ground for positing an inclusio.

shifts from Timothy to the others.[50] Using a participial clause (ἔχων),
Timothy is urged to maintain faith and a good conscience, but the others
are described by a participial clause (ἀπωσάμενοι) as having rejected these
very qualities. As a result of this rejection these people have made a
shipwreck of their faith rather than fighting the good fight as Timothy is
urged to do. This contrast and the syntactical symmetry bind 1.18–20
together.

2.1–7

Boundaries

The next textual unit is commonly considered to be 2.1–7, with some
disagreement as to whether the unit ends at v. 7 or v. 8. Though 2.1
continues in first person singular as in 1.18, there is a significant shift in
topic. The concern in 2.1 clearly becomes prayer and this issue is not in
view in 1.18–20. Also, though in both sections Paul is exhorting Timothy,
the communicative situation does seem to be different in some degree.
There is similarity because in 1.18 and in 2.1–2 an exhortatory statement is
given followed by a ἵνα clause denoting the purpose/result of the
exhortation. However, in 1.18–20 it is clear that Paul exhorts Timothy
(σοι, τέκνον Τιμόθεε) and the purpose concerns what Timothy himself
should do (second singular verb, στρατεύῃ). By contrast, the exhortation of
2.1–2 does not express an indirect object and the verb in the ἵνα clause is
first person plural (διάγωμεν). Thus, the exhortation of 2.1–2 seems to
apply to a group larger than just Timothy as in 1.18.[51] Indeed, Quinn and
Wacker note that while in 1.18 there is an explicit second person singular
reference, there is no such reference in 2.1 (in fact, from 2.1–3:13).[52] There
is also a shift in the participant field, as the opponents are not mentioned in
2.1–7. In addition to these shifts both οὖν and παρακαλέω are used in
ancient letters to mark transitions.[53] All of these shifts support understanding 2.1 as beginning a new unit.

Diverging from the majority opinion, Bernard, Guthrie, and Knight all
include v. 8 with 2.1–7 in their listing of the structure of 1 Timothy.
However, in the actual commentary Bernard groups v. 8 with the following

---

50. It is also interesting to note that while the verbs in vv. 18–19a when Timothy is in view
are all present tense, when the subject shifts to the opponents the verbs are almost entirely
aorist (4 out of 6, with ἐστιν and βλασφημεῖν being the exceptions).

51. It is true, as Reed has argued (1993b), that the exhortation is still directed to Timothy.
The point here is that the exhortation of 2.1–2 is one expected not simply to be applied by
Timothy to himself but to be passed on by Timothy to a wider audience (presumably the
Church).

52. Quinn and Wacker 2000: 170.

53. Cf. White 1986: 211; Aune 1987: 188; Boers, 1975: 154–55; Kim 1972: 61.

verses and Guthrie acknowledges that v. 8 resumes the topic of prayer and is essentially connected with vv. 9ff.[54] Neither Bernard nor Guthrie gives argumentation for including v. 8 with 2.1–7. Knight suggests that v. 8 has links to both the preceding and following verses and should therefore be seen as a transitional verse.[55] While there are indeed links in both directions, it is hardly possible to remove v. 8 from v. 9 leaving v. 9 without a main verb, especially since the ὡσαύτως in v. 9 links the two verses and suggests the verb in v. 8 is to be supplied in v. 9.

Cohesion

The cohesion of this unit and the next has not been viewed very highly by some scholars. Easton says both 2.1–7 and 2.8–15 are 'discontinuous and illogical' and totally lacking in any 'regular scheme.'[56] Miller divides the passage into the following pieces, which he suggests were originally independent, traditional materials: w. 1–2, 3, 4, 5–6, 7.[57] The linguistic cohesion of 2.1–2, which is not contested, will be assessed briefly. Following the demonstration of a shift between 2.2 and 2.3, the connections between 2.3–7 will be assessed. Finally, the relation between 2.1–2 and 3–7 will be discussed.

2.1–2 cohere well. They are grammatically one sentence and focus on prayer for all people. The word πᾶς occurs four times, including early in v. 1 and late in v. 2. The sentence is also characterized by completeness in description with four words being used for prayer ('all sorts of prayer for all sorts of people') and couplets (joined by καί) for people in authority, for the type of life sought, and the manner in which this life will be lived. 2.1 calls for all sorts of prayer for all sorts of people and 2.2 gives a specific example of the people to be prayed for, rulers.

2.3, however, seems to involve a shift in topic. Prayer is no longer explicitly in view and the focus shifts to God (four occurrences in vv. 3–5), Jesus (v. 5 and a relative pronoun referring to him in v. 6), and salvation (σωτῆρος, 2.3; σωθῆναι, 2.4; and the discussion of Christ's work in 2.6). Thus, there seems to be a significant shift in topic from 2.2 to 2.3. There is also a shift in genre since 2.1–2 is an exhortation but 2.3ff. appear more to be a doctrinal statement. Whereas the actor in 2.2 was Paul, exhorting Timothy, in 2.3ff the actors are God and Christ Jesus. Thus, it may be suggested that a new unit begins at 2.3. However, some features display a strong link between 2.3 and 2.1–2. First, the use of the pronoun, τοῦτο, in 2.3, links 2.3ff. to 2.1–2 because it refers back to the material of 2.1–2. 2.3

54. Guthrie 1990: 84.
55. Knight 1992: 130.
56. Easton 1947: 125.
57. Miller 1997: 67.

then acts as a bridge, connecting vv. 1–2 with vv. 3ff. by saying the prayer encouraged in vv. 1–2 is pleasing to the God described in vv. 3ff. Secondly, the couplet of adjectives joined by καί which modify τοῦτο in 2.3 (καλὸν καὶ ἀπόδεκτον) mirrors the use of couplets joined by καί in 2.2 (ἤρεμον καὶ ἡσύχιον, εὐσεβείᾳ καὶ σεμνότητι). Third, the occurrence of πάντας ἀνθρώπους in 2.4 and πάντων in 2.6 connects with πάντων ἀνθρώπων in 2.1 (and the other three occurrences of πᾶς in 2.1–2). These connections make it clear that 2.3–6 flow out of 2.1–2, and that the shift in cohesion fields is not drastic. The idea of 'all people' unites 2.1–7,[58] but the topic concerning 'all people' differs. 2.1–2 address prayer for all people and 2.3–7 address salvation for all people. Thus, though there is some shift between 2.2 and 2.3 there are clear linguistic and logical connections between them.

It remains now to discuss the coherence of 2.3–7. Miller isolates 2.3 because he identifies it as a 'marker' of traditional materials. It is indeed a validation statement affirming 2.1–2, but this does not mean it cannot have been penned by the author of the surrounding material or that it does not cohere with the surrounding material. According to 2.3, the One to whom the prayers of 2.1–2 are acceptable is 'God our savior.' This not only gives divine approval but also describes God as 'savior' (σωτήρ). 2.4, then, follows naturally with its discussion of God's desire to save (θέλει σωθῆναι). Thus, 2.3 appears as a typical communicative bridge, restating the given information (τοῦτο) and introducing the new material (τοῦ σωτῆρος ἡμῶν θεοῦ) which is discussed further in the following verses. 2.3 and 2.4 show no necessary discontinuity, as they are both concerned with the God who saves.

Then 2.5–6 are structurally similar to 2.3–4. 2.3 opens with reference to the given information (τοῦτο) and introduces 'God our savior,' a new topic,[59] at the close of the verse. 2.4, then, by means of a relative clause discusses this new topic, God, in terms of his salvific interest. Similarly, 2.5 begins with the given information (θεός), and at the close of the verse introduces a new topic, 'Christ Jesus.'[60] 2.6, then, in much the same way as 2.4, by means of a relative clause discusses the new topic in terms of his salvific work. Also, in both 2.4 and 2.6, the salvific interest/work concerns 'all people' (πάντας ἀνθρώπους, 2.4; πάντων, 2.6).[61] This literary-linguistic similarity directly contradicts Miller's assertion that the literary style of

---

58. Cf. Mounce 2000: 78, 'The use of ἄνθρωπος, "person," ties the passage together.' Cf. also Lock 1924: 24.

59. There is no reference to 'God' in 2.1–2.

60. There is no reference to 'Jesus' in 2.1–2.

61. Bassler, commenting on 1 Timothy 2.6, writes, 'It states, however, more radically than … any other New Testament text, the efficacy of Jesus' self-giving death for *all* humankind' (1996: 53).

2.5–6 is 'notably different from the materials surrounding it.'[62] This similarity suggests that 2.3–4 and 2.5–6 go together and that 2.5 follows naturally from 2.4, grounding the availability of salvation to all in God and Christ.

Having shown linguistic connections between 2.3–4 and 2.5–6, there is still the logical problem concerning the function of the γάρ in 2.5. How does the existence of one God and one mediator serve as a basis either for God's desire for all to be saved or for the universal availability of salvation more generally? Dibelius and Conzelmann and Miller argue that a logical connection is hard to find, with Miller even stating that the independent nature of 2.5–6 'is confirmed by its inclusion of ideas that appear unmotivated by the context (for example, the mention of monotheism and the reference to Jesus' mediatorial role).'[63] Help for this question can be found in the fact that other New Testament writers used the basic truth of monotheism as a ground for the availability of salvation to all (see Rom. 3.30; 10.12; Eph. 4.6).[64] This is exactly the point being made in 1 Timothy 2.5.[65] The idea is that since there is only one God, he must be the God of all people, and his salvation must then be for all people; and, 'Since there is only one God and not several, there can therefore only be one way of salvation.'[66] W. Kramer, in fact, argues that the εἷς θεός formula was a 'technical term' used in the mission to the Gentiles and had been taken over from Jewish missionary activity.[67] The argument of 1 Timothy 2.5, grounding the universal availability of salvation in monotheism, is then an argument common to early Christianity and the reference to monotheism is not out of place as Miller suggests.[68] The inclusion of reference to the one mediator as well as one God is unique but follows the same logic as the appeal to one God. Since the writer appeals to the salvific interest of God and Jesus, then having appealed to the uniqueness of God, it is logical for him to also appeal to the uniqueness of Jesus as mediator. This mention of the uniqueness of God and Jesus, then is logical in this salvific context and serves to ground the universal availability of salvation in a manner common to the time. Thus, the suggestion of Merkel and Houlden that v. 5

---

62. Miller 1997: 69.

63. Miller 1997: 69; Dibelius and Conzelmann 1972: 41.

64. The point made here is not dependent on any theory of authorship for the three letters mentioned. The important point is that early Christian writers used the truth of monotheism to support the universal availability of salvation.

65. Towner 1989: 51 writes, 'In a manner similar to Rom 3.29–30 ... the *heis theos* formula in 1 Tim 2.5 provides theological substantiation for the claim in v. 4 that God, indeed, desires to save all men – hence the presence of the *gar*.' Cf. also Marshall 1999: 428–29; Barrett 1963: 51; Bernard 1906: 41; Bassler 1996: 52.

66. Marshall 1999: 429.

67. Kramer 1966: 95. See also Peterson 1926: 216.

68. Miller 1997: 69.

has no place in the larger argument is disproven.[69] Thus, 2.4–6 work together to argue for the universal availability of salvation.[70]

Having argued for the coherence of 2.3–6, 2.7 must now be addressed. There are some shifts in cohesion fields at 2.7. The verbs (ἐτέθην, λέγω,[71] ψεύδομαι) shift back to first person singular and Paul returns explicitly as the primary actor, like 2.1. However, there are significant connections between 2.3–6 and 2.7. First, the relative pronoun that introduces 2.7 (εἰς ὅ) connects back to the characterization of the work of Christ as a testimony (μαρτύριον).[72] In fact, this characterization of the work of Christ may be intended to serve as a transition to 2.7 or at least trigger the mention of Paul's ministry of bearing witness to Christ. Already in 1 Timothy 1.11 a mention of the gospel prompted the author to refer to the entrusting of this gospel to Paul and this is seen elsewhere in letters attributed to Paul (Eph. 3.7; Col. 1.23, 25).[73] That the topic is still related to the doctrinal concerns of 2.3–6 is noted by the words κῆρυξ, ἀπόστολος, and διδάσκαλος, each of which in this context clearly refers to the communication of the doctrinal truths mentioned previously.[74] Also, the description of Paul as a teacher of the Gentiles in faith and 'truth' connects with the desire of God that all people come to the knowledge of the 'truth' in 2.4. Lastly, the mention of ἔθνη connects to the emphasis on 'all people' in the previous verses, since as was noted above, other New Testament passages referring to the universal availability of salvation often had Gentiles in view. In fact, the ministry of Paul to the Gentiles is in essence another confirmation of the argument for the availability of salvation to all. What God desired and Jesus died for, Paul has been called to bring into effect as a 'teacher of the Gentiles.' Thus, 2.7 fits well in the argument of 2.3–6 both linguistically and logically.

Since 2.7 does connect well with the preceding verses, the shifts in cohesion fields may actually function as a sort of inclusio. The unit begins with a first person singular verb and there is no other reference to first person singular until the beginning of v. 7. Accordingly, Paul comes to the fore in 2.1 as the one giving the exhortation, but then fades from view as

---

69. Merkel 1991: 24; Houlden 1976: 67.

70. Cf. Lau 1996: 72–90.

71. The major textual variants here do not effect the argument since λέγω is found in the variant as well. Only minuscules 1984 and 1985 (in UBS) do not have λέγω.

72. Donelson 1986: 166 writes, 'The "into which (εἰς ὅ)" of Paul's appointment can only refer to the doctrinal assertion in 1 Tim. 2.5–6; he is witness of the salvation event produced by Jesus' epiphany.'

73. Knight 1992: 124 writes, 'As is Paul's practice elsewhere, having mentioned the person and work of Christ, he adds the fact that he was appointed to minister for Christ.'

74. Each of these three words is classified by Louw and Nida in 1989: 33, 'Communication.'

the discussion moves to the idea of people living proper lives and the salvific interest of God and Christ. Following the discussion of salvation, Paul is reintroduced as the herald of this message, thus bracketing the section as the command of Paul.

So far, then, it has been argued that 2.1–2 and 2.3–7 are coherent textual units. Along the way in the argumentation, connections between the two units have been mentioned but not developed. Now these connections need to be developed. First, it is interesting that doublets occur throughout this unit: kings and all those in authority (2.2); quiet and peaceful life (2.2); in all godliness and sincerity (2.2); good and acceptable (2.3); to be saved and to come to knowledge (2.4); preacher and apostle (2.7); faith and truth (2.7). This is suggestive of a common style. Secondly, and more importantly, phrases in the semantic range of universality or inclusiveness occur throughout this unit:[75]

2.1 – Pray for **all people**
2.2 – (Pray) for **all those in authority**
2.4 – God desires **all people** to be saved
2.6 – Christ gave himself as a ransom for **all**

Included in this should be the εἷς θεός formula (v. 5) with its traditional association with universal mission.[76] Even the mention of ἔθνη (v. 7) could have this same connotation.

Then, key for understanding the logical relationship between 2.1–2 and 2.3–7 is the identification of the antecedent of τοῦτο in 2.3. It could conceivably refer to εὐσεβείᾳ καὶ σεμνότητι, or to ἤρεμον καὶ ἡσύχιον βίον, or more generally to the exhortation to pray for all people. The fact that the One to whom τοῦτο is pleasing is discussed in the following material as desiring the salvation of 'all people' suggests that the antecedent is the general exhortation to pray for all people.[77] 2.3–7, which argues for the availability of salvation to all, provides a doctrinal basis for the exhortation to prayer for all in 2.1–2.[78] As Kelly wrote, 'it is the fact that Christ died for all men, without any kind of favouritism, that makes it obligatory for Christians to pray for them all without distinction.'[79] Thus, 2.1 gives the basic exhortation, 2.2 provides a common example of praying

---

75. Cf. Mounce 2000: 76, 78.

76. Towner 1989: 87, 'The integral place of the traditional material within the passage is evident from its contribution to the "all" theme...'

77. So most, including Marshall 1999: 424; Quinn and Wacker 2000: 179; Roloff 1988: 119.

78. That this was the understanding of some early scribes is suggested by the addition of γάρ in a number of MSS (NA 26 lists Aleph [2nd correction], D, F, G, H, Ψ, the majority text, the Old Latin witnesses and the Vulgate, all the Syriac witnesses). So also, Elliot 1968: 35.

79. Kelly 1963: 64.

for all people, and 2.3–7 provides a doctrinal basis for the exhortation.[80] The entire unit is then bound by mission concern which unites the discussion of salvation and prayer.[81]

2.8–15

Boundaries

Most commentators agree that a new unit begins at 2.8, though as noted above some connect 2.8 with 2.1–7. A number of elements argue for understanding 2.8 as beginning a new unit. First, the topic returns to prayer after an apparent digression to a doctrinal grounding. This suggests οὖν is functioning in a resumptive sense, taking up again the topic of prayer while also drawing inference from the preceding discussion of prayer and its doctrinal undergirding.[82] Second, the subject shifts from ἄνθρωπος in 2.1 to ἀνήρ in 2.8. Since γυνή follows, this suggests an intentional shift from discussing people in general to specific issues concerning men and women. This corresponds to a shift from prayer in general to specific things to be avoided at prayer. Thus, 2.8 begins a renewed discussion of prayer rather than closing the previous discussion.

There is also some debate concerning the conclusion of this unit. The question is whether πιστὸς ὁ λόγος (3.1a) goes with this unit or with the following one. It would seem best to take 3.1a with the following unit,[83] but this issue does not materially affect the current study. As a statement of affirmation it could easily conclude this section or introduce the following one.

Cohesion

1 Timothy 2.8–15 has been particularly criticized regarding its literary coherence or incoherence.[84] Abrupt and sudden transitions have been noted by commentators at v. 9 and at v. 11. However, it will be argued here that 2.8–15 is bound together linguistically. Miller has mounted the most vigorous attack so he will provide the starting point for this analysis.

---

80. So also Roloff 1988: 108.

81. Similarly, Lau 1996: 86–90.

82. Heckert 1996: 104; BDF § 451. So also Knight 1992: 127. Quinn and Wacker 2000: 207 write, 'The recurrence of the first person singular with the particle *oun* marks the second division within the apostolic exhortations that began in 2.1 with the same pattern.'

83. So also Marshall 1999: 475; Mounce 2000: 167; Knight 1992: 152–53; Roloff 1988: 148; Oberlinner 1994: 112; Brox 1969a: 139; Spicq 1969: 427f; and Ellingworth 1980: 443–45. But recent defenders of the other view include Quinn and Wacker 2000: 234f. and Johnson 2001: 203.

84. E.g. Bassler 1996: 56, writes, 'The passage [2.8–3.1a] is oddly disjointed. There are several awkward grammatical transitions...'

It does seem that this passage falls into three distinct pieces: (1) v. 8 on men at prayer, (2) vv. 9–10 on women's adornment (probably also at prayer), and (3) vv. 11–15 on women and teaching.[85] Miller, however, argues that this 'cluster' (rather than passage or unit) is made up of five distinct pieces. This is the result of dividing vv. 11–15 into three parts: v. 11, v. 12, and vv. 13–15. Perhaps the best starting point, then, will be to examine any indications of cohesion within 2.11–15.

First, Miller presents surprisingly little argument for isolating 2.11 from 2.12. He simply states that 2.12 is another traditional regulation concerning the role of women and that the 'phrase ἐν ἡσυχίᾳ in its present context [in 2.12] seems unnecessary in light of its appearance in 2.11.'[86] This leads him to suggest 2.11 and 2.12 were previously independent regulations here combined because of word association. However, this is thin ground for such a leap.

Perriman contends for a similar position with more argumentation.[87] He argues that v. 12 is a parenthetical aside based on several observations. First, after claiming that v. 12 is grammatically 'awkward and elliptical,'[88] he says v. 12 does not follow on naturally from v. 11, particularly with the shift from imperative (μανθανέτω) to indicative (ἐπιτρέπω).[89] However, shifts from imperative to indicative, in and of themselves, are not uncommon and need not suggest any lack of connection. More importantly, Perriman's argument betrays an overly wooden understanding of the moods of Greek verbs.[90] Ἐπιτρέπω with an infinitive here functions as a command just as παρακαλέω in 2.1 and βούλομαι in 2.8. There is then no lack of continuity between vv. 11–12. Secondly, Perriman is bothered by the repetition of ἐν ἡσυχίᾳ just as Miller was. Perriman goes as far as to write that the repetition would 'be more easily explained if the verse were something of an afterthought, a rather hurriedly constructed interpolation.'[91] However, both scholars have failed to acknowledge that lexical repetition was a common device in ancient writing. Since ἐν ἡσυχίᾳ occurs at the beginning of v. 11 and at the end of v. 12, it is likely that the phrase is functioning here as an inclusio binding together a statement on women and

---

85.   So also Marshall 1999: 437.
86.   Miller 1997: 73.
87.   Perriman 1993: 129–42.
88.   Perriman 1993: 129.
89.   Perriman 1993: 130.
90.   This error is not uncommon in the literature on this verse. See for e.g., Spencer 1990: 57.
91.   Perriman 1993: 130. It seems that Perriman has used 'interpolation' in an unusual way, since it normally refers to something added later, but he nowhere argues this. Elsewhere in the article he seems to be arguing that v. 12, while a part of the original text, is an aside and not part of the general flow of the argument.

teaching and, in doing so, emphasizing silence.[92] Lastly, he states that the γάρ of v. 13 refers back to v. 11 and not to v. 12, since, according to Perriman, the deception of Eve is 'clearly' ground for the need for women to learn but not a ground for prohibiting them from teaching.[93] However, this is not as clear as Perriman assumes. This is simply asserted rather than argued. Once Perriman's other arguments are disproved, this statement has no basis.[94] The arguments which follow on close links between v. 11 and v. 12 only further damage Perriman's case.

On the positive side, vv. 11–12 function well together stating the point positively and negatively. Verse 11 states what women should do (learn quietly) and v. 12 states what women should not do (teach or have authority over men). A number of scholars have underscored this connection by arguing for some sort of chiasm in vv. 11–12.[95] While there is disagreement among the proposals, common to each of them is the recognition of the inclusio created by the occurrence of ἐν ἡσυχία at the beginning and ending of the verses. In fact the most common chiasm is little more than an acknowledgement of this inclusio and the double prohibition in v. 12.[96] More convincing and useful are the contrasts between v. 11 and v. 12 as noted by Schreiner: learn (μανθανέτω) but not teach (διδάσκειν); in all submission (ἐν πάσῃ ὑποταγῇ) not exercising authority (αὐθεντεῖν).[97] Thus, v. 11 and v. 12 take up the same issues in order, stating the positive and the negative respectively: A, B, not A, not B. This parallelism bracketed by an inclusio firmly supports the cohesion of vv. 11–12.

Second, there are connections between 2.11–12 and 2.13–15. Miller's arguments for isolating vv. 13–15 rely on the notorious exegetical

92. So also, Mounce 2000: 117; Schreiner 1995: 124–25; Fung 1987: 336, n. 186; Bowman 1992: 202–203, n. 32.

93. Perriman 1993: 130.

94. Perriman also says that the emphatic position of διδάσκειν in v. 12 may support his case (1993: 130). How this would support his case is unclear to me. Also, once the arguments for effectively removing v. 12 are refuted, Perriman's larger chiastic structure for vv. 11–14 fails (1993: 130).

95. Moo 1980: 64; Fung 1987: 336, n. 186; Bowman 1992: 202–203, n. 32; Barnett 1989: 228–29; Harris 1990: 340.

96. Fung 1987: 336, n. 186; Bowman 1992: 202–203, n. 32; Barnett 1989: 228–29; Harris 1990: 340. This proposed chiasm is:

A Γυνὴ ἐν ἡσυχία μανθανέτω ἐν πάσῃ ὑποταγῇ·

    B διδάσκειν δὲ γυναικὶ οὐκ ἐπιτρέπω

    B' οὐδὲ αὐθεντεῖν ἀνδρός,

A' ἀλλ' εἶναι ἐν ἡσυχία

97. Schreiner 1995: 124, n. 88. This is also noted by Köstenberger, 1995: 179. Roloff 1988: 138, notes a part of the contrast. There is of course debate on the meaning of αὐθεντεῖν but the point made here is in no way dependent on the gloss I have given.

difficulties found here. However, ambiguities do not necessitate disparate sources. The γάρ in v. 13 designates this section as a ground for the injunction on the silence of women. Two grounds are then given: (1) creation order (v. 13) and (2) Eve and not Adam was deceived (v. 14). Verse 15 then closes the discussion with a positive note on the salvation of women, stressing the positive alternative to the behavior being prohibited. It is typical in Pauline writings for discussions of judgment, etc., to close with a more positive note and that seems to be what is occurring here. The fact that v. 15 opens with a singular verb is not problematic, and it can easily refer to γυνή in vv. 11–12 rather than Eve since δέ regularly introduces a shift to something new, often a new subject.[98]

If 2.11–15 cohere, then we are left with the three main sections mentioned at the first. Now possible links between these sections must be considered. First, the relation between 2.8 and 2.9 will be considered. Miller writes, 'The admonition to women (2.9) ... is only loosely connected to 2.8 and presents significant translation problems owing to its lack of any main verb.'[99] This is simply not so, since ὡσαύτως provides a clear connection with the preceding material, comparing 'a fresh comment with a preceding one.'[100] Miller contends that ὡσαύτως provides a link only in a formal sense and that it does not carry over to women all that has been said to men. There is no need to think of the word applying to women everything that was said to men. It simply identifies the statement to women as another authoritative statement, makes apparent the verb intended to be supplied in the ellipsis,[101] and keeps the injunction to women within the context of corporate worship.[102] The ellipsis itself creates a connection with 2.8 as the reader intuitively looks back to 2.8 to supply the verb.[103] Thus, though there is clearly a shift from men to women from 2.8 to 2.9–10, there is no serious disjunction and commonly used devices are present to signal cohesion. The lack of a main verb, then, in 2.9 is no anomaly but part of the common device of ellipsis.

Therefore, we now have two sections: (1) instructions to men and women concerning corporate prayer, probably focusing on issues

98.   Levinsohn 1999: 320–25; Bakker 1993: 275–311. Bakker gives examples in which δέ marks a return to the primary subject or point of view in a discourse.

99.   Miller 1997: 69.

100.   Marshall 1999: 446.

101.   Ὡσαύτως may also carry over the setting of corporate prayer to the discussion of women's dress. This would not require the supplying of προσεύχεσθαι in 2.9 but would suggest that the focus (but not limit) of the discussion on dress is the setting of corporate prayer.

102.   This is not to say the injunction is limited to dress at worship, but that this topic is raised within the discussion of conduct at corporate worship.

103.   Reed 1999a: 40–41, classifies ellipsis (or zero-anaphora) as a type of co-classification (a type of componential tie). 'The simple act of elision invokes a cohesive interpretation by the reader' (41).

particularly problematic for each gender and (2) prohibition of women teaching.[104] Many scholars have noted that a significant shift, marked by asyndeton, occurs at 2.11. Some scholars have understood this shift to be so stark that they have concluded that 2.11–15 is a later addition or at least did not originally follow 2.10.[105] The asyndeton does create an abrupt feel in the text, but asyndeton was a common device in the ancient world. This may be a resumptive asyndeton marking a more explicit return to the setting of corporate worship since the discussion of women's adornment did not specifically mention corporate worship and had broader applications. It may also mark another shift. Having discussed men and women separately, the author may now be turning to particularly problematic issues concerning the relationship *between* men and women in corporate worship, i.e., that women should not teach or have authority over men.

There are also linguistic elements that bind 2.8–10 with 2.11–15. First, the authoritative tone of v. 8 (βούλομαι) continues through the section, being implied in v. 9 and explicitly reiterated in v. 12 (ἐπιτρέπω).[106] Second, the setting of corporate worship (prayer and teaching) unites these verses. Third, there are some interesting similarities in sentence structure between 2.9–10 and 2.11–12 (each a single sentence). Both begin with γύνη, then a prepositional phrase using ἐν describing proper behavior, and the verb following. Both employ the 'not this but (ἀλλ᾽)' structure in the argumentation:

> 'not with braided hair and gold ... but that which is fitting ...'
> (vv. 9–10)
> 'not to teach but to be in silence' (v. 12)

These verses are also bound by the recurrence of σωφροσύνη in v. 9 and v. 15,[107] which is all the more significant since these are the only two occurrences of the word in the letter. Even the idea of v. 15 is similar to vv. 9a, 10, with the exhortation to good works appropriate for godly women being similar to the call to remain in faith, love, and sanctification.[108] Therefore, 2.8–15 should be seen as a cohesive unit.

---

104. The question of how this is to be applied today is not in view here.

105. E.g., Miller 1997: 72; Holtz, 1972: 72–73.

106. Johnson 1996: 134. Bassler's statement that in vv. 11–12 the author shifts from persuasion to authoritative command (1996: 59) wrongly assumes βούλομαι has no nuance of authoritative command.

107. So also Schreiner 1995: 151; Barnett 1963: 228–29.

108. The occurrence of σωφροσύνη at the very end of the sentence renders very unlikely the argument of Falconer, Diaz, and Michel that all or part of v. 15 is a later addition (Falconer 1941: 375–79; J. Alonso Diaz, 'Restricción en algunos textos paulinos de las reivindicaciones

3.1–7

Boundaries
Whether or not this unit includes πιστὸς ὁ λόγος, it opens with asyndeton and several obvious shifts in cohesion fields. The topic shifts away from the roles of men and women or corporate prayer to the qualifications of an overseer.[109] Whereas the previous unit had concluded with primarily aorist verbs, 3.1 opens with a series of present tense verbs. The subject is no longer γυνή or ἀνήρ, but τίς and ἐπίσκοπος. Τίς has not been the subject since 1.19, and nowhere previously has it dominated a section as it does here. Almost every commentator notes an abrupt shift between the previous unit and this one.

Cohesion
3.1–7 appears to be a cohesive unit simply because of its form as a catalogue of qualifications for an office. The different phrases all cohere because they refer to ἐπίσκοπος (or to τις which refers to ἐπίσκοπος) and to the necessary qualifications for such office. This recognition is sufficient for arguing the cohesiveness of the unit, but it is also interesting to note that the list of qualifications opens and closes with a statement of necessity (δεῖ; 3.2, 7).[110] Towner also notes the similarity between the first qualification, 'irreproachable' (ἀνεπίλημπτος) and the last qualification, having a 'good witness with outsiders.'[111] The last two statements are particularly similar since they list a qualification and then state a possible negative result of failing to have the qualification in similar terms – ἵνα μή ... εἰς ... ἐμπέσῃ τοῦ διαβόλου (v. 6 and v. 7). These observations may explain why there is little discussion of the incoherence of this unit. Even Miller says comparatively little against this unit, but he does argue for some disjunction in this unit on two grounds. First, he notes, as most scholars have, the marked difference in style between the one or two word items in vv. 2–3 and the more syntactically complex items of vv. 4–7. For Miller, 'These changes in style and content suggest the likelihood that different sources have been combined here.'[112] However, catalogues, like this one, in

de la mujer en la Iglesia,' *Estudios Eclesiásticos* 50 [1975]: 77–93; Michel 1948: 93). Porter 1993b: 90 particularly critiques this view as 'not exegetically or historically sound' and as 'pure conjecture meant to deal dismissively with admittedly difficult verses.'

109. Cf. Roloff 1988: 148–49.

110. Note the similar observation by Quinn and Wacker 2000: 260: 'The final sentence of this whole section on the bishop, verse 7, appears to echo verbally (with forms of *dei* and *kalos*) the opening of 3:1b-2.'

111. Towner 1989: 230–31 concludes, 'Thus the list is no mere catalogue of virtues and standards, but rather a thoughtfully constructed, or perhaps modified, device designed to examine the reputation of candidates for the office of bishop.'

112. Miller 1997: 76.

ancient literature often did not have a consistent style running throughout their constituent items. Indeed, Fitzgerald notes that it was common for items at either the beginning or end to be expanded, thereby showing their importance.[113] This may likely be what is going on in 3.1–7.[114] In any case, the difference in syntactic complexity between items in the list is not sufficient grounds for positing a seam in the text. Miller also bases his argument for a break at v. 4 on a supposed difference in content, but ancient catalogues often had items of varying content.

Secondly, Miller calls the repetition of ἐμπέσῃ τοῦ διαβόλου in vv. 6 and 7 'strange' and says its supports his 'conjecture' that different sources are in use. However, Miller does not explain the basis from which he declares this repetition 'strange.' Since repetition was a common literary device it could be used to link these two items, as suggested above. Also, Fitzgerald notes that it was common specifically in ancient catalogues for words to be repeated for emphasis.[115]

Therefore, 3.1–7 is a cohesive unit bound by unity in topic, literary form, and smaller linguistic devices (e.g., repetitions).

3.8–13

Boundaries
That a new unit begins at 3.8 is signaled by several shifts. The subject shifts from ἐπίσκοπος to διάκονοι. Whereas in the previous unit the verbs were all third person singular, in 3.8–13 they are all third person plural.[116] The topic is still qualification for office, but now the office of 'deacon' rather than 'overseer.' The presence of ὡσαύτως, though not requiring a shift to a new unit, signals a change to another group of people. That this is clearly a new unit is universally accepted.

Cohesion
The cohesion of this unit, however, is doubted by some. Easton and Falconer suggest the unit suffers from poor arrangement, with Falconer even suggesting the verse order has been disturbed.[117] However, Falconer does not provide any basis for his conjecture, nor does he point to glaring problems which necessitate such a radical solution which is devoid of any

---

113. Fitzgerald 1997: 290–91.
114. Bassler 1996: 67 reaches a similar conclusion.
115. Fitzgerald 1997: 287.
116. The contrast holds for participial forms in the two units as well, with all participles in 3.1–7 being singular and all participles in 3.8–13 being plural.
117. Easton 1947: 133; Falconer 1937: 136 suggests the order may have originally been 3.8, 9, 12, 10, 13, 11.

manuscript support. These suggestions are enough, however, for Miller to suggest this unit is composed of disparate documents.[118] Miller also points to the ambiguity of the identity of the γυναῖκες and the ὡσαύτως in 3.11 as evidence of seams in the text. However, ambiguity (in the minds of modern readers and not necessarily for the original recipients) need not necessitate the combination of independent documents.

In contrast to the alleged incoherence of the text, a number of elements support a cohesive view of this unit. First, this unit coheres as a catalogue of qualifications. As noted above, these catalogues were a common ancient literary form and could include diverse items in the same catalogue. Second, there is a continuity of verbal person and number throughout (third plural) and the subject is διάκονοι throughout (with a form of the word occurring in vv. 8, 10, 12, 13), except for v. 11 which appears almost as a parenthesis. This could suggest that v. 11 does not cohere with the rest of the unit, and that issue will be dealt with below. Third, there is an apparent inclusio binding the unit. The first list of qualifications for deacons closes with 'holding the mystery of the **faith**' (3.9). The unit then closes with the reward of 'having much confidence in the **faith** which is in Christ Jesus' (3.13). The idea seems to be that those who hold on to the faith and serve well grow in confidence of that very faith.

As noted above, v. 11 does stand out from the rest of the unit. In effect, its presence creates three pieces in the unit marked by shifts in subject: vv. 8–10 (deacons), v. 11 (women), vv. 12–13 (deacons). However, significant connections between these pieces show they are all part of a cohesive unit. There are obvious connections between vv. 8–10 and vv. 12–13, primarily the same subject. The issue, though, is connections between these pieces and v. 11. A compelling case for the cohesion of 3.11 with the rest of the unit has been made by Jennifer H. Stiefel.[119] Following Roloff, she notes a parallelism between the qualifications for deacons in 3.8 and for women in 3.11.[120] Significantly, both lists begin with σεμνός, an adjective which, although Stiefel did not note it, does not occur elsewhere in the letter. This repetition along with the fact the word is not used elsewhere suggests a deliberate connection intended by the author. Then, the other items in the list, though not identical are quite similar. The women are to be μὴ διαβόλους, and the deacons are to be μὴ διλόγους. The form of the qualification is the same with a negated adjective, and the adjectives themselves are semantically similar as both refer to sinful speech. Next, the call to sobriety in v. 11 (νηφάλιος), though quite possibly wider in

118. Miller 1997: 76–77.
119. Stiefel 1995: 442–57.
120. Marshall 1999: 494–95 makes the same comparisons, stating, 'The list of qualifications for the female deacons corresponds closely to that for the male deacons in v. 8' (494).

connotation, still includes a prohibition on drunkenness as μὴ οἴνῳ πολλῷ προσέχοντας in 3.8. Lastly, both lists conclude with an element referring to πίστις. While πιστὰς ἐν πᾶσιν in 3.11 could simply refer to reliability, the other parallels with 3.8 may suggest that this qualification refers more to maintenance of Christian faith in all areas of life, similar to 'holding fast to the mystery of the faith' in 3.9.[121]

In addition to these lexical parallels, Stiefel notes that '3.11 repeats the syntax of 3.8.'[122] Both verses begin with an anarthrous noun in accusative plural, taken as governed by an understood δεῖ εἶναι from 3.2, followed by the adverb ὡσαύτως. Then, 3.10 and 3.12 have very similar syntactic structures. Both verses begin with a nominative plural subject (οὗτοι, 3.10; διάκονοι, 3.12) followed by third person plural imperatives (δοκιμαζέσθωσαν, διακονείτωσαν, 3.10; ἔστωσαν, 3.12), the only imperatives in the unit. This creates an alternating structure within the unit:

A   3.8–9 acc. pl. noun + adv. modified by adjectives/participles in accusative
   B   3.10 nom. pl. noun + imperative, participle, imperative
A'   3.11 acc. pl. noun + adv. modified by adjectives in accusative
   B'   3.12 nom. pl. noun + imperative + participle

This is then followed by a generalizing statement with a nominative plural substantival participle and a finite indicative verb, both of which occur for the first time in the unit here. Though there are some irregularities in this structure (e.g., two imperatives in 3.10, but only one in 3.12), it does suggest this passage fits together. 3.11 does not obtrude from the structure of the rest of the passage, but fits well in the overall scheme of the passage, appearing even as an abbreviated summary of 3.8–9.[123] Thus, Stiefel is justified in concluding that this 'passage exhibits a balanced and coherent structure.'[124]

While the argument so far shows that the verses connect with each other semantically and syntactically, the logical question of why there is a shift from 'deacons' to 'women' and back to 'deacons' remains. It can be noted that the movement is from men to women to family life. Since the γυνή in 3.12 clearly refers to a 'wife,' it may be that γυνή in 3.11 also means 'wives.' In that case, there would be a logical progression: qualities of deacons, qualities of their wives, and further domestic issues concerning the deacon. Hence, the mention of the wives in deacons in 3.11 prompts a mention of

---

121.   Roloff 1988: 165–66; Stiefel 1995: 444. Followed by Johnson 2001: 229. Marshall 1999: 494–95 also notes this interpretation as a possibility.
122.   Stiefel 1995: 447.
123.   Stiefel 1995: 450; Roloff 1988: 149–50, 165.
124.   Stiefel 1995: 450.

faithfulness to one's wife in 3.12. This is offered only as a possible solution to the shifting found in this unit.

3.14–16

Boundaries

Another clear shift occurs at 3.14 with the disappearance of the διάκονος vocabulary and the close of the catalogue at v. 13. In addition, the verbs shift from entirely third plural in the previous unit to first person singular in 3.14. This corresponds to a shift in participants as Paul and Timothy come to the forefront again as the discussion becomes a more explicit interaction between these two. This is indicated by the collocation of first person singular verbs and second person singular verbs and pronouns, which have not occurred together since 1.18. Indeed, the second person singular has not occurred at all since 1.18 and the first person singular has not occurred since 2.12.[125] No unit so far in the letter has had such a high occurrence of second person singular forms.

Cohesion

There does not seem to be any contention against the cohesiveness of 3.14–15. The continuity of participants (Paul to Timothy) unites the two verses, with the first four verbal forms referring to Paul and the fifth verb shifting to Timothy's response. The content of what Timothy is to know introduces the topic of the church, which is then the focus of 3.15b. Accordingly the verb shifts to third person singular here. The discussion of the church closes with a mention of 'truth,' and v. 16 further expounds what this truth is.

The connection between 3.15 and 3.16 is found in the relations between ἀναστρέφω, ἀλήθεια, and εὐσεβείας μυστήριον. First, ἀλήθεια and μυστήριον are both terms referring to the basic Christian message with differing nuances. Already in the early Pauline letters ἀλήθεια had come to be one of the terms used for God's saving revelation. In the Pastoral Epistles ἀλήθεια is used to refer to 'the authentic revelation of God bringing salvation'[126] vis-à-vis aberrations of this message. μυστήριον refers to God's plan for salvation in Christ which has now been revealed.[127] Already in 3.9 μυστήριον τῆς πίστεως has been used to clearly refer to the content of the Christian message. Thus, 3.15 closes its discussion of the church by

---

125. Quinn and Wacker 2000: 306–307 notes also that after 2.12 Paul 'vanished completely into the subject matter until this section begins.'

126. Marshall 1999: 122. Cf. Towner 1989: 122.

127. Towner 1989: 87–88; Marshall 1999: 490–91; Bornkamm *TDNT*: 4, 822; Bockmuehl 1990: 226; Marshall also cites H. Krämer, 'μυστήριον', *EDNT* 2: 446–9.

referring to the church's role in relation to the 'truth,' and 3.16 continues by further expounding what the content of this 'revealed' truth is.[128] Secondly, μυστήριον is characterized by εὐσέβεια, a word which refers to the whole of Christian existence as a way of life resulting from acceptance of the Christian message.[129] The clear ethical overtones of the use of this word connects with the discussion of how one should 'behave' (ἀναστρέφω) in church in 3.15.

The so-called 'hymn,' itself is clearly cohesive. It contains six balanced clauses each having a third person singular aorist passive indicative verb and a dative noun. Five of the clauses also have the preposition ἐν. Since this is such a clearly defined unit, one could argue that this piece should be considered a self-contained unit. However, it is clearly intended to be an explication of εὐσεβείας μυστήριον, and this phrase has been shown to have links with v. 15. Therefore, 3.14–16 should be seen as one cohesive unit.

4.1–5

Boundaries
At 4.1 the so-called 'hymn' has clearly ended and a new unit has begun as the string of aorist passive verbs is broken with the appearance of present active and future middle verbs. Whereas the subject in the hymn was clearly the risen Christ, in 4.1 the subject is πνεῦμα, for the only time in the letter. Similarly, the topic shifts at 4.1 to the problem of the opponents. As will be shown below, at 4.6 there is a shift to specific exhortation to Timothy with the return of second person singular verbs. Thus, a new unit begins at 4.1 and continues through 4.5 dealing with opponents.

Cohesion
It seems there has been no one who has argued against the cohesiveness of this unit, though some have commented on the awkward syntax found within it. It coheres around the topic of opponents within the Church, as they are introduced in 4.1 (τινες) and their activities are described into 4.3. From the middle of 4.3 to 4.5 the position of the opponents is refuted. There is also a significant interest in supernatural beings (Louw and Nida's domain 12 [1989]) throughout the unit with πνεῦμα occurring twice in v. 1, δαιμόνιον (v. 1), and θεός in vv. 3,4, and 5.[130] Marshall notes how the section is structured with pairs (with and without καί): spirits and

---

128. Marshall 1999: 523 writes, 'μυστήριον (3.9) is another way of referring to the 'truth' (v. 15).'

129. Cf. Towner 1989: 147–52; Marshall 1999: 523.

130. θεός is of course common throughout the letter (22 occurrences) but only one other unit (2.1–7) has this many occurrences.

teachings; liars and branded; to marry and to abstain from foods; believers and people who have come to know the truth; good and not to be rejected; word of God and prayer.[131] Also, there is significant lexical cohesion between vv. 3 and 4:

4.3	**4.4**
Θεός ἔκτισεν	κτίσμα θεοῦ
μετάλημψιν	λαμβανόμενον
μετὰ εὐχαριστίας	μετὰ εὐχαριστίας
forbid foods	refuse nothing

These connections suggest careful composition. Indeed, there seem to be several deliberate contrasts within the unit. Doctrines of demons are connected to hypocrisy and seared consciences, but the word of God is associated with sanctifying. Those who turn away from the **faith** (πίστις) for **deceitful** spirits in the hypocrisy of **liars** are contrasted with those who **believe** (πίστοις) and know the **truth**. These semantic and structural observations indicate a strong cohesiveness in this unit, and suggest intentionality in composition even though the syntax may be awkward at times.

4.6–10

Boundaries

A new unit clearly begins at 4.6 as reference to the second person singular, which had been prominent in 3.14–15 but completely absent from 4.1–5, appears quite prominently with five occurrences in vv. 6–7.[132] In fact the two imperatives in 4.7 are the first second person singular imperatives in the entire letter! This marks a shift to exhortations to Timothy specifically concerning himself, rather than concerning the church as in chapters 2–3 (where the imperatives that occur are third singular[133] or plural[134]). The exhortations to Timothy (with the accompanying high occurrence of second person singular) concerning Timothy carry on through 4.16, causing some scholars to consider 4.6–16 as one unit. However, it is interesting to note that references to second person singular occur in vv. 6–7, are absent entirely from vv. 8–10, and then occur at least once in every verse in vv. 11–16. This observation plus the accompanying fact that vv. 8–

131. Marshall 1999: 531, n. 3.
132. Cf. Marshall 1999: 547, 'Verse 6 clearly brings the previous sub-section to a conclusion and provides a transition to the next one....'
133. 2.11.
134. 3.10 (2x), 3.12.

10 appear to function as a ground for vv. 6–7 (γάρ in vv. 8, 10) suggest that there may be reason to consider 4.6–10 and 4.11–16 as distinct units. 4.6–7 begin exhortations to Timothy followed by a sort of theological grounding (vv. 8–10) which almost digresses. 4.11, with a ταῦτα statement similar to 4.6, then resumes the exhortations to Timothy which continue through 4.16.[135] This structure would be quite similar to what has been observed in 2.1–15.[136]

Cohesion

Miller despairs of any cohesion within 4.6–10, referring to this unit as 'a cluster of miscellaneous admonitions and proverbial sayings,' which he distinguishes as 4.6, 4.7a, 4.7b, 4.8, 4.9, 4.10. Little argumentation is given, however, for these divisions, with most of the argument resting on two points: (1) the suggestion that many of these verses have a 'proverbial' character with similar parallels in other literature, and (2) the ambiguity in the intended referent of certain words such as ταῦτα (4.6) and εἰς τοῦτο (4.10). In response, even if the first point is granted it proves neither incoherence nor that sources are being directly borrowed. An author can use sources creatively and coherently, can compose original material with a 'proverbial' character, and can write in ways simply influenced by common sayings. On the second point, a certain amount of ambiguity is common in communication (especially when read by a distant third party) and does not necessitate incohesiveness. To be compelling, Miller's observations would need other argumentation. Miller's only real argumentation is that 'No thread of logic drives this unit along; only the loosest thematic link (training in godliness?) holds the diverse materials together.'[137] To investigate this assertion, it is necessary to examine each verse looking for possible connections.

In 4.6 there is a strong emphasis on teaching not only with the two noun phrases, τοῖς λόγοις τῆς πίστεως and τῆς καλῆς διδασκαλίας, but also with the two participles, ὑποτιθέμενος and ἐντρεφόμενος, which are both classed by Louw and Nida (1989) within the lexical domain of teaching.[138] The key concern is for Timothy to remain in this true teaching with him being encouraged to be nourished or trained in them and being reminded that he

---

135. So also Knight 1992: 204. Some scholars take 4.11 with 4.6–10 and see 4.12 as beginning the new unit. As mentioned above, I think the parallel with 4.6 suggests 4.11 is resuming the topic and thus beginning the new unit. For more argumentation to this effect see below, section on connections between consecutive units.

136. Having argued for this division, it must be said, however, that there are connections between the units (as will be argued subsequently) and the argument here is not adversely affected if 4.6–16 are viewed as one unit.

137. Miller 1997: 80.

138. ὑποτιθέμενος, 33.230; ἐντρεφόμενος, 33.242.

has followed them.[139] Verse 7a, then, provides a very clear and logical contrast introduced naturally by δέ. In contrast to proper teaching there are 'myths.' Whereas the teaching in v. 6 was 'good' (κάλος), these myths are 'profane' (βέβηλος);[140] and, whereas Timothy himself has followed the true teaching, these myths are of such a quality as to inspire a following only among the most gullible (γραώδης). Also, and perhaps most importantly, Timothy's response to these two should be quite different. Whereas he is to follow and be nourished in the true teaching, he is to avoid (παραιτοῦ) the myths. Thus, semantically, syntactically, and logically v. 7a provides a fine contrast to v. 6.

4.7b, then, provides another contrast with 4.7a again introduced by δέ. Verse 6 mentioned the positive, v. 7a contrasts with the negative, and v. 7b contrasts by returning to the positive. 4.7b also moves the argument along by introducing two new elements which will be developed in the following verses: 'training' (γυμνάζω) and εὐσέβεια. 4.7b is not an entirely new and disconnected statement, however, because (in addition to the syntax) εὐσέβεια links back to the previous discussion of the proper way in 4.6. The usage in 3.16 shows that εὐσέβεια refers at least in part to the content of the Christian message just as τοῖς λόγοις τῆς πίστεως and τῆς καλῆς διδασκαλίας do in 4.6. The new element which εὐσέβεια introduces in the argument here is the idea of the ethical outworking of the Christian message. This may indeed be the intended contrast with v. 7a since the previous mention of 'myths' (1.4) stated that these myths led only to quarrels rather than to ethical living, expressed as 'love' (1.5).

Next, 4.8 provides a ground for 4.7b, a reason for exerting oneself in training for godliness, namely that εὐσέβεια brings with it the promise of eternal life. However, Miller says the logical link between 7b and 8 is not clear, though he concedes a lexical link with the recurrence of εὐσέβεια. He does not elaborate on why the link is not clear, but presumably his problem is with the fact that v. 8 opens with a surprising reference to 'bodily exercise,' a heretofore unmentioned subject. There is no logical problem here, however, as v. 8a clearly acts as a foil for the real point which is made in v. 8b, the profitability of εὐσέβεια.[141]

---

139. 4.6 is further bound together by the repetition of κάλος which suggests the good servant is the one who adheres to the good teaching (Bassler 1996: 83).

140. Perhaps also faith contrasts gullibility; words characterized by faith may contrast myths that are devoid of any divine or sacred character. Cf. Hort 1894: 138, on βέβηλος.

141. So also, Knight 1992: 198–99; Heckert 1996: 47. For 'foil' as a discourse device see Stephen Levinsohn, *Discourse Features of New Testament Greek: A Coursebook* (Dallas: Summer Institute of Linguistics, 1992): 84. Levinsohn defines a foil as 'a constituent that is presented for the purpose of being contrasted or added to in the following material. The foil comes into temporary focus in anticipation of a switch of attention to the corresponding constituent' (84). As cited in Heckert 1996: 47.

4.8 itself is bound together as another clear contrast. Knight has noted the parallelism and lexical repetitions which bind 4.8. These elements can be clearly seen when the verse is laid out in the following way:[142]

ἡ γὰρ	σωματικὴ	γυμνασία	πρὸς ὀλίγον	ἐστὶν ὠφέλιμος
ἡ δὲ		εὐσέβεια	πρὸς πάντα	ὠφέλιμος ἐστιν

The portion of 4.8 not represented here (4.8c) introduces the new element which cinches the contrast and advances the discussion – the promise of life now and to come.

Next, 4.9 appears perfectly logical as an affirmation of the statement in 4.8. Although Miller refers to confusion over the identity of the faithful saying in 4.9, the majority of commentators agree that it refers to some or all of 4.8.[143] As such, it fits perfectly well into the flow of the argument.

4.10 then links back to 4.8. This is argued by commentators, but can be further confirmed by noticing semantic links between the two verses. First, 4.10 returns to the idea of hard work and exertion. Timothy had been exhorted with γύμναζε, and now Paul refers to his own efforts with κοπιάω and ἀγωνίζομαι. Since the ἀγών word-group is used in the accepted Paulines to refer to his mission work for the gospel and the care of the churches and since κοπιάω is used later in this letter (5.17) for the work of elders, it can be argued that what is in view here is strenuous effort for the gospel's sake.[144] This is then also similar to the effort called for from Timothy for personal advance in appropriating the message of the gospel. This idea of hard work for the sake of the true message then encompasses vv. 7b–10. Second, just as Timothy's effort is grounded in the promise of life, so v. 10b grounds (ὅτι) Paul's efforts in hope in the 'living God' who is savior. Lastly, there also seems to be an inclusio within the participant field. As noted by many commentators, 4.6–10 focuses on Timothy personally. He is to be nourished on good teaching and to train 'himself' (σεαυτόν) for godliness because it will lead to salvation. However, the corporate church does appear at the beginning (v. 6, ἀδέλφοι) and at the very end (v. 10, πιστῶν), enclosing the exhortation to Timothy within an ecclesial setting.

---

142. Knight 1992: 198.

143. Knight 1992: 198 writes, 'the vast majority of commentators … agree that part or all of v. 8 is the saying.' Apparently, subsequent commentators have continued in this line: Marshall 1999: 554; Quinn and Wacker 2000: 378–79; Bassler 1996: 84.

144. Cf. Marshall 1999: 555; also Pfitzner, 1967.

4.11–16

Boundaries

As noted above this unit is closely linked with 4.6–10, so the shifts between the units are not great. However, there is a shift back to the predominant second person singular after this faded from view in the last part of the previous unit. Accordingly, there is also a return of σύ (Timothy) as the subject. 4.11 resumes the topic begun in 4.6 by repeating ταῦτα and words concerning teaching (παραγγέλλω and διδάσκω in v. 11 and ὑποτίθημι in v. 6).[145]

Cohesion

Miller criticizes this unit as 'another collection of loosely connected admonitions and sayings that seem to be strung (like beads on a string) around the theme of "commands to Timothy."'[146] He then suggests that v. 11, v. 12, v. 13, v. 14, v. 15, v. 16a, and v. 16b are all previously independent pieces which have been incoherently merged in this text.[147] As grounds for this assertion, Miller lists three elements that 'suggest that the material has been gathered from various sources:' (1) the accumulation of 10 imperatives; (2) the vague use of ταῦτα and τοῦτο; and (3) 'the lack of any internal cohesion.'[148]

In response, it may be noted first that Miller underestimates the cohesive value of unity in genre, topic, and participant ('commands to Timothy'). The facts that the entire unit is exhortatory, that ten out of 14 finite verbs are imperatives, each one addressed to Timothy from Paul, and the high concentration of second person singular references (15, more than any other unit in the letter) suggest some cohesion in what the author is writing. Such strings of commands were common in exhortatory literature in the ancient world, which makes the accumulation of ten imperatives no evidence for disparate sources.

By the vague use of ταῦτα and τοῦτο Miller refers to the fact that the referent of these words is not easily discernible. Miller then suggests the reason for this ambiguity is that these statements have been lifted from sources without their original referent and strung together. However, this is only a supposition. Ταῦτα and τοῦτο occur in this way so often in the Pastoral Epistles that it could just as easily be argued that this represents

145. The similarities between the openings of these units will be discussed further in the following chapter.
146. Miller 1997: 82.
147. Quinn and Wacker 2000: 402ff. separate vv. 15–16 as a separate unit but I cannot find any reason given or argumentation to support this.
148. Miller 1997: 82.

the style of the author. Thus, this observation, though interesting in itself, has no probative value in the argument.

Miller's third argument is that this unit lacks any sort of internal cohesion. This has already been shown to be false by the observations concerning cohesion of genre, topic, participants, and verbal forms. There are also some semantic chains running through the unit. First, there is a concern for teaching represented most notably by the διδασκ- root (διδάσκω, v. 11; διδασκαλία, v. 13 and v. 16), but also παραγγέλλω (v. 11), ἀνάγνωσις and παράκλησις (v. 13), and possibly λόγος (v. 12).[149] Thus, this chain runs throughout the unit with clusters in vv. 11 and 13 and with the διδασκ- root occurring at the beginning and end of the unit. Secondly, there is a semantic chain concerning perseverance or endurance. Three words in this unit are listed in Louw and Nida's subdomain 68b, 'Continue:' προσέχω (v. 13),[150] μελέτα (v. 15),[151] and ἐπιμένω (v. 16).[152] In addition, the imperatival use of εἰμί in the phrase ἐν τούτοις ἴσθι (v. 15) also has the idea of continuing in these things.[153] Then, μὴ ἀμέλει is a negative way of calling for continued faithfulness. Also, ἔπεχε σεαυτῷ καὶ τῇ διδασκαλίᾳ (v. 16) seems to fit in with this chain. In the context, the point of the enjoined watchfulness is to ensure continuance in proper faith and practice. Thus, this chain of endurance runs throughout the unit as well. Lastly, the chains of teaching and endurance interact in that teaching is one of the areas in which Timothy is to endure.[154]

Also, as was noted above, pairs have been common in parts of 1 Timothy. This is true of the imperatives in this unit: 'command and teach' (v. 11); 'practice these things' and 'be in them' (v. 15); 'watch closely . . .' and 'remain in them' (v. 16). The imperatives in 4.12 are a contrasting pair: 'let no one despise . . . but be an example.' Thus, eight of the ten

149.   There is some debate whether this word in this instance refers simply to conversation or to more official speech by Timothy, i.e., teaching. See Marshall 1999: 561 for discussion.

150.   Louw and Nida 1989: 68.19.

151.   Louw and Nida 1989: 68.20.

152.   Louw and Nida 1989: 68.11.

153.   Louw and Nida 1989: 68.20 (p. 657) say this phrase is essentially synonymous with the use of μελετάω in the same verse.

154.   It could be argued that there is also a semantic chain relating to conduct in this unit. There definitely is a cluster of such words in v. 13 with τύπος followed by several words relating to behavior. However, to be a significant chain through the unit it would need to recur elsewhere. If σεαυτῷ in v. 16 is understood to refer to personal conduct then this chain would be established, and along with the chain on teaching would provide the objects of the chain on endurance. Indeed, if σεαυτῷ refers to personal conduct, then v. 16a is a particularly apt conclusion restating the concerns of vv. 12–13 in parallel order:

4.12 – behavior

4.13 – teaching

4.16 – Watch yourself (behavior) and your teaching

imperatives occur in explicit pairs.[155] This continuity in style also argues for cohesion.

Also, there is significant similarity in the syntactic structure of vv. 15 and 16. Both verses consist of a second person singular imperative, followed by another second person singular imperative with a dative noun (of general referent) expressing the object of concern, following a clause stressing the outcome of obedience to the command:

imperative + imperative with dative + clause stressing outcome
μελέτα + ἴσθι + ἐν τούτοις + ἵνα ἡ προκοπὴ φανερὰ ᾖ
ἔπεχε + ἐπίμενε + αὐτοῖς + γὰρ ... σώσεις

The structure of the two verses is not identical (especially the objects of the first imperative), but the similarities are striking. The similarity is strengthened by the similarity in parallel verbs. The second imperative in both sentences calls for being in, or remaining in, the things that are being urged. The idea of continuance is clear. The first imperative in both sentences is the one that calls for more specific action. Both verbs urge care in carrying out the exhortations: 'take pains with,' 'pay close attention to.'

Lastly, there is also a strong continuity in the participant field. Timothy is, of course, in view throughout, as in the previous unit. Paul is also in view implicitly as the one exhorting Timothy. Additionally, the church becomes a prominent participant throughout this unit though it was only mentioned in the opening and closing of the previous unit. 4.11 assumes a group whom Timothy will teach. In v. 12 those who might despise Timothy's youth at least include the church, and Timothy is explicitly told to be an example to 'those who believe.' 4.13 addresses Timothy's role in public, corporate ministry. 4.14 refers to the πρεσβύτεροι. The stated purpose for the charge to faithful perseverance in 4.15 is that Timothy's progress be evident to 'all,' undoubtedly including the church. Similarly, the continued call to faithfulness has in view not only his own salvation (as in 4.7–8) but also that of those who hear him.[156] Thus, 4.11–16 are unified by a focus on Timothy in relation to the church.

---

155. One could also argue that προσέχω (v. 13) and μὴ ἀμελέω are a pair. They are similar in meaning (one positive, the other negative), but it is not clear that they are intended to be seen as a pair.

156. Thus, Roloff 1980: 250, notes that 'In spite of the terse, apodictic style,' there is a clearly recognizable organized theme of the relationship between church leaders and the church.

5.1–2

Boundaries
It seems to be universally accepted to consider 5.1–2 as an individual unit. The primary shifts signaling a new unit are the introduction of new participants (the different age groups) and a slight shift in topic (from Timothy's behavior and teaching ministry to treatment of age groups). While these shifts can support viewing 5.1–2 as a new unit, it must be noted that the shifts are not dramatic since this is still exhortation from Paul to Timothy and the predominant second person singular imperatives continue.

Cohesion
There seems to be no dispute of the cohesion of this short unit. The fact that it is brief and is syntactically one sentence makes it difficult to subdivide. The topic is united as proper treatment of age and gender groups and the proper treatment is framed in familial language. Thus there is a semantic chain of age/gender grouping (πρεσβύτερος, νεώτερος, πρεσβυτέρα, νεώτερα)[157] and a semantic chain of familial relationship (πατήρ, ἀδελφός, μητήρ, ἀδελφή). These interact as the familial relations provide the perspective for proper treatment of the age/gender groups. Also, the use of ὡς with ellipsis (implying the verb παρακαλέω from 5.1) serves to bind the clauses together. Thus, this is a clearly defined and cohesive unit.

5.3–16

Boundaries
Just as in the previous unit, an initial asyndetic noun representing a new participant signals a new unit. The primary shifts from 5.1–2 are the new participants (widows and families) and topic (the provision for widows). While the unit begins with a second person imperative addressed to Timothy it moves on to address other people directly as well (v. 4).[158] Also, though imperatives do occur with some frequency in this unit, it is not as dominated by imperatives as the previous units have been. The topic of widows and the occurrence of the word (χήρα) runs throughout the unit and ceases at 5.16, where this unit ends.

---

157. The fact that there are actually only two terms used here (just masculine and feminine forms) serves to bind the unit even more.

158. Of course Timothy is again directly addressed in 5.7 and 11. The point here is not that Timothy ceases to be addressed but that others are addressed as well.

Cohesion

The unity or disunity of this passage may have received more discussion than any other passage in 1 Timothy, probably due to the fact that, as Bassler and Towner note, the interpretation of this passage hinges to a great extent on the structure of the passage.[159] Indeed Verner writes, 'Most of the particular interpretive problems connected with this passage are related to the problem of the structure of the passage as a whole.'[160] Most scholars, even Miller, concede that this unit does have a thematic unity concerning the care of widows.[161] The problem, however, is in the arrangement of the material and how the different verses relate to one another. Thus, Parry says 5.3–8 is 'curiously ill-arranged,'[162] and several suggest v. 16 should have followed v. 8[163] and that v. 7 must be an editorial insertion.[164] Bassler suggests we need to ask 'what is wrong with the text? The primary problem here is the apparent lack of unity in this passage, though it seems to deal with a single issue.'[165] Some commentators, particularly older ones, have conjectured radical rearrangements of the text (e.g., Parry and Falconer).[166] Hanson represents a common position when he writes that the passage is 'confused and obscure in some places, probably because the author is adapting an existing church order source.'[167] Miller takes an even more radical position that there is not even one main source but a variety of separate sayings have been combined here. Miller identifies these separate sayings by dividing the text as follows: 3, 4, 5–7, 8, 9–10, 11–15, 16.

What then are the primary problematic elements identified by these scholars? Miller bases his arguments on three observations: (1) 'frequently rough and obscure transitions,' (2) the presence of statements which seem to mark traditional material (vv. 4b and 7), and (3) the lack of linguistic precision.[168] Miller's only example of the lack of linguistic precision is the shift in subject from singular to unexpressed plural in 5.4. Other scholars mention as problematic the apparent repetition in vv. 4, 8, and 16 (which Miller also alludes to) and whether the 'real widows' of 3–8, 16 and the catalogued widows in 9–15 are the same group.

---

159. Bassler 1984: 33; Towner, 1989: 180–81.
160. Verner 1983: 161.
161. Miller 1997: 84. Verner 1983: 166 writes, 'When one views the whole of 5:3–16 together one finds that to a certain extent it does reflect a unified perspective after all.' Oberlinner 1994: 221 says the verses form a literary and thematic unity.
162. Parry 1920: 30.
163. Houlden 1976: 94. Miller also includes Spicq 1969: 538, and Scott 1936: 63.
164. Quinn and Wacker 2000: 434–35; Falconer 1937: 147.
165. Bassler 1984: 33.
166. Parry 1920: 31; Falconer 1937: 147–48.
167. Hanson 1982: 96.
168. Miller 1997: 84.

However, some scholars have maintained the literary unity of this passage. Indeed Karris refers to this passage as 'the author at his creative best,'[169] referring to the manner in which different traditions are merged here. However, the brevity of the space allowed in his commentary does not allow one to see how this provides cohesion for the entire passage. Johnson also suggests 'the discussion of widows is not without literary structure,'[170] though he does not specifically spell out this structure. He notes the alternation of commands, 'case law' (conditional statements) and antithetical descriptions of true and false widows, and seems to suggest the section hangs on what he calls the four apodictic commands in the section (vv. 3, 9, 11, 14). While this is helpful, it is only suggestive, and his choice of commands is neither clear nor substantiated since vv. 4, 7, 16 also contain imperatives but are not included. Most significantly, J. Müller-Bardorff has argued for the following chiasmus within this unit:[171]

A The Command: Honor widows who are real widows (v. 3)
  B Conditions of Qualification: No supporting relatives, conduct (vv. 4–6)
    C Admonition to the Family (v. 8)
  B' Conditions of Qualification: Age, conduct (vv. 9–15)
    C Admonition to the Family (v. 16a)
A' The Command Restated: Help widows who are real widows (v. 16b)

This suggestion will be considered in the following analysis of cohesive elements within 5.3–16.

What elements in 5.3–16, then, suggest or provide cohesion? First, as others have noted, the word χήρα occurs eight times in this unit (3 [2x], 4, 5, 9, 11, 16 [2x]) including the beginning and end of the unit. Also, the word occurs nowhere else in the letter. This observation led Bassler to state, 'Thus a clear word pattern is established that points to the unity of the passage.'[172] The term αἱ ὄντως χῆραι seems to especially set off the unit. It occurs at the beginning (v. 3) and then occurs at the very end of the unit (v. 16b, the 2nd and 3rd to the last words) seeming to serve as an inclusio.[173] The term does occur again in v. 5, but in the singular. It seems the term is used in v. 5 to distinguish those described there from the flanking contrary descriptions of those who are not true widows (vv. 4, 6). Marshall notes that the plural χήρας is surprising in v. 16b. This may simply strengthen the case for an inclusio, suggesting the author has deliberately used a plural

---

169.   Karris 1979: 92.
170.   Johnson 1996: 177; similarly in his more recent *Anchor* commentary (2001: 270).
171.   Müller-Bardorff 1958: 116.
172.   Bassler 1984: 33.
173.   Quinn and Wacker 2000: 448; Oberlinner 1994: 222; Bassler 1996: 92; Towner 1989: 181.

here to connect with the only other occurrence of this term in the plural in v. 3.

The case for the inclusio can be strengthened further by noting similarities between v. 4 and v. 16a. They are both conditional sentences beginning with εἰ and τις and refer to the care of widows using the verb ἔχω. It is as if v. 16a-b takes up the concerns of vv. 3–4 in reverse order.

A (v. 3) Honor **true widows**

  B (v. 4) If (εἰ δέ τις) a *widow* **has** (ἔχω) *children*, they should care for her

  B' (v. 16a) If (εἴ τις) a *believer* **has** (ἔχω) a *widow*, should take care of her

A' (v. 16b) **True widows** will be cared for

This arrangement is strengthened if Marshall is correct that ἔχει is used, as in v. 4, of "having relatives."[174] Then the same verb would be used in the same way, and in both instances it would be relatives who are being called to care for widows. This provides cohesion for 5.3–16, and points to a weakness in the chiasm suggested by Müller-Bardorff. While he correctly noted a connection between v. 16a and v. 8 (C' and C in the diagram), v. 16a also has significant links to v. 4 since these three verses are the only three conditional sentences in the unit and all refer to familial responsibility for widows.[175] While his chiasm holds at some level, lexical and syntactic repetitions suggest the connections may be more complex.

Having noted the significant inclusio which binds the entire unit, it can be noted that there are indeed three pieces within the unit: vv. 3–8, 9–15, and 16, each marked by asyndeton with asyndeton occurring nowhere else in this unit. These divisions are noted by several with some of the debate on this passage centering on whether or not vv. 3–8 and vv. 9–15 refer to the same group. That issue will not be the concern here at the moment, but the concern will be cohesion within each piece before considering cohesion between the pieces.

First, having suggested that there are three pieces within this unit, one might then suggest these are separate units. However, the strong affinity of v. 16 with vv. 3–8 suggests that these two pieces belong together enveloping vv. 9–15. Several elements support the cohesion of vv. 3–8 with v. 16. First, there is the inclusio just argued above. Second, the term 'true widows' occurs only in vv. 3–8 and v. 16. Third, the concern for families to take care of their own widows occurs only here (4, 8, 16) and not in 9–15. Thus, there are actually two pieces within this unit: (1) vv. 3–8, 16 and embedded

---

174. Marshall 1999: 606. Cf. also Winter 1988: 93.
175. For more on the connections between vv. 4, 8, and 16a, see below.

within that, (2) vv. 9–15. Attention must now be given to the cohesion of each piece.

5.3–8 is the portion of this unit where the unity is most contested. Yet, there are clear indications of cohesion. First, there is an apparent bracketing of this piece between v. 4 and v. 8.[176] 5.4 and 5.8 are both conditional sentences (the only other one in this unit is v. 16) and begin with the same three words, εἰ δέ τις. They refer to one's own household in strikingly similar language (not found elsewhere in the unit): τὸν ἴδιον (v. 4) and τῶν ... οἰκείων. Indeed, the point of both verses is the responsibility of families to care for their widowed relatives.[177] In both verses this familial responsibility is presented as part of Christianity. In v. 4 it is referred to as 'practicing godliness' (εὐσεβεῖν) and as 'pleasing before God.' In v. 5 failure to take such responsibility is tantamount to a denial of the faith! Thus, v. 3 sits atop this piece (indeed the entire unit) stating the major theme. Verses 4 and 8 then bracket the first piece emphasizing familial responsibility.

Within 5.3–8 there is a basic progression advancing primarily by contrasts (marked by δέ).[178] It can be represented as follows:

Honor true widows (v. 3)
BUT not widows with families (v. 4)
BUT true widows, alone and pious (v. 5)
BUT not the impious (v. 6)

Then, vv. 7–8 provide a strong closing exhortation on familial responsibility. Verse 7 need not be seen as a mere editorial insertion as some have said. Rather it provides a sharp apostolic command to the families of widows returning, along with v. 8, to the concern of v. 4. The

---

176. Wagener 1994: 150 also notes the tight connection between these two verses.

177. While this is the majority view (see Marshall 1999: 583–85; Oberlinner 1994: 225; Mounce 2000: 280; Quinn and Wacker 2000: 430–31), some have argued that the subject of the verb μανθανέτωσαν in v. 4 is not to the 'children and grandchildren' but the widows themselves (for e.g. Roloff 1988: 287f. and Wagener 1994: 149–54). Wagener provides the most thorough argument for this contrary view. She bases her argument to a large degree on the parallel between 5.4 and 5.8, affirming the connection I have argued above. In fact, the cohesion argued for here remains even if her arguments are accepted. However, her arguments do not persuade me. She argues that since the subject is the same in both the protasis and apodosis of v. 8, then the subject of both parts of v. 4 should be the same. This does not necessarily follow from the parallel between these verses. She also argues, no doubt correctly, that the words ἀμοιβή (151) and πρόγονοι (152) can have meanings more broad than that which they are assigned in the more common interpretation. The point, however, is how this context shapes the use of these words. The familial context already signaled in 5.1–2 as well as the obvious concern for the care of widows in 5.16 argue against her construction which seems overly subtle (see Marshall 1997: 584–85, for more discussion of Wagener).

178. Quinn and Wacker 2000: 433 note that δέ occurs 7 times in this unit, more than in any other unit, and call this a 'telltale stylistic feature' of this unit.

return of the imperative in v. 7 links to the last imperative which is in v. 4. If μανθανέτωσαν in v. 4 refers to the families, then the third person plural in ὦσιν in v. 7 likely refers to the families as well. 'Widow' has been singular from v. 4 onward as well and the only plural entity has been the children and grandchildren. Thus, the third plural verb and the imperative in v. 7 suggest a return to the concern of v. 4, and the content of v. 8 confirms this as it urges in strong terms familial responsibility.

The cohesion of 5.9–15 is not quite as disputed as that of 5.3–8, though Miller divides vv. 9–10 and vv. 11–15. 5.9–10 coheres as a list of qualifications in support of the imperative in v. 9. The last five items in the list demonstrate a particular cohesion with each one being introduced with εἰ and containing an aorist active indicative third person singular verb. 5.11–15 cohere as instruction on younger widows. The structure hangs on two commands:

v. 11 – Negative – Don't enroll young widows
v. 14 – Positive – Let them marry, etc.[179]

These two commands are then both buttressed by supporting statements introduced by γάρ (vv. 11b–13 and v. 15). The basis for both commands displays a concern lest the young widows experience spiritual failure (v. 12, 'rejecting their first faith'; v. 15, 'turning aside after Satan').[180] There is also a clear contrast between the description of what the young widows would be like if enlisted in vv. 12–13, and what they are exhorted to do in v. 14. Thus, 5.11–15 is coherent and cohesive.

5.9–10 and 11–15 then go together as two items in contrast (note the δέ in v. 11). The first qualification for those to be enrolled is that they be no less than sixty and νεωτέρας directly contrasts this. Then, the positive description of female activity in vv. 9–10 contrasts the negative description in vv. 12–13. For example, the diligence in good deeds of widows to be enrolled (εἰ παντὶ ἔργῳ ἀγαθῷ ἐπηκολούθησεν, v. 10) is in direct contrast to the laziness of the younger ones (ἀργός, v. 13). Whereas widows to be enrolled have a reputation for good deeds (v. 10), it is feared the younger widows may give occasion for someone to speak evil of the community (v. 14). The behavior commanded of young widows in v. 14 is then very similar to the qualifications listed in vv. 9–10. They are exhorted to live in such a way now as to be eligible for enrollment if they find themselves widowed in older age. Thus, 5.9–15 cohere as contrasts, stating who is to be enrolled and a significant group who is not to be enrolled.

---

179. βούλομαι is correctly recognized by most scholars as representing a command.

180. Both of these statements have connections to discussions of the opponents. This will be discussed under connections across units.

Having now argued for cohesion within 3–8, 16 and 9–15, connections between these two pieces must be examined. The simple fact that 3–8, 16 envelopes 9–15, as noted above, suggests these pieces are intended to be read together. Then v. 3 and v. 9 both open with asyndeton and the first word is χήρα, followed by an imperative and a phrase or phrases clarifying who is meant by χήρα. Both pieces are concerned to identify a certain group of widows and provide behavioral guidelines for this identification.[181] However, the greater stress in both sections seems to be on a group which may fail to act properly (families in 3–8, 16 and young widows in 9–15). It is these groups who are to be exhorted, with the widows only being discussed.[182] Both groups are considered to be in spiritual danger. Irresponsible family members will 'deny τήν πίστιν' (v. 8), and it is feared younger widows may 'reject their first πίστιν' (v. 12).[183] Family members need to learn (μανθάνω, v. 4) to practice godliness by caring for their widowed relatives, but young widows may learn (μανθάνω, v. 13) to be lazy. Thus there seem to be parallel concerns uniting 5.3–16 under the theme of provision for true widows (v. 3), which does not include those with families or younger widows. Additionally, these true widows are marked by a life of prayer (v. 5) and active good deeds (vv. 9–10). This continuity can also be seen in a chart from Marshall which shows how specific issues recur throughout this unit:[184]

The families of widows	4	7–8	16a
Pious widows	5	9–10	16b
Impious/young widows	6	11–13	14–15

Therefore, 5.3–16 is a cohesive unit with repetitions serving as emphasizing structural markers rather than as evidence of a writer's anxiety or of disparate sources being combined.

5.17–25

Boundaries

The beginning of a new unit is signaled by the disappearance of the term χήρα and the introduction of οἱ πρεσβύτεροι.[185] The singular πρεσβύτερος

---

181. This observation is true whether one considers the 'true widows' and 'enrolled widows' to be identical or separate groups.

182. This is of course dependent on some of the exegetical decisions made above.

183. Marshall 1999: 600 touches on this connection, noting that, 'The writer is concerned throughout with conduct which is in effect a denial of the faith that they previously held.'

184. Marshall 1999: 581.

185. So also Roloff 1988: 304–305.

occurred in 5.1, but the context here shows this plural use refers not simply to an age group, as did the singular in 5.1, but to a position in the church.[186]

The final boundary of this unit is more debated. Apparently most commentators regard vv. 17–25 as one unit. Others, however, discern a break at v. 20 or v. 22 with the solemn adjuration of v. 21 serving as a transition. Those who think v. 20 begins a new unit say the participle τοὺς ἁμαρτάνοντας refers not to sinning elders but to sinners in general, thus creating a shift in topic.[187] While it is true that τοὺς ἁμαρτάνοντας is plural and the closest occurrence of πρεσβύτερος is singular (v. 19), such alternation in number is not uncommon in this letter (cf. 2.9–15; 5.1–2), and other arguments weigh heavily against a shift in topic as most recent commentators agree.[188] J. P. Meier presented the conclusive argument for this view showing among other things that, (1) in the NT the noun ἁμαρτώλος is most often used for a generic substantive and the participle τοὺς ἁμαρτάνοντας is rarely (if ever) used this way; (2) in 5.1–6.2 all other units refer to specific groups within the church, so a general discussion of those who sin would be out of place.[189]

The other potential boundary is at v. 22. Those who think a new unit begins in v. 22 suggest v. 22 takes up the subject of reinstating repentant sinners rather than the ordination of elders. However, once again it seems most recent commentators have been persuaded by strong arguments against this view.[190] First, the practice of laying on hands to restore sinning believers is not attested until the third century.[191] Second, the laying on of hands as a ritual of appointment was already known in the early church and it is already mentioned in this sense in this letter (4.14). Third, all of the Greek fathers understood v. 22 to refer to appointment of elders.[192] Fourth, 1 Timothy has already shown particular interest in the appointment of leaders. Therefore, it seems best to consider 5.17–25 as one unit.

---

186. So most commentators, for e.g., Quinn and Wacker 2000: 458, write, 'The *presbyteroi* of this section are all but certainly not simply the older men of the community (contra Jeremias)....' See also Marshall 1999: 610–11; Mounce 2000: 307; Johnson, 2001: 286–87; Oberlinner 1994: 249f.; Roloff 1988: 305–309.

187. A key proponent of this position was P. Galtier, 'La réconciliation des pécheurs dans Saint Paul', *RSR* 3 (1912): 448–60; 'La réconciliation des pécheurs dans la première épître a Timothée', *RSR* 39 (1951): 317–20.

188. E.g., Marshall 1999: 618; Quinn and Wacker 2000: 465; Roloff 1988: 310; Oberlinner 1994: 250; Brox 1969a: 200; Bassler 1996: 100–101; Knight 1992: 236.

189. Meier 1973: 331.

190. For e.g., Marshall 1999: 620–22; Quinn and Wacker 2000: 470–74; Roloff 1988: 313; Oberlinner 1994: 259f.; Knight 1992: 239.

191. Quinn and Wacker 2000: 473–74 says even the evidence from Tertullian should be re-examined. See also Quinn 1989.

192. So Marshall 1999: 621; Spicq 1969: 547; Roloff 1988: 314, n.447.

Cohesion

As the discussion on the boundary of this unit has already hinted, the cohesion of this passage is quite contested. The fact that some have discerned two different sections here shows that some have found it difficult to find the connections between these verses. Even many of those who consider this whole section to deal with elders still find little coherence. Easton refers to 5.17–25 as a 'collection of miscellaneous rules.'[193] Johnson, who argues for coherence elsewhere in 1 Timothy (most notably 5.3–16), writes, 'In contrast to the fairly well structured discussion of the widows in 5:3–16, this section of text really does resemble a loose connection of *mandata* without any visible organizing principle apart from the need to address certain issues in the community ...'[194] The admittedly surprising placement of v. 23 and the fact that every verse but one (v. 18) begins with asyndeton makes this conclusion understandable. Also, Roloff finds very little homogeneity ('sehr wenig homogen') in this passage, suggesting it consists of four individual directives (vv. 17–18, 19–21, 22, 23) of entirely different formal character followed by a wisdom saying serving as a conclusion (vv. 24–25).[195]

As elsewhere, the most thoroughgoing criticism of coherence comes from Miller. Miller, as others mentioned above, discerns two units here with vv. 17–21 addressing elders and vv. 22–25 being miscellaneous admonitions.[196] He criticizes vv. 17–21 as lacking 'any internal development of thought' and as having a disjointed sequence of material.[197] In his view, then, vv. 17–21 is composed of the following distinct statements: 17, 18a, 18b, 19a, 19b, 20, 21. Concerning vv. 22–25, Miller says their order 'defies attempts at systemization and they are so lacking in order and coherence that he concludes, 'No author could write in this way.'[198] As a result he divides vv. 22–25 into the following separate pieces: 22a, 22b, 23, 24–25.[199]

While 5.17–25 can on first reading appear to have little interconnection (usually lacking any explicit connecting particles), there are several

---

193. Easton 1947: 159. So also Barrett 1963: 78.

194. Johnson 1996: 187. Cf. also Verner 1983: 156, n.97.

195. Roloff 1988: 304–305.

196. Miller 1997: 85–87. According to Marshall 1999: 608, n.115, Oberlinner (1994: 260f.) and Brox (1969a: 203) also regard vv. 23–25 as a separate set of interjections with no real connection to what precedes or follows.

197. Miller 1997: 85.

198. Miller 1997: 86, 87.

199. In his discussion on v. 23, Miller cites Calvin as suggesting this verse may have been a marginal note that made its way into the text by scribal error. However, this seems to misrepresent what Calvin actually wrote. Calvin allowed for the possibility of the erroneous inclusion of a marginal note, but went on to say such a view is unnecessary if one bears in mind Paul's tendency to make sudden shifts in topics. See Calvin's commentary *loc. cit.*

cohesive elements totally missed by Miller and others. Meier and Quinn and Wacker have led the way in illuminating these elements.[200] Their arguments will be combined and augmented in what follows.

There are a number of characteristics which are common throughout the unit. First, as even Miller admits, a common topic of elders unites at least vv. 17–21, and, according to the arguments given above and held by most commentators today, the topic of elders probably unites all of 5.17–25. This need not be dismissed as lightly as Miller does. Also, the sheer fact that asyndeton occurs so often in this unit provides some stylistic cohesion. The section opens with asyndeton and it occurs seven other times. Only 4.11–16 is close to this in 1 Timothy. Third, an authoritative tone permeates this unit. There are eight imperatives (vv. 17, 19, 20, 22 [3x], 23 [2x]) occurring throughout the unit. The solemn charge in v. 21 contributes greatly to this tone and is itself equivalent to another imperative. Since none of these elements is similarly characteristic of the previous unit (5.3–17), they provide a distinctive and cohesive character to 5.17–25. Lastly, ethical vocabulary permeates this unit. Terms from Louw and Nida's Domain 88 include καλῶς (v. 17); κάλος (v. 25); ἁμαρτάνω/ἁμαρτία (vv. 20, 22, 24); ἁγνός (v. 22); πρόκλισις (v. 21) and in the same verse though not Domain 88, πρόκριμα. Also ἀξιόω/ἄξιος (vv. 17, 18) belong to Domain 65 but have the ethical connotation here.

Next it may be useful to take up each of Miller's separate pieces to see if there are cohesive elements between them. Miller does not provide argumentation for the divisions he makes but simply suggests them on the basis of a perceived overall lack of internal order and logical development. Miller's first two pieces are v. 17 and v. 18a. It is hard to see why these pieces should be separated since they are joined by the only connective particle in the section (γάρ). The call to honor elders is grounded in a citation of scripture. This is basic logical development. As the text reads, a second quotation (v. 18b) is used to ground v. 17, but Miller separates this. There are however strong lexical links between v. 18b and v. 17:[201]

---

200. Quinn and Wacker 2000: 450–78; Meier 1973: 323–45. Although Quinn and Wacker obviously appeared well after the publication of Miller's monograph, it is interesting that Miller fails to interact with or even mention Meier since Meier's article appeared in 1973.

201. Quinn and Wacker 2000: 450.

5.17	5.18b
ἀξιούσθωσαν	ἄξιος
οἱ κοπιῶντες	ὁ ἐργάτης
τιμῆς	τοῦ μισθοῦ

The first link is obvious as the words are cognates and they function similarly in the argument. Marshall says the verb ἀξιόω 'is doubtless chosen in anticipation of the use of the saying of Jesus in v. 18b.'[202] In the second link, the group in consideration is viewed in terms of labor. Both κοπιάω and ἐργάτης are classified in Louw and Nida's Domain 42D, 'Work, Toil.' Both items in the third link refer to the recompense which the worker deserves. The argument is then:

> An elder who **works** hard is to be considered **worthy** of double **honor**
> Because a **worker** is **worthy** of his **wage**

Thus, the striking semantic and conceptual links between v. 17 and v. 18b show that v. 18b has been specifically chosen to support v. 17, and there is no reason for separating this statements.

Next, Miller divides v. 19a ('Do not receive an accusation against an elder') and 19b ('except on two or three witnesses'), apparently because v. 19b is a traditional citation. However, it is difficult to imagine v. 19a without v. 19b. Would there be a place for an unqualified dismissal of any accusation against an elder? It is hardly conceivable. 5.19a–b make perfect sense together, and there is no reason for separating them. With vv. 17–18 and v. 19 intact, a parallel can be seen between the two passages. They both contain an admonition on the treatment of elders grounded by a scriptural citation, though the scriptural nature is made explicit in v. 18 and only implicit in v. 19.

5.20 then connects logically with 5:19, providing the next step in dealing with accusations against elders. One must be careful in receiving accusations, but if the accusations are found to be true, discipline must be administered. Meier also suggests the substantival participle used here (τοὺς ἁμαρτάνοντας) links back to the previous two substantival participles in the unit (v. 17) which both refer to elders. All three participles are present active masculine third plural. This links vv. 17–20 and suggests the elders are still in view in v. 20.[203]

5.21 does appear sudden, but that is reasonable for a solemn injunction. It follows in the authoritative tone already established in the unit and has links to the previous verses. 5.19–21 have almost a court room setting. Accusations are to be taken only on the basis of two or three witnesses, sin

---

202. Marshall 1999: 612.
203. Meier 1973: 332; Brox 1969a: 202.

is to be rebuked in the presence of (ἐνώπιον) all, and Timothy is charged in the presence of (ἐνώπιον) of three witnesses (God, Christ, and elect angels). Even the idea of proper fear seems to connect with the solemnity of the charge in v. 21.

A logical connection between v. 21 and v. 22 is readily available. In light of the solemn necessity of rebuking sinning elders, candidates for such a position must be chosen carefully. Miller, however, divides v. 22a and v. 22b, calling the former an admonition on restoration and the latter an admonition on purity. However, a call to purity makes perfect sense after a warning not to share in the sins of another. One is the positive restatement of the other.

5.23 is admittedly a digression.[204] It is not totally out of place, however. As Quinn and Wacker note, the series of five commands in vv. 22–23 move from the general to the more specifically personal culminating in the quite personal statements in v. 23. A logical connection with v. 22b, as explaining the purity called for has been argued by many commentators.[205]

The closing two verses of this unit are not separated even by Miller, and for good reason. They are bound by ὡσαύτως plus ellipsis and the repetition of πρόδηλος (vv. 24, 25). The two verses are parallel making the same point of the eventual revealing of deeds whether they be sinful or good. The interesting thing about vv. 24–25 is how they recapitulate the main points of this unit. The occurrence of αἱ ἁμαρτίαι in 5.24 links back to the occurrences of the same word in vv. 20 and 22. The mention of 'good' (καλὰ) deeds in v. 25 links back to the elders who rule 'well' (καλῶς) in v. 17. This suggests an almost chiastic arrangement.

A few other things support this observation. Attention to the progression of verbs also suggests a chiastic development. The verbs are as follows:[206]

17 – **3p** imperative
    18 – γάρ [only non-asyndeton verse] 3s & 2s
19 – 2s imperative
20 – 2s imperative
    ἵνα – 3p
21 – 1s
    ἵνα – 2s
22 – 2s imperative
    2s imperative

---

204.   Falconer 1937: 149 labels v. 23 an interpolation.
205.   Quinn and Wacker 2000: 475, even says v. 23 emerges 'easily from the preceding command.'
206.   The chart is taken from Quinn and Wacker 2000: 476, and modified slightly from my own analysis of the verbal structure.

    2s imperative
23 – 2s imperative
    2s imperative
24 – **3p** indicative
    3p indicative
25 – **3p** indicative

The third person occurs in v. 17 but does not occur again until vv. 24–25, thus enveloping a series of almost uninterrupted second singular imperatives with the first singular command functioning similarly to a second singular imperative. Thus, there is a loosely chiastic structure:[207]

A Positive vv. 17–18 – Good (καλῶς) elders
  B Negative vv. 19–22 – Dealing with sin
      Digression v. 23 – providing break between the corresponding pieces
  B' Negative v. 24 – Dealing with sin
A Positive v. 25 – Those with good (κάλος) deeds

This is not to suggest an overly sophisticated arrangement here but simply to show that similar topics are taken up in reverse order. This arrangement, along with the many smaller linking devices already demonstrated, argues for cohesion in this unit, and seriously challenges Miller's assertion that 'No "author" would write in this way.'[208]

6.1–2

Boundaries
The disappearance of 'elders' and the appearance of slaves (v. 1) and masters (v. 1, 2), both for the first time in the letter, signals the beginning of a new unit. In the verbs, the third person, which occurred at the close of 5.17–25, dominates 6.1–2b, and quite unlike 5.17–25 there are no second person imperatives in 6.1–2b. Thus, a new unit on slaves and masters begins at 6.1.

    The final boundary of this unit is debated. With 6.3ff. slaves and elders are no longer in view, so this along with other shifts to be mentioned below suggest that the unit on slaves and elders cannot go beyond the end of v. 2.

---

207.   Adapted from Meier 1973: 336. Meier's diagram also shows the other smaller linking devices within the unit. Meier does not label the digression in v. 23 'C,' as Marshall does when citing Meier (1999: 608, n.116). Labeling v. 23 as 'C' makes the suggested chiasm look more formal and seems to suggest a special importance to v. 23 which is not intended in Meier's argument. Lock 1924: 61 noted something similar as recurring themes but did not make any structural suggestions or give much discussion to lexical and syntactic links to support this.
208.   Miller 1997: 87.

The question, though, is whether Ταῦτα δίδασκε καὶ παρακάλει (6.2c) goes with what precedes or with what follows. Most scholars combine this sentence with 6.3ff. though they understand ταῦτα to refer backward. Usually whether one places this summary statement with what precedes or what follows, it is understood to have a transitional function with connections both backward and forward. It is clearly distinguishable from 6.1–2b since there is a shift from entirely third person to entirely second person. In 6.3ff. there is a return to the third person and the imperatives disappear from view. Thus, in some ways 6.2c is isolated from its neighboring verses. However, ταῦτα provides some connection with the previous material and the emphasis on teaching does connect with some of the following material. Therefore, at this point in the study, 6.2c will be set apart as a transitional statement and its function will be discussed in more detail in the section on connections across units.

Cohesion
Though the commentators seem to sense no problems with internal cohesion of this unit, Miller suggests these are unrelated admonitions. He does not list where he would make divisions, but simply asserts that the compiling of admonitions on slaves was common. While such a practice may have been common and he may have examples of such, 6.1–2b have significant indications of cohesion. The semantic concept of slavery permeates the unit with δοῦλος (6.1), δουλεύω (6.2), δεσπότης (6.1, 2), and ζυγός (6.1). Also, 6.1 and 6.2a–b are parallel statements moving from the general to a specific case. In 6.1 the concern is on any that are in slavery and their masters. 6.2 moves specifically to those slaves who have believing masters. In 6.1 slaves are to consider their masters worthy of honor, and in 6.2 this honor is specifically not despising but serving. Even the motivation shifts from the concern of the church's reputation with outsiders in 6.1, to interrelations within the church in 6.2. Thus, there is a parallelism and perfectly logical progression. 6.2a–b even has a clear structure as the diagram below will show:[209]

οἱ δὲ πιστοὺς ἔχοντες δεσπότας
    μὴ καταφρονείτωσαν, ὅτι ἀδελφοί εἰσιν
ἀλλὰ μᾶλλον
    δουλευέτωσαν, ὅτι πιστοί εἰσιν καὶ ἀγαπητοὶ
οἱ τῆς εὐεργεσίας ἀντιλαμβανόμενοι

---

209. Quinn and Wacker 2000: 485–86 points out some of these connections without any diagram. They also suggest, on p. 483, an 'abccba' development in 6.1 but the value of that observation was not as obvious to me.

The sentence begins and ends with a substantival phrase consisting of an articular participle and a direct object. The placing of the second participial phrase at the very end of the sentence even seems deliberate. Between the participial phrases are contrasting verbs with synonymous ὅτι clauses. This is not intended as evidence of particular literary skill, but simply to show that these statements are crafted coherently rather than being unrelated admonitions.

6.3–10

Boundaries
Several shifts make it clear that a new unit begins at 6.3. The topic returns to the opponents who have not been explicitly in view since 4.1–5. Also, there are no imperatives in 6.3–10 in stark contrast to all of chapter 5, and indeed 4.6–16 as well. The concluding boundary of this unit is more debated. A number of scholars discern a break after v. 5, resulting in two units: 6.3–5, on opponents, and 6.6–10 on contentment vs. greed. This division is often based on the idea that the opponents are no longer specifically in view in vv. 6–10. The following discussion of the cohesion of this unit will argue that vv. 3–10 cohere with the opponents in view throughout. Since some scholars, including Miller, separate vv. 3–5 and vv. 6–10, the cohesion of each piece will first be considered before turning to cohesive links between the pieces.

Cohesion
Miller does not contest the cohesion of vv. 3–5. However, Falconer, commenting on these verses, stated,

> The construction of these verses is faulty. It might have been expected that the conclusion to 'if any man teacheth', &c. (ver. 3) would be, not 'he is puffed up' (ver. 4), but 'he is corrupted in mind and bereft of the truth, supposing &c.'[210]

This view simply fails to recognize the climactic arrangement of the appraisal of the opponents which is found in the predicate of this long sentence. The finite verb is expanded by two participles, the last of which is furthered by a prepositional phrase with a double object both of which are expounded by a relative clause leading to a five point vice list. The vice list itself, in a common ancient literary device, builds to a climax in the last element.[211] The nouns, initially singular, lead to plural. The first three elements are single nouns, with the fourth element adding an adjective. The

---

210.   Falconer 1937: 153.
211.   Cf. Fitzgerald 1997: 291–93.

fifth element adds a genitive clause which includes three participles and an infinitive, thus dwarfing the previous four items. Thus, the conclusion which Falconer wants to follow the protasis is actually the logical conclusion as he sensed but it is delayed because of the climactic rhetorical development used by the author. Additionally, this climactic development argues for the cohesion of vv. 3–5.

Lastly, the repeated use of doublets in these verses also suggests some cohesion. The first four doublets are particularly interesting:

ἑτεροδιδασκαλεῖ καὶ μὴ προσέρχεται (v. 3)
  ὑγιαίνουσιν λόγοις ... καὶ τῇ ... διδασκαλίᾳ (v. 3)
μηδὲν ἐπιστάμενος ἀλλὰ νοσῶν (v. 4)
ζητήσεις καὶ λογομαχίας (v. 4)

In v. 3 the opponent is described with two verbs (ἑτεροδιδασκαλεῖ καὶ μὴ προσέρχεται), and the last verb is expanded with a double object (ὑγιαίνουσιν λόγοις... καὶ τῇ ... διδασκαλίᾳ). 6.4 continues to describe the opponent, this time with two participles (μηδὲν ἐπιστάμενος ἀλλὰ νοσῶν), with the last participle being further modified by a prepositional phrase with two objects (ζητήσεις καὶ λογομαχίας). This shows not only the repeated use of doublets but also some parallelism between the protasis and apodosis. This parallelism is strengthened, when it is noted that the first and third doublets, the verbal phrases, seem to take up the same issues in reverse order. The opponents' heterodoxy includes the unhealthy interest in speculations and their description as knowing nothing likely refers to the fact that they do not hold to sound teaching (i.e., they know nothing of value).

The other doublet occurs at the close of v. 5, where the men involved in constant irritation are described as 'depraved in their minds and devoid of the truth.' This doublet occurs as part of the expansion on the mention of the opponent's morbid interest in speculations but returns to the cognitive failure of 'knowing nothing.' Therefore, it ties together the description of the opponent in vv. 4–5.

So, the climactic development, parallelism and the use of doublets all show vv. 3–5 to be cohesive.

Miller and Dibelius and Conzelmann see no real cohesion or development in 6.6–10. Dibelius and Conzelmann say these verses are just sayings listed in a series, and Miller describes them as a 'cluster of loosely connected epigrammatic sayings on moderation.'[212] Miller seems to suggest that each verse is a separate isolated saying.

Within vv. 6–10, vv. 6–8 argue for contentment and vv. 9–10 reflect on the ill fate of those who are not content but seek riches. Far from being

212. Dibelius and Conzelmann 1972: 84; Miller 1997: 90.

isolated sayings, vv. 6–8 have a basic unity, with v. 8 serving as a repetition and augmentation of v. 6. Both verses encourage contentment using cognate words in inclusio fashion (αὐταρκεία, v. 6; ἀρκέομαι, v. 8). This binds the verses around v. 7 which acts as a ground to the call to contentment by emphasizing the ephemeral nature of material goods. This is clear even though the import of ὅτι is unclear. Verse 8 then returns to the idea of contentment, contrasting the idea of taking material goods out of this world with being content with basic necessities.

6.9–10 then turn to those who desire riches rather than contentment. The two sentences are parallel to each other, with v. 9 making a basic statement and v. 10 grounding (γάρ) that statement in a more theoretical restatement. 'Those who desire to be rich' are those who have a 'love for money.' The desire to be rich leads people into 'temptation, a snare, and many foolish and harmful desires,' just as the love of money is the root which produces all sorts of evil.[213] The foolish desires of v. 9 weigh people down to ruin and destruction just as the love of money causes people to stray from the faith and to pierce themselves through with sorrows. It seems there is a bit of progression between v. 9 and v. 10 as well with the descriptions in v. 10 being harsher and more explicitly linked to rejection of the faith. This parallelism may also explain why the author uses two words to denote destruction in v. 9, a feature which has caused considerable discussion in the commentaries.[214] In addition to the author's favor of doublets in general, closing v. 9 and v. 10 with a double description of the destruction which results from seeking riches strengthens the parallelism, not to mention heightening the impact of his argument.

Thus, it is argued, there are three coherent pieces in vv. 3–5, 6–8 and 9–10. How then do they relate to one another? The disputed connection between vv. 5 and 6 will be taken up first. Dibelius and Conzelmann say vv. 6–10 'is only superficially connected with the polemic against heresy in 6.3–5.'[215] Miller agrees, writing that although the words πορισμός and εὐσέβεια recur in v. 6, they occur with opposite meaning, there is no logical connection, and 'the thought begun in 6.5 is suddenly discontinued.'[216] First, the recurrence of two identical words in the same construction (joined by εἰμί) in consecutive verses ought not be dismissed so lightly. It suggests some connection unless proven otherwise. Miller's proof to the otherwise is that the words are used with different meanings. However, it seems εὐσέβεια is used with the same meaning; the nuanced word is

---

213. Johnson 2001: 295, says 'There is a stunning alliteration'. within v. 9 with its repetition of 'p'.

214. E.g., Hanson 1982: 108 writes, 'It is difficult to see why the author needed to use two words for the disaster which riches bring.'

215. Dibelius and Conzelmann 1972: 84.

216. Miller 1997: 90.

πορισμός. Far from suggesting incohesion, however, this binds the verses together as the author makes a play on words reversing the idea of the opponents and giving the proper view of 'gain.' The change in meaning is intentional and clear. It was argued above that vv. 3–5 reached a climax with v. 5. The last participial phrase at the end of v. 5, not explicitly connected to the participial doublet, then stands at the close as the key issue of concern- the opponents, greedy use of godliness. 6.6–8, then, counter this (δέ) by redefining 'gain' and introducing the idea of 'contentment.'[217] Far from discontinuing the idea of v. 5 as Miller suggests, vv. 6–8 counter the idea of v. 5 with a proper view of contentment.[218]

How then are vv. 9–10 connected with the preceding verses? First, vv. 9–10 serve as a contrast to vv. 6–8 as denoted by the δέ.[219] This contrast is also found in the use of key words. It was shown above that vv. 6–8 are bracketed by αὐτάρκεια and its cognate verb. In vv. 9–10 a key term is φιλαργυρία, which was used in other literature as an antonym of αὐτάρκεια.[220] Secondly, vv. 9–10 return to the problem of greed which vv. 3–5 brought to the fore. Although Miller says the opponents are no longer in view in vv. 6–10, it is entirely likely that those who think εὐσέβεια is a way to turn a profit, are also those who desire to be rich (v. 9) and as a result turn away from the faith (v. 10). Indeed, Mounce suggests there is an intentional play on words between πορισμός (vv. 5–6) and πειρασμός (v. 9).[221] In addition, 6.9–10 has connections with descriptions of the opponents elsewhere in the letter.[222] Every other section which discusses the opponents at any length refers to them leaving the faith similarly to the statement in v. 10. Indeed, in every section but one, the reference occurs as a relative clause with a form of τίς, just like the statement in 6.10. 1.18–20 mentions the destruction which comes as a result of their apostasy as vv. 9–10 do as well. These striking parallels suggest the opponents are in view in vv. 9–10 as well.[223] Thus, vv. 6–10 are not simply general teaching on contentment and greed but such teaching given in response to the

---

217. Quinn and Wacker 2000: 501 argue for this strong contrast also on the basis of word order: 'The unusual word order of this sentence [v. 6], with its initial *estin*, characteristic of definitions and very solemn affirmations with an oath … places the following statement in emphatic contrast … with what the false teachers suppose.'

218. So similarly, Mounce 2000: 341.

219. So also Marshall 1999: 644. Marshall 1999: 643, writes, 'the passage [vv. 6–10] is carefully constructed.'

220. Kittel, 'αὐτάρκεια', *TDNT*, vol. 1, 466.

221. Mounce 2000: 335.

222. See the discussion of connections between units concerning the opponents in the following chapter.

223. The referent could be broader than the opponents, but the argument here is that it does include the opponents. Similarly, Mounce 2000: 335, 341f.

opponents. The teaching on contentment is then bracketed by reference to greedy opponents. This is part of a pattern of shifting contrast which runs throughout the unit:

> 6:2b – Positive – Teach these things
> 6:3–5 – Negative – But (δέ) those who don't teach this way, and are greedy
> 6:6–8 – Positive – But (δέ) contentment
> 6:9–10 – Negative – But (δέ) the ruin of those who pursue riches

The cohesive function of these contrasts is strengthened by the arrangement of each piece. For instance, the contrast between 6.2c and 6.3–5 is achieved because 6.3–5 open with a discussion of false teaching. However, 6.3–5 move on to the point that the opponents seek to make a profit from εὐσέβεια, thus providing a direct contrast with 6.6–8. The closing word of v. 8 is, then, a verb denoting contentment, providing a clear contrast with the opening words of v. 9, 'those who want to get rich.' Thus, the use of language here shows that these contrasts are not merely thematic accidents occurring from the compiling of statements on a similar theme, but the deliberate progression of an argument. Lastly, it is worthwhile to note that the unit opens and closes with reference to those who have departed the faith: those who do not hold to the sound words (v. 3) and those who abandoned the faith (v. 10).

6.11–16

Boundaries
That a new unit begins at 6.11 is clear to most scholars.[224] The vocative of address is a key indicator here. The use of the vocative was a common indicator of transition in papyri letters.[225] The use here also signals a strong shift in the person and number of the verbs. Second person singular, which had not occurred at all in 6.3–10, occurs six times in uninterrupted succession in vv. 11–12. Similarly, though imperatives had disappeared in 6.3–10, the first four verbs of 6.11f. are imperatives. These elements demonstrate a shift in topic and tone as well. The topic shifts to direct exhortation to Timothy, thus bringing the person of Timothy back to the fore. The tone returns to an authoritative one with an elevated feel. The fact that a doxology occurs in vv. 15–16 and that doxologies often serve a concluding function (as argued above) suggest that this unit ends at 6.16.

---

224. For e.g., Marshall 1999: 634, writes, 'A clear break at v. 11 signals the beginning of a section addressed to Timothy personally concerning his own conduct.'
225. White 1972a: 29.

Cohesion

The primary problem regarding 6.11–16 and cohesion is how it connects to the surrounding materials, which will be considered later. There is also, though, some skepticism concerning the internal cohesion of this unit. Miller says the internal order of this unit is 'puzzling,' but he does not elaborate.[226] Instead, he notes several phrases which appear to him to signal formulaic material (for e.g., Σὺ δέ, 'man of God,' 'flee … pursue'). Whether or not these phrases actually do signal formulaic material can be debated, and an author can use, shape, or simply allude to existing materials or well-known ideas without compromising the coherence of his argument. The question is whether or not the language used here is cohesive.

A number of characteristics of this unit suggest cohesiveness. First, there is an elevated tone throughout, beginning with the address to Timothy as 'man of God' in v. 11, then references to the 'good fight' and the 'good confession,' the solemn adjuration in v. 13 and the lofty doxology in v. 15–16. These statements all cohere as a serious and profound exhortation. Indeed, four of the five main verbs are second person imperatives, creating the sense of exhortation and specifically exhortation directly to Timothy. The fifth main verb continues this idea since the first person verb of exhortation (παραγγέλλω) with infinitive (τηρῆσαι) functions as an equivalent of an imperative. Thus, all the main verbs denote exhortation to Timothy. Each of these exhortations is also related to the idea of perseverance.[227] The idea of fleeing evil and pursuing good is to stay on the right track. Fighting the good fight and laying hold of eternal life both refer to enduring as well. Then the final and most solemn command is to keep the command, which doubtless connotes faithfulness and perseverance as well. Thus, the main verbs of this unit in their syntactic form and semantic connotation provide cohesion for the unit.

Some have suggested a break between vv. 11–12 and vv. 13–16, noting a difference in style as the short imperatives in vv. 11–12 give way to an indicative verb with an infinitive.[228] However, it has just been shown that though the style is technically different the idea is the same. There is also no indication that this shift in style should indicate a break in argument or

---

226. Miller 1997: 91.

227. Mounce 2000: 351, though not referring to the verbs, writes, 'The predominant emphasis in this section is perseverance.'

228. No one was found who disputed the connections within vv. 11–12. It is interesting to note that the four main verbs occur in rhyming pairs: φεῦγε and δίωκε; ἀγωνίζου and ἐπιλαβοῦ. φεῦγε and δίωκε are obviously linked by δέ, and ἀγωνίζου and ἐπιλαβου seem to be connected also as they both have an occurrence of a double cognate. Pfitzner states, 'The command to carry on the good contest of the faith follows on smoothly from v. 11, the metaphor itself being easily suggested by the verb διώκειν' (1967: 178–79).

a move to a new 'source.' Indeed, it could be argued that this interchange of imperatives and first person admonitions is part of the style of the author. First person admonitions occur commonly in the letter (2.1, 8, 12; 5.14, 21), and sometimes they occur amidst imperatives. In fact, the construction in 5.17–25 is very similar to 6.11–16. All the main verbs in 5.17–20 are imperatives, but 5.21 switches to a first person admonition using very similar language to 6.13. Thus, the shift in style between 6.12 and 6.13 is well within the bounds of the style elsewhere in the letter.

There are also lexical and semantic links between vv. 11–12 and v. 13. Timothy, having been reminded that he 'confessed the good confession' (ὡμολόγησας τὴν καλὴν ὁμολογίαν) before (ἐνώπιον) many witnesses (μαρτύρων; v. 12), is exhorted in the presence of (ἐνώπιον) Christ Jesus who bore witness (μαρτυρήσαντος) to 'the good confession' (τὴν καλὴν ὁμολογίαν; v. 13). These three instances of strong lexical cohesion suggest that these verses have been intentionally worded in order to connect to each other. Additionally, there is a semantic chain of ethical concern uniting all of the exhortations: the virtue list in v. 11; καλός twice in v. 12; ἄσπιλον and ἀνεπίλημπτον in v. 14. It is also sensible that the 'man of God' should be exhorted 'in the presence of God.' Lastly, a semantic chain concerning 'life' runs throughout all the exhortations and the doxology: τῆς αἰωνίου ζωῆς (v. 12), τοῦ ζωογονοῦντος (v. 13), ἀθανασίαν (v. 16).[229]

All of these connective elements show 6.11–16 to be a cohesive unit. A series of exhortations to perseverance reaches its climax with a solemn adjuration and concludes with a grand doxology.[230]

6.17–19

Boundaries
That a new unit begins at 6.17 is unquestioned; indeed, the key issue discussed here is the abruptness of the shift. The close of the doxology in 6.16 marks the end of one unit and therefore the beginning of another. Many scholars have stated that the tone of this unit differs from the elevated tone of the previous unit. There is a shift from exhortation about Timothy's actions to exhortations to Timothy concerning the behavior of others. Then, most importantly, the topic switches to the behavior of those who are already rich.

---

229. Lock 1924: 70, notes this emphasis on life.
230. There seems to be no contention against the coherence of the doxology itself. Quinn and Wacker 2000: 537–38 mention several cohesive elements within the doxology including alliteration and repetition.

Cohesion

There seems to be no contention against the cohesion of this unit. Even Miller seems to understand these verses as a single piece.[231] These verses are all one sentence clearly centered on instruction to those who are rich. As noted by various commentators, the fourfold repetition of cognates for 'rich' (πλουσίοις, πλούτου, πλουσίως, πλουτεῖν) binds these verses together and suggests a deliberate wordplay: Those who are **rich** are not to trust in **riches** but in God who gives **richly**, and they are to be **rich** in good deeds. The use of ἀποθησαυρίζω (v. 19) would also contribute to a semantic chain concerning riches. Indeed Quinn and Wacker conclude, 'The formal variations with *plousiois, ploutou, plousiôs* (v. 17) and *ploutein* (v. 18) as well as the assonance with *p* leave no doubt about the inner coherence of this paragraph. ...'[232]

In addition to this commonly noted cohesive feature, there are other symmetrical features in this unit which contribute to cohesion. First, there are some clear contrasts between the opening and closing of the unit. 6.17 opens with a reference to the present age (ἐν τῷ νῦν αἰῶνι), and 6.20 closes with a reference to the future age (εἰς τὸ μέλλον).[233] Indeed, what is contrasted is riches in this present age and things treasured up for the age to come, perhaps implying that the former does not ensure the latter. Further, the riches of the present age are 'unstable' (ἀδηλότης) whereas that which is treasured up for the future age is referred to as θεμέλιος, 'foundation,' a word which can connote stability.[234] Commentators puzzle over the mixed metaphor here ('treasuring up a foundation'), but perhaps the odd use of words is intended to contrast with the instability of riches in the current age. Within these inclusio-like contrasts the asyndetic exhortations in v. 18 occur in doublets. ἀγαθοεργεῖν and πλουτεῖν ἐν ἔργοις καλοῖς are roughly synonymous, as are εὐμεταδότους and κοινωνικούς. All of these features confirm and strengthen the view of 6.17–19 as a cohesive unit.

6.20–21

Boundaries

The shift to a new unit is marked again by the vocative plus ὦ, as in 6.11. The occurrence of Τιμόθεε clearly marks a shift as well from discussion of a

---

231. Miller 1997: 94. Mounce 2000: 365, writes, 'The structure of the passage is simple. Paul gives six admonitions built around five imperatives. ...'

232. Quinn and Wacker 2000: 550. Quinn often makes much of repetition of sounds.

233. Towner 1989: 191, briefly touches on this contrast but does not develop it in terms of structure or cohesion.

234. Cf. 2 Timothy 2.19.

group within the church to exhortation for Timothy personally. The rich are no longer in view, but the topic is Timothy's faithfulness in contrast to the opponents. The closing grace marks the close of this unit.

Cohesion
The coherence of this one sentence unit is not contested. Timothy is to remain faithful while avoiding the errors of the opponents because they lead to apostasy. Thus, the opening call to faithfulness is in direct contrast to the closing description of apostasy. The contrast between Timothy and the opponents, common throughout the letter, closes the letter.

Conclusion

The goal of the preceding discussion was twofold: (1) to divide the text into discrete units of thought, (2) to examine the coherence of each unit. The discussion focused primarily on the latter. Within each unit of 1 Timothy significant cohesive elements were found, often in direct contradiction to Miller and others who have argued for incohesive seams in 1 Timothy. From the preceding arguments it is clear that each unit in this letter has been carefully constructed even if the interpretation of certain elements eludes modern readers. Throughout the letter doublets were a common stylistic device. Also, many units were found to have symmetric structures even if some were not highly developed.

Now the connections between these units must be investigated. The division of the text into units provides the basis for this next step.

Chapter 3

Connections Between Units in 1 Timothy

The last chapter identified discrete units within 1 Timothy and argued that these units cohered within themselves. Such cohesion is important, but for the entire letter to cohere these units must connect in some way with each other. Examining such interconnection between units is the focus of this chapter.

The analysis will take place in three parts. First, there will be an examination of connections between contiguous units, between each unit and the one which follows. In a cohesive document one will expect there to be some coherent flow from one unit to the next, though the level of connection may vary since discourses do not develop only linearly. Specific attention will be given to conjunctions, transitional devices (e.g., hooked keywords, etc.), and continuities in cohesion fields.

The second part will shift to the macroperspective examining semantic chains which run through significant portions of the letter. These chains consist of recurring elements related to each other lexically or semantically and reveal a common concern throughout the letter. If these chains themselves overlap and are interrelated the cohesive function is even greater.

The third part will focus on how the units may form larger sections and how this affects the shape of the whole. Once larger section and transitional units are identified, the connections and relationships between these sections will be examined. Due to the length of 1 Timothy, this part of the analysis is more complex and is more involved than the similar analysis of 2 Timothy.

Connections Between Contiguous Units

1.3–7 and 1.8–11

Miller appears to be alone in disputing a connection between 1.3–7 and 1.8–11. He writes, 'It is difficult to identify any clear development of thought between 1:7 and that which follows.'[1] However, several scholars

---

1. Miller 1997: 61.

(including some who find little cohesion elsewhere) do not even posit a break between v. 7 and v. 8, keeping all of 1.3–11 together as one unit.[2] Scholars commonly note a connection concerning the use of the Law. This argument can be enhanced, though, since 'Law' provides not simply a common theme but a hooked keyword. In the previous chapter, it was noted that though 1.7 cohered with 1.3–6, it contained some shifts in cohesion fields and introduced new information.[3] The key new point introduced in 1.7 is that the opponents desire to be 'Law teachers' (νομοδιδάσκαλοι). 1.8–11 then opens with three occurrences of 'Law' vocabulary (νόμος, v. 8; νομίμως, v. 8; νόμος, v. 9).[4] These are the only occurrences in the entire letter of νόμος vocabulary. Thus, there is a clear and strong connection formed as 1.7 closes the discussion of the opponents by introducing the topic (teaching of the Law) which will be further developed in the following unit.

Additionally, there is another hook. 1.7 describes the opponents as not knowing what they try to teach (μὴ νοοῦντες), i.e., the Law. This is the first occurrence of noetic vocabulary in the letter. In contrast (δέ), 1.8–9 state that Paul and those with him ('We') do know (οἴδαμεν, v. 8; εἰδώς, v. 9) how the Law is properly used.[5] This suggests that 1.8–11 follows 1.3–7 logically, providing the corrective to the opponents' false understanding of the Law. Thus, these two hooks provide clear cohesion between these two units.

1.8–11 also closes with a similar idea to that which opened 1.3–7. 1.10 refers to that which is contrary to sound doctrine (εἴ τι ἕτερον τῇ ὑγιαινούσῃ διδασκαλίᾳ ἀντίκειται), and 1.3 referred to those who teach contrary (ἑτεροδιδασκαλεῖν). Both the wording and the idea are very similar, and surely the same group is in mind. Thus, following the vice list, v. 10b serves to bring the discussion back to the idea of those who are not in accord with Pauline teaching, suggesting 1.8–11 was composed in light of 1.3–7.

1.8–11 and 1.12–17

Miller sees a serious disjunction between these two units primarily because he says this 'sudden outburst' of thanksgiving is unexpected following the vice list of 1.9–11. Quinn and Wacker also say that the appearance of the thanksgiving at this point is surprising, writing, 'here in First Timothy it

---

2. E.g., Roloff 1988: 59f.; Merkel 1991: 18f.; Easton 1947: 108f.; Falconer 1937: 119f.
3. Cf. also Marshall 1999: 372.
4. Quinn and Wacker 2000: 91, also note a connection of 'repeated *m* sounds' from 1.7. However, the value of such repetitions (including not only initial sounds, but any sounds within any word) is uncertain.
5. Cf. Johnson 2001: 167, 'The contrast with the ignorance of the would-be teachers is deliberate and emphatic ... .' The contrast is also noted by Quinn and Wacker 2000: 91; Bassler 1996: 40. These, however, do not note how the positioning of the words creates a hooking device.

appears dislocated, from the point of view of the normal positioning of the thanksgiving prayer in the ancient epistolary genre as well as in other letters of Paul.'[6] There are then two issues raised in criticism of the connection between these two units: (1) the place of the thanksgiving in the letter in comparison with the ancient epistolary genre, and (2) disjunction between a vice list and a thanksgiving. These will be dealt with in order.

First, while it is true that the placement of the thanksgiving is unusual in comparison with the other letters attributed to Paul, Quinn and Wacker are simply wrong in stating that its position is somehow abnormal in comparison with the use of thanksgivings in ancient epistolary literature in general. Two recent articles (by P. Arzt and J. T. Reed) provide the most extensive treatment of thanksgivings in the papyri to date.[7] Both articles conclude, with copious examples, that thanksgivings in the papyri letters are not confined to the introduction of letters but occur in various places with a wide range of uses. Arzt concludes:

> There are no formal 'introductory thanksgivings' in the proemia of letters contemporaneous with the Pauline and other New Testament letters; hence any reconstruction of such an 'introductory thanksgiving' shatters on the lack of evidence.[8]

While Reed contests several points of Arzt's argument he agrees that thanksgivings should not be referred to as 'introductory' since they can be found in the openings, bodies and closings of Hellenistic letters.[9]

> It is clear from the papyri that thanksgiving was not a matter to be limited to either the opening or the closing sections ... In other words, an epistolary thanksgiving *formula* may appear in various locations within the discourse.[10]

Thus, the placement of the thanksgiving in 1 Timothy is not abnormal in comparison with ancient letters. There is, then, nothing amiss concerning the location of 1.12–17.

Secondly, Miller, in suggesting a stark shift between a vice list (1.9–11) and a thanksgiving (1.12–17), misses the important function of v. 11. As

6. Quinn and Wacker 2000: 122. This idea appears to be what motivated the view mentioned by Moffatt that 1.12–17 have been accidentally misplaced and originally came between 1.2 and 1.3 (Moffatt 1918: 402).

7. Arzt 1994: 29–46; Reed 1996a: 87–99. Arzt describes his article as 'a more extensive examination of papyrus letters than has been undertaken previously, so far as I am aware ....' Reed, who writes in response to Arzt, affirms this appraisal while advancing yet more evidence himself.

8. Arzt 1994: 44.

9. Reed 1996a: 87, 89, 99. One example is P. Oxy 1.113.13. Reed 1996a: 87 also notes that expressions of thanksgiving also occur in the opening, body, and closing of Pauline letters.

10. Reed 1996a: 96.

noted in the previous chapter, 1.11 while cohering with the previous verses introduces a number of shifts or new points. These shifts serve as 'hooks' preparing the way for 1.12f. Four such shifts are of particular interest here. First, εὐαγγέλιον occurs in 1.11 for the first (and only) time in the letter. Though this word coheres with the previous mentions of proper teaching, it introduces a more specific reference to the saving message. Secondly, the idea of Paul being entrusted with a special ministry ('the gospel') occurs in 1.11 for the first time in the body of the letter.[11] Third, the mention of Paul's receiving a ministry uses the verb πιστεύω, the only occurrence of the πιστ- root in 1.8–11. Fourth, the mention of Paul being entrusted with the gospel (ὃ ἐπιστεύθην ἐγώ) brings Paul back to the forefront with the only occurrence of a first person singular referent in 1.8–11, and indeed the first such occurrence since 1.3. Each of these new elements become major components of 1.12–17 showing that 1.11 was deliberately constructed to introduce 1.12–17. First, vv. 12–17 spell out the message of the εὐαγγέλιον by rehearsing Paul's conversion replete with a discussion of Christ's salvific intent and use of common words associated with the gospel such as χάρις, πίστις, σῴζω, ζωὴ αἰώνιος, and Χριστὸς Ἰησοῦς.[12] Second, while 1.12–17 discusses Paul's conversion, it begins by explicitly referring to his being strengthened and placed in ministry (v. 12), a clear connection with Paul being entrusted with the gospel in 1.11. Third, the πιστ- root, which occurred in 1.8–11 only at the end of v. 11, becomes a keyword in 1.12–17 occurring five times (πίστον, v. 12; ἀπιστίᾳ, v. 13; πίστεως, v. 14; πίστος, v. 15; πιστεύειν, v. 16).[13] Fourth, while in 1.8–11 a first person singular referent occurred only in 1.11, 1.12–17 begins with a first person verb (ἔχω) and first person referents occur a total of seven times in 1.12–17, one of the densest collections of first person referents in the letter.[14] Indeed, after occurring in 1.11, the pronoun ἐγώ occurs only four more times in the letter, three of which are in 1.12–17 (vv. 12,15,16).[15] That these four elements (lexical, semantic, and deictic) are introduced in 1.11 and carry on through 1.12–17 argues strongly that these two units were intended to be contiguous and that they were written in light of each other.[16] The transition then is clearly signaled and not unexpected.

11.   Knight 1992: 92 writes, 'V.11 with its assertion that the gospel was entrusted to Paul provides the setting for vv. 12–17.' Cf. Barrett 1963: 44.

12.   Johnson 2001: 183, also suggests vv. 12–17 expound the 'healthy teaching' of vv. 10–11.

13.   Cf. also Mounce 2000: 47, 50.

14.   1.12 – ἔχω, με; 1.13 – ἠλεήθην, ἐποίησα; 1.15 – εἰμι ἐγώ; 1.16 – ἠλεήθην, ἐμοί. The two words in 1.15 are considered one occurrence since they function together.

15.   The other occurrence is 2.7.

16.   Marshall 1999: 361 also notes this 'hook' and the one in 1.7 and agrees (in n. 1) that it appears that these hooks were 'deliberately introduced to prepare for what follows.'

In addition to these hooks, the two units seem to have parallel closings. Both units close with their only mention of θεός (1.11, 17) and in both instances 'glory' (δόξα) is associated with God along with other honorific modifiers.[17] The only other occurrence of δόξα in the entire letter is 3.16. 1.11 seems to be a 'mini-doxology' preparing a way for the proper doxology in 1.17. The presence and number of these connections directly contradicts Miller's assertion that 1.12–17 has only a 'loose tie' to its context and, therefore, was probably just inserted as a preformed block of material.[18]

Lastly, there is a significant continuity between the units in their focus on sin. 1.9–10 contains a list of vices and 1.13, 15 also contain a list, this time referring to the pre-conversion Paul.[19]

1.9–10	1.13–15
ἄνομος (v. 9)	βλάσφημος (v. 13)
ἀνυπότακτος (v. 9)	διώκτης (v. 13)
ἀσεβής (v. 9)	ὑβριστής (v. 13)
ἁμαρτωλός (v. 9)	ἀπιστία (v. 13)
ἀνόσιος (v. 9)	**ἁμαρτωλός (v. 15)**
βέβηλος (v. 9)	
πατρολῴας, μητρολῴας (v. 9)	
ἀνδροφόνος (v. 9)	
πόρνος (v. 10)	
ἀρσενοκοίτης (v. 10)	
ἀνδραποδιστής (v. 10)	
ψεύστης (v. 10)	
ἐπίορκος (v. 10)	

The repetition of ἁμαρτωλός further strengthens this continuity as both sections relate to the issue of sinful people, marking a development in thought from 'The Law and sinful people' to 'The Gospel and a sinful person.'

1.12–17 and 1.18–20

Miller argues that 1.18–20 'does not follow smoothly after 1.17' and suggests it 'probably followed originally on 1.7,' since it has only a loose connection to the surrounding context.[20] Brox also found the placement of 1.18–20 problematic and suggested it should follow 1.11, with 1.12–17

17. Mounce 2000: 59 briefly notes some of this parallel.
18. Miller 1997: 65.
19. Mounce 2000: 47, 51, also notes this connection between the units.
20. Miller 1997: 65–66.

being an interpolation.[21] Others who are not so skeptical find connections further back in the letter, but very little is found by way of connection between 1.18–20 and 1.12–17.[22]

However, there are some connections between these two units, some of which have been noted by Mounce.[23] The connections center around Paul, so it can first be noted that Paul remains a constant in the participant field in both units (from 'Paul and Jesus' to 'Paul, Timothy and opponents'). Thus, first person singular referents which were a common feature of 1.12–17 continue in 1.18–20 (παρατίθημι, παραδίδωμι). The other connections can be subsumed under the idea of 'Paul as example' which was alluded to in 1.16. Paul's authority is established by the fact that he was entrusted with a ministry by Christ Jesus (vv. 11–12). That authority sets the stage for him to entrust a charge to Timothy (1.18).[24] The 'good fight' language in 1.18 refers to ministry (Timothy's), as 1.12f. focused on Paul's ministry.[25] As Paul needed to be strengthened for his ministry (1.12), so Timothy is reminded of the resources by which he can endure his calling (1.18).[26] Paul was considered faithful (πιστός), and Timothy is to hold on to his faith (πίστις). The opponents however shipwrecked their faith (πίστις). Lastly, there is a lexical connection between βλάσφημος (1.13) and βλασφημεῖν (1.20).[27] While Paul was *formerly* a blasphemer, these individuals still need to be taught not to blaspheme. Thus, there is a noticeable continuity between 1.12–17 and 1.18–20.

It can be conceded, though, that there is not as direct a connection between these two units as has been observed between the previous units. There are no hooking devices, for example. This suggests there may be further things to explore here later in this chapter when larger connections are considered.

1.18–20 and 2.1–7

It is commonly noted that a significant shift occurs at 2.1. Miller and others argue that the shift is so stark that 2.1 bears no relation to 1.18–20. Miller bases his case on (1) a shift from personal comments (1.18–20) to

21. Brox 1969a: 117.

22. A fault of Miller's is that he considers only contiguous connections. The oft noted connection between 1.18–20 and 1.3–7 will be dealt with below.

23. Mounce stands out among the commentators in pointing out connections between these units.

24. Similarly, Mounce 2000: 64.

25. That the military metaphor is used here of ministry is supported by Marshall 1999: 410–11; Roloff 1988: 103f. Cf. Pfitzner 1967: 177–68. Marshall 1999: 410, commenting on this phrase, states, 'ministry is viewed as warfare.'

26. Mounce 2000: 64. The resources in both cases also come from a divine source. This is explicit in 1.12 and implicit in 1.18 as the source of prophecy here would obviously be divine.

27. Mounce 2000: 64.

'unexpected' formal regulations' in 2.1f and (2) the ambiguity of οὖν in 2.1.[28] For his conclusion he approvingly quotes another scholar, 'whoever wrote II,1 … can have written neither I,3–11 nor I,18–20.'[29]

In response, first, disagreement among scholars over the referent of οὖν is a slim basis for discontinuity since many scholars do find a connection, whether to 1.3–5, 1.18, or to all of 1.3–20.[30] Secondly, the shift from more personal remarks to Timothy in 1.18 to the 'regulations' in 2.1f. may well be what οὖν signals, as Paul in 1.18 reiterates the general commission and then moves on to the particulars of how the commission is to be accomplished.[31] Furthermore, the personal nature of 1.18–20 is not altogether lost in 2.1–7. There is no real shift in the person and number of the main verbs, with first person singular verbs continuing in prominence. The communicative situation remains the same. Paul is urging Timothy. Indeed, Marshall writes, 'The tone of the instructions [in 2.1–7] is personal and somewhat urgent … the verb παρακαλῶ … expresses a command within the context of mutual relationship.'[32]

Therefore, there are continuities between 1.18–20 and 2.1–7 which allow one to see a logical progression and development. There are not, though, strong connections or transitional devices as found elsewhere.

2.1–7 and 2.8–15

There is not a lot of direct argument against the connection between these units though some are skeptical. Miller suggests that 2.8–15 is placed after 2.1–7 simply because of the catchword προσεύχεσθαι, though he does not argue a lack of connection.[33] In fact there are a number of indications of connection between these units.

First, the most commonly noted connection is the theme of prayer, seen most clearly in the lexical repetition noted by Miller. Several scholars note that 2.1–7 explains the goal or motive prayer (salvation of all people) and that 2.8–13 discuss the manner of prayer (peacefully, without disruption).[34] Secondly, the mention of prayer forms parallel introductions for the two

---

28. Miller 1997: 66.

29. Miller 1997: 67, citing A. Hilgenfeld, 'Die Hirtenbriefe des Paulus', *ZWT* 40 (1897): 17.

30. Cf. thorough discussions in Mounce 2000: 76–77; Marshall 1999: 418.

31. So also Mounce 2000: 77; Bernard 1906: 37; Ellicot 1856: 24; apparently also Marshall 1999: 418.

32. Marshall 1999: 418. He says this is also the way the verb is used 'in the earlier Paul' (Rom. 12.1; 1 Cor. 1.10; 2 Cor. 10.1; cf. 1 Pet. 2.11).

33. Miller 1997: 70.

34. Quinn and Wacker 2000: 207, 'The previous section articulated the goal and reason for public prayer; this section now turns to the questions of by whom and how Christian prayer is to be offered.' Similarly, Mounce 2000: 105; Oberlinner 1994: 82; Bassler 1996: 55; Towner 1989: 207; Barrett 1963: 53.

units. Both 2.1 and 2.8 begin with οὖν + a first person singular verb of authoritative exhortation,[35] and then have a call to prayer with a phrase using πᾶς which creates a universalistic tone.[36]

2.1   Παρακαλῶ οὖν   ποιεῖσθαι ... προσευχάς   ὑπὲρ πάντων ἀνθρώπων
2.8   Βούλομαι οὖν   προσεύχεσθαι   ἐν παντὶ τόπῳ

This significant parallel suggests 2.8 picks up and expounds the topic introduced in 2.1. Third, πᾶς seems to function not only in the parallel introduction, but also as a hooked keyword. It is a keyword in 2.1–7, occurring five times undergirding the unit's universalistic emphasis. It then occurs only at the beginning of 2.8–15, thus providing cohesion across the transition.[37] Fourth, the parallel introductions also point to an authoritative tone which permeates both units and is built on three key verbs: παρακαλέω (v. 1), βούλομαι (v. 8), ἐπιτρέπω (v. 12).[38] Authority is also connoted by the reference to Paul's role as apostle (2.7) and the grounding of one exhortation in the will of God (2.3–4).

Fifth, 2.7 appears to function as a transition for 2.8f. in a number of ways. As noted in the previous chapter, 2.1–7 opens with the first person singular (Paul), then the first person disappears from view until 2.7 where the first person singular (Paul) returns forming an inclusio. This return to first person singular in 2.7 also serves as a bridge preparing the way for 2.8 which opens with a first person singular verb. 2.7 also sets up the command of 2.8 by first stating Paul's position as preacher, apostle, and teacher.[39] Thus, after the doctrinal statement of 2.4–6, 2.7 brings Paul (first person singular) back to the forefront and states his credentials. 2.8 then builds on 2.7 by continuing in the first person and stating a command in keeping with the credentials given.

Sixth, the two units are connected by a common desire for peace and proper living. One of the goals of prayer in 2.2 is to live a peaceful, quiet (ἡσύχιος) life. 2.8 then deals explicitly with issues which are disrupting the peace within the church, and it appear that the issues raised in the rest of the unit were also points of contention.[40] Indeed, one thing prescribed for the peaceful worship is the quietness (ἡσυχία) of the women (2.11, 12).[41]

---

35.   So also Mounce 2000: 104; Oberlinner 1994: 85.
36.   The universalistic idea in 2.1 is clear, while in 2.8 it is debatable. Towner 1989: 205–207 argues well for the universalistic sense in 2.8.
37.   Towner 1989: 207, though not identifying a hooked keyword, notes the connection created by the use of πᾶς in 2.8.
38.   Johnson 2001: 198. Similarly, Towner 1989: 207; Oberlinner 1994: 85.
39.   Bassler 1996: 56; Roloff 1988: 130.
40.   Johnson 2001: 204; Bassler 1996: 56.
41.   This connection may suggest a more positive view of the quietness enjoined.

Further, the desire in 2.2 is also to live in 'all godliness and dignity' (ἐν πάσῃ εὐσεβείᾳ καὶ σεμνότητι). This description is expounded in 2.8–15 as it forbids vices (ὀργή, διαλογισμός) and enjoins virtues (ὅσιος, κόσμιος, αἰδώς, σωφροσύνη, θεοσέβεια, ὑποταγή, πίστις, ἀγάπη, ἁγιασμός). The lexical connection between εὐσέβεια and θεοσέβεια is particularly strong.

Lastly, 2.11–15, which is particularly criticized regarding connection, has some particular affinities with 2.1–7 with the language of proclamation and salvation. The strong statement of Paul's position as a teacher (διδάσκολος, v. 7) connects naturally with a discussion of who should and should not teach (διδάσκω, v. 12). Then 2.15 picks up the concern over salvation which was so crucial in 2.3–6 (among other terms σῴζω occurs in v. 4 and v. 15).

Therefore, the common view that 2.1–7 and 2.8–15 are significantly linked has a strong basis in lexical and semantic connections as well as transitional devices. Miller's assertion that they are only connected by the repetition of prayer vocabulary fails to account for all these other connections.

2.8–15 and 3.1–7

Many commentators do not even consider the relation between these two units, but those who do give it thought commonly note that the transition between the two units appear abrupt and sudden.[42] Marshall sums up the general consensus writing, 'The section [3.1–7] at first sight has no connection with what has just preceded.'[43] This is enough for Miller to declare, 'There is no development of thought that links 2:15 with 3:1b.'[44] However, several scholars, like Marshall, who acknowledge the abruptness of the transition still point out logical connections.[45] For example, having just declared that women were not allowed to teach, the text moves logically to those who should.[46] And discussion of behavior at prayer leads naturally to those who should lead.[47]

Undergirding these logical connections is a significant continuity in theme which contains some lexical connections as well. As noted above, 2.8–15 is full of ethical vocabulary including some virtue lists (vv. 9–10, 15). 3.1–7 continues this focus with an extensive virtue list. While the group in view is different, the focus in both is peace and propriety. The men in 2.8

---

42. E.g., Miller 1997: 74; Quinn and Wacker 2000: 251; Bassler 1996: 63.

43. Marshall 1999: 473.

44. Miller 1997: 74.

45. Even Easton 1947: 130, who is not a proponent of cohesion in the Pastoral Epistles, writes, 'The directions about men and women in chapter 2 are continued naturally by instructions about church officers.'

46. Marshall 1999: 473; Bassler 1996: 63.

47. Quinn and Wacker 2000: 251.

are exhorted to pray without 'wrath' (ὀργή); similarly, the overseer must not be 'violent' (πλήκτης) but be 'gentle' (ἐπιεικής) and 'peaceable' (ἄμαχος). Then a number of words in the semantic range of propriety, respectability are shared between the units: σωφροσύνη (2.9, 15), σώφρων (3.2)[48] and σεμνότης (3.4); κόσμιος (2.9; 3.2) and κοσμέω (2.9).[49] Most of the other qualities listed fall within this range as is often noted by those who point out that these characteristics would be those recognized as respectable in the broader Greco-Roman culture at the time. Connected with this is a shared concern for order as seen in submission to the proper authority: ἐν πάσῃ ὑποταγῇ (2.11) and ἐν ὑποταγῇ (3.4).

Thus, while someone could argue that the logical connections mentioned earlier are only the accidents of placement, the significant continuity in genre (virtue lists) and outlook (peace and propriety) along with the lexical repetition holds these two units together and supports the logical connections.

3.1–7 and 3.8–13

A connection between these two units is rarely contested. Even Miller concedes the connection formed by the common concern over qualifications for leadership.[50] Indeed, the very genre is the same since both units are composed largely of virtue lists. In fact there are striking similarities between the qualifications stated in each list.[51]

Overseer (3.1–7)	**Deacons** (3.8–13)
μιᾶς γυναικὸς ἀνήρ	μιᾶς γυναικὸς ἀνήρ
νηφάλιος	νηφάλιος
μή πάροινος	μή οἴνῳ πολλῷ προσέχοντας
τοῦ ἰδίου οἴκου καλῶς προϊστάμενον τέκνα ἔχοντα ἐν ὑποταγῇ	τέκνων καλῶς προϊστάμενοι καὶ τῶν ἰδίων οἴκων
σεμνότης	σεμνός
	σεμνή (women)
ἀφιλάργυρος	μὴ αἰσχροκερδής
ἀνεπίλημπτος	ἀνέγκλητος

---

48. Johnson 2001: 214, notes the connection between σωφροσύνη (2.9, 15) and σώφρων (3.2).

49. Also Johnson 2001: 214.

50. Miller 1997: 74, 'This block of materials (3:1b-13) is unified by its concern for establishing proper leadership standards within the community.'

51. Mounce 2000: 195, 'The similarity of this list [3.8–13] to the preceding one for overseers is striking.' Various commentators have noted some of these connections. E.g. Marshall 1999: 489f.; Mounce 2000: 195; Johnson 2001: 227–29; Hanson 1982: 78–79; Barrett 1963: 60.

Also, 'holding to the mystery of the faith' (deacons) and 'apt to teach' (overseer) have some connection in that both involve a clear grasp of the Christian message.[52] The concern for propriety and peaceableness noted earlier in 3.1–7 continues in 3.8–13 as well. There are of course interesting and important differences as well, which is what one would expect in lists for different offices, but these striking similarities suggest the two lists were formed in light of each other.

Next, these two lists are connected by the use of ὡσαύτως with elision. This creates clear cohesion as the ὡσαύτως sends the reader back to 3.2 to supply the verb (δεῖ) for 3.8f.[53] This sharing of the same main verb is matched by some similarity in basic structure. Both lists begin with a virtue/vice list and then move on to some more extended discussion. Also, as noted by Knight, the bishop passage begins with a commendation and the deacon passage ends with a commendation creating a sort of inclusio around the two units:[54] the work of overseer is a 'good' (καλός) work, and those who serve 'well' (καλῶς) as deacons obtain a 'good' (καλός) standing.[55]

3.8–13 and 3.14–16

The previous chapter showed that there was a significant shift in cohesion fields at 3.14. Thus, commentators commonly note an abrupt transition at 3.14.[56] Some find the transition so rough that they conclude that there is no connection between 3.14–16 and what precedes or follows.

> In its present context, the passage fits awkwardly both in tone and subject matter with that which immediately precedes ... and that which follows.[57]

> Thus we are at a loss to find the connection between our verse and the previous and following ones, but even the internal order of the verse is no better.[58]

---

52. Hanson 1982: 79, suggests they are roughly equivalent, but this is probably overstating the connection since 'holding to the mystery' does not connote any necessary aptitude in passing on that message as 'apt to teach' does.

53. So also, Marshall 1999: 489.

54. Knight 1992: 167, 173. Cf. also Marshall 1999: 495; Roloff 1988: 166.

55. It may be significant that the word διάβολος occurs three times in the letter, and all three are shared between these two units: 3.6, 7, 11. The usage in 3.6, 7 is different from 3.11, but one wonders if a wordplay was intended.

56. E.g. Quinn and Wacker 2000: 606.

57. Miller 1997: 77.

58. Schleiermacher 1836: 304.

> This passage is without grammatical or doctrinal connection with the
> material which immediately precedes or follows.[59]

Miller concludes that 3.14–16 is an original piece of Pauline material that
originally followed 1.18–20.

However, such a drastic view is unnecessary. First, the unit opens with
ταῦτα which would commonly be interpreted as referring backward as a
summary as is common elsewhere in the Pastoral Epistles.[60] A summary,
then, might be expected to be different in form from the material directly
preceding it. Furthermore, the sphere of concern in 3.14–16 is still the
church. The previous unit(s) has been describing the behavioral qualities
'necessary' (δεῖ; 3.2, 7, and by ellipsis in 3.8, 11) for church leadership, and
now 3.14–16 refer to writing about the behavior 'necessary' (δεῖ; 3.15) in
the church. Similarly the concern with the deacon's leadership of his
household (οἶκος, v. 12; cf. 3.4), corresponds with the description of the
church as God's household (οἶκος, v. 15). Thus, the concerns are similar,
though 3.14–16 speaks more generally, as would be expected in a
summary.

Lastly, the mention of τὸ τῆς εὐσεβείας **μυστήριον** in 3.16 links back to the
reference to τὸ **μυστήριον** τῆς πίστεως in 3.9.[61] These are the only two
occurrences of μυστήριον in the letter and both refer to the basic gospel
message. Thus, 3.16 functions to expound the passing reference to the
'mystery of the faith' in 3.9.[62]

These connections hold 3.14–16 to 3.8–13 in a plausible manner.[63]
Scholars usually discuss connections between 3.14–16 and units further
back in the letter but this will be addressed in a later section.

3.14–16 and 4.1–5

As noted above, Miller and others have argued that 3.14–16 has no
connection whatsoever with 4.1–5. Several commentators do not seriously
discuss connections between this passage since they understand 4.1 to
introduce a new section after 3.14–16 concluded the previous one. This is
especially true among those who see 1 Timothy as a church order and

---

59.   F. Gealy, *The Epistles to Timothy and Titus* (The Interpreters Bible, vol. 11; New
York: Abingdon Press, 1955): 418.

60.   Marshall 1999: 505, 'The demonstrative pronoun is usually anaphoric in the PE,
pointing backwards to what has just been said and summarising or concluding sections of
teaching' (e.g., 1.18). Also Mounce 2000: 219, who says this is also a common use in other
letters attributed to Paul.

61.   So also Marshall 1999: 523. Towner 1989: 88, says the two phrases are commonly
taken as equivalents. Also Lau 1996: 110, 113.

62.   Lau 1996: 113. Lau also notes (107) that the contextual function of 3.16 is often
ignored (he cites Easton, Dibelius and Conzelmann, Scott, and Houlden as guilty of this).

63.   Johnson 2001: 226f., does not even separate 3.8–13 and 3.14–16.

therefore see 3.14–16 as merely a pause between the church order material.[64] However, there are some significant links between these two units. First, there appears to be a sort of hook word between 3.14–16 and 4.1–5. The rarity of explicit references to the Spirit in the Pastoral Epistles is commonplace. In fact πνεῦμα occurs only three times in 1 Timothy, and all three occurrences are in these two units, at the close of one and the beginning of the next (3.16, 4.1 [2x]).

In spite of the debate concerning the meaning of ἐν πνεύματι in 3.16, it is most likely that the Holy Spirit is in view.[65] Thus, the seemingly abrupt appearance of the Spirit in 4.1 has been prepared by the reference in 3.16. This also plays a part in the direct contrasts which link these two units, as the triumph of the gospel envisaged in 3.16 is balanced by the apostasy of some in 4.1ff. The Spirit who was involved in the vindication of Christ (3.16) also clearly says that some will turn away (4.1).[66] Also there is a contrast in the involvement of other spiritual beings in the units. Angels are associated with the gospel (3.16) but lying spirits and demons are associated with the message of the opponents (4.1). In 3.16 Christ is believed in (πιστεύω), but in 4.1 some turn away from the faith (πίστις). The general deceitfulness of the opponents' message (πλάνος, ψευδολόγος) contrasts the role of the church as the foundation and pillar of the truth.[67] Thus, there is a significant connection between the two units.[68]

4.1–5 and 4.6–10

The connection between these units is not often disputed, with most commentators seeing a contrast between the opponents and Timothy.[69] However, Falconer suggested a lack of cohesion since he argued that 4.6–7a interrupted the argument and were probably an editorial

---

64.   E.g. Easton 1947: 135, who also cites, without reference, Dibelius.

65.   This would be the case whether one interpreted the phrase as 'in the realm of the Spirit' (Marshall 1999: 525–26; Towner 1989: 90–91; Quinn and Wacker 2000: 334–37; Lau 1996: 100; Fee 1994: 766) or whether one interpreted the phrase instrumentally as 'by the Spirit' (Barrett 1963: 65). As Fee states, the question of which of these two is correct is moot. This is in contrast to Gundry who argues that the phrase refers to Jesus' human spirit (Gundry 1970: 211–14).

66.   Quinn and Wacker 2000: 348. Fee 1994: 768.

67.   Quinn and Wacker 2000: 348–49, note how 'the content of the passages [3.14–16 and 4.1–5] both complements and yet contrasts with each other.'

68.   Indeed, Quinn and Wacker 2000: 290f. keep the two units together as one, stating, 'All the literary signals indicate that 3:14–16 is to be read along with 4:1–5' (349). Mounce 2000: 233, while separating the units, writes, '1 Tim 4:1–5 does not begin a new topic.'

69.   E.g. Fee 1988: 102, 'The instructions in the first paragraph (vv. 6–10) are clearly given vis-à-vis the false teachers.' See also Bassler 1996: 82; Roloff 1988: 240. Barrett 1963: 68 sees a logical flow from theological response to opponents in general to how Timothy, himself, should handle them specifically.

insertion.[70] Miller also sees no connection. Therefore, potential connections need to be investigated.

First, the ταῦτα in 4.6 sends the reader to previous material in search of a referent. Miller contests the connecting function of ταῦτα here on the basis that its intended referent is ambiguous.[71] While it is true that the exact referent of the pronoun is debated, it is widely agreed that it refers backward and it most likely refers to the refutation of the opponents in 4.3b–5.[72] This interpretation of the referent of ταῦτα is confirmed by lexical and semantic connections between 4.6–7a and 4.1–5. The opponents have rejected τῆς πίστεως (4.1), but Timothy is to be nourished on τοῖς λόγοις τῆς πίστεως (4.6). They hold to διδασκαλίαις δαιμονίων and **deceitful** spirits (v. 1), but Timothy is to be nourished on τῆς καλῆς διδασκαλίας and **faithful** words (v. 6).[73] Whereas the 'word of God' sanctifies (v. 5), the myths in v. 7 are 'defiling.' Whereas the opponents hold to (προσέχω; v. 1) the false teaching, Timothy is to avoid it (παραιτέομαι; v. 7a). These clear contrasts with lexical repetition bind these verses suggesting ταῦτα links to the previous unit and contradicting Falconer's assertion that 4.6–7a interrupt the flow of the argument.

There are also structural indicators of cohesion between these two units. First, though future verbs are not common in the letter,[74] both of these units open with a future tense verb creating a continuity in temporal frame. Both units are looking forward: though difficult times are coming, Timothy will be (in such times) a good servant if he does these things. Second, 4.1–5, though dealing with false teaching, closes with a refutation and a mention of 'the word of God' (λόγος θεοῦ). This provides the transition to the discussion of proper ministry based on faithful words (λόγοι). The discussion of proper ministry, then, also contains a restatement of the false teaching to be avoided. In this way, the author has knit together these two contrasting units by closing one unit with a foreshadowing of what is to come in the next and then opening the next with a brief recapitulation of what was in the previous.

> False teachers ... refutation (Proper ministry)
> Proper ministry ... false teachers ... proper ministry

This strongly suggests that 4.1–5 and 4.6–10 were composed together and in light of each other.

---

70. Falconer 1937: 142.

71. Miller 1997: 79–80.

72. Cf. also Marshall 1999: 548; Roloff 1988: 241; Wolter 1988: 146; Bassler 1996: 83.

73. Also Marshall 1999: 549. Collins 1975: 158 also notes that κάλος appears in both units (vv. 4, 6) and the contrast between ψευδολόγος (v. 2) and λόγοι of faith (v. 6).

74. Including the two occurrences here, there are 8 uses of future tense verbs in 1 Timothy: 2.15; 3.5; 4.1, 6, 16; 5.18; 6.8, 15.

4.6–10 and 4.11–16

It was noted in the previous chapter that the shifts in cohesion fields between these two units were not great. As a result a connection between these units is almost unanimously accepted, with many commentators not even placing a break at 4.11.[75] Those who do separate the units usually connect them at a higher level.[76] Miller apparently sees no connection, but he does not argue for incoherence here.[77] The general consensus has a good basis, some of which has not been explicitly noted before.

First, there is a significant continuity in genre and participant. Both units are exhortation from Paul to Timothy, and, as a result, second person referents and imperatives are prominent in both units. Second person referents, which were absent from 4.1–5, occur five times in 4.6–10 and 15 times in 4.11–16. Then, there are two imperatives in 4.7 and 10 in 4.11–16.[78] This common characteristic is even more striking when it is realized that second person singular imperatives do not occur in the letter until 4.7. Thus, 4.6 seems to mark a shift to direct exhortation to Timothy in second person singular imperatives which, after a bit of doctrinal grounding in 4.8–10, really come to the fore in 4.11–16 and continue through the rest of the letter. Thus, 4.6–16 demonstrates a particular continuity as direct exhortation to Timothy.

Secondly, there is some similarity in both the introduction and closing of both of these units. Both units open with ταῦτα + a verb of instruction: Ταῦτα ὑποτιθέμενος (4.6); Παράγγελλε ταῦτα καὶ δίδασκε (4.11).[79] Both passages refer to Timothy teaching the church.[80] In their closings both units contain statements referring to hard work in ministry and salvation. 4.10 refers to laboring and striving (κοπιάω, ἀγωνίζομαι) because of hope in God who is savior (σωτήρ) of all. 4.15–16 calls Timothy to 'remain in' (εἰμί, ἐπιμένω)

---

75. E.g. of those keeping the units together: Johnson 2001: 249f.; Mounce 2000: 244f.; Hanson 1982: 89f.

76. E.g. Dibelius and Conzelmann 1972: 70, 'In 4:11, the exhortation to the leader of the congregation, which was begun in 4:6, is continued.' However, several German commentators do posit a strong section break at 4.12.

77. Miller 1997: 82–83.

78. Even the introductory participle in 4.6 (ὑποτιθέμενος) could be understood as the semantic equivalent of an imperative. Mounce 2000: 246 also notes this feature and its cohesive effect. Mounce further notes the continuity created by the fact that all the imperatives, as well as the participle mentioned, are present tense. He goes on to suggest this continuity in linear aspect gives a sense of urgency to the instructions, but I am not sure the present tense or the aspect does this.

79. Mounce 2000: 246, also notes the parallel. Several commentators note the linking function of v. 11. There is then no need to label 4.11 perfunctory as Falconer does (1937: 143).

80. Louw and Nida (1989) classify ὑποτίθεμθαι (33.230) and διδάσκω (33.224) in the subdomain of 'Teach.' They classify παράγγελλω (33.327) in the subdomain 'Command, Order.'

and 'take pains with' (μελετάω) what he has been taught because in doing so both he and his hearers will be saved (σῴζω). Both verses use the τοῦτο γάρ construction.

Third, there are striking similarities between v. 6a and v. 16b which envelop the two units. First, both statements have the structure: τοῦτο + participle + second person singular future verb, with the future verb describing future benefits of the faithfulness called for in the participle.

4:6a – Ταῦτα ὑποτιθέμενος τοῖς ἀδελφοῖς καλὸς ἔσῃ διάκονος Χριστοῦ Ἰησοῦ
4:16b – τοῦτο γὰρ ποιῶν καὶ σεαυτὸν σώσεις καὶ τοὺς ἀκούοντάς σου

No other future verbs occur between these verses, and indeed these are the only two places where second person singular future verbs are used of Timothy. There is only one other second person singular future verb in the letter (5.18) and it is entirely different since it is part of a quotation and is used in an imperatival sense. Thus, this repetition of verbal form here is all the more significant. Both statements function to urge Timothy to faithfulness by laying out the future benefit both to himself and his hearers, and provide a fitting summary of this section.

Fourth, there is another continuity in the participant field. The church shows up in both units. As noted in the previous chapter, 4.6–10 is bracketed by references to the congregation ('brothers ... those who believe), though the congregation is not prominent as the unit focuses on Timothy personally. In 4.11–16, as shown in the previous chapter, the congregation is in view throughout. Thus, the return to the congregation in 4.10 brings back to the fore a participant who will be prominent in the following unit. This is similar to a hooked construction. This hook is further strengthened by lexical repetition as 4.16 closes with a reference to those who believe (πιστῶν) and the instructions of 4.11–16 begin with a reference to 'those who believe' (πιστῶν).[81]

Finally, the continuity of theme in the two units can be seen in the topic of teaching. Running through both units is a chain of words referring to proper teaching along with calls to receive or hold to this teaching.

Verse	Proper teaching	Reception
4:6	ὑποτιθέμενος	
4:6	οἱ λόγοι τῆς πίστεως	ἐντρεφόμενος
	ἡ καλὴ διδασκαλία	
4:9	πιστὸς ὁ λόγος	πάσης ἀποδοχῆς ἄξιος

---

81. These are the only two occurrences of the verb πιστεύω in these two units. There are three occurrences of cognates (vv. 6, 9, 12), but the verb forms are substantially different here as they refer to people, the church.

4:11　παραγγέλλω
　　　διδάσκω
4:12　λόγος
4:13　ἀνάγνωσις　　　πρόσεχω
　　　παράκλησις
　　　ἡ διδασκαλία
4:16　**ἡ διδασκαλία**　　ἐπέχω
　　　　　　　　ἐπιμένω

In summary, 4.6–10 and 4.11–16 are strongly bound by various repetitions, transitional devices, and continuity of themes. There is then little basis for skepticism regarding this connection, and the common view has been given further support.

4.11–16 and 5.1–2

Miller in his customary fashion disputes any connection between 5.1–2 and the preceding material saying it abruptly and unexpectedly introduces a discussion of the proper treatment of individuals within the community. Thus, he concludes, 'The independent character of 5.1–2 can hardly be denied.'[82] Kelly also writes, 'At this point the tone and content of the letter change abruptly.'[83] However, this skepticism is not shared by most commentators, with many noting the possibility of keeping 5.1–2 with 4.11–16.[84] Fee states that 5.1–2 'flows naturally out of 4.11–16.'[85] A number of features favor this more favorable assessment of the connection between the two units.

The most obvious connection is the continuity of second person singular referents and imperatives which were so prominent in 4.11–16 and continue straight through 5.1–2. Both verbs in 5.1–2 are second person singular and are imperatival.[86] More specifically, both units begin with two imperatival verbs connoting authoritative speech.[87] Secondly, the context and relational matrix is the same in both units: Paul exhorting Timothy concerning his relationship with the community.[88] Having mentioned

---

82. Miller 1997: 83.
83. Kelly 1963: 109.
84. The possibility is weighed, for example, by Quinn and Wacker 2000: 409; Mounce 2000: 268; Bassler 1996: 90; Fee 1988: 112. Roloff 1988: 250, and Dibelius and Conzelmann 1972: 72, argue for this position.
85. Fee 1988: 112.
86. The negated subjunctive μὴ ἐπιπλήξῃς functions as an imperative, as is common.
87. So also, Fee 1988: 112; Mounce 2000: 268. This continuity in imperatives is apparently what led Bassler 1996: 90, to suggest that 5.1–2 is grammatically part of 4.11–16.
88. So also Fee 1988: 112.

'those who hear you' in 4.16, 5.1–2 further distinguish these people.[89] Within the context of Timothy's relationship with the church, 5.1–2 and 4.12 have a similar concern about Timothy's youthfulness.[90] 4.12 refers to people not despising Timothy and 5.1–2 deals (among other things) with Timothy not despising the older members. Though he has authority, Timothy is not to use it harshly.[91] Also, in 4.12 Timothy is to be an example of ἁγνεία and in 5.2 ἁγνεία is to characterize his treatment of the young women.[92] The treatment of the young women, then, is to be one area in which Timothy is to be an example of purity.[93]

Thus, a significant level of continuity between 4.11–16 and 5.1–2 militates against the view of incoherence. Instead, Mounce is justified in writing, 'There is a strong connection between these two verses and the preceding section.'[94]

5.1–2 and 5.3–16

Miller suggests these units are disconnected and come from different sources but he does not actually discuss it.[95] Quinn and Wacker and Easton also suggest the transition is abrupt since 5.1–2 contain short statements and 5.3–16 is a long detailed discussion.[96] However, neither Quinn and Wacker nor Easton goes on to suggest a lack of cohesion between the two units.[97] Most commentators understand 5.1–2 as introducing the units which follow.[98]

There are, in fact, several indicators of cohesion between 5.1–2 and 5:3–16. There is an ecclesial context to both units. Both units open with a second person singular imperative concerning proper treatment of a certain group. 5.1–2 closes with mention of women groups in the church and 5.3 opens with one specific such group – widows. 5.2 takes up older women then younger women. 5.3–16 seems to follow the same order, with 5.3–10 dealing with older women as made clear in v. 9 and 5.11–15 dealing with younger women.[99] Similarly, as older women are to be treated as

---

89.   Mounce 2000: 268; Knight 1992: 213.

90.   So also, Roloff 1988: 250.

91.   Fee 1988: 112; Knight 1992: 213; Marshall 1999: 572.

92.   These are the only two occurrences of ἁγνεία in 1 Timothy.

93.   So also Bassler 1996: 92.

94.   Mounce 2000: 268.

95.   Miller 1997: 83. Concerning 5.1–22 as a whole he writes, 'That the collection derives from various sources is apparent from the discontinuity both among and within the collected traditions.'

96.   Quinn and Wacker 2000: 426; Easton 1947: 151.

97.   Quinn and Wacker 2000: 409 does suggest 5.3–16 comes from a different source than 5.1–2.

98.   E.g. Mounce 2000: 273; Marshall 1999: 572–73; Quinn and Wacker 2000: 409.

99.   νεωτέρας occurs in vv. 2, 11, 14 – the only occurrences in the letter.

mothers (5.2), part of the qualifications in 5.3–10 for the widow is her 'motherly' status (5.10). Also, younger women are to be treated in all purity, and one of the concerns for younger widows in 5.11–15 is purity. Lastly, 5.3–16 continues the familial tone set in 5.1–2. 5.1–2 describes the relationships within the church with the terms father, mother, brother, and sister. 5.3–16 is then deeply concerned with responsibilities of children, grandchildren, and households.[100] Thus, there is a natural flow from 5.1–2 to 5.3–16.

5.3–16 and 5.17–25

Miller says 5.17–25 comes from a different source from 5.3–16 and probably was placed here simply due to the repetition of τιμάω/τιμή.[101] Some other commentators note an abrupt shift but usually do not suggest a lack of coherence.[102] While there is not a significant discussion of connections between the two units, most note a continuity in broad topic in that 5.17–25 continues the discussion of various groups within the church.[103]

This general recognition can be expanded. First, there is a continuity in genre since both units are framed as exhortation. Indeed both units are full of imperatives. In 5.3–16, seven out of 28 finite verbs are imperatives, and an even greater percentage of the main verbs in the sentences. In 5.17–25 eight out of ten finite verbs are imperatives.[104] Second, there is a striking similarity in the structure of the introductions of the two units. Both open with a fronted plural noun announcing the particular group in view followed by a call to give those in view proper honor (τιμάω/τιμή). This similarity does not appear accidental as Miller suggests, but indicates that specific groups are being taken up intentionally in a similar way. The idea that the discussion of the two groups is intentionally framed in a similar manner is bolstered by a few other similarities. In both units the group in view has good and bad examples: true widows and those that are not; elders who work hard and those who sin.[105] In both units, judgment is mentioned in reference to the sinning group (κρίμα, v. 12; κρίσις, v. 24), and 'good works' (ἔργα καλά, v. 10; τὰ ἔργα τὰ καλά, v. 25) are mentioned in reference to the good group. Diligence seems to be a mark of the good

---

100. Louw and Nida's (1989) Domain 10 contains 'Kinship Terms.' 5.1–2 contains four words in this domain (πατήρ, μήτηρ, ἀδελφός, ἀδελφή). 5.3–16 contain seven words in this domain (χήρα, τέκνον, ἔκγονον, οἶκος, πρόγονος, μονόομαι, ἀνήρ).

101. Miller 1997: 85.

102. E.g., Quinn and Wacker 2000: 458.

103. E.g., Marshall 1999: 609; Mounce 2000: 304; Knight 1992: 231.

104. The numbers increase if verbs like βούλομαι and διαμαρτύρομαι, which are not in imperative mood but function as commands, are included.

105. So also, Marshall 1999: 609; Quinn and Wacker 2000: 458.

group in both units in contrast to the laziness of the excluded younger widows. The presence of good and bad in both groups leads to a concern over who is included in both groups (e.g., vv. 9, 22). Thus both units call for honor for specific groups and provide criteria for determining who is actually entitled to receive this honor.

There is also a sense of seriousness about the issues addressed, denoted not only by the reference to judgment, but also by the fact that both units contain an exhortation to enforce the guidelines given (vv. 7, 21). Both of these statements use ταῦτα (the only two occurrences of ταῦτα in 5.3–25) and have ἵνα- clauses. This weighty sense is then also created by the use of ἐνώπιον τοῦ θεοῦ, appearing in both units (vv. 4, 21) and indicating that this is all done in the presence of God, himself.

Lastly, there is a concern in each unit about inappropriate behavior which might bring reproach. Younger widows are given instruction so that they might give no occasion for reproach from the enemy (5.14); the sin of elders is to be dealt with publicly (5.20), indeed it cannot be hidden (5.24), and it could implicate Timothy if he is not careful (5.22)

5.3–16 and 17–25 are clearly distinct units, but the similarities in their structure and content suggest that different (though related) topics are being treated in a similar way which creates cohesion between the two units. While the need to address a list of subjects may create a significant shift between the units, the similarities suggest these units do in fact cohere.

5.17–25 and 6.1–2

The connection between these two units is significantly more disputed than that between 5.3–16 and 17–25. A number of scholars consider 6.1–2 to be significantly different from what precedes. A loose connection with the preceding material is acknowledged because of the repetition of honor and the continuation of exhortations. However, four observations suggest to some that the connection is very loose, leading Roloff to say 6.1–2 is simply tacked on.[106] The observations are: (1) 6.1–2 does not concern an official church group,[107] (2) the word 'honor' is used in a very different way (without any financial overtones),[108] (3) there is not a good and bad group in 6.1–2,[109] and (4) it bears no obvious relation to the age groups which provide 'the general rubric of this section.'[110]

In response, it can be noted that the first objection assumes that the widows of 5.3–16 constituted an office-bearing group within the church, a

106.   Roloff 1988: 318.
107.   Bassler 1996: 103; Roloff 1988: 318.
108.   Bassler 1996: 103; Marshall 1999: 627, though Marshall does not suggest a lack of cohesion.
109.   Fee 1988: 136.
110.   Bassler 1996: 103.

position which, though arguable, is not certain.[111] The use of 'honor' here is different from what precedes but in a way necessary considering the subject – slaves are not going to be urged to give financial remuneration to their masters. If one conceives of an author free to choose (create) any three topics in order to use honor in the same way, then the shift here in 6.2 would be quite bothersome. If, however, one conceives of an author with three real and differing issues confronting him, then the fact that he has packaged his response to each of them in terms of honor is significant and creates cohesion. On the third objection, while this unit does not directly connect with age groups, it does connect with the family context created by 5.1–2 for the discussion of groups within the church. Slaves were considered part of the household. Furthermore, one of the key bases for the exhortation in 6.1–2 is that believing masters are 'brothers' to believing slaves. Thus, it is not necessarily incongruous with 5.1–2.[112] Lastly, while it is true that there is not a good and bad group in 6.1–2, the exhortation is presented in terms of two groups – slaves in general and slaves with believing masters. While these groups overlap and the others would seem to be mutually exclusive, it is significant that each unit takes up two groups.

Beyond these objections, there are some links between 5.17–25 and 6.1–2. First, 6.1–2 begins with a fronted nominative plural identifying the group under consideration just as the previous two units did, and particularly similar to 5.17 (οἱ … πρεσβύτεροι and ὅσοι … δοῦλοι.). Secondly, the wording of the call to honor is strikingly similar between 5.17 and 6.1. 5.17 has διπλῆς τιμῆς ἀξιούσθωσαν and 6.1 has πάσης τιμῆς ἀξίους ἡγείσθωσαν. The wording is virtually synonymous. Third, the continuity of imperatives should not be minimized. Even if one does not count 6.2c (whose place is disputed), three of the seven finite verbs in 6.1–2 are imperatives. Fourth, in both units the exhortation is linked to a concern about 'teaching' (διδασκαλία, 5.17; 6.1). Lastly, it was noted in the previous chapter that 5.17–25 began with a third plural verb, shifts to first and second singular verbs, and then returns to third plural verbs in vv. 24–25. This formed a bit of inclusio for 5.17–25, but also forms a transition to 6.1–2 which is dominated by third plural verbs.[113]

In summary, while there are shifts between 5.17–25 and 6.1–2, there are still linguistic connections binding the two together.

---

111. The following recent commentaries do not view the widows as a church office: Johnson 2001: 271–72; Mounce 2000: 273–75; Marshall 1999: 573–77; Knight 1992: 222–23.

112. This objection would not seem to be as cogent for those like Roloff and Oberlinner who do not connect 5.1–2 with 5.3–6.2. The connection with 5.1–2 will be explored more fully later in this chapter.

113. Quinn and Wacker 2000: 482 note this phenomena as well.

6.1–2 and 6.3–10

Miller says 6.3f. 'returns abruptly to the subject of false teachers' and is 'unmotivated by what precedes.'[114] However, a number of scholars have noted that 6.2c (Ταῦτα δίδασκε καὶ παρακάλει) serves as a transition linking 6.3f. with what precedes.[115] 6.2c can be labeled a 'hinge.' As the previous chapter showed, 6.2c stands apart both from what precedes and what follows as its second person singular imperatives are not found in the units on either side of it. Ταῦτα, though, connects with the previous material as a summarizing statement.[116] It then provides the foil for 6.3f. Timothy is to teach (διδάσκω) these things, but there are others who 'teach otherwise' (ἑτεροδιδασκαλέω).[117] By summing up the previous material in terms of teaching (especially with the use of διδάσκω), a transition is created for addressing those who do not teach these things. This begins a series of switching contrasts which runs through 6.3ff.[118] Thus, the return to false teachers in 6.3f. is neither 'abrupt' nor unmotivated by what precedes.'

Furthermore, there are some connections between 6.1–2b and 6.3–10 beyond the hinge in 6.2c. First, in a very general sense, 6.3–10 continues the concern with groups within the church, since presumably the opponents were within the church. Whereas 6.1–2 (and previously) had been concerned with those due proper honor, 6.3–10 switches to those not due honor. Whereas 6.1–2 (and previously) had been concerned with proper behavior, the opponents are marked by improper behavior. More specifically, there are at least two significant lexical connections between 6.1–2 and 6.3–10. The behavior of the slaves is to be motivated by a desire that the name of God and the teaching (διδασκαλία) not be slandered (βλασφημέω). However, the opponents fail to hold to godly teaching (διδασκαλία; v. 3) and their disputings produce slander (βλασφημία; v. 4) among other things.[119]

6.3–10 and 6.11–16

This connection is among the most doubted in the letter. Miller claims there is 'no logical connection' with the preceding material.[120] Dibelius and

---

114. Miller 1997: 89.

115. Cf. Marshall 1999: 634, 'Verse 2b is transitional, summing up the previous material and stressing the need to teach it. At the same time, it provides the positive statement to which the activity of the opponents forms a contrast.' See also Mounce 2000: 335; Barrett 1963: 83.

116. Marshall 1999: 637, 'Despite the minority opinion that it refers forwards (Scott 1936: 72f.), ταῦτα must refer backwards ...' So also e.g., Johnson 2001: 291; Mounce 2000: 336; Oberlinner 1994: 267–68; Roloff 1988: 325.

117. So also Roloff 1988: 326; Marshall 1999: 638.

118. The fact that 6.2c is so well suited to this function as a hinge critically damages Falconer's position that 6.2c is an insertion (1937: 152).

119. There may also be a contrast between the thought of rendering benefit to another (εὐεργεσία) in 6.2 and the greed of 6.9–10.

120. Miller 1997: 91.

Conzelmann represent a common view when they suggest vv. 11–16 appear to be an intrusion between v. 10 and v. 17.[121] Some have even suggested vv. 11–16 may be a later editorial insertion.[122]

However, there are a number of linguistic connections between these two units. First, as in the last unit, the connection is primarily one of contrast.[123] A sharp contrast is denoted by Σὺ δέ in v. 11. Having discussed the improper motives of the false teachers, Paul urges Timothy not to be like them. Both vv. 8–10 and vv. 11f. give the sense of striving after something, but while some have yearned for riches (βούλομαι, v. 9; ὀρέγω, v. 10), Timothy is to flee this and pursue (διώκω) virtues. Whereas the greed of the opponents would lead to destruction (ὄλθερος, ἀπώλεια; v. 9), the virtues urged on Timothy would allow him to take hold of eternal life (v. 12).[124] Also, whereas vv. 3–10 open with a vice list, vv. 11–16 opens with a virtue list.[125] Secondly, there is a structural parallel between 6.2b and 6.11a. Both sentences begin with a second person singular imperative with ταῦτα and neither ταῦτα nor imperatives nor any second person referent occurs between. In both sentences, the imperative serves as a link with previous material (affirming in 6.2b, contrasting in 6.11a) and provides a foil for what follows. Thus v. 11 serves as a hinge with 11a ('flee these things') restating (in contrast) the previous material as a foil and 11b ('but pursue righteousness,' etc.) moving (by means of another contrast) to the new material. This is a thoroughly logical and common transitional device. Involved in this hinge are contrasting references to 'faith.' Πίστις occurs three times in these two units, once at the close of 6.3–10 (v. 10) and twice at the beginning of 6.11–16 (vv. 11, 12). Whereas the opponents wander away from the faith (v. 10), Timothy is to pursue 'faith' (v. 11) and fight the good fight of 'faith' (v. 11). Lastly, εὐσέβεια appears to function as a hooked keyword connecting the two units. The word occurs three times in vv. 3–10 and is an important point. It then recurs in v. 11, the beginning of the next unit. Timothy is to flee the vices of the opponents as described in vv. 3–10 but to pursue εὐσέβεια, which has been clarified in contrast to the opponents in vv. 3–10.

Thus, 6.11–16 is significantly connected to 6.3–10 in ways that suggest 6.11–16 have been intentionally shaped to follow 6.3–10.

---

121. Dibelius and Conzelmann 1972: 87. So also Läger 1996: 55; Easton 1947: 165; Houlden 1976: 100.

122. E.g., Brox 1969a: 212. Falconer 1937: 156 suggests at least part of v. 11 is an editorial addition.

123. Cf. Roloff 1988: 340, 'Der Abschnitt [6.11–16] hat die Funktion einer Antithese zu VV3–10...'

124. The desires of the opponents are even called 'harmful' (βλαβερός).

125. So also Roloff 1988: 341.

6.11–16 and 6.17–19

The connection between these two units has been hotly contested as well, since many scholars have assumed that vv. 17–19 should follow on from v. 10. Thus, Miller says this section abruptly returns to theme of 6.6–10 and 'breaks any thread of continuity between 6.16 and 6.20.'[126] For this reason, some have regarded vv. 17–19 as a later addition[127] or have attributed it to a pause in dictation.[128] It is true that the doxology in the preceding verses creates a sense of closure so that v. 17 seems like a fresh start, but there are several indicators of continuity between 6.11–16 and 17–19.

First, 6.17 continues the second person singular address which is common in the previous unit. Additionally, vv. 17–19 are presented as an exhortation to Timothy built on an imperative just as vv. 11–14. There are also a number of lexical connections between the two units. First, παραγγέλλω occurs in v. 13 and v. 17. It is the last main verb of vv. 11–16 and the first main verb of vv. 17–19. As Paul exhorted Timothy, so Timothy is to exhort those who are rich.[129] The shift from calling Timothy to personal faithfulness to calling him to exhort others to faithfulness has occurred often in this letter. Secondly, almost the exact phrase is used to call both Timothy and the rich to take hold of life (ἐπιλαβοῦ τῆς αἰωνίου ζωῆς, v. 12; ἐπιλάβωνται τῆς ὄντως ζωῆς, v. 19). This is similar to the use of παραγγέλλω, in that what Timothy receives personally as exhortation from Paul, he then passes on to others. Third, αἰών and αἰώνιος occur in vv. 12, 16, and 17. 6.11–16 is concerned with taking hold of 'eternal' life (v. 12) and with the one who has 'eternal' power (v. 16). 6.17–19 then opens by referring to those who are rich 'in this present age.' The use of the same root in contrasting ways suggests a contrast is being made between the two units. This serves to lessen the significance of the riches which these people have, because those riches are only for this present age, whereas there is life which is eternal and comes from the God who has eternal power. Lastly, the exhortation in v. 17 for the rich to hope in God with the implication that God is more reliable than riches works well following the exalted doxology of vv. 15–16.

These links between 6.11–16 and 6.17–19 suggest that, although there is a significant shift between these two units, there is sufficient continuity to

126. Miller 1997: 93. Similarly, Dibelius and Conzelmann 1972: 91; Lock 1924: 73; Easton 1947: 169–70. According to Quinn and Wacker 2000: 550, Käsemann (1972) in *Essais*, 112, called the abrupt transition 'brutal.'

127. Easton 1947: 170; Falconer 1937: 158; Gealy 1955: 456–57. Gealy also mentions A. von Harnack, *Der Chronologie der altchristlichen Litteratur bis Eusebius* (Leipzig: J. C. Hinrichs, 1897), I: 482, as a proponent of this view.

128. Spicq 1969: 575.

129. Cf. Oberlinner 1994: 303.

hold them together and there seems to be some deliberate play on words between the two units.

6.17–19 and 6.20–21
Some scholars have found very little connection between these two units. For example, Easton and Falconer suggest vv. 20–21 may be another later addition,[130] and Miller suggests vv. 20–21 are the original ending of a short letter into which the preceding material was incorporated.[131] However, there are some significant continuities between the two units. First, both units begin with a second person singular imperative and have no other imperative in the rest of the unit. Accordingly, there is a continuity in genre as both units are exhortation to Timothy concerning his role in the church.[132] The units also have contrasting endings with the rich laying for themselves a good foundation for the future and taking hold of true life and the opponents straying from the faith. As Timothy is to exhort the rich to shun evil and to prepare well for eternity, so Timothy is to shun evil knowing that it will not lead to life but lead to the destruction of faith.

Semantic Chains Running Throughout the Letter

Having shown a connection from unit to unit through the letter it will be helpful to consider the letter from the macro-perspective noting themes (with semantic and lexical connections) which occur through significant portions of the letter. Each theme or semantic chain does not necessarily occur in each unit of the letter, but they occur in a significant number of units. Therefore they bind the letter together not as one strand around the whole, but as various adhesive strips across various units overlapping one another.

Participants
More work has been done on 1 Timothy in this area than on 2 Timothy, due to the work of J. T. Reed who has written two important articles demonstrating a level of cohesion within 1 Timothy.[133] Reed has persuasively argued that 1 Timothy coheres at the level of participant structure. The use of epistolary conventions in the letter's opening and closing, as well as the use of personal referents, shows that throughout the

130. Easton 1947: 170; Falconer 1937: 160.
131. Miller 1997: 94–95.
132. The shift from opponents to Timothy is common in this letter and has just happened above in 6.11.
133. Reed 1992: 131–47; 1993b: 90–118. Cf. also Reed 1993a: 228–52.

letter Timothy is the one being addressed.[134] It can also be shown that the church is in view throughout the letter.[135] As noted by Reed, the discussions of the opponents (1.3–7, 18–20; 4.1–5; 6.3–10, 20–21) have the church in view since the opponents apparently come from within the church. This is seen by the fact that they are described as abandoning the faith (1.6, 19; 4.1; 6.10, 21) and can be handed over to Satan (1.20). Even in the statement of Paul's conversion in 1.12–17, Paul is designated an example for those who will believe, which certainly includes the current church. The church is in view in 2.1–15 as the discussion focuses on corporate prayer (2.1–7; note the first person plural verb in v. 2) and the behavior of men and women. These men and women are seen as under Paul's authority (Βούλομαι, 2.8; ἐπιτρέπω, 2.12). 3.1–13 focuse on church leadership (with the first occurrence of ἐκκλησία) and 3.14–16 state as the intent of the letter explaining how to behave in ἐκκλησία. The exhortation to Timothy in 4.6–16 is given with the church in view as was shown above. 5.1–6.2, 17–19, clearly refer to different groups within the church as evidenced by the familial language, the fact that Timothy is to exhort them, and the fact that they have the potential of bringing disrepute on the gospel (5.14; 6.1). The charge to Timothy in 6.11–16 reminds him of his confession before 'many witnesses,' presumably the church. Thus, throughout the letter, the church is in view.[136] This creates a certain amount of cohesion as all of 1 Timothy hangs together as communication from Paul to Timothy concerning the church and Timothy's relation to it. Reed has a good chart illustrating the interrelation between these participants, or 'identity chains' as he calls them.[137]

Virtue and Vice
Reed's chart also points out 'virtue' and 'vice' as 'central tokens' within this letter. Indeed vocabulary describing acceptable and unacceptable behavior dominates the letter. The following table demonstrates how pervasive such vocabulary is in 1 Timothy.

---

134. See esp. Reed 1993b: 101–107, 117–18.
135. Reed 1992: 141–43 divides this group into believers and apostates but notes that the distinction is one of degree since the opponents come from within the church.
136. The continuous concern with the church has of course been a common point made by those who see 1 Timothy as a church manual. The point is established here as an indicator of cohesion.
137. Reed 1992: 141.

Reference	Virtue	Vice
1.4	πίστις	ἐκζήτησις
1.5	ἀγάπη	
	καθαρὰ καρδία	
	συνείδησις ἀγαθή	
	πίστις ἀνυπόκριτος	
1.6		ματαιολογία
1.8	καλός	
1.9–10	δίκαιος	ἄνομος
		ἀνυπότακτος
		ἀσεβής
		ἁμαρτωλός
		ἀνόσιος
		βέβηλος
		πατρολῴας, μητρολῴας
		ἀνδροφόνος
		πόρνος
		ἀρσενοκοίτης
		ἀνδραποδιστής
		ψεύστης
		ἐπίορκος
1.12	πίστος	
1.13	ἐλεέω	βλάσφημος
		διώκτης
		ὑβριστής
		ἀπιστία
1.14	χάρις	
	πίστις	
	ἀγάπη	
1.15	πιστός	ἁμαρτωλός
	ἄξιος	
1.16	ἐλεέω	
	μακροθυμία	
1.17	τιμή	
	δόξα	
1.19	πίστις	
	ἀγαθὴ συνείδησις	
1.20		βλασφημέω
2.2	ἤρεμος	
	ἡσύχιος	
	εὐσέβεια	
	σεμνότης	
2.8	ὅσιος	ὀργή
		διαλογισμός

2.9–10	κόσμιος	
	αἰδώς	
	σωφροσύνη	
	θεοσέβεια	
	ἔργον ἀγαθόν	
2.11–12	ἡσυχία	
	ὑποταγή	
	ἡσυχία	
2.14		ἀπατάω
		παράβασις
2.15	πίστις	
	ἀγάπη	
	ἁγιασμός	
	σωφροσύνη	
3.1a	πιστός	
3.2–7	ἀνεπίληπτος	
	μιᾶς γυναικὸς ἀνήρ	
	νηφάλιος	
	σώφρων	
	κόσμιος	
	φιλόξενος	
	μὴ πάροινος	
	μὴ πλήκτης	
	ἐπιεικής	
	ἄμαχος	
	ἀφιλάργυρος	
	ὑποταγή	
	σεμνότης	
	(μὴ) τυφόω	
	μαρτυρία καλή	
3.8–13	σεμνός	
	μὴ δίλογος	
	μὴ οἴνῳ πολλῷ προσέχων	
	μὴ αἰσχροκερδής	
	ἀνέγκλητος	
	σεμνή	
	μὴ διάβολος	
	νηφάλιος	
	πιστός	
	μιᾶς γυναικὸς ἀνήρ	
3.15	ἀναστρέφω	
3.16	εὐσέβεια	

4.2		ὑπόκρισις ψευδολόγων
		κεκαυστηριασμένοι
		συνείδησιν
4.4	καλός	
4.5	ἁγιάζω	
4.6	καλός [2x]	
4.7	εὐσέβεια	βέβηλος
4.8	εὐσέβεια	
4.9	πιστός	
	ἄξιος	
4.12	λόγος[138]	
	ἀναστροφή	
	ἀγάπη	
	πίστις	
	ἁγνεία	
5.2	ἁγνεία	
5.4	εὐσεβέω	
	ἀπόδεκτος	
5.6		σπαταλῶσα
5.7	ἀνεπίλημπτος	
5.8		χείρων
5.9–10	ἑνὸς ἀνδρὸς γυνή	
	ἐν ἔργοις καλοῖς μαρτυρουμένη	
	ἁγίων πόδας ἔνιψεν	
	θλιβομένοις ἐπήρκεσεν	
	ἔργον ἀγαθόν	
5.11		καταστρηνίαω
5.13		ἀργή [2x]
		φλύαρος
		περίεργος
		saying what they ought not
5.14	Acceptable activities	
	Not giving occasion for λοιδορία	
5.20		ἁμαρτάνω
5.21		πρόκριμα
		πρόσκλησις
5.22	(μή) ἁμαρτία	
	ἁγνός	
5.24		ἁμαρτία
5.25	ἔργα καλά	

138. Λόγος here is commonly understood to refer to 'speech' in general and thus another area of Timothy's lifestyle. Cf. Marshall 1999: 561.

6.1–2	ἄξιος	βλασφημέω
		καταφρονέω
6.3	εὐσέβεια	
6.4–5	εὐσέβεια	τυφόω
		νοσέω
		ζήτησις
		λογομαχία
		φθόνος
		ἔρις
		βλασφημία
		ὑπόνοια πονηρά
		διαπαρατριβή
		διαφθείρω
6.6–8	εὐσέβεια	
	αὐτάρκεια	
	ἀρκέομαι	
6.9–10		πειρασμός
		ἐπιθυμία ἀνόητος καὶ
		βλαβεράς
6.11	δικαιοσύνη	
	εὐσέβεια	
	πίστις	
	ἀγάπη	
	ὑπομονή	
	πραϋπαθία	
6.14	ἀνεπίλημπτος	
6.17–18	ἀγαθοεργέω	ὑψηλοφρονέω
	ἔργον καλόν	
	εὐμετάδοτος	
	κοινωνίκος	
6.20		βέβηλος

While there could be some discussion about the inclusion or exclusion of a word here or there, the chart clearly shows that ethical behavior is a major concern throughout 1 Timothy. This further enhances cohesion as much of the communication from Paul to Timothy concerns the behavior of Timothy, church groups, and the opponents. However, some might say the occurrence of so many terms for virtue and vice is coincidental. Several factors argue against this.

First, the behavior in view has many similarities throughout. Many of the vices in view concern sinful speech,[139] which contrasts the silence called for from the women in 2.12 and the example in speech which Timothy is to give (4.12). There is also a pervasive concern for propriety. This chain would include words for dignity, self-control, and concern for reputation.[140] This concern for propriety is noted by those who have pointed out that many of the virtues prescribed are those which would be esteemed by the culture of the day.[141] There is also a chain of gentleness/peacefulness vs. violence running through the ethical vocabulary. These continuities within this large chain of ethical vocabulary, along with other lexical repetitions evident within the chart, serve to bind this chain together showing that not only is there a concern for behavior throughout, but the behavior in view is consistent throughout.

Within this chain on ethics there are also several terms referring to improper use of wealth. In 2.9 there is a concern about proper adornment without the trappings of gold, pearls, and rich garments. Both bishops (ἀφιλάργυρος, 3.3) and deacons (μὴ αἰσχροκερδής, 3.8) are explicitly required to be free of greed. Also, the widow who lives indulgently, i.e., who has means but squanders it selfishly, is excluded from the provision of the church (5.6).[142] The opponents are implicated as being greedy (φιλαργυρία, 6.9–10). There is also similarity in the result of greed in that the self-indulgent widow is dead while she lives and those who desire riches come to ruin and destruction (6.9–10).

Furthermore, there are distinct contrasts, both semantic and lexical, within the ethical vocabulary. Virtue is connected primarily with Timothy and the appropriate leadership, bishops and deacons. Vice is connected primarily with the opponents and pre-conversion Paul (1.12–17).[143] Beyond this general contrast (good/bad) there are striking similarities which suggest these groups have been intentionally contrasted. For example, while the characteristics of the bishop are in general contrast with that of the opponents, there are strong connections with the description of the opponents in 6.3–10, as shown in the following table.

139.   E.g., ἐκζητήσις, 1.4; ματαιολογία, 1.6; ψεύστης, ἐπίορκος, 1.10; βλάσφημος, ἱβριστής, 1.13; βλασφημέω, 1.20 and 6.1; διαλογισμός, 2.8; ὑπόκρισις ψευδολόγων, 4.2; φλύαρος, 5.13; ζήτησις, λογομαχία, ἔρις, βλασφημία, διαπαρατριβή, 6.4–5; κενοφωνία, 6.20.

140.   It may be significant to note that of the five words listed by Louw and Nida (1989) in the subdomain 'Modesty, Propriety,' four occur in 1 Timothy. In fact, over half (7/13) of the New Testament occurrences of words from this domain are found in 1 Timothy.

141.   Cf. e.g., Dibelius and Conzelmann 1972: 39–41, 50, and throughout; Marshall 1999: 472.

142.   Cf. Marshall 1999: 588, who suggests this widow is probably among the rich women addressed in 2.9b.

143.   The various groups within the church are urged to virtue and warned of vice (2.1–15; 5.3–6.2; 6.17–19).

Bishop (3.1–7)
Able to teach (v. 2)
Good desire (ἐπιθυμέω) (v. 1)

αφιλάργυρος (v. 3)
τυφόω (v. 6)
παγίς (v. 7)
ἐμπίμπτω (vv. 6 and 7)
ὀρέγω (v. 1)
not a neophyte (v. 6)
restrained, not violent, gentle, peaceable

Opponents (6.3–10)
Teaches wrongly (v. 3)
Many foolish desires (ἐπιθυμία) (v. 9)*

φιλαργυρία (v. 10)*
τυφόω (v. 4)*
παγίς (v. 9)*
ἐμπίμπτω (v. 9)*
ὀρέγω (v. 10)*
knows nothing (v. 4)
disputes, strife, constant arguing

The items marked with an asterisk represent the only occurrences of the word or root in 1 Timothy. The high number of such instances (six!) strongly suggests that the connection between these lists is more than accidental.[144]

One further example of the connections between the ethical lists may be helpful. There is a strong connection between the description of the pre-conversion Paul and the opponents.

Paul (1.12–16)
βλάσφημος (v. 13)
persecutor and violent aggressor (v. 13)
ἀπιστία (v. 13)

ἁμαρτωλός (v. 15)

Opponents
βλασφημέω (1.20), βλασφημία (6.4)
murderers (1.10)

rejected faith (1.6, 19; 4.1; 6.10, 21)
shipwreck of faith (1.19)
ἁμαρτωλός (1.9)*

This connection between Paul and the sort of people for whom the Law is intended, including the opponents, again suggests the chain of ethical terms is intentionally crafted and interlinked. This comparison may serve to further discredit the opponents suggesting their behavior is the sort that is found among those who have not come to faith.

Then, in the units concerning groups within the church, there is a concern to prevent sin. There is a concern about men sinning as they gather for prayer (2.8) and apparently sinful behavior of women elicits a

---

144. Other scholars have noted verbal connections between these and other lists; cf. Marshall 1999: 473f.; Mounce 2000: 153f. Mounce 2000: 153 notes the general contrast: 'Almost every quality Paul specifies here has its negative counterpart in the Ephesian opponents.'

discussion of Eve's sin (2.14). Steps are to be taken to prevent sin on the part of the overseer (3.6–7). Then in 5.3–6.2 there is a concern about certain ones in each of the three groups sinning: families and young widows, sinning elders, and potentially rebellious slaves. Also, Paul's past sin is dealt with (1.12–16). This pervasive concern, not only for vice in general but for sin amongst specific groups within the church, serves to bind the letter together.

Lastly, bound up with this chain of virtue and vice is a chain of words relating to desire. It occurs most often in reference to evil desires of the opponents. They have an 'unhealthy desire for' (νοσέω) controversy (6.4), desire (βούλομαι) to get rich, are marked by many harmful and foolish desires (ἐπιθυμία), including the 'love of money' (φιλαργυρία), and they desire (ὀρέγω) money (6.9–10). They also wrongly desire (θέλω) to be teachers (1.7). Young widows are also prone to evil desires such as 'lusting against' Christ (καταστρηνιάω) and as a result desiring (θέλω) to marry (5.11).[145] In contrast, especially to 1.7, there is an appropriate desire to teach and lead since one who 'desires' (ὀρέγω) to be an overseer 'desires' (ἐπιθυμέω) a good work. The ultimate contrast to the selfish desires in the letter is the desire of God (θέλω) that all be saved (2.4).[146]

Thus, the pervasive chain of virtue and vice binds the letter together by its presence throughout the letter and by the many connections and deliberate contrasts within the chain.

Teaching/Word/Message

The second major semantic chain running alongside 'virtue and vice' is one relating to teaching or doctrine. The letter opens with a reminder that Timothy's role is to 'command' (παραγγέλλω) and the 'command' (παραγγελία), or basic message, is summarized. A chain of related words then runs through the letter, signifying the message which Timothy is to proclaim in contradistinction to the opponents. The occurrences are shown in the following table.

Reference	Semantic	Lexical
1.5	Command	παραγγελία
1.8	Law	νόμος
1.10	Sound Teaching	ὑγιαινούσῃ διδασκαλία
1.11	Gospel	εὐαγγέλιον
1.15	Gospel summary	λόγος
1.18	Command	παραγγελία

145. While there is debate on what is intended by this statement, it is clear that sinful desire is in view.

146. Βούλομαι also occurs in 2.8 and 5.14, but in those instances the connotation is command more than desire so they have not been included in this discussion.

2.4–6	Summary of message	ἀλήθεια
2.7	Faith and truth – content of Paul's preaching (?)[147]	πίστις, ἀλήθεια
3.9	Mystery of the faith	μυστήριον, πίστις
3.15	Truth	ἀλήθεια
3.16	Mystery of godliness	μυστήριον
4.5	Word of God	λόγος θεοῦ
4.6		οἱ λόγοι τῆς πίστεως, καλὴ διδασκαλία
4.13		ἀνάγνωσις, παράκλησις, διδασκαλία
4.16		διδασκαλία
5.17		λόγος καὶ διδασκαλία
5.18	Scripture	
6.1		διδασκαλία
6.3	Sound words	ὑγιαινούντες λόγοι
	Teaching which accords with godliness	ἡ κατ' εὐσέβειαν διδασκαλία
6.5	Truth	ἀλήθεια
6.20	Deposit	παραθήκη

This table shows that proper teaching is mentioned throughout the letter, though it is not enumerated in the same detail as the chain on proper behavior. In addition to the semantic link running throughout there are significant lexical repetitions as διδασκαλία occurs seven times and λόγος occurs five times. Both of these terms are described as 'sound,' and they are used in conjunction with each other twice (4.6; 5.17). The message is also connected with faith as it is 'the mystery of the faith' (3.9), 'the words of the faith' (4.6), and Paul teaches 'faith and truth' (2.7). A continuous theme of doctrinal fidelity might be dismissed as accidental in view of the sort of materials compiled (theoretically), but the continuity of terms used and the manner in which they are used argues strongly for intentional cohesion.

This chain on 'teaching' is also intertwined with the chain of 'virtue and vice.' The goal of the command in 1.5 is love. In 1.8, 10, the law and sound teaching are in contrast to vice. In 1.15 the gospel summary concerns salvation for 'sinners.' The mystery of the faith in 3.9 is connected with a clear conscience and is part of a virtue list. The statement about the church as the pillar of 'truth' (3.15) occurs as part of a discussion of how one should 'behave' in the church. In 3.16 the gospel summary is termed the

---

147. So Mounce 2000: 93; Knight 1992: 127; Fee 1988: 67; Bernard 1906: 43; Guthrie 1990: 83. Marshall 1999: 435 does not take it this way. He interprets it as 'truthfully and faithfully.' Quinn and Wacker 2000: 190; Hanson 1982: 70, also disagree.

mystery of εὐσέβεια, a term with strong ethical connotations.[148] In 4.5 the 'word of God' sanctifies. In 4.16 what Timothy is to 'watch over' is not only his teaching but also 'himself,' which is commonly understood to refer to his conduct.[149] In 6.1 the 'teaching' can be blasphemed by bad behavior, and in 6.3 'teaching' is further qualified as that which is in accordance with 'godliness.' Lastly, in 6.5, the rejection of 'truth' is connected with vice. Thus, there is a significant interconnection between these two predominant chains which creates cohesion.

There is also a counter-chain of terms related to a message contrary to the Pauline one which Timothy is to uphold.

Reference	Semantic	Lexical
1.3	Teach otherwise	ἑτεροδιδασκαλέω
1.4	Myths & genealogies	μῦθος
		γενεαλογία
1.7	Wanting to be law-teachers	νομοδιδάσκαλος
	Don't know what they are	λέγω
	saying and asserting	διαβεβαιόομαι
1.20	Blaspheme	βλασφημέω
4.1	Doctrines of demons	διδασκαλίαι δαιμονίων
4.3	Summary of message	
4.7	Myths	μῦθος
6.3	Teach otherwise	ἑτεροδιδασκαλέω
6.20	Foolish talk	κενοφωνία
	Contradictions of falsely	ἀντιθέσεις τῆς
	called 'knowledge'	ψευδωνύμου γνώσεως

One could argue that other words referring to divisive or disruptive speech refer to the teaching of the opponents and, therefore, should be included here.[150] However, the occurrences represented portray the major portion of this chain. These occurrences are clustered and do not cover as much of the letter as the references to the proper message, as might be expected. This chain is in actuality a part of the larger chain on teaching, clearly serving as

148. Cf. Marshall 1999: 135–44 for a recent thorough discussion. Marshall writes, 'as employed in the PE, εὐσέβεια expresses a strongly Christian concept of the new existence in Christ that combines belief in God and a consequent manner of life' (144).

149. E.g., Mounce 2000: 264; Marshall 1999: 571; Johnson 2001: 254; Knight 1992: 210.

150. 5.13 might also be included with the young widows 'saying things which they ought not.' However, it is not clear whether this refers to teaching or something more along the lines of gossip. Marshall 1999: 603 says λαλέω does not refer to teaching but the 'things which ought not be said' does refer to heresy so that the young widows are furthering the false teaching in a less formal manner. So similarly, Mounce 2000: 294–95.

the contrast to the chain on the proper message. Whereas the proper message is the 'sound teaching' (1.10) and 'good teaching' (4.6), the message of the opponents is the 'teaching of demons' (4.1) and 'false (or "other") teaching' (1.3; 6.3). Whereas the Pauline message is described as sound and trustworthy, the message of the opponents consists of myths and foolish talk. Whereas the proper message is referred to as 'truth,' the message of the opponents is associated with lying spirits (πλάνος, 4.1), and the hypocrisy of liars (ψευδολόγος, 4.2), and is falsely called (ψευδώνυμος, 6.20) knowledge.[151]

While the proper message connected to virtues, the opponents' message connects with vices. The myths and genealogies of 1.4 lead to 'disputes.' The myths in 4.7 are described as 'vile' (βέβηλος), and in 4.1 and 6.3 the false teaching is associated with vice.

Thus, there is running through 1 Timothy a semantic chain concerning teaching which falls into two parts – proper and improper teaching. The two parts are contrasted both semantically and lexically. Both parts of the chain are also intertwined with the chain for virtue and vice. Indeed, as there is a chain on ethics with two sides, virtue and vice, so there is a chain on teaching with two sides, truth and heresy. These prominent chains and their significant interaction creates cohesion within the letter.

Salvation
Related to the chain on proper teaching is a chain concerning salvation. The chain begins in the letter opening with the reference to God as 'our Savior' and continues through the letter built largely on occurrences of σώζω and its cognates and ζωή.[152]

Reference	Semantic	Lexical
1.1	God our Savior	σωτήρ
1.12–16	Shown mercy	ἐλεέω
	Grace of our Lord abounded,	χάρις, πίστις, ἀγάπη
	with faith and love in Χριστὸς Ἰησοῦς	κύριος, Χριστὸς Ἰησοῦς
	Χριστὸς Ἰησοῦς came to save sinners	σώζω, Χριστὸς Ἰησοῦς
	Shown mercy	ἐλεέω
	Believe in him unto eternal life	πιστεύω, ζωή
2.3–6	God our Savior	σωτήρ
	Desires *all* to be saved	σώζω

---

151. The vice list of 1.9–10, which may refer to the opponents, also mentions 'liars' (ψεύστης).

152. One might could include 6.13 with the reference to God as the one who gives life (ζῳογονέω) to all things. However, it is less than certain that salvation is the intended point here. Cf. Marshall 1999: 662, 'The thought of God as the giver of the eternal life in v. 12b may well be included, but does not seem to be stressed.'

	Knowledge of truth	ἐπίγνωσις ἀληθείας
	Χριστὸς Ἰησοῦς only mediator	Χριστὸς Ἰησοῦς
	Χριστὸς Ἰησοῦς, ransom for *all*	Χριστὸς Ἰησοῦς, ἀντιλύτρον
2.15	Women saved	σῴζω
3.16	Gospel summary	πιστεύω
4.8	Promise of life to come	ζωή
4.10	Living God, savior of *all*, those who believe	ζάω, σωτήρ, πιστεύω
4.16	Timothy save self and hearers	σῴζω
6.12	Take hold of eternal life	ζωή
6.19	Take hold of real life	ζωή

This chain occurs across the whole letter though it skips significant portions. Within the chain, continuity is seen in the concern for eternal life or life which is to come and the fact that salvation is often linked explicitly to faith. In the three gospel statements (1.12–16; 2.3–6; 3.16), Christ Jesus is more explicitly prominent than God is.[153] The universal offer of salvation figures prominently in 2.3–6, 3.16, and 4.10. 2.3–6 and 4.10 makes this point with the recurrence of πᾶς, and 3.16 makes this point with reference to being preached among the 'nations' and believed on in the 'world.'

Additionally, all three of the major soteriological statements refer to the incarnation. 1.15 refers plainly to Christ Jesus coming 'into the world.' 2.5 says salvation is dependent on the one mediator who is the 'man Christ Jesus.' The wording seems to stress the humanity, and thus incarnation, of Christ.[154] Then, the mention in 3.16 of 'being revealed in the flesh' is usually understood to refer to the incarnation.[155]

It is also interesting to note that many of the occurrences in this chain emphasize the point of human responsibility in salvation. In 2.15 salvation is contingent upon the women abiding in virtue. In 4.8 the promise of life to come is mentioned as an accompaniment of εὐσέβεια, for which Timothy is to exert himself (γυμνάζω). 4.16 stresses Timothy's responsibility for his own salvation and that of the congregation as well. In 6.12 and 6.19 there are exhortations for people to 'take hold of' eternal life, again stressing the human responsibility. A similar idea is probably in view in both 1.19 and 3.9 where Timothy and deacons are expected to 'hold on to' the faith. Even

153. Though the subject is not made explicit in 3.16 it is commonly understood as referring to Jesus with its reference to incarnation and ascension.

154. Cf. Marshall 1999: 430; Lau 1996: 81.

155. Cf. Towner 1989: 89, 'most have rightly concluded that Christ's incarnation (in one aspect or another) is the far more likely object of line 1.' So also Marshall 1999: 523–25; Lau 1996: 92; Barrett 1963: 66; Brox 1969a: 160; Hanson 1982: 85; Kelly 1963: 90. Lau provides a lengthy list of proponents.

the key statement in 2.4–6 stresses the desire of God rather than his decisive action. Thus there is a significant continuity in this theological emphasis in the salvation statements.[156]

The stress on human responsibility is often used in such a way as to connect this semantic chain with the chain of virtue and vice. The point of the passages urging perseverance unto salvation (2.15; 4.16; 6.12, 19) is to call the people in view to proper living (virtue). Thus 2.15 contains a virtue list and 6.19 occurs in the midst of a virtue list. 6.19 is the climax of a call to good works. Also, in 2.3–6 and 4.10 this salvific intent of God grounds the ethical exhortations given. Thus virtue and salvation are interlinked.

Further, as might be expected the chain on salvation is linked with the chain on the proper message. First, the summaries of the proper message in 1.12–16, 2.3–6, and 3.16 also show up in the salvation chain as they refer to salvation or belief which leads to salvation. Second, in 4.16 it is diligence in doctrine as well as lifestyle which will ensure salvation. Thus as the proper message promotes virtue, so it also leads to salvation.

These connections can be drawn out further by noting the presence of another contrasting chain, the semantic chain referring to apostasy or loss of salvation.

Reference	Semantic	Lexical	Louw and Nida
1.6	Rejection	ἀστοχέω	31.68
		ἐκτρέπω	31.65
1.19	Rejection, shipwreck of faith	ἀποθέω	31.63
4.1–2	Rejection of faith	ἀφίστημι	34.26
5.6	Dead while alive	θνῄσκω	
5.8	Rejection of faith	ἀρνέομαι	31.25
5.12	Rejection of faith[157]	ἀθετέω	31.100
5.15	Turned aside after Satan	ἐκτρέπω	31.65
6.5	Deprived of the truth	ἀλήθεια	
6.10	Rejection of faith	ἀποπλανάω	31.67
6.21	Rejection of faith	ἀστοχέω	31.68

This table shows that apostasy is mentioned across the letter, primarily in the explicit discussion of the opponents but also in the discussion of the

---

156. The point of God's sovereignty and graciousness is not absent, however. 1.12–16 present more of the side of God's action. Cf. Lau 1996: 65–66.

157. There is debate as to whether πίστις in this passage refers to 'faith' as elsewhere (and thus apostasy) or to something else. Among recent commentators, Marshall 1999: 600, and Mounce 2000: 291–92, interpret the verse as referring to apostasy, while Johnson 2001: 266, and Quinn and Wacker 2000: 442 do not. The similarity of the statement with the others on apostasy throughout the letter suggest it should be understood as referring to apostasy. At least it appears the statement has been shaped to resemble the other statements on apostasy.

widows. The similarity of the wording is striking. The Louw and Nida (1989) domain assignments have been given to illustrate this further. Six of the occurrences have verbs which refer to turning away from a belief and in each instance πίστις is at least part of the object of the verb. Twice there is reference to turning aside to other things (including Satan). Thus, the role of 'faith' is one of the key contrasts between the salvation chain (believe) and the apostasy chain (reject faith). This is what one might expect from a coherent document. Further, the salvation chain included a reference to 'knowledge of the truth' (2.4) but the apostasy chain refers to being 'devoid of the truth' (6.5). Whereas 'life' was a key element of the salvation chain, 'death' is a part of the apostasy chain (5.6).[158] Also, the discussion of people who turn away from the faith connects logically to the emphasis on human responsibility found in the salvation chain and is a direct lexical contrast to the call to 'hold on to' the faith in 1.19 and 3.9.

The rejection language shows how the apostasy chain is connected to the chain concerning the proper message. Apostasy is the result of rejecting the goal of the command (1.5–6, 19) and being deprived of truth (6.5). Those who stray from the faith in 6.21 are those who profess the false teaching.

The apostasy chain also connects to the chain for virtue and vice in that the goal of the command which is rejected in 1.6, 19, is stated in terms of virtues. The widow who is dead while still living in 5.6 is the one who lives immorally. Those who deny the faith in 5.8 are those who fail to behave properly toward their families. Lastly, those who deny the faith in 6.9–10 are those who have pursued the love of money.

Thus, there are contrasting chains throughout the letter referring to salvation and apostasy. These chains are actually components of each other and exhibit a high level of continuity within themselves. They are also intricately linked with the previously mentioned chains concerning proper teaching and virtue and vice.

Opponents

The opponents have already been mentioned under most of the chains previously discussed, so it might be argued that it is not legitimate to discuss them under another heading. However, since the opponents are discussed in five major units it will be worthwhile to consider similarities between the descriptions, especially since Miller argues that significantly different groups are in view in 1.3–7 and 4.1–5.[159] Table 1 lists similarities between the units.

158. One might could include here the many references to destruction in the discussion of the opponents. Cf. especially 1.19 and 6.9–10.
159. Miller 1997: 79.

Table 1: Connections Between Sections on the Opponents in 1 Timothy

1.3–7	1.18–20	4.1–5	6.3–10	6.20–21
ὧν τινες ἀστοχήσαντες / ὧν refers to πίστις (among other things)	ἥν τινες ἀπωσάμενοι / ἥν refers to πίστις (among other things)	ἀποστήσονται τινες / direct object- πίστις	ἧς τινες ... ἀπεπλανήθησαν ἀπὸ τῆς πίστεως	ἥν τινες ... ἠστόχησαν περὶ τὴν πίστιν
ἐξετράπησαν	----	----	ὀρεγόμενοι wealth	ἐκτρεπόμενος
προσέχειν myths & genealogies	----	προσέχοντες lying spirits and doctrines		ἐπαγγελλόμενοι falsely called knowledge
ματαιολογίαν	----	----	λογομαχίας (λογ- root)	κενοφωνίας (idea of emptiness)
ἐκζητήσεις			ζητήσεις	
συνειδήσεως ἀγαθῆς	ἀγαθὴν συνείδησιν	seared συνείδησιν	depraved νοῦν	----
Produces negative: περέχουσιν speculation	----	----	Produces negative: ἐξ ὧν γίνεται envy, strife, etc. ruin and destruction pierced with pains	----
	shipwreck, handed over to Satan [need to be taught]	----	μηδὲν ἐπιστάμενος	Falsely called knowledge
μὴ νοοῦντες	----	----	ἀνοήτους	----
θέλοντες	taught not βλασφημεῖν	----	βουλόμενοι, ἐπιθυμίας result in βλασφημίαι	----
τις ἑτεροδιδασκαλεῖν / Followed by refutation	Followed by refutation	Followed by refutation	τις ἑτεροδιδασκαλεῖ / Followed by refutation	----

These are striking similarities between the units specifically addressing the opponents, including repetition of words, syntactic patterns, and themes. The strongest connection between these units is the statement in each unit on 'certain ones' turning from the faith. 1.3–7, 18–20, 6.3–10, 20–21, in their statement of the opponents turning from the faith all have the following elements in order: relative pronoun, indefinite pronoun, participle, finite verb. Each one also has a prepositional phrase occurring either immediately before (1.19; 6.21) or immediately after (1.6; 6.10) the finite verb. In three of the units the object of the preposition is πίστις. In 1.6 and 1.19 the verb of 'rejection' is the participle, that which is rejected is relative pronoun which refers back to similar statements in both units (ἀγάπη ἐκ καθαρᾶς καρδίας καὶ συνειδήσεως ἀγαθῆς καὶ πίστεως ἀνυποκρίτου, 1.5; πίστις καὶ ἀγαθή συνείδησις, 1.19). The finite verb with the prepositional phrase then states the results of this departure: they turn aside to empty talk and they make shipwreck concerning the faith. In 6.10 and 6.21, however, the verb of rejection is the finite verb and that which is rejected (faith) is stated in the prepositional phrase. In this construction the abandonment of the faith is even more explicit. The participle then states what these people have adhered to instead of the faith, the relative pronoun, which refers back to greed and doctrinal error. 4.1 is then most like 6.10 and 21 in that there is a finite verb of rejection with πίστις as its object and a participial phrase referring to what has been adhered to in preference to the faith.

This abandonment of the faith is perceived as primarily a doctrinal problem. In 1.3 and 6.3 the opponents are introduced as 'certain ones' who 'teach wrongly' (τις ἑτεροδιδασκαλεῖ). This doctrinal problem is seen as well in the basis of the opponents' teaching. They 'hold to' (προσέχω) myths and genealogies (1.4), 'hold to' (προσέχω) lying spirits and **doctrines** of demons (4.1), fail to agree with (προσέρχομαι) sound words of our Lord Jesus Christ and the **doctrine** which is in accordance with godliness (6.3), and they 'profess' (ἐπαγγέλομαι) to have 'knowledge' but it is a false knowledge associated with worldly, empty chatter. 1.4 and 4.1 share the same verb and 4.1 and 6.3 form a clear contrast. The spiritual source of the opponents' teaching is lying spirits and demons as opposed to our Lord Jesus Christ. The doctrine of the opponents is associated with demons rather than with godliness.

There are connections as well in the results of the opponents' teachings. In 1.4 they produce (παρέχω) disputes rather than the work of God. This is contrasted with the goal of love out of a clean heart, good conscience, and sincere faith. In rejecting these things, they turn aside to empty talk (ματαιλογία). In 1.19 as well they reject faith and good conscience and apparently engage in blasphemy (βλασφημέω). In 4.2 the opponents are characterized by the hypocrisy of liars and a seared conscience. In 6.4 the opponents have a morbid interest in disputes and word battles which lead to strife, envy, blasphemy (βλασφημία), and evil suspicions. In 6.20, also, the opponents are associated with worldly empty chatter. Thus there is a common thread of spurning of conscience and engagement in useless disputes which are engendered by their teachings.

There is also a similar reference to the opponents' lack of knowledge. They desire to be teachers of the Law, but they 'do not know' (μὴ νοέω) what they are talking about (1.7). They 'know nothing' (μηδὲν ἐπίσταμαι, 6.4), and though they profess to have knowledge it is not really knowledge (6.20). This could be connected to references to the opponents having depraved minds (6.5) and needing 'to be taught' not to blaspheme (1.20). This stands in contrast to Paul and those with him who do 'know' (οἶδα, 1.8–9).

Instruction to Timothy, Personally
There are also five corresponding sections with instructions addressed specifically to Timothy: 1.3–7, 1.18–20, 4.6–16, 6.11–16, 6.20–21. The similarities between these sections are demonstrated in the table below (see Table 2).

This table demonstrates a continuity between sections directed expressly to Timothy similar to what was demonstrated between sections on the opponents. The contexts in which these sections occur are similar in that each one is in the context of the discussion of the opponents. In 1.3–7, 18–20, and 6.20–21, the exhortations to Timothy are intermixed with the discussions of the opponents. 4.6–16 and 6.11–16 follow units discussing the opponents, though they both also briefly exhort Timothy to avoid the errors of the opponents: 4.7, 'But avoid worldly foolish myths'; 6.11, 'But you ... flee these things.'

As noted in the table there is also continuity in regard to Timothy's message and task. In 1.3 he is left in Ephesus to 'command' (παραγγέλλω) certain ones not to teach in opposition to the truth. The idea is that he is to keep the people faithful to the proper teaching, referred to in 1.5 as the 'command' (παραγγελία). In 1.18 his message is again called a 'command,' and it is something entrusted to him by Paul (παραγγελία). 4.6 seems to refer to Timothy's message when it encourages him to be nourished in 'the words of the faith and the good teaching.' The wording envisions continuation in the true message and is thus an implicit call to faithfulness. Timothy's message is also in view in a more general way in 4.13 when he is urged to give himself to public reading, exhortation, and teaching and in 4.16 when he is urged to watch carefully over his teaching. Here again the call to watchfulness involves a concern for faithfulness. In 6.13–14 the language of command returns as Paul commands (παραγγέλλω) Timothy to keep the command (ἐντολή) spotless. Here again Timothy's message is referred to as a command and faithfulness (this time as preservation) is the

Table 2: Connections between sections of personal instruction to Timothy

	1.3–7	1.18–20	4.6–16	6.11–16	6.20–21
	Intermixed with discussion of opponents	Intermixed with discussion of opponents	Follows discussion of opponents (which had no 2nd person referents)	Follows discussion of opponents (which had no 2nd person referents)	Intermixed with discussion of opponents
Vocative		Vocative τέκνον Τιμόθεε		Vocative ὦ ἄνθρωπε θεοῦ	Vocative Ὦ Τιμόθεε
Faithfulness		Faithfulness to a received message παραγγελίαν παρατίθεμαί	Faithfulness to a received message ἐντρεφόμενος τοῖς λόγοις τῆς πίστεως καὶ καλῆς διδασκαλίας continued nurture in message ἔπεχε ... τῇ διδασκαλίᾳ guard the message	Faithfulness to a received message τηρῆσαι ... ἐντολήν	Faithfulness to a received message παραθήκην φύλαξον
Message		message entrusted		obey the message	guard the message
Avoidance of error	Avoidance of error: Command them not to hold to μύθος, γενεαλογίας παραγγέλλω (v. 3) παραγγελία (v. 5)		Avoidance of error: Refuse (παραιτέομαι) βεβήλος, μύθος παραγγέλλω (v. 11)	Avoidance of error: Flee (φεύγω) these things (greed) παραγγέλλω (v. 13)	Avoidance of error: Avoid (ἐκτρέπω) βεβήλος κενοφωνία, etc.
		παραγγελία (v. 18)	ἀγωνίζομαι (only other occurrence with 6.12)		
Fight the good fight		Fight the good fight: στρατεύῃ ... τὴν καλὴν στρατεία		Fight the good fight ἀγωνίζου τὸν καλὸν ἀγῶνα τῆς πίστεως	
Call to exertion			Call to exertion connected to obtaining eternal life: γύμναζε ... ζωῆς now and to come	Call to exertion connected to obtaining eternal life: ἀγωνίζου ... ἐπιλαβοῦ τῆς αἰωνίου ζωῆς	
Reminder of Timothy's spiritual beginnings		Reminder of Timothy's spiritual beginnings: κατὰ τὰς προαγούσας ἐπὶ σὲ προφητείας	Reminder of Timothy's spiritual beginnings: χαρίσματος, ὃ ἐδόθη σοι διὰ προφητείας μετὰ ἐπιθέσεως τῶν χειρῶν τοῦ πρεσβυτερίου Exercise for εὐσέβεια	Reminder of Timothy's spiritual beginnings: ὁμολογήσας τὴν καλὴν ὁμολογίαν ἐνώπιον πολλῶν μαρτύρων Pursue εὐσέβεια	

concern. In 6.20 Timothy's message is a deposit to be guarded. This echoes the entrusting of the message in 1.18 as well as the preservation of 6.13–14, thus connecting to the general theme of faithfulness to a received message. There is thus a continuity through these units in concept and vocabulary as Timothy's task and message are repeatedly referred to as a 'command' and as something entrusted to which he and the congregation are to be faithful.

There are other links in the exhortations to Timothy. As noted by others, the calls to 'fight the good fight' in 1.18 and 6.12, though using different vocabulary, are strikingly similar. These exhortations connect to a broader theme of a call to exertion for the faith. In 4.7–8 Timothy is urged to 'train' himself for godliness because it leads to life. Similarly, in 6.12, following the exhortation to fight the good fight, Timothy is urged to 'take hold of life.' Thus, in both of these places there is call for exertion connected to obtaining life. Connected to this, in theme and lexical repetition, is Paul's statement in 4.10 that 'we labor and strive' (κοπιῶμεν καὶ ἀγωνιζόμεθα) because we have hoped in the living God who is the savior. Here again is the language of exertion connected with life and salvation. Also, as Timothy is called to train himself for εὐσέβεια in 4.7, he is called to pursue εὐσέβεια in 6.11. Lastly, in 1.18, 4.14, and 6.12 reference is made to Timothy's spiritual beginnings, each time as a source of help or strength or the basis of an exhortation. 1.18 refers to the prophecies made about Timothy and it is by means of these that he is to fight the good fight. In 4.14 mention is made again of prophecies (the only other occurrence in 1 Timothy), this time in conjunction with the laying on of hands by the elders. This is mentioned to buttress the exhortation to Timothy not to neglect his gift in the context of teaching the congregation faithfully.[160] Lastly, in 6.12 there is a reference to Timothy being called to eternal life and making the good confession before many witnesses. This is connected to the call to take hold of life and to fight the good fight (as in 1.18) most likely giving support to these exhortations. In other words, Timothy is to take hold of that life to which he has already been called and of which he has already made public confession.

As might be expected there is also a common thread of Paul urging Timothy to avoid the errors of the opponents. 4.7, 6.11, and 6.20 all have verbs of avoidance with similar connotations as was noted above. The recurrence of μῦθος (1.4; 4.7) and βέβηλος (4.7; 6.20) further binds these units.

---

160. Marshall 1999: 565, 'The solemn responsibility to do so [cultivate his gift] is underlined by a reminder of the circumstances in which Timothy received his charisma.'

Authority
Authority is also a key theme in 1 Timothy and one which overlaps some of the previous chains while incorporating some new material. Paul's authority is established and he is shown speaking authoritatively. The opponents are shown to have no authority since they know nothing and behave wickedly. Timothy, however, is entrusted with and called to authority. Also, within the congregation authority is denied to some and entrusted to others.

First, then, Paul is presented from the very beginning as the one with authority. The letter opens with the description of him as an apostle according to the command of God (κατ' ἐπιταγὴν θεοῦ, 1.1). He then is the one directing and exhorting Timothy (1.3). 1.11 refers to Paul being entrusted with the gospel and 1.12–17 elaborates this in what is in effect an exposition of the reference to Paul's apostleship in 1.1. Paul's authority is grounded in the act of Jesus Christ himself. Christ Jesus has placed him in service and intends him to be an example to other believers. The doxology in 1.17 serves to heighten further the authoritative tone of this authentication of Paul's place. Paul then possesses authority to entrust a command to Timothy and to hand over two of the opponents to Satan for discipline.

In the rest of the letter, Paul gives authoritative directives for the congregation and Timothy: 2.1, Παρακαλέω; 2.8, Βούλομαι; 2.12, ἐπιτρέπω; 5.14, Βούλομαι; 5.21, Διαμαρτύρομαι; 6.13, παραγγέλλω. It is Paul who lays down the qualifications for overseer and deacon (δεῖ, 3.2, 7) as well as instructions to Timothy.[161]

Second, Timothy is legitimated as the recipient of authority from Paul. Following the attribution of Paul's apostleship to God's command in 1.1, Timothy is identified as Paul's genuine, authentic (γνήσιος, 1.2) son and thus heir of Paul's authority.[162] Then the letter body opens with a recounting of Paul's direction for Timothy to 'command' (παραγγέλλω) others. Timothy is called by Paul to act authoritatively. Also, following the thorough grounding of Paul's authority in 1.12–17, Timothy is entrusted with a command (hence authority) from Paul in 1.18. This authority is further based on previous prophecies which were made concerning Timothy. Thus, Timothy too has a divine basis for authority.

4.6–16 furthers the discussion of Timothy's authority. Timothy is again to 'command' (παραγγέλλω) and 'teach' (διδάσκω) the congregation. He is not to allow himself to be despised (4.12). Timothy's public ministry is backed up by the fact of his gifting which is associated again with prophecies and also this time with the laying on of hands by the elders

161. Cf. Lohfink 1981: 106.
162. Cf. Mounce 2000: 7–8; Marshall 1999: 357; Oberlinner 1994: 5; Fee 1988: 36; Brox 1969a: 99.

(4.14). Still he is to exercise this authority in a proper way (5.1–2). He is to command (παραγγέλλω) people concerning widows (5.7) and even to rebuke (ἐλέγχω) elders when necessary (5.20). In 6.2 he is again charged to teach and exhort (διδάσκω, παρακαλέω) the congregation. Timothy is obviously in a position of authority in relation to the congregation. Then, the reference to Timothy as 'man of God' in 6.11 serves to highlight his authority and the letter closes with the picture of Timothy as the guardian of the Pauline deposit. Thus, Timothy is authenticated as an appropriate authority and this authority is often seen in teaching.

Third, authority within the congregation beyond Paul and Timothy is regulated. Women are not to teach or exercise authority over men (2.12). However, the overseer is to be able to teach and his very title suggests he is to exercise authority. Deacons (deaconesses) are also legitimated for a sphere of service. Deacons by serving well will gain proper confidence (παρρησία, 3.13), but the opponents speak confidently without grounds (διαβεβαιόομαι, 1.7). It may be that 5.13 intends to show that the young widows are not to be seen as having teaching authority. Elders on the other hand (5.17f.) are to be respected especially as they engage in the hard work of teaching.

Thus, running through the letter is the concern for authority – who has it, who does not, who should, and how should it be used.[163] This observation fits well with the suggestion that 1 Timothy fits is the genre of *mandata principis*.[164]

Summary of Chains

It has been shown that there are a number of significant semantic chains running through significant portions of 1 Timothy. No doubt others could be added. The chains mentioned have significant overlap, and this only strengthens their cohesive effect. It has also been shown that throughout the letter there is significant continuity in the various discussions of opponents and the personal instructions to Timothy.

Grouping Units into Larger Sections

So far it has been argued that there is a cohesive flow from one unit to the next within 1 Timothy and that across these units there are a number of interrelated semantic chains running throughout the letter. On these points rests the primary weight of the argument for cohesion. This last section will examine how the cohesion works, i.e., how the different units fit together

---

163. Mounce 2000: 14–15, cites a lengthy passage from Warfield which touches on some of these points (from 'Some Exegetical Notes on 1 Timothy: I. "The Progress of Thought in 1 Timothy i.3–20"', *Presbyterian Review* 8 [1921]: 500–502).

164. Cf. Wolter 1988: 164–70; Johnson 2001: 139–41.

to form the whole. It must be asked whether the different units group together in any way to form larger sections. It is entirely possible that a document could consist simply of a series of units, but the varying degrees of connectedness between the various units suggest that some units may cohere especially with one another forming sections. Indeed, at some points the connection between one unit and the following unit was not very strong. It needs to be considered whether there are links which bind such units to other parts of the letter. Some commentators do not address any larger groupings (e.g., Hanson (1982), Oberlinner (1994)), but most who display any concern with structure do.

The analysis will not move linearly through the letter, but will first take up potential section groupings which are fairly clear (1.3–20; 2.1–15; 3.1–13; 4.6–16; 5.3–25; 6.3–20). Then it will turn to the intervening material concerning which there is less unanimity and examine two possible ways of viewing the macrostructure of the letter.

1.3–20

1.3–20 is commonly considered by commentators to hold together as a section.[165] Previously in this chapter strong connections were found between 1.3–7, 8–11, and 12–17. Thus, it has already been shown that 1.3–17 are firmly bound. Connections were found between 1.12–17 and 1.18–20 but these connections were not as strong as those between the previous units. What can be discussed now is that 1.18–20 links back to 1.3–7 forming an inclusio around the larger section. Others have noted this connection. Here the arguments will be collated and supplemented.

First, in 1.18 Timothy returns to the forefront of the discussion. After 1.3, there is no further occurrence of a second person referent until 1.18. Indeed, the previous unit, 1.12–17, focused almost exclusively on Paul and Christ. Thus, in 1.18 there is a significant return to direct address to Timothy with three second person singular referents and the use of Τιμόθεε. Thus, the communicative situation is 'I to you,' Paul to Timothy, as it was in 1.3–7 but has not been in between.[166] Secondly, παραγγελία in 1.18 connects back to παραγγέλλω in 1.3 and παραγγελία in 1.5.[167] The fact that παραγγελία in 1.18 is introduced by a demonstrative (ταύτην), strongly suggests that it refers to the previous occurrence of παραγγελία.[168] Not only

---

165. E.g., Marshall 1999: 27; Mounce 2000: 14; Quinn and Wacker 2000: 47; Roloff 1988: 48–49; Knight 1992: 70. The opinion is virtually universal.

166. Quinn and Wacker 2000: 147, also note that the occurrence of the name 'Timothy' in 1.18 connects back to the only prior occurrence in 1.2. This also suggests 1.18–20 returns to the beginning of the letter. Cf. also, Bassler 1996: 45; Roloff 1988: 101.

167. So also, e.g., Marshall 1999: 408; Mounce 2000: 64; Quinn and Wacker 2000: 147.

168. Quinn and Wacker 2000: 147 say that the presence of the demonstrative 'emphatically specifies' a referent back to 1.3 and 5.

is there a return to Paul addressing Timothy, but the address is still concerned with the 'command.' Also, in both units, this command involves a task which has been given to Timothy. In 1.3 it is what Timothy was left in Ephesus to do and is reminded to continue; and in 1.18 it is something entrusted to Timothy. Third, in 1.5 the goal of the command involved a 'good conscience and sincere faith' (συνειδήσεως ἀγαθῆς καὶ πίστεως ἀνυποκρίτου), and in 1.19 Timothy also is to hold onto 'faith and a good conscience' (πίστιν καὶ ἀγαθὴν συνείδησιν).[169] It is hard to escape the impression that this exact repetition of terms is intended to cause the reader to connect these two passages. Additionally, in both units this faith and good conscience is rejected by some. This connects 1.3–7 and 1.18–20 simply because they both refer to opposition while there is no explicit mention of opposition in the two intervening units. Even more significantly, this rejection is stated in highly similar language:

1.6	1.19
ὧ τινες ἀστοχήσαντες	ἥν τινες ἀπωσάμενοι

In both instances the opponents are designated by τινες and the virtues are referred to by a relative pronoun in the accusative as the direct object of an aorist participle denoting rejection.[170] In both instances, the opponents' rejection of proper virtues leads to trouble (futility, v. 6; shipwreck, v. 20), though in 1.20 it is more drastic. In v. 7 the opponents do not know what they are talking about and in v. 20 they need to be taught. Also, in 1.3 and 1.20 there are similar uses of a ἵνα- clause with μή. In 1.3, Timothy was left in order that he might command certain ones not to **teach** wrongly, and in 1.20 Hymenaeus and Alexander (who apparently have taught wrongly) have been handed over in order that they might be **taught** not to blaspheme. These connections then suggest a structural similarity between vv. 5–7 and vv. 18–20, which could be shown in the following way:

The goal of παραγγελία is love, **good conscience, & faith**
  ὧν τινες swerved away
    description – desiring to be law teachers
      lack of understanding
I entrust παραγγελία to you Tim … keep **faith & good conscience**
  ἥν τινες rejected
    description – naming of Hym and Alexander
      need to be taught

---

169. So also, e.g., Mounce 2000: 64; Quinn and Wacker 2000: 147; Roloff 1988: 104.

170. Both verbs are classified by Louw and Nida (1989) in subdomain 31H, 'Change an Opinion Concerning Truth.'

These diverse connections between 1.3–7 and 1.18–20 argue strongly that they are intended to be seen together, thereby acting as an inclusio around 1.3–20. 1.3–20, then, bound by charges to Timothy in light of the opponents and connected by a series of significant transitional devices (argued previously), constitute a strongly cohesive unit.[171]

2.1–15

Previously in this chapter it was noted that scholars largely agree that there is a significant shift at 2.1. Also, while connections were found between 2.1–7 and 1.18–20, these connections were not as strong as many others in the letter. Therefore, it is logical to look for a new larger section beginning at 2.1. It has been shown above that 2.1–7 and 2.8–15 are strongly bound by lexical and semantic repetition as well as transitional devices. Since 3.1 introduces a new topic, the links between 2.1–15 support the commonly held view that 2.1–15 form a coherent section.

3.1–13

The connections between 3.1–7 and 3.8–13 have been argued above. The connections are strong and clear. Therefore, 3.1–13 is commonly considered a section.[172]

4.6–16

The German commentators tend to understand 4.1–11 as a section with 4.12 starting a new thought.[173] However, strong connections have already been found between 4.6–10 and 4.11–16. Indeed, the shifts in cohesion fields were so slight as to question the need of positing a break between the two units. Thus, based on previous arguments, 4.6–16 will be considered together as a larger section.[174]

5.1–2 – A Hinge

The place of 5.1–2 is debated. Some connect this unit with what precedes and others with what follows.[175] It has already been shown that 5.1–2 has significant connections in both directions. 5.1–2 continues the string of

---

171. Marshall 1999: 27 argues for a chiastic structure in 1.3–20.

172. So virtually all commentaries. Marshall 1999: 28 writes, 'The two sections on bishops and deacons clearly belong together.'

173. E.g. Roloff 1988: 250; Oberlinner 1994: 200–201; Merkel 1991: 37f.; Brox 1969a: 13

174. Cf. Marshall 1999: 28, 'It emerges that there are no grounds whatever for making a break at 4.11 (12) since the same theme of Timothy's personal conduct as a teacher continues.' Cf. also Quinn and Wacker 2000: 50; Mounce 2000: 245–46; Knight 1992: 193; Bassler 1996: 82–83.

175. Roloff 1988: 250 is a representative of those who link it strongly to what precedes. Guthrie 1990: 111–12 is an example of those who connect 5.1–2 only with what follows.

second person imperatives from 4.11–16 while also introducing the idea of dealing with different groups within the church which continues in 5.3–6.2. Thus, Bassler writes that 5.1–2 'is grammatically part of the personal instructions to Timothy (4.6–16) ... but has content that anticipates the verses that follow (5.3–6.2).'[176] As a result a growing number of scholars recognize 5.1–2 as a transitional passage, a hinge.[177]

5.3–6.2b

The next relatively clear section is 5.3–6.2. These three units (5.3–16, 5.17–25, 6.1–2) are usually considered together whether or not they are considered cohesive as they clearly provide instructions regarding various groups within the church. Whether or not 5.1–2 should be included with this section is debated and will be discussed later. The concern here is whether or not 5.3–6.2 cohere as a larger section. Miller contends that these are miscellaneous admonitions compiled with no sense of order or connection.[178] It has already been shown, however, that there are significant connections between each unit and the following unit. Now links across all three units need to be examined.

First, the three units are connected by a common genre, since all three units are instructions concerning specific groups. Each unit is full of imperatives. In 5.3–16, seven out of 28 finite verbs are imperatives, and an even greater percentage of the main verbs in the sentences. In 5.17–25 eight out of ten finite verbs are imperatives. In 6.1–2a three out of seven finite verbs are imperatives. The numbers increase if verbs like βούλομαι and διαμαρτύρομαι, which are not in imperative mood but function as commands, are included.

The foremost connection between the three units, however, is the repetition of τιμή/τιμάω. The concern in each unit is that proper honor be shown, as most scholars point out. The fact that the connotation of honor in each unit varies is cited by some as evidence for discontinuity, but this does not follow. In each group, the proper honor to be shown would be quite different, and that is to be expected. The fact that the concern in regard to each group has been stated in terms of 'honor' suggests a deliberate crafting of each unit in order to cohere with the others. Indeed, there seems to be a progression in the three units with reference to honor – honor widows, elders are worthy of honor, masters are to be considered worthy of honor. The commands become increasingly distant. Conversely, the intensity of the honor increases in the progression – honor, double

---

176. Bassler 1996: 90.

177. Though they do not use the word, 'hinge,' some who interpret 5.1–2 in this way include: Mounce 2000: 268–69; Marshall 1999: 572; Fee 1988: 112; Bassler 1996: 90.

178. Miller 1997: 83–88.

honor, all honor. This sense of movement supports the idea of an author at work crafting these units in light of each other.

Also there is a concern in each unit about inappropriate behavior which might bring reproach. Earlier it was shown that concern over sin within the church occurred throughout the letter, and it is especially prominent in these units. Younger widows are given instruction so that they might give no occasion for reproach from the enemy (5.14); the sin of elders is to be dealt with publicly (5.20), indeed it cannot be hidden (5.24), and it could implicate Timothy if he is not careful (5.22); and slaves are to respond properly to their masters lest the name of God and the teaching be blasphemed (6.1).

6.2c – A Hinge
It has already been argued above that 6.2c functions as a 'hinge' linking preceding and following material.[179] The exhortation to 'teach and exhort these things' (Ταῦτα δίδασκε καὶ παρακάλει) naturally refers to the preceding teaching,and has a lexical link with the previous transitional hinge in 5.1–2 (παρακαλέω). The exhortation to teach properly (διδάσκω) then serves as the foil for the discussion of those who 'teach otherwise' (ἑτεροδιδασκαλέω).

6.3–21
Miller considers this section as a 'miscellany of diverse materials' and says most commentators take this view as well.[180] This view does indeed have many supporters among commentators, including several from widely divergent perspectives. For example, Dibelius and Conzelmann say 6.6–10 is 'only superficially connected' to 6.3–5, vv. 11–16 'appears to be an intrusion between vss 10 and 17', and 17–19 also seem out of place and show a 'lack of logical coherence.'[181] Guthrie agrees stating, 'The concluding portion of the Epistle contains no clear sequence of thought.'[182]

However, this is not the majority view today. The turning point came with Jukka Thurén's 1970 article, 'Die Struktur der Schlußparänese 1. Tim. 6,3–21,' in which he argued for the cohesiveness of 6.3–21 countering what he said was a widespread opinion that the section was incoherent ('uneinheitlich').[183] Though it took some time,[184] his arguments seem

179. Cf. Marshall 1999: 634, who writes, 'Verse 2b is transitional, summing up the previous material and stressing the need to teach it. At the same time, it provides the positive statement to which the activity of the opponents forms a contrast.'

180. Miller 1997: 88–89.

181. Dibelius and Conzelmann 1972: 84, 87, 91, respectively.

182. Guthrie 1990: 122. Roloff 1988: 326, also mentions Brox and Käsemann as proponents of this view.

183. Thurén 1970: 241. It is surprising that Miller does not interact with Thurén.

184. Writing in 1990, P. G. Bush complained that Thurén's work had not received its due attention ('A Note on the Structure of 1 Timothy,' 1990: 152–56).

largely to have won the day with most recent commentators accepting his conclusion (most notably Roloff, Oberlinner, Marshall, and Mounce).[185] Thurén's argument rests on three observations: (1) the section is connected by contrasts at key places, (2) there is an alternation between warnings and exhortations (with summary warnings), and (3) there is a parallel with 1.3–20. While these observations have been widely accepted by subsequent commentators, they have not been greatly advanced; and they do not address fully the connections between each individual unit which is the point at which Miller makes his criticisms. Earlier in this chapter significant links were found between each unit and the one which follows it. What remains now is to investigate links and patterns which may unite the entire section.

First, it can be noted that there are significant links between non-contiguous units within this section. Three such areas will be mentioned.

6.3–10 and 17–19. It is commonly noted that these two units are related, especially vv. 9–10 and 17–19. They both are concerned with issues relating to wealth. The πλου- root occurs five times in these verses and nowhere else in the letter (vv. 9, 17 [3x], 18), not to mention other words for wealth or desire. Both units point to the transient nature of material wealth. 6.7 makes the point that one cannot take his riches out of this world. 6.17, by referring to those with wealth as 'those rich in the present age,' highlights that material wealth is only for 'this age.' There are also some clear contrasts between the discussion of wealth in vv. 9–10 and vv. 17–19. Though v. 9 and v. 17 open with an adjectival phrase used as a substantive, v. 9 refers to those who desire to be rich but v. 17 refers to those who are in fact rich in the present age.[186] The lust to have in vv. 9–10 is contrasted with a willingness to share in vv. 17–19.

6.11–16 and 6.20a. There are significant connections between these two passages which both give direct address to Timothy about himself. Both passages begin with the interjection Ὦ and a vocative referring to Timothy (ἄνθρωπε θεοῦ, v. 11; Τιμόθεε, v. 17). These are the only occurrences of vocatives in this section (indeed there is only one other occurrence in the entire letter) and the only occurrences of Ὦ in the letter. The idea in both passages is a call to enduring faithfulness in light of the opponents, who precede vv. 11f. and follow v. 20a. This call to faithfulness is expressed in similar phrases as well: τηρῆσαί σε τὴν ἐντολὴν (v. 14) and τὴν παραθήκην

185. Thurén does not appear in the bibliography or index of Quinn and Wacker (2000) or Johnson (2001).

186. Kidd 1990: 95–96, argues that the same group is in view in both units. While this is not convincing to me, it does not affect the argument here since the necessary point for the argument is that there is a literary or linguistic relation between the two units.

φύλαξον (v. 20). The two verbs used have similar connotations and are both listed in Louw and Nida's subdomain for 'Guard, Watch Over.'[187] The object in both phrases in context refers to a message which has been handed on to Timothy. Thus, there are significant connections between these two passages.

6.3–10 and 6.20b–21. Both of these passages refer to the opponents and follow an imperative which urges Timothy to faithfulness (v. 2b and v. 20a). In 6.3–10 the opponents 'know nothing' (v. 4), and in v. 20 their teaching is 'falsely called knowledge.' In v. 9 they have 'foolish desires' and in v. 20 they engage in 'foolish talk.' Both passages refer to the opponents abandoning the faith in strikingly similar ways, with syntactic and semantic similarities. In both statements there are the following elements: mention of something negative, relative pronoun, indefinite pronoun, participle denoting attachment to the previous negative, and then a verb denoting rejection of truth along with a prepositional phrase denoting faith as that which has been rejected. The elements are in the exact order in both statements except for the verb and prepositional phrase, which swap places.

v. 10 – greed   ἧς τινες ὀρεγόμενοι ἀπεπλανήθησαν ἀπὸ τῆς πίστεως

v. 21 – false teaching   ἥν τινες ἐπαγγελλόμενοι περὶ τὴν πίστιν ἠστόχησαν

Lastly, not only do both passages refer to the opposition as lacking knowledge, being foolish and rejecting faith, but they also connect the opponents to divisive verbal arguments. In 6.3–10 the opponents have a morbid interest in 'disputes and word battles' (ζήτησις καὶ λογομαχία, v. 4) and these produce, among other things, 'quarrels' (ἔρις) and 'constant arguing' (διαπαρατριβή). In 6.20 the opponents are characterized by 'worldly foolish talk' (βέβηλος κενοφωνία) and 'contradictions' (ἀντίθεσις). All of these similarities in spite of the fact that 6.20b-21 is much shorter than 6.3–10 suggest a close connection between the two units.

Thus, in 6.3–21 there are links between each contiguous unit and there are other (sometimes stronger) links between non-contiguous units. This suggests some degree of cohesion since it seems that different units in the passage treat similar issues. However, it raises the biggest issue concerning the coherence of 6.3–21 – why are the units which discuss similar issues separated? This is the largest criticism against the coherence of this section. 6.11–16 is said to be problematic because it interrupts vv. 6–10 and

187. τηρέω, 37.122; φυλάσσω, 37.119.

vv. 17–19 which are about wealth.[188] 6.17–19 is problematic because it interrupts vv. 11–16 and 20f. which address Timothy specifically.[189] If these units are as strongly connected as has been argued here, why are they separated? In answer it should be noted that since the topics of wealth, direct address to Timothy, as well as the opponents, all occur more than once, perhaps this is part of the design of the author. The critics of this passage assume that units on a similar topic must occur together, but this need not be so. Rather there seems to be a certain symmetry to the unit. The opponents occur at the beginning and the end of the unit, forming an inclusio. Noting the occurrence of discussion of money and direct address to Timothy could result in the following structure:

A Opponents (wrong teaching & behavior) (3–5)
  B Money, negative (6–10)
    C Timothy (11–16)
  B' Money, positive (17–19)
    C' Timothy (20a)
A' Opponents (wrong behavior & teaching) (20b–21)

These units cannot be quite so neatly separated (the opponents are still in view in vv. 6–10), but this shows a pattern of thought which can explain the recurrence of topics within the section. The connections noted previously support the paralleled sections in this outline.

At root the structural key to this unit is, as others have noted, the contrast between the opponents and the right way of Christian life (usually represented by Timothy).[190] This can be helpfully combined with Thurén's observation on the shifts between warning and exhortation. Thurén noted that the section alternates between exhortations and warnings, with the shift being marked each time by a summary statement.[191] He represented this patterns as follows (S = summary statement):

Exhortation	Warning
2b(S)	
	3–10
	11a(S)
11–19	
20a(S)	
	20b–21a

---

188. Roloff 1988: 326 identifies this as the key issue in discerning the coherence of this section. Cf. Dibelius and Conzelmann 1972: 87.

189. Cf. Miller 1997: 93.

190. E.g. Marshall 1999: 635, who provides a chart tracking the contrasting shift through the section.

191. Thurén 1999: 244.

6.2b exhorts Timothy to teach 'these things,' summarizing the previous instruction. 6.3–10 then warns about the opponents. 6.11a summarizes vv. 3–10 by warning Timothy to flee 'these things.' 6.11b–19 then proceed by exhorting Timothy in his role. 6.20a summarizes Timothy's role by urging him to 'guard the deposit,' with vv. 20b–21a serving as a concluding warning. The exhortation then is each time concerned with the proper way (Timothy and those who are rich), and the warnings are concerned with the opponents. This results in the contrast running throughout the unit as Timothy is exhorted to the right way and warned of the wrong way.

This also points to the fact that the opponents are a unifying factor in this section. Not only are they explicitly mentioned at the beginning and ending of the section, but the whole section is framed in response to them. As was shown above, the exhortation to Timothy in vv. 11–16 is set in clear contrast to the opponents and the exhortation to the rich is also in clear contrast to the opponents. Thus, concern about the influence of the opponents unites this section.

The Remaining Portion (3.14–4.5)
It is more difficult to be certain or clear in the placement of these two units. Most commonly 3.14–16 is thought to conclude 2.1–3.13.[192] However, a number of scholars, including some who place 3.14–16 with preceding material, note connections between 3.14–16 and 4.1ff.[193] Quinn and Wacker even argue that 3.14–4.5 form a section independent of 2.1–3.13.[194] Both units have significant connections with what precedes and what follows. To place too strong a break before or after either unit would be unjustified and would obscure the transitional function of 3.14–16.[195]

Where one places these two units affects how one sees the overall structure of the letter. To do justice to the transitional nature of 3.14–16, the macrostructure of 1 Timothy can be viewed in two different ways corresponding to two different placements of 3.14–16 in particular. Both perspectives show the letter to be coherent and cohesive. To demonstrate the strengths of both perspectives they will need to be laid out in some detail. The first view follows the more common placement of 3.14–16 at the close of 1.3–3.13. The second takes a more novel approach.

---

192. E.g., Marshall 1999: 28; Roloff 1988: 49–50; Oberlinner 1989: 151–52; Merkel 1991: 32–33; Towner 1989: 87.
193. E.g., Marshall 1999: 498; Lau 1996: 107–14; Mounce 2000: 214–15; Karris 1979: 81; Fee 1988: 97.
194. Quinn and Wacker 2000: 50, 289ff.
195. Dibelius and Conzelmann 1972: 60 also refer to this unit as a transitional passage. Cf. also Lau 1996: 108.

1.3–3.16 and 4.1–6.21. If the backward referring connections of 3.14–16 are stressed, 3.14–16 can be seen as the conclusion of the first half of the letter. This results in two main sections of the letter, 1.3–3.16 and 4.1–6.21. This general view of the letters' structure is fairly common (at least among the few who give attention to the macrostructure of the letter) with various modifications.[196] There is at least some support for this 'two halves' view in the participant and verb structure of the letter. First person singular referents are more common in the first half and second person singular referents are more common in the second half. Of the 23 discrete first person singular referents in the letter, 19 occur in 1.3–3.16. Of the 55 occurrences of second person singular referents, 49 are in the second half of the letter.[197] Furthermore, there are only four imperatives in the first half of the letter and 39 in the second half. All 30 of the second person singular imperatives occur in the second half of the letter.

In order to develop and establish this view of the letter's structure several points will be argued. First, connections between 3.14–16 with previous material beyond 3.8–13 (e.g., 3.1–7, 1.3–20) will need to be demonstrated if 3.14–16 is to be seen as a concluding summary. Connections between 1.3–20 and 2.1–15 will also need to be noted. Then, the second half of the letter will need to be examined.

In addition to links to 3.8–13 which have already been argued, 3.14–16 has a number of lexical connections with material further back which substantiates its backward connection. As already mentioned, ταῦτα would normally be considered to refer backward. Further, δεῖ (3.2, 7) is the main verb of 3.2–7 and, with the ὡσαύτως of 3.8, 11, it is the main verb of 3.8–11 as well. Thus, the use of δεῖ in 3.15 connects 3.1–15 with what is 'necessary.' This is even more significant since what is 'necessary' in all three units concerns behavior and is focused within the church. Also, the words οἶκος (3.4, 5, 12, 15) and ἐκκλησία (3.5, 15) cluster in 3.1–15, accounting for all but one occurrence of each word in the letter.[198] These words are also used similarly as 'household' and 'church' are closely related in both 3.5 and 3.15. In 3.5 the handling of one's 'own household' (ὁ ἴδιος οἶκος) is said to be indicative of how they would handle 'God's church' (ἐκκλησία θεοῦ). 3.15 then connects with this as it mentions 'God's household' (οἶκος θεοῦ) which is 'God's church' (ἐκκλησία θεοῦ). Thus, it is because the church is God's household that household management is important for church leaders. Thus, 3.14–16 coheres well with 3.1–13.

---

196. Cf. Marshall 1999: 30; Bassler 1996: 7–8. Quinn and Wacker 2000: 47 basically hold this view as well even though they separate 3.14–4.5 as a 'piece in pause.'

197. Cf. Roloff 1988: 218, who notes that second person singular referents are a distinguishing mark of the second half of the letter.

198. Οἶκος also occurs in 5.4, and ἐκκλησία also occurs in 5.16.

3.14–16 also connects with several elements of 1.3–20. Second person referents and the resulting 'I-you' communication, which are prominent in 1.3–7, 18–20, disappear in 2.1–3.13 and reappear in 3.14–15. In 1.3–7 and 18–20 Paul spoke directly to Timothy. In 2.1–3.13 it shifts to less direct exhortation. Then, in 3.14–15 the personal interaction between Paul and Timothy resurfaces, thus creating linking back to Chapter 1 and enveloping 2.1–3.13. Furthermore, in both 1.3–7 and 3.14–15 the relational setting between Paul and Timothy includes issues of travel, purpose, and Timothy's mission. 1.3 refers to Paul apparently passing through Ephesus and going to Macedonia. In 3.14 he hopes to come to Timothy. 1.3 refers to Paul's purpose in leaving Timothy in Ephesus, and 3.14–15 refers to Paul's purpose in writing to Timothy. In both instances the purpose is bound up with Timothy's mission in relation to the church. These connections hold 1.3–7 (with 1.18–20) and 3.14–16 together enveloping 2.1–3.13. This suggests cohesion within 1.3–3.16.

There are further indications of cohesion within 1.3–3.16. The three main gospel summaries of 1 Timothy all occur within these verses (1.12–16; 2.3–6; 3.16). It has already been shown that these passages share several commonalities including an emphasis on universality.[199] A further connection can here be noted, since the reference to being preached among the nations (ἐκηρύχθη ἐν ἔθνεσιν) in 3.16 connects strongly to the description of Paul's role in 2.7 as a preacher to the nations (κῆρυξ ... ἐθνῶν). These terms occur nowhere else in the letter. Also the statements in 1.12–16 and 2.3–6 are both closely associated with Paul's call to ministry (θέμενος εἰς διακονίαν, 1.12; εἰς ὃ ἐτέθην ἐγὼ κῆρυξ καὶ ἀπόστολος, 2.7). 2.1–15 and 3.1–13 hold together with a common focus on church life, in addition to lexical connections within the virtue/vice chain.

The connection within this larger passage most often contested is between 1.3–20 and 2.1–15. However, a continuous stream of first person singular referents connects these sections. Of the 23 discrete occurrences of first person singular referents in 1 Timothy, 11 occur in 1.3–20 and six occur in 2.1–15.[200] Indeed each unit opens with a first person (usually singular) verb:

1.3 – I urged you (παρακαλέω)
1.8 – We know

---

199. Cf. Marshall 1999: 527–28; Oberlinner 1994: 169. Bassler 1996: 77, notes 'the worldwide audience that the hymn foresees for this gospel and the worldwide faith that it will elicit echo the universal message' of 2.5–6a.

200. These occurrences consist of 21 first person singular verbs and two other instances where ἐγώ occurs but is not the subject of one of these verbs (1.3, 11, 12 [2x], 13 [2x], 15, 16 [2x], 18, 20; 2.1, 7 [3x], 8, 12; 3.14, 15; 4.13; 5.14, 21; 6.13). All five occurrences of ἐγώ are also found here (1.11, 12, 15, 16; 2.7).

1.12 – I give thanks
1.18 – I entrust to you
2.1 – I urge (παρακαλέω)[201]
2.8 – I desire

First person referents are absent in 3.1–13 and then reappear in 3.14–16 as the unit opens with a first person verb (γράφω) thus linking back to 1.3–2.15.

In summary, 3.14–16 functions well as a conclusion of 1.3–3.13. Links between 3.14–16 and 1.3–7, 18–20, and links within 1.3–3.16 reveal a cohesive major section.

If 1.3–3.16 is a cohesive major section, 4.1–6.21 needs to be examined. As noted previously, second person singular referents dominate 4.1–6.21. 2.1–3.13 was completely devoid of such references and 3.14–16 shifted back to direct second person address (as in 1.3, 18) preparing the way for 4.1–6.21. This section is presented then especially as instruction to Timothy directly. However, there are two units (and only two) in this section where no second person referents occur: 4.1–5 and 6.3–10. These are the two units directed at the opponents. Their total lack of second person referents in the midst of such a preponderance of such referents in 3.14–6.21 causes them to stand out and suggests there are two key figures in this section – Timothy and the opponents. In fact a basic symmetrical structure can be suggested.

4.1–5 – Opponents
    4.6–10 – Timothy, personally
    4.11–16 – Timothy, concerning church
        5.1–6.2a – specifics of Timothy's instruction to the church
    6.2b – Timothy, concerning church
6.3–10 – Opponents
    6.11–16 – Timothy, personally
    6.17–19 – Timothy, concerning church
    6.20 – Timothy, personally
6.21 – Opponents

Of course too rigid a division between instruction given to Timothy personally and that given to him concerning the church cannot be maintained since Timothy's personal behavior has an important impact on the church as well. The point here is that there does seem to be an emphasis in one direction or the other in different units and there is a flow to the

---

201.   The repetition of παρακαλέω further binds 1.3–20 and 2.1–15. 2.1, with a resumptive οὖν, picks up the charge begun in 1.3. Having reminded Timothy of the charge in 1.3–20, Paul begins to expound it in 2.1f. Cf. Oberlinner 1994: 65; Quinn and Wacker 2000: 171.

thought. Connections already established between 4.1–5, 6.3–10, and 6.21 (opponents) and 4.6–16 and 6.11–16 (Timothy) affirm this structure.

The outline proposed above suggests 5.1–6.2a is bracketed by 4.11–16 and 6.2b and grows out of 4.11–16. That 5.1–6.2 grows out of 4.11–16 is suggested by the flow of the letter. After the mention of the opponents in 4.1–5, 4.6–10 deals primarily with Timothy's personal response to this problem focusing on his being a good minister, training himself and attaining life himself. A shift occurs in 4.11–16 to a concern for Timothy's public ministry in the church – being an example, engaging in public teaching, and making progress personally which is evident publicly. This shift to what Timothy is to teach publicly prepares the way for specific instruction he is to give to specific groups within the church. While there is indeed a shift from the general to the particular, the continuity of second person imperatives from 4.11 through 5.1–6.2 shows that the directives are a continuation of what Paul tells Timothy to teach. 5.1–6.2 is not simply general church information, but specific instruction directly to Timothy concerning the church. Other continuities confirm this. Just as in 4.11–16 there is a concern that Timothy's behavior be exemplary and his progress be publicly evident, so there is (as noted above) a concern for each group specifically addressed in 5.3–16 that their behavior not bring public reproach. There is also a chain of ταῦτα commands to Timothy concerning teaching that unite 4.11–6.2:

4.11 – command and teach these things (Παράγγελλε ταῦτα καὶ δίδασκε)
4.15 – cultivate these things (ταῦτα μελέτα)
5.7 – command these things (ταῦτα παράγγελλε)
5.21 – obey these things (Διαμαρτύρομαι ... ἵνα ταῦτα φυλάξῃς)[202]
6.2b – teach and exhort these things (Ταῦτα δίδασκε καὶ παρακάλει)

Since there are no other ταῦτα commands concerning teaching in the letter, the repetition of this phrase through this section unites it as specific instruction to Timothy.[203]

The greatest similarity is between 4.11 and 6.2b with both statements occurring at the opening or closing of units, using two verbs for teaching, one of which is διδάσκω. It is this correlation which suggests 4.11 and 6.2 bracket the intervening section of teaching, providing a structural parameter for the continuity of teaching that was just observed. The use of παρακαλέω in 6.2b also links back to the previous occurrence of the word in 5.1, the beginning of the specific instructions.

---

202. Though not in the imperative mood, this statement functions as a command.

203. 4.6 contains a ταῦτα saying with a participial and it could be argued that the participial has imperatival force. If this is so, it only ties 5.1–6.2 more firmly to the instruction to Timothy in Ch. 4.

In summary, 4.1–6.21 display a significant level of cohesion with symmetrical arrangement, continuity, and lexical repetitions.

So, if one stresses the concluding function of 3.14–16, the result is two letter-halves which cohere well by various means, with each half opening and closing on the same note. These two halves are then held together by the various semantic chains delineated previously.[204] These two parts have then been joined by noticing similarities between 1.3–20 and 6.3–21. Since the connection between 1.3–20 and 6.3–21 has played a significant role in the discussion of the cohesion of 1 Timothy, it must be examined in some detail. This examination also leads to the second way of viewing the placement of 3.14–16 and the macrostructure of 1 Timothy.

The argument that parallels between 1.3–20 and 6.3–21 suggest an inclusio was first put forth by Thurén in 1970.[205] Thurén noted four parallels between Chs. 1 and 6: (1) a grace wish (1.2; 6.21), (2) a warning about those who are straying from the faith (1.5f.; 6.20f.), (3) a doxology (1.17; 6.15–16), and (4) an exhortation to Timothy to remember his ordination and to fight the good fight (1.18–20; 6.11f.).[206] The last parallel actually has three significant pieces: the reference to Timothy, reference to ordination, and 'fight the good fight.' While it may be noted that the repetition of the grace wish is not very helpful, since this regularly occurs at the opening and closing of every letter in the Pauline corpus, the other parallels are striking. These parallels have then been expanded upon by others, perhaps most notably Bush, Roloff, and Oberlinner.[207]

There are similarities in the exhortations to Timothy. Foremost, Roloff has noted that each of these sections remains almost entirely on the level of communication directly from Paul to Timothy, or as he calls it, 'sender recipient communication.'[208] Related to this, the vocative Τιμόθεε occurs in 1.18 and 6.20 and nowhere else in the letter. Though Bush was wrong to say these were the only occurrences of vocative address in the letter, the

---

204. Marshall 1999: 31 faces the possibility that the 'two halves' approach might suggest that two similar letters have been joined. He rejects the possibility because 'there is sufficient unity of theme between the two parts to suggest that they belong closely together.' The delineation of specific semantic chains further strengthens his point. The transitional nature of 3.14–16 also serves to hold the two halves together.

205. Thurén 1970: 241–53.

206. Thurén 1970: 242–43.

207. Couser 2000: 279–82, further expounds the connections between the doxologies already noted by Thurén, and concludes, 'It is apparent that the author intended 1:17 and 6:15–16 to be seen in relationship to one another both on the conceptual and functional level' (281–82).

208. Roloff 1988: 49: 'Wie das Proömium, so bleibt auch der ausführliche Sclußabschnitt fast ganz auf der Ebene der Absender-Empfänger-Kommunikation, mit Ausnahme der kontextbedingten Abschweifung 6,17–19.'

other occurrence is also found within these sections (6.11).[209] 'Deposit' language is found in both 1.18 (Ταύτην τὴν παραγγελίαν παρατίθεμαι σοι) and 6.20 (τὴν παραθήκην φύλαξον), where Timothy is seen as the recipient of a message or task from Paul.[210]

There are also similarities in the discussions of the opponents. For example, both sections open with reference to ἑτροδιδασκαλέω (1.3; 6.3). Dibelius and Conzelmann also noted that in both sections those who teach wrongly are characterized as ignorant (μηδὲν ἐπιστάμενος, 6.4; μὴ νοοῦντες, 1.7),[211] and Oberlinner noted they are associated with disputes using similar words (ἐκζήτησις, 1.4; ζήτησις, 6.4).[212] Oberlinner also noted the presence of vice lists in both 1.9–10 and 6.4.[213] Then, Roloff expanded on Thurén's recognition of a warning on those straying from the faith in 1.5f. and 6.20f. by noting that the statements employ almost identical vocabulary.[214] Different scholars have noted a continuity in that there are warnings about those straying from the faith, though interestingly they have connected different passages. Thurén connected 1.5f and 6.20f. Bush connected 1.19 and 6.21. Roloff connected 1.19 and 6.11. The differences here may point to an area in which the parallel between these sections can be enhanced.

Little has been made of the fact that both 1.3–20 and 6.3–21 both open and close with a discussion of the opponents, forming parallel inclusios around these sections, as was argued above. This means there are within these sections four discrete discussions of the opponents, and this is why different scholars have made different connections regarding the warnings about opponents as mentioned above. In fact there is a high degree of similarity between all four units, as was shown in Table 1 on p. 120. The following table re-presents the parallels within the units in view here.

---

209. Couser 2000: 272 follows Bush in this error.
210. Bush 1990: 153; Roloff 1988: 49; Oberlinner 1994: 309. However, Couser 2000: 272, n. 47, disputes this connection since the charge in 1.18 is simply the task at Ephesus while the 'trust' in 6.20 refers to the Christian message more broadly. This is a valid critique, but the use of similar language and the picture of Timothy as the recipient of Paul may still create a significant link.
211. Dibelius and Conzelmann 1972: 83.
212. Oberlinner 1994: 270.
213. Oberlinner 1994: 270.
214. Roloff 1988: 327.

1.3–7	1.18–20	6.3–10	6.20–21
ὧν τινες ἀστοχήσαντες	ἥν τινες ἀπωσάμενοι	ἧς τινες ... ἀπεπλανήθησαν ἀπὸ τῆς πίστεως	ἥν τινες ... ἠστόχησαν περὶ τὴν πίστιν
ὧν refers to πίστις (among other things)	ἥν refers to πίστις (among other things)		ἐκτρεπόμενος
ἐξετράπησαν	-----	-----	ἐπαγγελλόμενοι falsely called knowledge
προσέχειν myths & genealogies	-----	ὀρεγόμενοι wealth	
ματαιολογίαν	-----	λογομαχίας (λογ- root)	κενοφωνίας
ἐκζητήσεις	-----	ζητήσεις	-----
συνειδήσεως ἀγαθῆς	ἀγαθὴν συνείδησιν	depraved νοῦν	-----
Produces negative: παρέχουσιν speculation	-----	Produces negative: ἐξ ὧν γίνεται envy, strife, etc.	-----
-----	shipwreck, handed over to Satan [need to be taught]	ruin and destruction pierced with pains	-----
μὴ νοοῦντες		μηδὲν ἐπιστάμενος ἀνοήτους	Falsely called knowledge
θέλοντες	-----	βουλόμενοι, ἐπιθυμίας	-----
-----	taught not βλασφημεῖν	result in βλασφημίαι	-----
τις ἑτεροδιδασκαλεῖν	-----	τις ἑτεροδιδασκαλεῖ	-----

This table incorporates the parallels previously noted by scholars while including some further observations. Perhaps most importantly it lays out clearly the great similarity in the way each unit refers to 'certain ones' who turn away from the faith. Most of these connections have already been observed under the discussion of semantic chains. Here it will be useful simply to mention connections between these units which this table contributes to the scholarly discussion.[215] First, the verb ἐκτρέπω occurs only twice in the letter, in the first and last units on the opponents (1.6; 6.20). In both instances it refers to the teaching of the opponents, though different nuances of meaning of the verb are used in the two places ('stray after' in 1.6, and 'avoid' in 6.20). Interestingly, another parallel is that the object of ἐκτρέπω in both instances refers to foolish talk (1.6, ματαιολογία; κενοφωνία, 6.20). These two words are practically synonyms. They occur as adjacent listings in Louw and Nida, both under the subdomain of 'Foolish

---

215. Some commentators may refer to the fact that these words recur in the letter, but what is claimed here is that these repetitions have not previously been advanced as part of an argument for connections between 1.3–20 and 6.3–21.

Talk.'[216] Marshall also says that according to Hesychius and Suidas these words were synonyms.[217] A third parallel is the statement that the opponents' teaching produces negative results. This occurs in 1.4 where the opponents' teaching gives rise to (παρέχω) speculation as opposed to God's work and in 6.4 where in reference to the opponents' speculations it says out of this comes (ἐξ ὧν γίνεται) strife, envy, blasphemies, evil suspicions, etc. In each instance this is connected with the speculations of the opponents. Fourth, in 1.7 as in 6.9–10 some of the problems with the opponents are presented as 'desires' for the wrong things (θέλω, 1.7; βούλομαι, ἐπιθυμία, ὀρέγω, 6.9–10). In both 1.3–7 and 6.3–10, the unit closes with these wrong desires and they provide the contrast from which the following unit develops. Lastly, there may be connection between βλασφημέω in 1.20 and βλασφημία in 6.4, though the word does also occur in 1.13 and 6.1.

Therefore, the structural, syntactic, and lexical parallels between these units on the opponents cause them to cohere and support seeing 1.3–20 and 6.3–21 as an inclusio around the entire letter. The opponents, thus, frame the entire letter by framing both the opening and closing sections of the letter.

It may be useful then to provide a similar table for the similarities in the exhortations to Timothy in these sections. Exhortations specifically to Timothy concerning his own behavior and belief are concentrated in 1.3–7, 1.18–20, 6.11–16, and 6.20–21.

---

216. See Louw and Nida 1989: 33 'Communication,' 33 'Foolish Talk' (33.374–33.381). Ματαιολογία is 33.377 and κενοφωνία is 33.376.

217. Marshall 1999: 677, n.135.

1.3–7	1.18–20	6.11–16	6.20–21
Intermixed with discussion of opponents	Intermixed with discussion of opponents	Follows discussion of opponents	Intermixed with discussion of opponents
	Vocative τέκνον Τιμόθεε	Vocative ὦ ἄνθρωπε θεοῦ	Vocative Ὦ Τιμόθεε
	Faithfulness to a received message παραγγελίαν παρατίθεμαί message entrusted	Faithfulness to a received message τηρῆσαι … ἐντολὴν obey the message	Faithfulness to a received message παραθήκην φύλαξον guard the message
Avoidance of error: Command them not to hold to μῦθος, γενεαλογίας		Avoidance of error: Flee these things (greed)	Avoidance of error: Avoid βέβηλος κενοφωνία, and contradictions of falsely called knowledge
παραγγέλλω (v.3) παραγγελία (v.5)	παραγγελία (v.18)	παραγγέλλω (v.13)	
	Fight the good fight στρατεύῃ ἐν αὐταῖς τὴν καλήν στρατεία Reminder of Timothy's spiritual beginnings: κατὰ τὰς προαγούσας ἐπὶ σὲ προφητείας	Fight the good fight ἀγωνίζου τὸν καλὸν ἀγῶνα τῆς πίστεως Reminder of Timothy's spiritual beginnings: ὡμολόγησας τὴν καλὴν ὁμολογίαν ἐνώπιον πολλῶν μαρτύρων	

This table largely condenses and presents the parallels previously found in these sections, though it subdivides these by units, resulting in four discrete units in which Timothy is specifically addressed in these sections, similar to the table for the opponents. This analysis by unit provides a clearer picture of the connections. One contribution this table makes is to note that the language of command often commented on in 1.3–20 also occurs in the address to Timothy in 6.13. Similarly, while, as stated above, it is often noted that 1.18–20 and 6.20–21 both refer to a message entrusted to Timothy which is to be guarded, a similar idea also occurs in 6.14. In 1.18, the message is a παραγγελία (Louw and Nida 1989: 33.328) and in 6.14 the message is an ἐντολή (Louw and Nida 1989: 33.330), with both words being in the vocabulary of command. Similarly, the verb in 6.14 (τηρέω) is virtually synonymous with the verb used in 6.20 (φυλάσσω). Both verbs have the connotations of guard and obey. Indeed Louw and Nida list them together under one heading for obey (1989: 36.19). Thus there is a series of connections between the exhortations to Timothy to be faithful to the received message in 1.18, 6.14, and 6.20. In both 1.18 and 6.14 the message is a command. In 6.14 and 6.20 it is to be kept (both guarded and obeyed). And in 1.18 and 6.20 it is referred to in the language of 'deposit.' These interwoven connections, using similar words to say similar things in similar ways bind these units together and suggest that these fit together by more than mere accident. This further substantiates the argument for a parallel between 1.3–20 and 6.3–21.

Thus, the parallel between 1.3–20 and 6.3–21 can function to bind together the two cohesive letter halves.

3.14–4.16 as a unit. Now the second and more novel approach to the placement of 3.14–16 can be considered. It arises from the unit's forward connections and the preceding analysis of parallels between 1.3–20 and 6.3–21.

In the previous view of 3.14–16, links with the preceding material were noted. Here links with the last half of the letter (beyond 4.1–5 which has already been discussed) can be pointed out. First, while the idea of behavior in the church (3.15) does connect well with 2.1–3.13, it also connects well with 4.1–6.21 as the analysis of the semantic chain of virtue/vice has shown.[218] Second, 3.15 and 4.10 link naturally since they contain the only references to 'the living God' in the letter. Third, the use of second person in 3.14–15, while it links back to 1.3–7, 18–20, also introduces the flood of second person singular referents which dominates the latter half of the letter. Roloff argues that 4.1 marks a new thought since second person singular referents become a common characteristic while they were not previously.[219] However, as will be mentioned below, there are no second person singular referents in 4.1–5! They are introduced in 3.14–16 and then continue in 4.6ff. Thus, second person referents connect 3.14–16 with what follows as well.

Next, having summarized and further substantiated the argument for parallels between 1.3–20 and 6.3–21, it must be noted, however, that this discussion is incomplete and only selective in its data. It was noted that the parallels between these sections hinged primarily on two poles: discussion of the opponents and exhortations specifically to Timothy. There is another cluster of these concerns within this letter. Explicit and extended discussion of the opponents occurs in just one other place, 4.1–5. Also, direct communication to Timothy about Timothy (Roloff's sender-

218. The connection of the statement in 3.15 with what follows would be even stronger if the subject of ἀναστρέφεσθαι is Timothy as some have argued (cf. Reed 1993b: 111–14). This would then connect well with the address to Timothy in 4.6–16 (where ἀναστροφή also occurs).
219. Roloff 1988: 218.

recipient level of communication) while characteristic to 13–20 and 6.3–21, is not unique to them, because it also very clearly occurs in 3.14–16 and 4.6–16. The combination of these results in a section, 3.14–4.16 which has similar concerns as 1.3–20 and 6.3–21.[220] It has already been shown in the discussion of opponents and instruction to Timothy under semantic chains that 4.1–5 has striking similarities with the other sections on the opponents and 4.6–16 has striking similarities to the other sections on Timothy. Thus, 3.14–4.16 can be considered a proper parallel to 1.3–20 and 6.3–21. In addition to the extensive connections shown in those previous tables, a comparison of 1.3–20, 3.14–16, and 6.3–21 can provide the following table (FT = False teachers).

1.3–20	3.14–4.16	6.3–21
3 – Timothy's proper corrective teaching	3.14 – for Tim to know right behavior	2b – Tim's faithful teaching
Summary of previous instruction to Timothy	Summary of previous instruction on church (ταῦτα)	Summary of previous instruction on church (ταῦτα)
3–11 – FT & Law with rebuttal	4.1–5 – FT & asceticism with rebuttal	3–10 – FT & greed with rebuttal
18–20 – exhortation to Timothy (no real shifting contrast)	4.6 – shift to contrasting exhortation to Timothy	11–16 – shift to contrasting exhortation to Timothy
	4.16 – a closing call to faithfulness	20 – a closing call to faithfulness

These structural similarities in addition to the syntactic, lexical, and thematic parallels previously noted all suggest that 1.3–20, 3.14–4.16, and 6.3–21 can be seen as parallel sections which have a high level of coherence with each other. These three major sections, occurring at the beginning, middle, and end of the letter, then contribute strongly to holding the entire letter together.

The identification of these three parallel sections leaves two intervening sections (2.1–3.13; 5.1–6.2) which both consist of instruction to the church. This produces an intriguingly simple outline of the flow of the letter.

---

220.   Couser 2000: 273–75 has recently noticed a parallel between 3.14–4.16 and 1.3–20 and 6.3–21 as well. He also develops a chart of comparison (276). The previous tables in this chart provide more extensive parallels, and, as his concern is not structure, he does not develop the observation in terms of what it means for the structure of the entire letter. This analysis is a confirmation of his suggestions.

1.3–20 – On Timothy and the Opponents
  2.1–3.13 – On Specific Church Groups
3.14–4.16 – On Timothy and the Opponents
  5.1–6.2 – On Specific Church Groups
6.3–21 – On Timothy and the Opponents

While such a brief outline cannot account for all the nuances in a letter, it does demonstrate important continuities in the development of the letter. It has already been argued that the main sections on Timothy and the opponents cohere. Commonalities in the sections on specific church groups can also been seen in the virtue lists, etc.

There are a number of lexical repetitions between 2.1–3.13 and 5.1–6.2 which suggest a common ethical or value system behind both sections. For example, the call to universal prayer in 2.1–2 is grounded in the fact that such prayer is acceptable before God (τοῦτο ... ἀπόδεκτον ἐνώπιον τοῦ σωτῆρος ἡμῶν θεοῦ), and 5.4 uses the same language (which does not appear elsewhere in the letter) to ground the call to children to care for aging parents in the fact that such care is acceptable before God (τοῦτο ... ἀπόδεκτον ἐνώπιον τοῦ θεοῦ). Also, 2.1 mentions prayer as a top priority in the church, using the words δέησις and προσευχή among others. The importance of prayer comes out again in the description of the godly widow as one who continues in δέησις and προσευχή both night and day (5.5). In the discussion both of bishops (3.2) and widows (5.7) there is a concern for being above criticism (ἀνεπιλήμπτος). Believing women in general (2.10), widows (5.10), and elders (5.25; as well as the rich, 6.18) are all urged to good works. It makes sense that if the proper adornment of godly women is good works, that in order for a woman to be enrolled as a widow she must have a reputation for good works. In 3.7 the bishop is to have a good (κάλος) reputation (μαρτυρία) and in 5.10 widows are to have a reputation (μαρτυρέω) for good (κάλος) deeds. This connects with the more general concern for propriety and avoidance of scandal found also in 2.2, 10; 5.14; and 6.1. Similar clusters of this concern are found in 3.6–7 and 5.12–14. 3.6 and 5.12 contain the only two occurrences of κρίμα, both times cautioning against including less mature people (neophytes and younger widows) lest they fall into condemnation. The concern that the overseer have a good reputation with outsiders lest he fall into 'insult' (ὀνειδισμός, 3.7) is similar to the concern that young widows give no occasion to slander (λοιδορία) from adversaries in 5.14.[221] Also, the negative connotations are in both passages associated with the devil or Satan. Similarly there is a high evaluation for family throughout. In 2.15 the women are encouraged to bear children (τεκνογονία). In 5.10 the good widow is one

---

221. Both words used for the possible offence are categorized by Louw and Nida (1989) in sub-domain 33, P', 'Insult, Slander.'

who has been involved in raising children (τεκνοτροφέω) and the younger widows are encouraged in 5.14 to have children (τεκνογονέω). In 3.5 and 5.8 there is a common high importance placed on caring for one's own family. If one does not know how to lead his own household (εἰ δέ τις τοῦ ἰδίου οἴκου) he cannot care for the church (3.5), and if one does not care for his own household (εἰ δέ τις τῶν ἰδίων καὶ μάλιστα οἰκείων) he has denied the faith (5.8). The discussions concerning overseers, deacons, and elders naturally cohere, and each group is called to rule well, with προΐστημι occurring in each unit (3.4, 5, 12; 5.17) usually modified by καλῶς (3.4, 12; 5.17).[222] Lastly, common to the qualifications for bishop, deacon and an enrolled widow is faithfulness to one's spouse (μιᾶς γυναικὸς ἄνδρα, 3.2; μιᾶς γυναικὸς ἄνδρες, 3.12; ἑνὸς ἀνδρὸς γυνή, 5.9).[223] Broader similarities between 3.1–13 and 5.3–16 have been noted by other scholars, even to the extent of arguing that these similarities show that the 'widows' refers to an established order within the church.[224] This conclusion need not follow, since both groups are to be recognized by the church, whether for leadership or for charity, but the similarities in the lists of character qualities does demonstrate a common view of propriety behind both lists.

Thus, 2.1–3.13 and 5.1–6.2 can be seen in parallel with each other both in terms of their subject matter (instructions for specific church groups) and in the common ethical concern represented by lexical links. This commonality creates significant cohesion between these two large sections.

Thus, the parallel of 3.14–4.16 provides another perspective of how the letter as a whole fits together.

It has been argued that the units of 1 Timothy form coherent larger sections. Then, the final grouping of larger sections can be viewed in two ways: (1) two main sections with their own coherent structures, (2) three large sections addressing Timothy in light of the opponents separated by instruction to specific church groups. Both perspectives demonstrate the cohesion of 1 Timothy. These views of the macrostructure are not mutually exclusive but demonstrate the nuance of the letter and how its units function together.

Summary

The preceding analysis argues first that each unit connects in some way with the unit which follows, though the strength of the connections vary. Devices which were found connecting units included hook words and even

---

222. This represents every occurrence of προΐστημι in the letter.
223. Whether this prohibits polygamy or sexual unfaithfulness more generally does not affect the point here.
224. E.g. Bassler 1996: 92.

a 'hooked' use of participants. Several verses function as hinges creating link between two sections (e.g., 1.7, 11; 2.7). Secondly, there are running throughout the letter various semantic chains which unite these smaller units. The semantic chains often had a positive and negative side revealing the tension between opposing parties (Paul/Timothy and opponents). Indeed the continuity in the discussions of the opponents and instructions to Timothy also served to bind the letter together. Third, the individual units of the letter combine to form coherent larger sections some of which were connected by transitional, hinge, units. There are then symmetrical patterns which unite these larger sections, and the pattern in which the larger sections unite can be viewed in two ways. The previously noted parallel between 1.3–20 and 6.3–21 has been further developed showing, among other things, the implausibility of Bush's suggested structure which relied on changing the location of 6.17–19. The structure of the letter argued for here affirms the plausibility of the fairly common view of the letter as two coherent halves (cf. generally Marshall, Roloff). However, the second view of the structure showed more of the connections within the letter which are rarely noted in structural outlines of 1 Timothy and supports the suggestions of Couser.[225] This second view also revealed errors in Roloff's too stringent division of the two halves of the letter.

225. Couser 2000: 276.

Chapter 4

THE TEXTUAL UNITS OF 2 TIMOTHY

This chapter will undertake the first two steps in the analysis of cohesion in 2 Timothy. The first step is the demarcation of the basic communicative units of the letter, the discrete 'units' or paragraphs. It is important to identify these units so the following chapter can analyze the level of cohesion between these units. However, before examining possible connections between units, one must ascertain whether or not these units are themselves unified. Miller contends that most are not. Thus, the second and most crucial step in this chapter is the analysis of the cohesion of each unit.

Units will be taken up consecutively through the letter. For each one an analysis of their boundaries will be given first, followed by a more extensive analysis of cohesion within the unit.

1.1–2

1.1–2 are clearly identified as the epistolary prescript and salutation in a form clearly recognizable for ancient Greek letters. The end of the salutation at v. 2 marks the close of this form and therefore the close of this unit. The cohesion of this unit is not seriously challenged since it follows a clearly established form for ancient letters, a form which was in fact fairly flexible.[1]

1.3–5

Boundaries
The cohesion shift analysis suggests that the first unit of the letter is 1.3–5. The initial boundary of the unit is obvious and noted by all. The epistolary salutation comes to an end at the close of 1.2 and the first words of 1.3

---

1. Miller 1997: 96–97 does conjecture that the elements concerning apostolic authority were added later since he finds them unnecessary for the letter. However, even he admits this is simply conjecture without evidence. In reality the mention of Paul's position fit well with the regular connection of the gospel with Paul in the letter.

(Χάριν ἔχω τῷ θεῷ) mark it as the beginning of a thanksgiving. Concerning the final boundary of this unit, however, Quinn and Wacker write, 'there is no agreement on where the prayer ends.'[2] This seems, though, to be an overstatement of the case. While many commentators see strong connections between vv. 3–5 and what follows,[3] most of them agree that vv. 3–5 form the thanksgiving.[4] The factors suggesting v. 6 begins a new unit will be examined at the beginning of the discussion of the next unit, but key among these factors is the fact that at v. 6 there is a shift to exhortation. Whereas in vv. 3–5 the topic and genre center on thanks and remembrance, in vv. 6ff. the genre becomes exhortation.

Cohesion

Miller seems to be alone among modern commentators in arguing for a lack of cohesion. Concerning this unit Miller writes, 'No clear train of thought drives the sentence on ... and the connections between the various clauses are not easily followed'; and, 'The material seems strangely fragmented and discontinuous.'[5] Miller's assertion of the lack of a 'clear train of thought' serves as his primary argument, with two examples of ambiguity in the connections between clauses: the meaning and function of ὡς and the referent of ἀδιάλειπτον. However, these points of exegetical debate do not in any way produce incoherence. That the statements are connected is clear.[6] What is debated is the manner of connection. The letter to the Philippians provides an example of a thanksgiving in a New Testament letter where some of the syntax is not clear.[7] In spite of Miller's claim the train of thought is essentially clear: Paul gives thanks to God in connection with his remembrances of Timothy in prayer; Paul desires to see Timothy, remembers his tears and is convinced of the sincerity of Timothy's faith. Thus Miller does not provide any real argumentation against the coherence of this unit.

In contrast to Miller, there are a number of factors which serve to bind this long sentence together. First, this unit is bound around remembrance both as a theme and in lexical repetition. Words for remembrance occur three times in the unit, once in each verse (μνείαν, v. 3; μεμνημένος, v. 4;

2. Quinn and Wacker 2000: 576.
3. This will be discussed further in the next chapter on links between units.
4. E.g., Marshall, Oberlinner, Quinn-Wacker, Mounce, Knight, and Fee. While Bassler lists 1.3–14 as the unit, in her exposition she notes that vv. 3–5 are the thanksgiving and vv. 6–14 are exhortations which flow from it (1996: 127).
5. Miller 1997: 98, 99 respectively.
6. This is seen in the fact that while other commentaries discuss the syntactical questions, no other commentaries suggest the unit is incoherent.
7. Cf. Marshall 1999: 689: 'The connections of thought are intricate, but not more so than, say, in the opening of Phil.'

ὑπόμνησιν, v. 5). The unit is also full of indicators of deep emotion: incessant memory of Timothy, longing to see him, tears, and fullness of joy. Even the confidence expressed of Timothy in v. 5 could fit in this category. It becomes clear then that the ideas of memory and emotion are intertwined establishing the relational setting of this unit and the letter. Even if the precise manner of the connections between certain clauses is uncertain, it is clear that these verses make sense as the thanks of one person over the memory of a dear friend whom he longs to see. This point is strengthened by the observation that expressions of fond remembrance and desire for reunion were common in Hellenistic letters of friendship and exhortation.[8]

This relational matrix is further strengthened by a look at the participant structure of the unit. The unit is dominated by the interaction between Paul and Timothy. Paul is the subject of every verb but one (ἐνοικέω, v. 5). Of the 17 personal referents in the unit, six are references to first person singular[9] and seven are second person singular references to Timothy.[10] The remaining four are third person singular and refer to God (1.3, necessary for the thanksgiving), faith, Lois, and Eunice, with the last three all occurring in v. 5 and describing Timothy's spiritual heritage.

Lastly, the idea of spiritual heritage forms an inclusio around the unit. As Paul serves God from his forefathers (1.3), so the sincere faith which is in Timothy is that same faith that dwelt in his mother and grandmother (1.5). This comparison is part of the interrelation between Paul and Timothy that was seen in the relational matrix and which continues through the letter.[11]

1.6–14

Boundaries
In the previous section it was noted that there is some debate on whether or not a new unit should be marked at v. 6. However, most commentators agree that there is a shift at v. 6, even though some keep vv. 6ff with the preceding verses because they are so closely connected. The primary reason for beginning a new unit at 1.6 is the shift from thanksgiving to

---

8. Bassler 1996: 128; Stowers 1986: 59. Examples may be found in Stowers' discussion and in Pseudo-Demetrius' *Epistolary Types* under his discussion of the friendly letter (Malherbe 1988: 33).

9. 1.3 (4x), 1.4, 1.5.

10. 1.3, 4 (2x), 5 (4x).

11. Cf. Mounce 2000: 466, 'Throughout the first half of the epistle Paul shows Timothy that their lives and ministries are intertwined and because of this Timothy can draw encouragement from Paul.' Cf. also Wolter 1988: 203; Dibelius and Conzelmann 1972: 98; Knight 1992: 366; Johnson 1996: 47.

exhortation. 1.6 marks the first time in the letter that Timothy is urged to do anything.[12] This is followed by the first occurrence of a second person singular verb and the first imperative in the letter in v. 8. The move to exhortation is mirrored by a shift in participants. While the participants are still primarily Paul and Timothy and Paul is still the subject of the first verb of 1.6, Timothy becomes the subject of a verb for the first time in 1.6 (σε ἀναζωπυρεῖν) and then is the subject of the hortatory verbs (imperatives and a subjunctive) which follow. This shift to Timothy as subject is also seen in the use of 'remembrance' language. 1.6 continues with 'remembrance' language (ἀναμιμνῄσκω), but, whereas in 1.3–5 it was Paul who was doing the remembering, now it is Timothy who is called to remember. On the basis of these shifts a new unit is posited at 1.6, though this does not dispute the strong connections with 1.3–5.[13]

There is practically universal agreement that there is a break between 1.14 and 1.15.[14] What is debated is whether vv. 6–14 should be held together or divided. While the majority of commentators seem to agree with the division made here,[15] some divide vv. 6–14 into smaller units.[16] The case for holding vv. 6–14 together as one unit will be considered in the discussion of cohesion.

Cohesion
The cohesion of this unit is challenged from two perspectives. First, some break 1.6–14 into two or three units without necessarily claiming incoherence between these smaller units. Three prominent examples can be given. First, Hanson (1982) breaks these verses into three units: vv. 3–8 (personal exhortation), 9–10 (liturgical fragment), 11–14 (commission). However, in keeping with his view of the Pastorals Hanson offers no real discussion of why these pieces are separated and demonstrates little concern for larger structure at all. Second, Marshall breaks the verses into three units, though at different points from Hanson: 6–7, 8–12, 13–14.[17] However, it is apparent that he does not see these as strong breaks since he can also write, '1.3–14 flows smoothly without any noticeable break.'[18] Indeed, he refers to vv. 6–8 as 'the appeal' of the larger section, expressing unity between 6–7 and 8–12.[19] The greatest distinction he makes is between

12. So also Mounce 2000: 475, 'V 6 grows out of vv 3–5, but a break is suggested here after v 5 because in v 6 Paul starts to encourage Timothy explicitly.'
13. Cf. Marshall 1999: 34, n.46.
14. Grounds for this will be discussed in the next section.
15. E.g., Oberlinner, Mounce, Knight, Fee, Bassler, Bernard.
16. Most notably Marshall (6–7, 8–12, 13–14) and Quinn and Wacker (6–12, 13–14).
17. Marshall 1999: 38.
18. Marshall 1999: 36.
19. Marshall 1999: 34.

13–14 and what precedes, saying that vv. 13–14 have a different theme from vv. 6–8, though vv. 13–14 are related to v. 7 and vv. 11f.[20] Third, Quinn and Wacker divide 1.6–14 into two pieces by separating off vv. 13–14. No explicit justification for this division is given. The outline given labels vv. 6–12 as 'The Present' and vv. 13–14 as 'The Future,' but the basis for such a distinction is neither obvious nor stated.[21] Among these three only Hanson suggests any lack of cohesion between the verses. For Marshall and Quinn and Wacker the only issue is whether or not vv. 13–14 should be combined with this unit, without suggesting incoherence.

The second, and more drastic, challenge to the cohesion of this unit is stated most thoroughly by Miller who suggests that various pieces of the unit are incongruous with each other. Of 1.6–14 Miller writes:

> One looks in vain for any sustained development of thought; the material is constantly disrupted by changing subject matter, variations in literary style, and the presence of seemingly unnecessary expressions. In short it reads poorly as a literary unit.[22]

As a result Miller suggests 1.6–14 is composed of the following independent bits: 6, 7, 8, 9–10, 11, 12a, 12b–14.

In order to address these challenges attention will first be given to the cohesion shift analysis of the unit. This analysis shows some points of shifting which could support division of 1.6–14. These will be considered in light of other cohesive features. This discussion will connect directly with the division suggested by Marshall and Quinn and Wacker. Following this, Miller's specific objections will be considered.

It must first be noted that the cohesion shift analysis does indicate some points of significant shift in cohesion fields within this unit which could suggest it should be broken into five separate units: 6–7, 8, 9–10, 11–12, 13–14. Each potential break will be taken up in order.

While 1.6–7 continues with the first person singular and third person singular indicatives which have occurred already in the letter, 1.8 shifts to second person singular and imperative for the first time in the letter. At first sight this appears to be a significant shift, and would confirm one of Miller's divisions. Miller gives no evidence for this break but simply isolates 1.8 as a 'traditional admonition.'[23] However, semantically v. 8 fits with 1.6–7 as a

---

20.   Marshall 1999: 35.

21.   Quinn and Wacker 2000: 565. This may be connected with later comments which distinguish between the imperatives of v. 8 and v. 12 because the former is aorist tense and the latter is present tense. If this is their intent (and it is not clear that it is), this will not hold for at least two reasons. First, the aorist imperative in 1.8 followed an exhortation in 1.6 built on present verbs. Second, though the imperative in 13 is present, the one in 14 is aorist.

22.   Miller 1997: 100.

23.   Miller 1997: 103.

continuation of the exhortation. While 1.6 does not contain an imperative, the verb construction (a first person singular verb of reminder with an infinitive) is used as an exhortation just as the imperatives in 1.8.[24] Similarly, though the verbs shift from first singular to second singular, this is due to the use of differing verbal constructions both of which result in Paul exhorting Timothy. Thus, 1.6–8 hold together directions from Paul to Timothy concerning Timothy's work. Lastly, there is a lexical and thematic link which binds the exhortation of v. 8 to the exhortation of vv. 6–7. Both exhortations are buttressed by a reference to the power (δύναμις, v. 7 and v. 8) which God provides. This connection is even stronger if, as several scholars argue, the power of God in v. 8 is an intentional restatement of 'the Spirit of power' in v. 7.[25] Thus, 1.6–8 hold together as parallel exhortations to faithfulness rooted in the power of God mediated by his Spirit.

The next significant shift occurs between v. 8 and v. 9. 1.9–10 stand out in the cohesion shift analysis not because they differ radically from the preceding material but because of the high level of homogeneity within. The six verbs are all aorist singular participles arranged in a symmetrical pattern: two genitive masculine singular, two accusative feminine singular, two genitive masculine singular. The subject throughout is deity or his plans. The verses are a distinctly doctrinal statement. These features could suggest the possibility of isolating vv. 9–10, which would coincide with breaks suggested by Hanson and Miller. Miller also adds that vv. 9–10 have a 'flowing, hymn-like' style, different from the preceding verses and that certain parts of vv. 9–10 are unnecessary to the context.

However, there are significant cohesive links between vv. 6–8 and vv. 9–10. First, and most basically, vv. 9–10 are connected grammatically to v. 8 in a proper manner. This grammatical connection is further supported by an inclusio created by the occurrence of εὐαγγέλιον in v. 8 introducing vv. 9–10 and again as the very last word in v. 10.[26] This connection is also logical as vv. 9–10 provide an exposition of the gospel for which Timothy is to suffer,[27] as well as a depiction of the sovereign and powerful acts of the God who is expected to give the power necessary for endurance.[28]

---

24. Marshall 1999: 695 says v. 6 is 'in effect a command.' On 696, he says the verb 'remind' is used here as 'a means of admonition.' Cf. also Wolter 1988: 215–16; Mounce 2000: 477; Bassler 1996: 129.

25. Marshall 1999: 704 says the reference of 'the power of God' in v. 8 'is clearly to the Spirit who gives power.' Quinn and Wacker 2000: 596 say 'the reference must be to the spirit of power,' referring to v. 6. So also, Fee 1994: 798–90, and Mounce 2000: 480.

26. Wolter 1988: 216, also notes the connection created by this repetition.

27. Towner 1989: 94 identifies 1.9–10 as a 'capsule summary of the gospel of salvation.'

28. Cf. Bassler 1996: 134, who writes that vv. 9–10 supports the preceding discussion 'by presenting the gospel as a demonstration of God's power. This power, revealed in both the manifestation of grace and the abolition of death, is the ultimate ground for confidence.' See also Lau 1996: 115; Lock 1924: 86.

Thus, the content of vv. 9–10 seems to fit the context quite well in spite of the criticisms of Miller and Dibelius and Conzelmann.[29] Dibelius and Conzelmann fail to mention any specific portion which does not fit the context and Miller only mentions 'before eternal ages.' Yet this reference to the eternal plan of God and other vaulted language only serve to further highlight the awesomeness of God who will provide power and the glory of the gospel for which Timothy is to suffer. Indeed, Mounce is correct to conclude, 'Vv 9–10 fit the context perfectly.'[30]

In this logical connection, vv. 9–10 seem to function as a ground for the exhortation in v. 8.[31] This creates a parallel between vv. 6–7 and vv. 8–10. 1.6–7 is an exhortation grounded in what God has given. 1.8–10 is an exhortation grounded in what God has done, with the ground in both instances referring to the power of God, as was mentioned above. These previous references to the work of God (θεός, vv. 6, 7, 8) prepare the reader for the longer discussion of God's work in vv. 9–10. Thus, the topic of vv. 9–10 does not protrude unseemingly from the flow of thought in vv. 6–8.

Additionally, on the level of participant structure, 1.7–10 are held together by a significant cluster of first person plural referents. Of the nine occurrences of ἡμεῖς in the letter, six occur in 1.7–10 with no occurrences for several verses preceding or following.[32] These verses represent the most significant clustering of the first person plural pronoun in the letter and the second largest significant cluster of first person plural referents in general.[33] This creates a connection between these verses as they discuss issues common to both Paul and Timothy and presumably the broader Christian community. This connects as well to the previous discussion of the concern with the work of God as many of the first person plural referents are used to discuss 'us' as the recipients of God's action (e.g., 1.7, 9 [2x]). Also, the mention of Paul as God's agent in this gospel connects with the reference to Paul in v. 8 as God's servant.

Lastly, it is often noted that 1.9–10 exhibit parallelism which is thought to be common in liturgical fragments, and this is used to suggest 1.9–10 stand out from the surrounding context. Parallelism is certainly evident in

---

29.   Towner 1989: 100 concludes his investigation of 1.9–10 by saying 'the traditional material appears to have been carefully chosen (or composed), in this case, in explication of the pregnant concept of *dynamis theou* (v. 8) inserted to motivate Timothy to participate in the preaching ministry ...'

30.   Mounce 2000: 475. Cf. also Marshall 1999: 701; Läger 1996: 67; Lau 1996: 114.

31.   Since 1.9–10 function as a ground for v. 8, it is not surprising that, as Miller states, 'the admonition of 1.8 gives way to a flowing hymn-like passage' (1997: 103). The admonition gives way to basis and it is entirely logical to present a creedal sort of statement in order to give a theological basis for an exhortation.

32.   Prior to 1.7 there is only one other occurrence (1.2) and following 1.10 the next occurrence is 1.14. Following 1.14 there is not another first person plural referent until 2.11.

33.   The largest is 2.11–13 where there are seven referents, six of which are verbs.

vv. 9–10 ('not according to our works but according to his plan and grace'; 'He gave us ... before eternity but now revealed'; 'destroying death but bringing to light life and immortality'). However, it must also be noted that this pattern of parallelism is not foreign to the context but has already begun in vv. 7–8 (spirit not of timidity but of power; do not be ashamed but suffer).[34]

Thus, while vv. 9–10 do have their own unique status, they function as a part of the preceding argument being connected grammatically, logically, stylistically, and in participant structure.

The next significant shift occurs at 1.11, which is to be expected following the tight cohesion of vv. 9–10. In vv. 11–12 there is a return to finite verb forms, indicative rather than imperative (the mood of the last finite verb, v. 8), and there is a return to a first person singular subject which has not occurred since 1.6. Of the eight verbs in vv. 11–12, six are indicative first person singular. Of the verbs, Paul is the subject of six and God is the subject of the other two acting in reference to Paul. A division here would correspond with the arrangements of Hanson and Miller.

In spite of these shifts, a number of factors show that vv. 11–12 should be connected with the preceding verses. First, 1.11 is syntactically linked to v. 10. The relative pronoun, ὅ, clearly refers back to εὐαγγέλιον, in v. 10. The mention of the gospel prompts a statement connecting it with the work of Paul as is common in the Pastorals (e.g., 1 Tim. 1.11; 2.7; Tit. 1.3). This tag is also sensible in the flow of thought of 2 Timothy 1. Throughout this unit, the work of God has been linked to Paul. In 1.6 the gift of God is within Timothy by the laying on of Paul's hands. In v. 8 Timothy is not to be ashamed of the Lord or of Paul. Instead Timothy is to suffer for the gospel (vv. 8–10), and v. 11 then identifies this gospel with Paul again. This answers the objection of Miller and others that the statement in v. 11 would be unnecessary for Timothy.[35] 1.11 does not function to present new, previously unknown information but fits a larger pattern in the larger passage of connecting the proper message with Paul. Thus, while there are shifts in cohesion fields at v. 11, the grammar and logic connect it to the preceding verses. It may be then that the shifts in cohesion fields serve to introduce v. 12 with its heavy concentration on Paul. The first person

---

34.   Mounce 2000: 475. The pattern of the words used is as follows:

   7 οὐ + verb + ἀλλὰ

   8 μή + verb + ἀλλὰ

   9 οὐ κατὰ ἀλλὰ κατὰ

   9–10 δὲ νῦν

   10 μὲν δὲ

The occurrences in vv. 7, 8, 9, represent the only three uses of the 'not this but that' formula in Ch. 1.

35.   Miller 1997: 103–104; Easton 1947: 44.

singular was absent from vv. 9–10, so v. 11 reintroduces it to prepare for v.
12 where it occurs six times (one of the largest such clusters in the letter).[36]
1.11 then functions as a hinge, connected grammatically and logically with
vv. 8–10 but connected by cohesion fields with v. 12.[37]

From what has just been argued, 1.12 is connected to 1.6–11 by the
hinge in v. 11, but such a hinge could create a link to a new unit rather than
a continuation of the same unit. Lexical and thematic repetition show that
1.12 is strongly connected with the preceding material. First, v. 12 mirrors
v. 8 with Paul serving as the example for Timothy. The two key verbs in v.
8 and v. 12 are related (lexically and semantically) and occur in chiastic
order. Timothy is urged not to be ashamed (ἐπαισχύνομαι) but to 'suffer
with' Paul (συγκακοπαθέω) for the gospel, and Paul suffers (πάσχω) in his
role of proclaiming the gospel and is not ashamed (ἐπαισχύνομαι).[38] Thus, v.
12 returns to Paul specifically to portray him as already doing what he
urges Timothy to do. 1.12 is then still connected logically with the
exhortation in v. 8, serving as further grounds for the exhortation. The
parallelism also envelopes the doctrinal statement in vv. 9–11 further
affirming the inclusion of these verses. There is then no basis for Miller's
division between 1.12b and the preceding material. Further, just as the
charges to Timothy in v. 6 and v. 8 are grounded in a statement about God
and his power (δύναμις), so Paul's statement about his experience is
grounded in a statement about God with particular reference to his power
(δυνατός). These three occurrences of the δυν- root are the only occurrences
in 2 Timothy 1. This binds v. 12 not only with the exhortation in v. 8 which
it supports but also with v. 6. 1.12 is further connected with v. 6 by its
repetition of δι' ἥν αἰτίαν, which only occurs in these two places in the
letter.[39] The symmetry and lexical repetition can be set out as follows:

v. 6 – δι' ἥν αἰτίαν
    οὐ γὰρ ἔδωκεν ἡμῖν ὁ θεὸς πνεῦμα ... δυνάμεως

v. 8 – οὖν
(A) μὴ ἐπαισχυνθῇς τὸ μαρτύριον τοῦ κυρίου ἡμῶν μηδὲ ἐμὲ τὸν δέσμιον αὐτοῦ

36. Quinn and Wacker 2000: 602 also note that v. 11 reintroduces the first person singular.
37. Mounce 2000: 486, though not mentioning participant structure, writes, 'V 11 not only looks backward but also forward to v 12.' Cf. also Fee 1988: 231.
38. Cf. Wolter 1988: 216. Quinn and Wacker 2000: 602, and Johnson 1996: 52; also note the verbal repetitions between v. 8 and v. 12.
39. Quinn and Wacker 2000: 602 also suggest the lexical repetitions between v. 12 and vv. 6, 8 suggest an 'inclusion.'

(B) ἀλλὰ συγκακοπάθησον τῷ εὐαγγελίῳ κατὰ δύναμιν θεοῦ

vv. 9–10 – statement of gospel closing with τοῦ εὐαγγελίου

   v. 11 – Paul's appointment

v. 12 – δι᾽ ἣν αἰτίαν
(B') καὶ ταῦτα πάσχω
(A') ἀλλ᾽ οὐκ ἐπαισχύνομαι
   οἶδα γὰρ ᾧ ... ὅτι δυνατός ἐστι

This layout shows the numerous lexical and thematic connections within 1.6–12. 1.6–12 coheres as two similar exhortations to service grounded in God with reference to his power. 1.12 specifically connects with v. 8 reiterating its main verbs while presenting Paul as the example for Timothy to follow.

The next significant shift in the cohesion shift analysis is at 1.13. Here the verbs return to second person singular imperatives and Timothy is the subject. Neither of these factors have occurred since 1.8. Both Quinn and Wacker and Marshall make a division between vv. 13–14 and what precedes. However, there is significant evidence for keeping vv. 13–14 with what precedes.

First, the last part of 1.12 introduced language of preservation (φυλάσσω) and of a deposit (παραθήκη) which is picked up in vv. 13–14. In 1.13 the context suggests ἔχω is used in the sense 'hold on to,' or 'maintain'; thus it is preservation language. Then, 1.14 uses the same verb as 1.12 (φυλάσσω), thus establishing not only a semantic but a lexical connection. Indeed v. 12 and v. 14 also use the same word for what is to be preserved, producing very similar phrases in both verses:

v. 12 – τὴν παραθήκην μου φυλάξαι
v. 14 – τὴν καλὴν παραθήκην φύλαξον

Thus, vv. 12–14 are held together by the idea of preservation and lexical repetition. Some scholars are troubled by the use of παραθήκη to refer to differing things. Indeed Miller suggests this difference in reference of παραθήκη may be 'the most significant indication' that v. 12 and v. 14 disagree with one another so much that they probably come from different sources.[40] However, if the word refers to different things in the two verses this only strengthens the case for the author intentionally stating his point in v. 12 in such a way as to prepare for vv. 13–14. The author employs a play on words: 'God is faithfully keeping what we have entrusted to him,

---

40. Miller 1997: 104–105. So also Falconer 1937: 78.

so we should in turn faithfully keep what he has entrusted to us.' In this way v. 12 holds vv. 6–11 and vv. 13–14 together. 1.12a repeats items from 1.6–8, and then 1.12b introduces the idea of God maintaining Paul's deposit. From this springs vv. 13–14 calling for Timothy to be faithful in maintaining God's deposit.

Second, 1.6–12 have been shown to be made up of two exhortations with supporting material. 1.13–14 continue in the genre of exhortation. In light of this, the return to second person imperatives in vv. 13–14 is not surprising. Imperatives were absent in vv. 9–12 because those verses were supporting material. 1.13–14 link back to 1.8 as the next exhortation. The unit, 1.6–14, is then a unit of exhortation resting on four specific exhortations to Timothy:[41]

1.6 – stir up your gift
1.8 – do not be ashamed but join in suffering
1.13 – keep the example of sound words
1.14 – guard the deposit

Though Marshall says 1.13–14 have a different topic, the four exhortations are linked, Marshall himself notes.[42] 1.6 and 1.8 call Timothy not to shrink back but to join the work in spite of the difficulty. 1.13–14 then state more specifically what the work is, or at least a specific part of the work. This connection can be seen in the fact that the objects of the exhortations are largely gospel oriented. In 1.8 Timothy is not to be ashamed of 'the testimony of our Lord,' but he is to suffer for the 'gospel.' In 1.13 what is to be kept is the 'standard of sound words,'[43] and in 1.14 what is to be guarded is the 'deposit' which most likely refers to the gospel. Thus these exhortations are united as appeals to Timothy to be faithful regarding the gospel.

Third, there seems to be a connection of thought between 1.6–7 and 1.14. The exhortations begin in v. 6 with a call to stir up the gift of God. Several scholars argue that v. 7 identifies this gift as the Holy Spirit.[44] If this is so, then vv. 6–7 call for readiness through the Spirit, the Spirit being the equipment necessary for ministry. 1.14 then closes the unit by stating once again that the work of preserving the truth must be done 'through the Holy Spirit.' Πνεῦμα occurs only once more in the letter (4.22) and there does not refer to the Holy Spirit. Thus, the entire unit of exhortations is

---

41. So also, Mounce 2000: 475.
42. Marshall 1999: 35.
43. Mounce 2000: 475 says the sound words of v. 13 are the gospel of vv. 9–10.
44. Marshall 1999: 698 says the gift referred to is clearly the Holy Spirit. Cf. also Fee 1994: 785–89.

bracketed by reminders of one's need of the Holy Spirit to carry them out.[45]

Taking 1.6–14 as a unit, then, other similarities in the exhortations can be seen. For instance, each exhortation is grounded in or connected to God. In 1.6–7 Timothy is to stir up his gift because God gave a certain type of Spirit. In 1.8 Timothy is to suffer according to the power of God. In 1.13 Timothy is to maintain the standard of sound words in the faith and love which are in Christ Jesus. This concerns more of the manner than the ground of the exhortation, but Timothy's expected activity is still connected to things which are found in the Godhead.[46] Lastly, in 1.14 Timothy's guarding is to be done 'through the Holy Spirit.' Each of these is linked to divine resources. Also all but one of the exhortations is tied to Paul as a source and example. The gift which is to be stirred up in v. 6 came from the laying on of Paul's hands. In 1.8 what Timothy is not to be ashamed of is not only the testimony of the Lord but also Paul himself. The exhortation of v. 8 is grounded in a statement of the gospel which is linked with Paul (v. 11). 1.12 presents Paul as a model for Timothy in obeying the exhortation of v. 8. In 1.13 the sound words which Timothy is to maintain are that which he heard from Paul. Only the charge in 1.14 is not explicitly tied to Paul though Paul is still in view in that verse since it refers to the Holy Spirit dwelling not simply 'in you' (Timothy) but 'in us.'

Before concluding the discussion of 1.6–14, one other critique of Miller's which was not addressed above must be answered. Miller characterizes 1.7 as a proverbial saying and isolates it from the rest of the unit. He notes that the γάρ suggests a link to 1.8, but he argues it is a loose link the legitimacy of which is disputed 'by a number of seemingly unmotivated changes in the mode of address.' He lists three such changes: (1) shift from personal admonition in v. 6 to a 'generalized, almost proverbial, character' in v. 7; (2) the three verbs of v. 6 are present tense and the verb in v. 7 is aorist tense; and (3) shift from second person singular to first person plural. However, these shifts are not significant and need cast no doubt on the connective function of γάρ. In fact the γάρ explains the shift from personal admonition to a generalized, proverbial statement, since γάρ introduces a basis or ground and a general truth would be a common choice for grounding an admonition. Regarding the shift in tenses, it is hard to base much on this alone since the tenses shift regularly within the letter. Of

---

45. Fee 1994: 787 also notes the connection though he does not develop it in terms of coherence. On the basis of this he does write, 'vv. 6–14 hold together as a single unit of appeal.' Mounce 2000: 477, 'Paul thus begins and ends (1.14) this paragraph on the same note: the role of the Holy Spirit in Timothy's life.' Cf. also Knight 1992: 382; Fee 1988: 225; Lau 1996: 127.

46. Mounce 2000: 489–90 also argues that 1.13 points to divine resources for carrying out the commands.

course one might suggest this shifting is further evidence of the piecemeal nature of 2 Timothy. However, similar examples can be found within the accepted Paulines. For example, Rom. 12.20 contains two present tense imperatives followed by γάρ and a future tense verb giving the basis. Romans 13.8 has a present tense imperative, γάρ, and a perfect tense verb providing the basis. Further examples could be given, for it is entirely sensible and common for an admonition and its basis to be presented in different time frames or in differing aspects.[47] Lastly, the shift from second person singular to first plural is neither surprising nor unmotivated. Gordon Fee has shown that such a shift is common in the accepted Paulines when an appeal or exhortation is followed by a theological basis.[48] For example, 1 Thess. 1.9–10 refers to 'how *you* turned to God from idols, to await his son Jesus, who delivers *us* from the coming wrath.' Also, 1 Cor. 15.1–3 refers to 'the gospel *you* believed, in which *you* stand; how that Christ died for *our* sins.' Again examples could be multiplied, but the point is clear.[49] Regardless of the authorship of 2 Timothy, the shift from 'you' to 'us' in this context is not surprising. Thus, these shifts which Miller notes, rather than disputing the connective function of γάρ, support it as they are found to be common in similar passages in other letters attributed to Paul.

Therefore, 1.6–14 should be considered as a single unit built on four exhortations concerning Timothy's work in being faithful to the Pauline gospel by dependence on divine resources. The recognition of symmetry, lexical repetition, and logical connections within the unit show that 1.6–14 hold together well as a logical unit.

1.15–18

Boundaries
There is widespread agreement among the commentaries that a new unit begins at 1.15. This is suggested by the presence of an epistolary disclosure formula at the opening of v. 15 (Οἶδας τοῦτο).[50] Significant shifts in cohesion fields also confirm this. Perhaps the most noticeable shift is the absence of the imperatives which formed the backbone of 1.6–14. This is indicative of a shift from exhortation to something more like a report. There is also a significant shift in the field of participants. The discussion so far in the

---

47. Simply in Romans cf. 1.19; 6.13–14. Examples which are similar but not as close include Rom. 2.11–12; 3.22–23. Time frame and aspect are both mentioned since this holds true regardless of how one views the function of verb tenses. Regarding time, it is sensible for a present exhortation to be grounded in a past event or a future promise. In an aspect approach, one reason for such a shift might be the foregrounding of the exhortation.

48. Fee 1994: 789.

49. Cf. also 1 Thess. 4.13–14; 1 Cor. 5.7–8; 2 Cor. 5.17–18; Gal. 4.6.

50. Quinn and Wacker 2000: 612 say the phrase is 'evidently transitional'.

letter has centered on Paul, Timothy, God, and Christ. 1.15–18 introduces a cluster of new participants: those in Asia, Phygelus, Hermogenes, and Onesiphorus. This is the first extended discussion of anyone other than Paul, Timothy, God, or Christ. As a result, third person singular referents, which occurred only four times in the previous 11 verses, now occur eight times in just four verses. Then, these referents disappear again in 2.1–3. By contrast Timothy recedes. Second person singular referents occur only twice and the first plural which occurred regularly in the previous section, even at the close of v. 14, do not occur at all in 1.15–18.[51] First singular referents continue through this unit as in the previous one. Thus, in this unit, the concern shifts from Timothy's engagement with Paul to the engagement of others with Paul.

Additionally, several scholars note a shift in style from 1.6–14 to 1.15–18.[52] These shifts are significant enough that the debate is not over whether there is a break at 1.15 but whether there is any connection. Basis for connection will be discussed in the next chapter.

Cohesion
There is little contention against the cohesion within 1.15–18. The only concerns seem to be whether the wish in v. 18a protrudes from the argument and/or whether v. 18b is an unnecessary tag. These will be addressed in assessing the cohesive elements in the unit.

It can first be noted that the unit both opens and closes with the statement 'You know,' establishing things as well known to Timothy.[53] Though different verbs are used in these two statements, these are the only two second person singular verbs in the unit, indeed the only second person referents of any kind. This serves to bracket the discussion of 'third parties' within the framework of address to Timothy. Also these statements concerning Timothy's knowledge are both placed within Timothy's geographical area ('in Asia,' 'in Ephesus'). Sandwiched between them will be a report from Paul's location.[54] So, there is, first, an inclusio around the unit.

Next, v. 15 and v. 16 are connected by way of contrast. Those in Asia abandoned Paul but Onesiphorus was not ashamed of Paul's chains and sought him out. The discussion of Onesiphorus is then bracketed by two prayer wishes which use very similar language:

v. 16 – δῴη ἔλεος ὁ κύριος τῷ Ὀνσιφόρου οἴκῳ
v. 18 – δῴη αὐτῷ ὁ κύριος εὑρεῖν ἔλεος

51. In fact first person plural referents do not occur again until 2.11.
52. Quinn and Wacker 2000: 611; Bassler 1996: 135–36; Fee 1988: 235.
53. Johnson 1978: 8, n. 30, also notes the framing function of these two verbs. He suggests they emphasize a note of urgency.
54. Quinn and Wacker 2000: 612.

The similarities are striking as the verb and subject are identical lexically and positionally. The repetition of the optative verb is all the more striking since this mood is so rare in general and occurs only once more in the letter (4.16). In both instances here the direct object is ἔλεος and the recipient is at least linked to Onesiphorus. These two verses are also distinct in being the first three times in the letter that κύριος is used absolutely (a feature unique to 2 Timothy in the Pastoral Epistles). Thus a significant inclusio holds vv. 16–18 together.

The new element in the wish in v. 18 is εὑρεῖν. This links back to v. 17 where εὑρίσκω occurs for the only other time in the letter and is in the aorist tense just as the occurrence in v. 18. It is likely that the wish in v. 16 has been intentionally modified to include εὑρεῖν in order to make a play on words: Onesiphorus sought and found me, so may he also find mercy from the Lord.[55]

In conclusion, 1.15–18 is held together by several well-used cohesive factors. From a linear perspective 1.15 connects with 1.16–17 as contrasts. Those in Asia, like Phygelus and Hermogenes, have abandoned Paul but Onesiphorus has been faithful. 1.16–17 then connect with 1.18 by a play on the verb εὑρίσκω. Bracketing this are two inclusios. 1.16 and 1.18a contain highly similar optative wishes and envelope the discussion of Onesiphorus. 1.15 and 1.18 both contain 'you know' statements with the only two second person singular verbs in the unit. This envelops the entire discussion of contrasting responses to Paul's imprisonment. The cohesion of the unit could be represented as follows:

'You know ... abandonment ... in Asia'
    Specific unfaithfuls: Phygelus & Hermogenes
  Specific faithful: Onesiphorus
    Wish: The Lord grant mercy to household of Onesiphorus
      He was not ashamed, but found Paul

    Wish: The Lord grant Onesiphorus to find mercy
'You know ... faithfulness ... in Ephesus'

2.1–13

Boundaries

That a new unit begins at 2.1 is widely accepted, and there is good reason for this. The opening of the verse with the emphatic Σὺ οὖν τέκνον μου clearly signals a transition.[56] Direct personal address, particularly

---

55. Similarly Quinn and Wacker 2000: 616; Marshall 1999: 721; Mounce 2000: 496.
56. Merkel 1991: 62 calls this a 'geläufigen Übergangswendung.'

vocatives, was commonly used to mark epistolary transitions. The placement of σύ at the very beginning of the sentence also clearly marks a return to a focus on Timothy after he had been less prominent in 1.15–18. As the second person singular referents return to prominence, the third singular disappears in 2.1–3 and there are no new proper names as there were in 1.15–18. The relational setting is now back to Paul and Timothy. The genre also shifts back to exhortation with the appearance of a string of imperatives which have not occurred since 1.14.

While the beginning of the new unit is clear, the ending is disputed. Commentators are divided as to whether the unit closes at 2.7 or continues all the way to 2.13.[57] Most of those who end the unit at 2.7 consider 2.8–13 to be a theological basis for 2.1–7, and therefore hold 2.1–13 together at a higher level. In this case there is little difference between considering 2.1–13 as one unit or as two closely related units functionally dependent upon each other. Additionally, there do not appear to be any significant shifts in cohesion fields between 2.7 and 2.8, nor are there any traditional transitional markers. Instead, 2.8 continues with a second person singular imperative just like 2.7 and the preceding ones in vv. 1, 2, and 3. The genre of exhortation continues with Paul exhorting Timothy in the light of or concerning Jesus Christ (vv. 1, 3, 7 [ὁ κύριος], 8, 10). Therefore in the absence of clear indications to the contrary, 2.1–13 will be considered as one unit here. The parallels between 1.6–14 and 2.1–13 considered in the next chapter further support this decision.

The chief objection to considering 2.1–13 as a unit comes from Oberlinner. Oberlinner argues that, although the motif of suffering is present in 2.1–7 and 2.8–13, it is handled differently in both sections.[58] Oberlinner has three main objections: (1) in vv. 8–13 it is Paul alone who suffers, (2) the suffering in v. 9 is different and more serious than the suffering in v. 3, and (3) vv. 1–7 are dominated by parenesis but vv. 8–13 are dominated by confession. However, these objections are not weighty. It is no problem that the suffering in 2.8–13 involves only Paul and seems more serious. As in 1.8–12, the call for Timothy to share in suffering (1.8; 2.3) is followed by the statement that Paul is already suffering (1.12; 2.9). Thus, Paul serves as Timothy's example. The analogy of 1.8–12 (which Oberlinner sees as belonging to the same unit) provides a precedent for the present unit. Secondly, if Paul's suffering is greater, then this only strengthens the example as Paul is already suffering even more than that to which he is calling Timothy. Third, the separation between the parenesis

---

57. Those who end the unit at 2.7 include Marshall, Oberlinner, Knight, Fee, Bassler, and Hanson. Those who end the unit at 2.13 include Mounce, Quinn and Wacker, Merkel, Brox, and Dibelius and Conzelmann. Miller also considers 2.1–13 together.

58. Oberlinner 1995: 75.

and confession is unnecessary since confession also occurred in the midst of 1.6–14 and there as here (it seems) served as a basis for the parenesis.[59] Thus, while there are some differences, they are only such as would fit in the flow of the argument.

Cohesion

The cohesion of 2.1–13 has been questioned at several points and these will need to be addressed one at a time. First, the cohesion shift analysis shows two pieces which stand out from the rest of the unit: 2.4–6 and 2.11–13. Miller and others also isolate these pieces. 2.4–6 contain proverbial statements rather than the explicit exhortation seen in vv. 1–3. 2.4–6 also shift to entirely third person singular in contrast to 2.1–3 which is dominated by second person singular and had no occurrences of third person singular. First and second person singular disappear from 2.4–6 though they appear in vv. 1–3 and 7. Thus, Paul and Timothy are replaced as participants by a general (thus proverbial) third person. There is clearly a shift here. However, there are other factors which integrate 2.4–6 into the section. The first proverbial statement (v. 4) is clearly linked to the preceding exhortation (v. 3) by lexical repetition: στρατιώτης (v. 3), στρατευόμενος (v. 4), στρατολογήσαντι (v. 4). Being a 'good soldier of Christ Jesus' (v. 3) involves pleasing one's commanding officer which v. 4 explains. Additionally, it has been shown that in the Hellenistic world there was an immediate association of the soldier with suffering, misunderstanding, and mockery.[60] Therefore there is a ready conceptual link between the call to suffer and the use of a soldier as an illustration. The following two statements do not have such a conceptual link so they are introduced with a conjunctive phrase (δὲ καὶ). Also, all three of these metaphors (soldier, athlete, farmer) were typical illustrations in Hellenistic moral teaching.[61] And, while the specific point of each statement may be different from the other, each one involves hard work and endurance. Thus, their use here in a call to suffering and endurance makes sense. Miller finds it suspicious that there is no explicit Christian element in the statements. However, there is no reason a Christian author could not take up common metaphors for his argument without needing to make the metaphors explicitly Christian. The Christian element is found in the exhortation not necessarily in its supporting metaphors. Lastly, it is true that the proverbial statements show up suddenly and without much explanation. However, the call to consider further these sayings in v. 7

---

59. Note also Marshall's disagreement with Oberlinner on this point (1999: 732).

60. Quinn and Wacker 2000: 637; Pfitzner 1967: 169.

61. Marshall 1999: 728 cites for example Epictetus 3.15, 24; 4.8. So also Bassler 1996: 140; Johnson 1996: 62–63.

suggests an author aware of the fact that all the connections have not been spelled out.

This leads to a discussion of 2.7, which Miller finds 'puzzling' and isolates as an independent saying. He says the function of 2.7a is 'not easy to determine.'[62] However, if one takes the ὅ as referring backwards, which is most likely, then it is altogether reasonable to call for a reader to ponder proverbial statements. In doing so with a second person singular imperative, the author returns to the Paul-Timothy exhortatory interaction which provides the main framework for the unit. The γάρ clause then provides encouragement for such thinking. Thus, 2.7 rounds out the use of the proverbial statements. Also, by return to a second person singular imperative, the use of cognitive language, and mention of Jesus (ὁ κύριος), 2.7 provides a transition to the fresh imperative of 2.8. All three of these elements had been absent since v. 3 but occur again in 2.8. The cognitive language (νοέω, v. 7; σύνεσις, v. 7; μνημονεύω, v. 8) is especially interesting since it has not occurred previously in the unit. Thus, 2.7 seems to function very well in the unit, concluding the proverbial illustrations and transitioning to the new imperative.

The next point of contention is 2.8. Miller and Läger, among recent works, argue that 2.8 contains elements unmotivated by the context.[63] Miller suggests the reference to 'seed of David' is 'irrelevant to the present context,' and Läger also says the reference to the resurrection is unmotivated. Additionally, Miller says the gospel summary in general is surprising at this point in the discourse. In response, it could first be noted that the gospel message has already been closely linked with the call to suffer in this unit and previously in the letter. In 2.3, the call to be strong is linked with passing on the message heard from Paul (2.3) and in 1.6–14 there is a strong link between suffering and the gospel (1.8, 12, 13–14). Therefore, it is not surprising that following the call to endurance in 2.1–7 there comes an exhortation to bear in mind the key aspects of the message. 'Jesus Christ' who has been in the background as the source of Timothy's strength (2.1) and the one he serves as a soldier (2.3–4), now comes to the fore as the core of the message and in all likelihood an example to follow. Thus, the gospel statement is not surprising here. Secondly, a reference to Jesus' resurrection is entirely logical within a unit which calls on Timothy to suffer. Jesus suffered even to the point of death but was victorious over death. This one who rose from the dead is also the one who will provide strength for Timothy (2.1).[64] This note of eschatological victory is part of a

---

62. Miller 1997: 108–109.
63. Miller 1997: 109; Läger 1996: 73.
64. So similarly Mounce 2000: 512; Fee 1988: 246. The resurrection of Jesus is used elsewhere in early Christian writings as encouragement to endurance (e.g. Rev. 2.8–11).

motif which runs through the unit. Both the athlete and farmer metaphors (2.4–5) explicitly mention future reward as a motivation. Likewise the motivation for Paul's endurance in 2.10 is the eschatological reward of the salvation of the elect; and the main point of the faithful saying of 2.11b–13 is eschatological reward or punishment. Thus the mention of Christ's resurrection in 2.8 is firmly entrenched in an important motif which binds the unit together.

The reference to 'seed of David' is not as clearly related to a major motif, though a number of broader theological connections are possible.[65] However, those who dismiss this statement as unrelated to the context fail to take adequate account of the connections between vv. 8–10 and vv. 11b–12a. 2.11b states that if one dies with Christ, he will also live with Christ. This mirrors the reference to Christ rising from the dead in 2.8. 2.11a then refers to reigning with Christ, which connects with the royal imagery of 'seed of David' in 2.8. This reigning comes after enduring (ὑπομένω; 2.12) which is what Paul says he in fact is doing in 2.10 (ὑπομένω).

vv. 8–10	vv. 11–12
Raised from dead	Die and live
ὑπομένω	ὑπομένω
Seed of David	Reign

Thus the statements of Christ's resurrection and kingship in 2.8 prepare the way for the reference to people sharing in that resurrection and reigning in 2.11a–12b.[66] These connections not only show how the Christological statements of 2.8 fit but also connect the two 'confessional' statements and thereby the unit.[67] This directly contradicts Läger's skepticism about the connection between the two statements.[68]

The previous discussion leads to a discussion of vv. 11b–13, which stand out in the cohesion shift analysis. It is evident that these verses have an identity of their own. Their structure with four brief conditional statements in a row suggests this immediately. Additionally there is a significant shift in the participant structure. First person singular referents disappear after occurring once in each verse in vv. 7–9. Inversely, first person plural

---

65. See, e.g. Mounce 2000: 512; Lau 1996: 144–49.

66. Wolter 1988: 216 also makes this point concerning Jesus and the resurrection. Knight, 401, and Marshall, 739, note the possibility that v.8 might be paraphrasing vv.11bf. but do not make any specific connections between the verses. Knight attributes the idea of v.8 as a preparatory paraphrase to Spicq, but does not cite where Spicq says this. I was unable to find any such discussion in Spicq's commentary.

67. 'Seed of David' and the resurrection are also used together in explaining the gospel in Rom. 1.3–4.

68. Läger 1996: 73.

predominates in vv. 11b–13 which contain the first occurrences of first person plural verbs in the letter. All of this contributes the sense that 2.11b–13 is in some sense a self-contained unit. However, this is not a surprise as it is suggested by the introduction of these verses as a 'faithful saying.'[69] Miller argues that since vv. 11b–13 have a self-contained identity, they must have been a preformed piece and therefore do not fit with the rest of the unit. However, whether or not this is taken up as a preformed piece says nothing about the coherence of the unit. The issue is whether or not this piece fits with the rest of the unit. As just noted above, 2.8–10 introduces some of the key concepts found in vv. 11b–12a. This suggests cohesion. Additionally it was noted that there is a motif of eschatological reward earlier in the unit which reaches its climax in vv. 11b–13. The whole theme of perseverance is admirably summed up in its pronouncement of blessing on endurance and cursing on denial. Indeed vv. 8–10 and vv. 11–13 are connected by the only two occurrences of ὑπομένω in the entire letter. Additionally, key themes from vv. 8–10 find counterparts in vv. 11–13 such as death/suffering, endurance/faithfulness, and live/salvation. As Towner has noted, the placement of the faithful saying after the reference to salvation suggests the saying is an exposition of that salvation.[70] 2.10 refers to Paul looking to the future and final salvation of the elect. That the reference is to final salvation and not simply to initial acceptance of the message is indicated by the phrase μετὰ δόξης αἰωνίου. Paul has in mind the final state of glory which is the culmination of salvation. This is further suggested by the use of τυγχάνω which is used by other NT writers to refer to final salvation (Luke 20.35; Heb. 11.35).[71] This concern for final salvation is the key issue then in 2.11b–13. As the desired salvation in v. 10 is accompanied with 'eternal glory,' so the faithful will reign with Christ. As the salvation in v. 10 is 'in Christ Jesus,' so in vv. 11f. the συν-prefixed verbs show that the dying, living, and reigning are all with Christ. The faithful saying is then a logical continuation of the preceding discussion.

Thus, 2.1–13 cohere as a unit. The semi-independent pieces are integrated into the whole and the perceived breaks of Miller and others have been answered. The whole unit has also been shown to cohere around certain motifs like eschatological reward and endurance. The endurance is also connected with a furtherance of the gospel. In 2.1–2 the call to be

---

69. There is now wide-ranging agreement that πιστὸς ὁ λόγος refers to what follows rather than to what precedes (so, for example, among recent commentators Marshall 1999: 739; Quinn and Wacker 2000: 648–49; Mounce 2000: 501; Bassler 1996: 143–44; Knight 1992: 400–402. See Knight for a listing of proponents of both sides). This conclusion is buttressed by the elements noted above which unite 11b–13 but distinguish it from the preceding material.

70. Towner 1989: 103–104.

71. Marshall 1999: 738. The other NT uses of the word do not refer to salvation.

strong is connected with the call to pass on the Pauline message (ἃ ἤκουσας παρ' ἐμοῦ). Similarly, the statement of Paul's endurance in 2.10 is connected with the desire for others to obtain salvation. The relational matrix throughout is Timothy, Paul, and Jesus. Each exhortation is directed to Timothy and is then connected with Paul, Jesus or both as the following table shows.

v. 1 – Be strong	in Christ Jesus	
v. 2 – Entrust		what you heard from me
v. 3 – Suffer	as a good soldier of Christ Jesus	with (me)
v. 7 – Consider	Lord will give understanding	what I say
v. 8 – Remember	Jesus Christ	according to my gospel

2.14–26

Boundaries

While 2.14 continues the exhortation based on second person singular imperatives which has been common in the letter so far, there are a number of indications that suggest a new unit begins here. The primary indication is the shift in participants. This can be seen in the first verb of 2.14. While ὑπομιμνῄσκω connects with the 'remembrance' language in the previous portion of the letter, there is a shift in who is to remember. In 2.8, the most recent occurrence of the 'remember' motif, it is Timothy who is to remember. Now, in 2.14, Timothy is to remind the congregation.[72] This is a significant shift since the letter so far has been almost entirely concerned with Timothy personally (the exceptions being 1.15–18; 2.2).[73] This shift can also be seen in the use of ἀκούω. This verb has occurred twice previously (1.13; 2.2), both times of Timothy learning from Paul. In 2.14 it refers to the congregation under Timothy's care. Also, first person referents disappear completely from 2.14–26. First person singular has been prominent in every unit to this point, and first plural dominated at the

---

72. There is exegetical debate on this issue. Although the majority of commentators interpret the verse as I have done above, some argue that in 2.14 Timothy is being urged to remind himself (e.g., Quinn and Wacker 2000: 672). This argument is based primarily on the lack of any stated direct object. However, the inclusion of a call to warn solemnly strongly suggests this verse has in view Timothy's interaction with the congregation.

73. Marshall 1999: 745 notes that the section begins with attention to what Timothy is to teach the church and that this is 'almost unique in this letter, concerned as it is more with Timothy's own behaviour.' So similarly Bassler 1996: 150; Knight 1992: 409.

close of the previous unit (2.11–13). From 2.14 to 2.26, then, first person referents are conspicuous in their absence.[74] Corresponding to the disappearance of first person is a significant increase in the occurrence of third person plural. In 1.1–2.13 there are only three occurrences of the third person plural,[75] but there are five such occurrences in 2.14–26 (vv. 16, 18 [2x], 23, 26). Each of these third plural referents in 2.14–26 refers in some way to some opponents. Thus, at 2.14 there is a shift in the participant fields or relational matrix from interaction between Paul and Timothy to the interaction between Timothy and the opponents.

The mention of opposition also points to a shift which occurs at 2.14. 2.14–26 contains the first explicit references to doctrinal error. Some opposition is implied by the calls to suffer in 1.6–2.13 and 1.15 mentions a desertion from Paul, but explicit opposition within the congregation occurs for the first time in this unit.[76]

For these reasons, 2.14 will be regarded as beginning a new unit, in line with the almost universal conclusion among the commentaries. This unit seems to end at 2.26 as 3.1 opens with a disclosure phrase and a new vice list. The shifts at 3.1 will be considered in more detail below.

Cohesion

While most commentators agree in grouping 2.14–26 together, they are often not clear on how or if these verses cohere. Miller despairs of finding the logical progression in the passage, and Houlden says the passage 'at first sight seems to lapse into a somewhat random collection of moral recommendations.'[77] Before examining connections between each verse, it will be helpful to consider the movement of the unit as a whole.

There are two key factors of the structure of this unit which have been noted by scholars. First, this unit, like many of those previous in the letter, is built on a series of second person singular imperatives.[78] Second, the unit moves in contrasts between positive and negative.[79] These contrasts occur at a number of levels and between various elements, but it will be helpful

---

74. First plural never occurs again in the letter. First singular occurs again at 3.10.

75. 1.15; 2.2, 10.

76. Oberlinner 1995: 91 says conflict with false teachers is already the theme in 2.8–10, but that is in no way clear or certain. His position seems to be dependent on his understanding of the situation behind the letter. Nothing is stated explicitly to confirm this. Though Oberlinner points to Paul's suffering and being in chains, nothing at least on the surface of the text suggests it is the false teachers who are responsible for his chains.

77. Miller 1997: 111; Houlden 1976: 120. Marshall 1999: 743, admits that the unit may at first seem disordered.

78. So also Marshall 1999: 743; Mounce 2000: 523; Bassler 1996: 149.

79. So also Mounce 2000: 523; Bassler 1996: 149; Karris 1979: 25; Johnson 1996: 72, who says this is 'classically paraenetic.'

first to note how the entire unit moves back and forth between the positive things to be sought and the negatives to be avoided.

Good	Bad
14 – remind these things	14 – [avoid] *word quarrels* → useless, destroys hearers
15 – seek divine approval • unashamed worker • right handling of *word* of *truth*	

	16 – [avoid] worldly foolish talk → more ungodliness
	 17 – their *word* spreads like gangrene
	     • 18 – stray from *truth*
	     • upset people's *faith*
	 19 – refrain from *unrighteousness* those who name the name of the Lord

21 – cleanse self-honor, set apart, useful, prepared	
22 – pursue *righteousness, faith* with those who call upon the Lord	22 – flee youthful desires
	23 – [avoid] foolish & ignorant speculations → *quarrels*
24 – must be gentle, able to teach, patient, correcting in gentleness • repentance unto knowledge of *truth* • freedom from devil	24 – must not be *quarrelsome*

This table shows first that two motifs (proper belief and behavior, and improper belief and behavior) run throughout the unit. Repetitions within each motif serve to unite them. On the negative side the μαχ- root occurs three times as quarrels are clearly associated with the opponents and are characterized as bad (vv. 14, 23, 24). In fact the exhortations to avoid evil begin with λογομαχεῖν (2.14) and end with οὐ δεῖ μάχεσθαι (2.24). In between these two exhortations there is also a chain of verbs used for 'avoiding' sin: περιΐστημι (v. 16), ἀφίστημι (v. 19), φεύγω (v. 22), and παραιτέομαι (v. 23).

There is also a repeated emphasis on the negative results of the opponents' ways: destroys the hearers (v. 14); leads to more ungodliness (v. 16); upsets faith (v. 18); and produces quarrels (v. 23). Thus both the characterization of the opposition and the proposed response to it cohere throughout these verses.

Within the motif of proper belief and behavior there are also connections, though not as many since most of the unit deals with avoidance of the negative. In v. 15 Timothy is urged to diligently seek divine approval and part of the point of the metaphor in vv. 20–21 is to be found 'useful to the Master.' The desire for divine approval undergirds the call to purity and faithfulness.

Then, the table also shows that these two motifs are interlinked not only by contrasting shifts ('not this but that') but also by contrasting uses of lexical and thematic items. 'Αλήθεια occurs three times in this unit, the first occurrences in the entire letter. Timothy is to properly handle the 'word of truth' (v. 15). The opponents, however, have abandoned the truth (v. 18), though hope is held out that they might yet come to the knowledge of the truth (v. 25). In contrast to the quarrels which have been seen to characterize the description of the opponents, Timothy is to pursue peace (εἰρήνη, v. 22), not to be quarrelsome (οὐ μάχεσθαι, v. 24), but to be gentle (ἤπιος, v. 24), patient (ἀνεξίκακος, v. 24), and gently to correct (πραΰτης, v. 25). There is also a clear contrast regarding purity. The metaphor in vv. 20–21 calls for cleansing (ἐκκαθαίρω), and v. 22 calls for the pursuit of virtues along with those who call on the Lord from a pure (καθαρός) heart. In contrast, the teaching of the opponents spreads like defiling gangrene (v. 17). Similarly, the relation of Timothy (and the rest of the faithful) and the opponents to the spiritual beings is antithetical. Timothy is to present himself to God (v. 15), the faithful are known to God (v. 19) and call on the divine name (vv. 19, 22), and Timothy is the Lord's servant. But, the opponents are held captive by the devil (v. 26). Lastly, the opponents upset people's faith (v. 18), but Timothy is to pursue faith (v. 22).

There is also a significant contrast between the results of true and false teaching. The following tables will list the chain of related words to demonstrate the prominence of the chain in the unit and to show how they contrast.

False Teaching	Result
λογομαχεῖν (14)	No use (14)
Profane empty chatter (16)	Destruction of hearers (14)
Their message (17)	Lead to further ungodliness (16)
Saying resurrection already occurred (18)	Spread like gangrene (17)
(youthful desires?) (22)	Turned away from truth (18)

Foolish & ignorant speculation (23)	Upset faith (18)
Those who disagree (25)	Produce quarrels (23)
	Held captive by the devil (26)

Right Teaching	**Result**
Word of truth (15)	Unashamed (15)
Gentle (24)	Depart from wickedness (19)
Able to teach (24)	Sanctified (21)
Patient (24)	Useful to the Master (21)
Correcting with gentleness (25)	Prepared for every good work (21)
	Pursue virtues (22)
	Possibly leading to salvation even
	of the opponents (25–26)

The difference in the results of the two 'ministries' is held up as further proof that the path Timothy is called to is the right one. In addition to the lexical links and contrasts already noted, this also highlights that while the opponents' talk is 'useless' (οὐδὲν χρήσιμον, v. 14), the proper way leads to being 'useful' (εὔχρηστος, v. 21). The opponents' teaching destroys faith (v. 18) but Timothy's can lead to repentance (vv. 25–26).

Thus, it has been shown that the unit as a whole moves by contrasts between two ways as is common in ancient parenetic material. Then the actual content is bound by major motifs and semantic chains centering on truth and error. The cohesive function of these motifs is enhanced by the fact that they are set in explicit opposition with each other. As a result, the unit achieves significant cohesion.[80]

Having argued the overall cohesion of the unit, some specific contested points should be addressed. First, Miller breaks v. 14, v. 15, and vv. 16–17a into three distinct, unrelated statements.[81] He argues that v. 15 has no clear connection with the preceding or following material and that vv. 16–17a

---

80. Cf. Marshall 1999: 36: 'Thus we can see that there is a theme running right through 2.14–26 which would encourage us to believe that this is one section.'

81. In fact Miller 1997: 112 also divides v. 14a and v. 14b, supplying a colon after θεοῦ, so the verse then reads, 'Remind [them] of these things, charging [them] before God: stop disputing about words...' However, no recent scholar was found who agreed with (or even discussed as a possibility) this view. Miller gives two bases for this view. First, he says this reading makes better sense of the 'list' quality of the admonitions which follow. This presumes the disparate view of the text which he holds. Given the cohesion already argued, there is no need to supply a colon. Second, he also appeals to 'the parallel in 2 Timothy 4:1' without further elaboration (112). It is not immediately clear why this would suggest his reading is better. In both cases the infinitive takes on the sense of a command (in Miller's reading or the more common reading). In 4.1 it is a bit stronger because διαμαρτύρομαι there is first person singular rather than a participle as in 2.14. Finally, even if one did supply a colon, it is not

'abruptly' return to the matter of empty words and babblings after v. 15.[82]
Miller fails to account for the regular shifting from positive to negative
throughout the unit which also occurs in vv. 14–17a. Apparently his focus
simply on contiguous connections did not allow him to see that v. 16 is
basically a restatement of v. 14.[83] Both verses forbid unhelpful talk and
comment on its negative results. This confirms the suggestion that the unit
moves intentionally back and forth between the positive and negative:
avoid useless talk, seek divine approval, avoid useless talk.

Miller also isolates vv. 17b–18, saying their reference to individuals is
'sudden' and the reference to a specific heresy is 'puzzling' and out of place
with the 'general and commonplace admonitions' elsewhere in the unit.[84]
However, reference to individuals is not that sudden. Timothy is addressed
as an individual in v. 15.[85] The mention of individual third parties has
already been introduced in the letter in 1.15–18. Secondly, it is not at all
puzzling that a specific heresy is mentioned here. It is entirely logical to
follow a warning with a specific illustration (or manifestation) of what has
been warned against.[86] Lastly, v. 18b and v. 16b both refer to the negative
result of the teaching of the opponents, thus providing some further
connection.

Miller also isolates v. 19 saying the connection to the context is unclear.
However, the connection is noted syntactically by the strong adversative
μέντοι. The relation to v. 18 is one of contrast, as is common in the unit.
The contrast is further strengthened by the words used: ἀνατρέπω (v. 18) vs.
στερεὸς θεμέλιος and ἵστημι (v. 19). Though the faith of some may be
overturned, God's work is still firm and steadfast.[87] Additionally, reference
to a house follows understandably from the imagery of a foundation.[88]
These connections also call into question the argument of Quinn and
Wacker that vv. 19–20 (and possibly v. 21) are not in alignment with the

---

evident that this would require a division between v. 14a and v. 14b. Miller contends that v.
14a is a literary signal (111–12), but an author can use a literary signal when shifting to a new
unit. Insufficient evidence is given to say v. 14 must be split.

82. Miller 1997: 112–13.

83. Cf. Marshall 1999: 750; Bassler 1996: 151.

84. Miller 1997: 114.

85. In fact the admonition in v. 14 is followed by reference to a specific individual
(Timothy) in v. 15; then, the admonition of vv. 16–17a is followed by reference to specific
individuals in v. 17b–18.

86. So also Marshall 1999: 751: 'a relative clause is loosely added to give an example as an
illustration and warning; the danger is real, not just a possibility!'

87. So also Marshall 1999: 755; Mounce 2000: 528; Fee 1988: 257. Marshall 1999: 756,
also writes, 'The point is that the true church, characterised by its possession of the truth and
as represented by the faithful believers in Ephesus, is certain to stand firm despite the activities
of the opponents.'

88. Marshall 1999: 759.

surrounding argument and therefore came from a different source, 'an authoritative source, not to be changed or redacted simply to bring it into alignment with the argument at hand.'[89] Quinn and Wacker contend that v. 19 introduces new problems, alien to v. 18, which v. 20 then addresses. In 2.21, then, the editor resumes but the seam created by the use of different material in vv. 19–20 is evident from the lack of an obvious antecedent for ἀπὸ τούτων in v. 21. In response, connections (syntactic, semantic, and logical) between v. 19 and v. 18 have just been highlighted. These connections challenge the idea that v. 19 is out of alignment with the preceding material. Additionally, it would not be unusual for a verse to further develop an issue as long as it fits with the preceding material as v. 19 has been shown to do.[90] 2.19–21 do move to a concern more with the church as a whole, rather than Timothy and the opponents, but this is simply a development from the mention of church members (τις) whose faith is being upset. Thus, there is development but not discontinuity.[91] Second, it is difficult to argue for a strong division between v. 20 and v. 21. 2.21 continues the discussion of σκεῦος which occurs only in these two verses. This indicates at least significant work at interweaving the two verses. Further, the call to purity in v. 21 echoes the similar call in v. 19,[92] and these fit in the context as an elaboration of the call to avoid the babblings of the opponents in v. 16. In the light of these connections, the ambiguity of the referent of τούτων does not threaten the overall coherence of the unit. If, as has been argued here, the unit is built on a series of imperatives, it may be useful to note that v. 21 occurs at the end of a lengthy collection of supporting material for the imperative in v. 16. Perhaps then v. 21 closes the supporting material by referring back to the

---

89.   Quinn and Wacker 2000: 691.

90.   It is not entirely clear what new 'problems' v. 19 raises, and Quinn and Wacker appear to be alone in this reading. Apparently the problem, as they see it, is the fact that there are indeed some within the church who cling to ἀδικία in spite of the 'seal' which calls for believers to put such things away. However, the intent of vv. 19–20 seems to be distinguishing between those who truly are the Lord's and those who are not, i.e., showing the distinguishing characteristics of those who follow the truth and those who do not. Thus, this is another shot at the opponents in line with the rest of the unit.

91.   It seems that the interpretation of v. 20 effects the understanding of the cohesion or lack thereof in this unit. Quinn and Wacker 2000: 691–94 understand the verse as saying both sorts of vessels are useful. In that case, v. 20 would not fit in the flow of this unit. However, such an interpretation is not required. In a unit where there is a constant contrast between two groups (Timothy and the opponents), it is most likely that contrasts between two sort of vessels correspond to these groups. The two sorts of vessels are then not two sorts of church members of differing usefulness, but represent the negative and positive options available to Timothy (and the church). Indeed in v. 21 it is only the vessel of honor who is 'useful.'

92.   So also Marshall 1999: 759; Fee 1988: 261; Mounce 2000: 530.

imperative, in which case the plural pronoun could refer to the plural βεβήλους κενοφωνίας.[93]

The last major objection to the unity of 2.14–26 is Oberlinner's argument for separating vv. 22–26 as a separate unit. He agrees that vv. 22–26 continue the series of imperatives begun in v. 14, but says vv. 22–26 have a different accent. Whereas vv. 14–21 concerned the relationship between church leaders (Timothy), the church, and the opponents, in vv. 22–26 the church recedes and the church leader and the opponents are more directly contrasted.[94] However, such a neat division is questionable. The congregation appears in v. 14 as those to be reminded and warned and then again in v. 18 as the 'some' whose faith is being upset surely refers to members of the congregation. So in vv. 14–18 the congregation appears explicitly in only two places. The rest of the material focuses on Timothy and the opponents. The church comes to the fore then in vv. 19–21 with 'the firm foundation,'[95] those who belong to the Lord, those who call upon the name of the Lord, and the various vessels of vv. 20–21.[96] The church appears again in v. 22 with the second reference to those who call upon the Lord. Thus, it seems that it would be more appropriate to say the congregation appears more prominently in vv. 19–21 where a general truth is expounded and vv. 14–18 and vv. 22–26 are more similar in focusing primarily on Timothy and the opponents. This can be further substantiated by examining the finite verbs. In vv. 14–18 the subject of every finite verb is either Timothy (three times) or the opponents (four times; personally or their teaching). In vv. 22–26 Timothy (four times) or the opponents (two times) are the subject of all but one of the finite verbs (with 'God' being the other subject). Even the proverbial statement in vv. 19–21,

---

93. Miller 1997: 115 also says vv. 20–21 do not fit because instead of invective against opponents these verses suggest that all members of the household, honorable and dishonorable, are necessary. However, the verses do not suggest that both are necessary but that both do in fact exist. As Marshall writes, 'The idea that the picture justifies the presence of heretics in the church ... is dubious; at most there is the recognition that their presence is unfortunately "normal"' (761).

94. Oberlinner 1995: 110.

95. Most commentators interpret this phrase as referring to the church. See Marshall 1999: 755–56 for a listing of those supporting this view as well as the alternate interpretations with their proponents.

96. Though some interpret the vessel metaphor as referring only to the opponents or to Timothy, it seems best to understand it as referring to any member of the congregation. Verse 19 with its general references to believers supports this. Cf. Marshall, 762: 'clearly the pronoun [τις] refers to "any member of the congregation", and further specification (e.g. the false teachers or those influenced by them, orthodox believers, or even a delicate reference to Timothy himself) is unnecessary. All members of the church are called on to cleanse themselves from anything that would defile them.'

though stated in general terms, is directly applied only to Timothy. Thus, the entire unit is focused on Timothy vis-à-vis the opponents.[97]

There are other connections between vv. 22–26 and the preceding material as well. First, not only does v. 22 continue the string of imperatives as Oberlinner concedes, it also continues the chain of exhortations to avoid evil (vv. 16, 19, 21, 23). In both v. 16 and v. 23 that which is to be avoided is characterized as foolish (v. 16, κενοφωνία; v. 23, μωρός, ἀπαίδευτος). Also, v. 19 calls for abstinence from ἀδικία, while v. 22 calls for pursuit of δικαιοσύνη, and both exhortations are related to those who call upon the Lord:

v. 19 – πᾶς ὁ ὀνομάζων τὸ ὄνομα κυρίου
v. 22 – μετὰ τῶν ἐπικαλουμένων τὸν κύριον

While there is a stronger emphasis on peace and gentleness in vv. 22–26, this theme was already mentioned in v. 14. Thus, it appears that Fee is right in concluding, 'The commands introducing this section [vv. 22–26] flow directly from the application of the analogy of verses 20–21, but all the time in the context of the concerns that began in verse 14.'[98]

3.1–9

Boundaries

That 3.1 begins a new unit is almost universally recognized by commentators.[99] A transition is indicated by the use of a disclosure formula (Τοῦτο δὲ γίνωσκε), a common transitional device in ancient letters.[100] The fact that similar statements (verb of cognition with οὗτος; 1.15; 2.14) have marked transitions to new units strengthens the argument for understanding Τοῦτο δὲ γίνωσκε in this way. Other shifts confirm that a new unit has begun. For example, second person singular verbs, which had been common in the previous unit, fade from view here. The unit is introduced by a second person singular verb, but then another one does not occur until v. 5 which is the last such verb within vv. 1–9. Instead, the

---

97. Johnson 1978: 10, writes: 'it is important to note that the emphasis here is entirely on Timothy's mode of teaching, and the description of the opponents serves as a contrast to the positive picture of 2:15'.

98. Fee 1988: 263. Another connection which could add to this could be the idea of conversion present in both vv. 20–21 and vv. 25–26. The reference to conversion in vv. 25–26 is accepted but the interpretation of the metaphor in vv. 20–21 is debated.

99. Cf. Marshall 1999: 36: 'By any account a new section starts at 3:1 ...'

100. White 1972a: 11–15.

verbs are predominately third person plural.[101] With the decrease in second singular imperatives, there seems also to be a shift in genre. 3.1–9 is not as much exhortation (though that is included, 3.5), as warning or description. The two vice lists serve to describe and to warn. Since there is a greater focus on third person (the opponents usually), there is less of the shifting contrast which was characteristic of the previous unit. There is a contrast at 3.5, but only one contrast out of nine verses is a significantly different pattern from the previous unit.

The closing boundary of this unit at 3.9 is also commonly agreed upon. 3.9 gives a positive or encouraging note in contrast (ἀλλ') with what has preceded. This has been seen to be a fairly common way to close units of exhortation or warning in this letter (cf. 2 Tim. 2.13; 2.25–26). Arguments for this boundary will be expanded in the following unit, but it can be noted that at 3.10 Timothy returns more clearly to the fore, the opponents recede, and the genre is more explicitly hortatory.

Cohesion

3.1–9 coheres primarily around the topic of the opponents and their characteristics. This is clearly the concern throughout. Opponents, whether eschatological (v. 2), present (v. 6), or historical/typical (v. 8), are the subjects of seven of the ten finite verbs of the unit and every participle in the unit is used of the opponents or their victims. The two vice lists (vv. 2–5, 6–8) and the discussion of the traditional opponents of Moses take up most of the unit. This combines to create a sense of a unified, coherent topic.[102]

There seem to be two major objections to the coherence of this unit. Miller sees as problematic the shift from future tense in v. 1 to present tense in vv. 5b–6.[103] Combined with this, he and Bassler both note difficulties in understanding how those described in vv. 2–4 could be said to have even the appearance of godliness.[104] While there is debate on the

101. Of the 10 finite verb forms, 5 are 3p, 3 are 3s, and 2 are 2s. All 10 of the participles are plural.

102. Smith and Beekman 1981: 82, similarly: 'There is strong referential coherence in this paragraph as seen in the numerous references to evil people...'

103. Miller 1997: 118.

104. Miller 1997: 118, n. 85; Bassler 1996: 159. Miller also cites John Calvin as agreeing that this combination is odd. However, Miller fails to acknowledge what Calvin goes on to write: 'But daily experience should be able to keep us from being too surprised, for such is the amazing audacity and wickedness of hypocrites that they are completely shameless in excusing even their grossest faults, having once learnt to shelter themselves falsely under God's name.' Calvin goes on to give examples (*Calvin's Commentaries: The Second Epistle of Paul the Apostle to the Corinthians and the Epistles to Timothy, Titus and Philemon*, trans. T.A. Smail, ed. D.W. Torrance and T.F. Torrance [Carlisle: Paternoster Press, 1996; first published by Oliver and Boyd, 1964]).

intention of the future tense in v. 1, even if it is taken to refer to a future time, the shift in verb tenses need present no especially difficult problem. 3.1 refers to a commonly known idea that in the last days people will be particularly bad. 3.5b–6 then connect the present opponents with this end-time evil, emphasizing their evilness and the need to avoid them. Additionally, the reference to having a form of godliness but denying its power need not refer to each person in view. The vice list does not necessarily intend to list qualities which are true of every person in view, but qualities which will be prevalent among people.[105] Thus, those who have only an appearance of godliness (like the opponents) are further stigmatized by being included in such a list (indeed coming at the climax of the list!).[106] They occur at the end of the list because it is this group that particularly resembles the opponents in view in the letter.

Within this overall coherence there are some other microlevel indicators of cohesion. First, it has often been noted that there are various connections within the vice list of 3.2–5. Verses 2–4 are bracketed by double occurrences of words based on the root φιλ-. The first two words are φίλαυτοι and φιλάργυροι, and v. 4 concludes with φιλήδονοι μᾶλλον ἢ φιλόθεοι. Quinn and Wacker even note that according to Philo, the′λαυτοι are the very opposite of the φιλόθεοι.[107] Within these brackets, nine of the 15 items contain a word beginning with α (often an alpha privative). Also, after being introduced with ἄνωρωποι, the list includes 14 other words which end with -οι. These factors enhance the cohesiveness of the list,[108] and serve to highlight ἔχοντες μόρφωσιν εὐσεβείας τὴν δὲ δύναμιν αὐτῆς

---

105. A number of scholars take the same basic view, but base it on the use of asyndeton in the list (Knight 1992: 429; Smith and Beekman 1981: 84; Quinn and Wacker 2000: 716 [though more cautiously]). Apparently this view is based on BDF §460.2, where this very point is asserted. However, since asyndeton was common in the ancient literary form of 'lists,' one cannot take much interpretive value from the use of asyndeton here (see Fitzgerald 1997: 287).

106. Miller 1997: 117 also appeals to the variant reading γινώσκετε in 3.1 as possibly supporting his argument. While he calls the variant 'well-attested' (A, F, G, 33, pc), the support is not terribly strong and no textual critics seem to have taken the variant seriously.

107. Quinn and Wacker 2000: 707, referring to Philo, *Fuga et inventione* 81. However, W. Grundman notes that for Aristotle φιλάγαθος is the opposite of φίλαυτος (*TDNT* 1.18). This would then provide a connection with ἀφιλάγαθοι in 3.4. J. Rendel Harris 1926: 565–66 argued that the similarity to Philo suggested a dependence on Philo, but this view has not gained much acceptance.

108. These factors enhance, not prove, the cohesiveness of this list since the 'list' or 'catalogue' was a known literary form and coheres as such. Ancient 'lists' do not always have any specific structure but are identifiable as part of this form simply by being a list (see Fitzgerald 1997: 292). Thus, E. F. Scott's evaluation of this list as incoherent misses the intended function of such lists (1936: 119).

ἠρνημένοι, since this element comes not only at the climax and with greater expansion, but also occurs outside of the inclusio.[109]

Second, in the microlevel cohesion, there are some links between the vice list of vv. 2–5 and the vice list of vv. 6–7. 3.5 refers to those who are 'lovers of pleasure' (φιλήδονοι: Louw and Nida 1989: 25.112) and 3.6 refers to women affected by the opponents as 'led by various desires' (ἐπιθυμία; Louw and Nida 1989: 25.12). In both lists there is an element which refers to a lack of power. In 3.5 they deny the power (δύναμις) of godliness, and in 3.7 they are never able (δύναμαι) to come to the knowledge of the truth. Also in both cases their lack of power is in contrast to appearance: they have an appearance of godliness but lack the power; they are always learning, but never come to knowledge. These conceptual and lexical links support the idea that these two lists are being used for a common purpose.

Lastly, and perhaps most tentatively, there are some interesting repetitions between the beginning and ending of the unit which may have cohesive value. First, ἄνθρωπος occurs only twice in this unit, both times in nominative masculine plural. The first occurrence introduces the first vice list (v. 2) and the second occurrence closes the description of the

---

109. Smith and Beekman 1981: 84–85, and Knight 1992: 429–30, argue for the same chiastic structure in this list (Holmes 2000: 125 seems to support this view but does not elaborate).

φίλαυτοι
φιλάργυροι
  ἀλαζόνες
  ὑπερήφανοι
  βλάσφημοι
    γονεῦσιν ἀπειθεῖς
    ἀχάριστοι
    ἀνόσιοι
    ἄστοργοι
    ἄσπονδοι
      διάβολοι
    ἀκρατεῖς
    ἀνήμεροι
    αφιλάγαθοι
  προδόται
  προπετεῖς
  τετυφωμένοι
φιλήδονοι μᾶλλον η
φιλόθεοι

The extreme ends represent the inclusion acknowledged above. The principle behind the other parts is basically that just within the inclusio there is a block of words without alpha privatives, then a group with alpha privatives, with διάβολοι standing out in the middle. While this is possible, it is not altogether convincing. It seems best to take the inclusio with assorted rhymes and wordplays (so also, Marshall 1999: 772; Quinn and Wacker 2000: 715–16). Quinn and Wacker refer to the list as 'nineteen sonorous assonant asyndetic entries' (716).

current opponents, just before the final statement of their end (v. 8). Howard Marshall notes that the occurrence in v. 8 is 'hardly necessary.'[110] This then could support the idea that this otherwise unnecessary word has been explicitly stated here to form a connection. Second, there are four future verbs in the unit: the second and third verbs from the beginning and the second and third verbs from the end.[111] There does seem to be a sense of temporal movement within the unit from well-known future trouble, to the present manifestation, and then the future of these contemporary opponents.

3.10–17

Boundaries

It is widely agreed among the commentators that a new unit begins at 3.10, and this is supported by a number of important shifts. Perhaps primary among the shifts is the shift in participants. First, in this area, there is a marked return to Timothy with the initial Σὺ δέ. While, the previous unit was addressed to Timothy (3.1, 5), the focus of the discussion was opponents and as a result the unit was dominated by third person referents. 3.10 marks a return to discussion of Timothy's behavior. While 3.1–9 had only two second person singular referents, 3.10–17 contains seven distinct such references (vv. 10, 14 [4x], 15 [2x]).[112] Thus, there is a significant shift in returning to Timothy's behavior. Secondly, in the participant field, first person referents occur again – the first time since 2:10![113] Thus Paul returns to the fore as there are four first person referents just in 3.10–11. There is then a return to the Paul/Timothy relational matrix so common in 1.3–2.13.

In addition to shifts in participants, there is the noticeable shift from negative to positive example, from vice (3.2–5, 6–8) to virtue (3.10–11). This is marked as well by the contrastive δέ in 3.10. These shifts make it clear that a new unit begins at 3.10.

The final boundary of this unit is more disputed. The majority favors v. 17 as the final boundary, as will be argued here.[114] Some, however, keep 3.10–4.8 together without breaking it up into smaller units.[115] Mounce

---

110. Marshall 1999: 779.
111. Smith and Beekman 1981: 82–83 also note these future tense verbs (with less specificity).
112. Instances where a 2s verb and an explicit subject occur are only counted once.
113. Smith and Beekman 1981: 89 also note the absence of first person referents from 2.11–3.9.
114. E.g., Marshall, Oberlinner, Knight, Smith and Beekman, Merkel, Brox, Fee, Kelly, and Easton.
115. E.g., Mounce, Dibelius and Conzelmann, and Hanson.

makes the strongest argument for this position. He says 3.10–4.8 is made up of four paragraphs (3.10–13; 3.14–17; 4.1–4; 4.5–8), but that they are bound together as a 'cohesive unit.'[116] The larger connection between 3.10–4.8 is not disputed here; indeed, such macroconnection will be discussed in the following chapter. Therefore, there is no serious disagreement with this position, though there will be a need in the following discussion on cohesion to examine whether or not there should be a division between v. 13 and v. 14.[117] Lastly, Quinn and Wacker and Bassler, who also consider 3.10–4.8 as the larger section, argue that 3.10–13 is one unit and that 3.14–4.4(5) is a separate unit.[118] Thus, while both commentaries see coherence in all of 3.10–4.8, the key issue here is whether 3.14–17 coheres primarily with 3.10–13 or with 4.1ff. Quinn and Wacker base their division on the three occurrences of σὺ δέ (3.10, 13; 4.5).[119] However, while it is a possible, and even an attractive, suggestion that σὺ δέ is functioning as a structural marker, they do not provide argumentation to support this. Rather, it seems that in 3.14 and 4.5 the intended connection is a contrast with the immediately preceding description of opponents. Indeed, in both cases material directed to Timothy (3.10–12; 4.1–2) is interrupted by references to opposition (3.13; 4.3–4), and the σὺ δέ then returns to the focus on Timothy, now in contrast to the opposition (3.14; 4.5).[120] This observation argues against taking σὺ δέ as an indicator of a new paragraph in these instances, and the broad similarities between 3.10–17 and 4.1–8 can suggest it is best to view these as individual units with significant connections. This suggestion is furthered by a slight difference in topic between 3.10–17 and 4.1–8. 3.10–17 focuses on the need for Timothy to 'remain' in what is right (hence the concern with the models and sources of truth), and is thus more defensive in posture. 4.1–8 is the offensive balance, focusing on what Timothy is to do. Therefore, 3.17 will be considered the final boundary of the unit begun in 3.10, while not disputing connections between these verses and 4.1ff.

Cohesion

3.10–17 coheres first of all as exhortation to Timothy. Since there is only one imperative (μένε, v. 14), the hortatory character of this unit might be

---

116. Mounce 2000: 555.

117. Bernard 1906: 135 makes a division between v. 14 and v. 15, but seems to be alone in this decision. The division seems to be thematic since v. 15 is a continuation of the sentence begun in v. 14 and Bernard does not argue for any strong break in the sentence.

118. Quinn and Wacker 2000: 567, 755–56, argues for 3:14–4:4 and Bassler 1996: 163, 166–70, argues for 3.14–4.5.

119. Quinn and Wacker 2000: 738.

120. Following the return to Timothy (3.14; 4.5) both units also provide further grounding material (3.15–17; 4.6–8).

disputed. However, this imperative is the central point of the unit.[121] The preceding statement about Timothy following Paul's model is implicitly hortatory since it is followed by the call to remain in what he has learned.[122] The material following the imperative in v. 14 then serves as a ground for remaining. Therefore, this is a unit of exhortation to Timothy. The second person singular pronoun occurs three times (3.10, 14, 15) and there are six second person singular verbs. Timothy is also at least implicitly included amongst 'those who desire to live godly' (v. 12) and the 'man of God' (v. 17). Thus, this unit coheres in its genre and major participant.

The unit opens with an extensive virtue list (vv. 10–11). Hanson criticized this list as a 'rather indiscriminate stringing together of disparate things' suggesting it lacked coherence.[123] However, as was noted above, 'lists' as used in ancient Greek writings often did not display a clear organization.[124] If this was common in the writings of the era, then it cannot be used as a criticism. However, it is not even clear that this list lacks organization. The list moves from teaching to behavior to suffering.[125] This connects to the ways Paul's example has functioned previously, especially his teaching (e.g., 1.11, 13; 2.2, 8) and suffering (e.g., 1.8, 12; 2.3). The arrangement also makes sense with teaching coming first in contrast to the false teachers just mentioned who opposed truth (3.8–9). As was common in these lists the final part is accented and stands out from the rest. The last two words, referring to suffering, are plural (in contrast to the preceding singulars) and are elaborated with historical discussion. The final singular word (ὑπομονή) prepares for this emphasis on suffering. The climax of the list in v. 11 is then enveloped by the two occurrences of διώγμος in the plural. This leads logically to a statement on the necessity of suffering in v. 12, with διωχθήσονται being a cognate of διώγμος.[126] Thus, vv. 10–12 are tightly connected by the theme of suffering, containing the following semantic chain:[127]

τῇ μακροθυμίᾳ (v. 10)
τῇ ὑπομονῇ (v. 10)
τοῖς διωγμοῖς (v. 11)
τοῖς παθήμασιν (v. 11)

---

121. So also Fee 1988: 275; Knight 1992: 438.
122. Marshall 1999: 787 also considers 3.10–11 to be an implicit exhortation.
123. Hanson 1982: 148.
124. Fitzgerald 1997: 292.
125. Fee 1988: 276, and Knight 1992: 439, argue similarly though they list teaching, way of life, cardinal virtues, endurance. Way of life and cardinal virtues both refer to behavior.
126. Louw and Nida (1989) list the two words together under entry 39.45.
127. So also Smith and Beekman 1981: 89.

οἴους διωγμούς (v. 11)
ὑπήνεγκα (v. 11)

This makes it hard to understand how Holtzmann (followed by Miller) could say of v. 12, 'the whole verse is without the necessary context.'[128] Dibelius and Conzelmann even say that the intention of the biographical allusions was to prepare for the statement of v. 12.[129]

3.13 stands out in the middle of this unit as the only reference to opposition. It functions as a contrastive hinge between the two pieces concerned directly with Timothy and introduced by σὺ δέ (vv. 10, 14). In contrast to the suffering of the godly in the previous verses, the 'evil men' will make progress.[130] In contrast to what follows, the evil men 'progress' into worse things but Timothy is to 'remain' in what he has learned. There may also be an intended contrast between the mention of the evil men being deceived (verb used twice) but Timothy having learned (v. 14; verb used twice), being convinced (v. 14), knowing (v. 15), and being wise (v. 15). 3.13 then serves as a hinge as the passage returns explicitly to exhort Timothy.[131] This results, as Howard Marshall has noted, in a symmetric structure:[132]

A – 10–12
 B – 13
A' – 14–17

Miller attacks the coherence of the unit because the thought of 3.13 is not developed.[133] There is no literary requirement that each point be developed further, however. He has failed to notice how the passage structure works and the hinge function of 3.13.

3.14–17 develop and apply much of what was stated in 3.10–13. That which Timothy is to remain in naturally includes the Pauline model in vv. 10–11. To 'learn' and 'be convinced of' in v. 14 are similar to what is meant by the 'following' in v. 10. Also the importance of 'from whom' Timothy has learned in v. 14 matches the emphasis on Paul's example in vv. 10–11, accentuated by the μου standing at the head of the list.[134] There is also a reference to things connected with Timothy's spiritual beginnings

---

128. Holtzmann 1880: 432f.; cited by Miller 1997: 119.
129. Dibelius and Conzelmann 1972: 119.
130. Cf. Marshall 1999: 786: 'The thought of the present affliction of the people of God is balanced by a reminder of the present triumph of the godless...'
131. Quinn and Wacker 2000: 746 says v. 13 is held together by the repetition of *p* sounds, climaxing with the wordplay with two words beginning with π.
132. Marshall 1999: 781.
133. Miller 1997: 120.
134. Quinn and Wacker 2000: 739 notes that μου standing before the list 'serves to stress the unity of all the individual things noted in the person of the apostle.'

in both parts. The persecutions referred to in v. 11 took place in Timothy's home area, with Lystra being his home town. These would have been familiar to Timothy from his first association with Paul.[135] This is balanced in v. 15 with a reference to Timothy's association with the scriptures from his infancy.[136] Thus the call to remain is grounded in what Timothy has always known since his affiliation with Paul and indeed from childhood. Lastly, Timothy has both a model of 'teaching' (διδασκαλία) in Paul (v. 10), and a source of teaching (διδασκαλία) in the Scriptures (v. 16). As these are the only two occurrences of this word in the letter, Smith and Beekman suggest they form an inclusio here.[137] The lexical repetition at least further supports the connections between 3.10–12 and 3.14–17.

Lastly, there is a significant chain of terms related to teaching and knowledge which runs throughout the unit:

παρηκολούθησάς (v. 10)
διδασκαλία (v. 10)
οἷς ἔμαθες καὶ ἐπιστώθης (v. 14)
ἔμαθες (v. 14)
ἱερὰ γράμματα (v. 15)
οἶδας (v. 15)
πᾶσα γραφὴ (v. 16)
διδασκαλία (v. 16)
ἐλεγμόν (v. 16)
ἐπανόρθωσιν (v. 16)
παιδείαν (v. 16)

This provides cohesion around this central semantic theme as the unit moves from Timothy being reminded of his following, learning, and knowledge (v. 10, 14, 15) to the divine source of this learning (vv. 15, 16), and then to Timothy's own ministry of teaching (vv. 16–17).[138]

---

135. So also Quinn and Wacker 2000: 756; Knight 1992: 440; Fee 1988: 276–77.

136. Some have disputed the historicity of Timothy's mother actually teaching him the OT scriptures from childhood since she did not have him circumcised. The historicity, while important, is not the issue here. The concern here is the presentation of the text at hand. For a clear and positive assesment of the historical situation see Marshall 1999: 788–89.

137. Smith and Beekman 1981: 89. Πίστις also occurs in v. 10 and then in v. 15.

138. In this context, 'every good work' most likely includes teaching as well and could be included in the chain (cf. Johnson 1978: 11, who says 'every good work' 'here clearly means teaching').

4.1–8

Boundaries
It has been argued above that 3.17 marked the end of the previous unit, making 4.1 the beginning of a new unit. It was also noted that there is a significant degree of connection between 4.1ff and that which precedes. Thus, the shifts at 4.1 are not drastic. However, there are some shifts. 4.1 opens with a first person singular verb. While first person referents occurred in the beginning of the previous unit, the only first person singular verb was in a dependent clause (ὑποφέρω, 3.11), whereas in 4.1 the first person verb is the main clause which shapes all that follows. The solemnity of the charge denotes a raising of the tone and, most importantly, introduces two strings of imperatives (nine in total). 3.10–17 contained only one imperative.[139] This shift in tone is mirrored in the content as 3.10–17 was concerned with Timothy's preparation (remaining in the Pauline model and Scripture) and 4.1–8 is the call to action (based on the preparation).

Regarding the final boundary, there is virtual unanimity among commentators on a unit break after 4.8. However, some also posit a break at the end of v. 4 or v. 5.[140] Even those who separate vv. 6–8 concede that these verses function as a ground for preceding material so it is difficult to isolate them.[141] 4.5 is a more reasonable point for beginning a new unit, but it will be argued below that there are significant parallels and repetitions which bind vv. 5–8 to vv. 1–4.

Cohesion
Regarding the cohesion of 4.1–8, it must first be noted that the cohesion shift analysis indicates significant shifts after verses 1, 2, 4, and 5, which corresponds to Miller's arguments that this unit is composed of the following pieces: v. 1, v. 2, vv. 3–4, v. 5 and vv. 6–8.[142] Those who see the unit as cohesive also note that the unit is composed of several parts roughly corresponding with these shifts.[143] However, Miller fails to offer much argumentation for the necessity of viewing these as *disparate* pieces.

---

139. This difference in the number of imperatives is blurred when Mounce 2000: 555 refers to 'the ten imperatives in 3:10–4:8.' He parenthetically mentions that there are nine in Ch. 4, though it is not immediately clear whether by Ch. 4 he means 4.1–8 or the verses which follow. This also questions Bassler's grouping 3.10–4.8 as the final charge (1996: 162ff.). With the solemn adjuration of 4.1 and the sharp increase in the number of imperatives, 4.1–8 stands out as a charge.

140. E.g., Quinn and Wacker, Bassler, Fee.

141. E.g., Bassler 1996: 171.

142. This is also similar to Harrison's reconstruction (1921: 127).

143. Cf. e.g., Marshall 1999: 797, who sees these four parts: vv. 1–2, 3–4, 5, 6–8.

Rather, it is relatively easy to see a pattern here. Verse 1 sets the solemn context for the charges which follow, at least those of v. 2. Verses 3–4 then shift to warning about opponents. Verse 5 then returns to exhortations, with vv. 6–8 shifting to testimony. Since both vv. 3–4 and vv. 6–8 are introduced by γάρ, there is a pattern of exhortation (vv. 1–2), ground (vv. 3–4), exhortation (v. 5), ground (vv. 6–8).[144] The second set of exhortations grows out of the warning in vv. 3–4 as a contrast (δέ). This creates a reasonable, coherent structure. Before discussing further the overall structure of the unit it will be useful to investigate the coherence of its various parts.

4.1 coheres as a charge though the shift from genitive with ἐνώπιον to accusative is awkward, as is noted by almost all the commentators.[145] However, the accusative is an acceptable usage in this context. 4.2 coheres as a list of five verbs, each one a second person singular aorist active imperative.[146] Four of the five verbs are explicitly concerned with speech in the context of teaching. Thus, the cohesion of the verbs is unmistakably tight.[147] However, Hanson criticizes the closing phrase, ἐν πάσῃ μακροθυμίᾳ καὶ διδαχῇ, saying that it clumsily puts together two things (teaching and patience) 'which belong to different dimensions.'[148] However, the two concepts occur together in 3.10 describing the Pauline model (διδασκαλία, μακροθυμία) and a similar idea is found in the exhortation to Timothy in 2.24–26 where his teaching is to be gentle. Indeed, ἐν πάσῃ μακροθυμίᾳ καὶ διδαχῇ could be an example of hendiadys: 'with all patience in teaching.'[149] Thus, it is not odd for these concepts to be joined in 4.2, nor is it unacceptable to call for exhortation (or perhaps some of the other verbs as well) to be done in the context of teaching.[150] Indeed, as Marshall states,

144. So also, Smith and Beekman 1981: 96. One could also suggest this structure: solemn charge (v. 1), exhortation (v. 2), ground (vv. 3–4), exhortation (v. 5), ground (vv. 6–8).

145. The awkwardness is noted in the manuscript tradition with several witnesses reading κατὰ rather than καὶ before ἐπιφάνειαν. Metzger notes the text accepted here has the more difficult reading and has wide support (1971: 648). Cf. also Quinn and Wacker 2000: 765–66; Marshall 1999: 798.

146. Marshall 1999: 799 says the fact that they are all aorist imperatives is 'surprising.' Mounce 2000: 572–73 says the aorist tense gives 'a serious tone appropriate for the pronouncements'; but, why the aorist tense itself would convey this is unclear.

147. Interestingly, Quinn and Wacker 2000: 769 note that this list does not follow the pattern commonly found elsewhere in the Pastorals: members do not gradually grow in length and alliteration and assonance are minimal. Perhaps the gradual growth in length of members should be considered more common to lists of nouns rather than verbs since it is not characteristic of the verbs in v. 5 either.

148. Hanson 1982: 153.

149. Cf. BDF §442 (16). I am indebted to Howard Marshall for this observation.

150. Malherbe 1984: 241 also refers to this phrase ('in all patience and teaching') as 'dangling' apparently suggesting it does not fit with the harsh words for rebuke which precede

'The point is that Christian exhortation is to be seen to have its basis in sound teaching of the gospel.'[151] Verse 1 then connects reasonably to v. 2, providing the solemn background. After the solemn charge of v. 1, one expects some sort of exhortation, which v. 2 provides.[152]

The next part is 4.3–4 where again the verbs show a high degree of similarity. All five finite verbs are third person future indicative, with four of the five being plural. The 'they' in view in these plural verbs are people opposed to Timothy's message, creating coherence around the theme of opposition which permeates these two verses. Structurally, Marshall has pointed out that vv. 3–4 consist of four clauses which alternate between negative attitudes toward truth and positive attitudes toward error.[153] This can be represented as follows:

A. τῆς ὑγιαινούσης διδασκαλίας οὐκ ἀνέξονται

B. ἀλλὰ κατὰ τὰς ἰδίας ἐπιθυμίας ἑαυτοῖς ἐπισωρεύσουσιν διδασκάλους κνηθόμενοι τὴν ἀκοὴν

A' καὶ ἀπὸ μὲν τῆς ἀληθείας τὴν ἀκοὴν ἀποστρέψουσιν

B' ἐπὶ δὲ τοὺς μύθους ἐκτραπήσονται

A and A' are the negative attitudes toward truth and B and B' are the positive attitudes toward error. Further lexical and semantic connections between the clauses can be noted. Between A and A' 'sound teaching' is equivalent to 'truth,'[154] and 'not endure' leads to 'turn away.' Between A and B, the contrast (ἀλλὰ) is strengthened by the use of διδασκαλία (sound teaching) and διδασκάλοι (teachers in accord with their own desires). There is also a contrast between a standard in A and a catering to their own desires and a penchant for novelty ('itching ears') in B.[155] A' and B' are tightly connected by the μέν … δέ construction. This connection is strengthened by the overt contrastive parallelism between the two clauses:

ἀπὸ μὲν τῆς ἀληθείας
ἐπὶ δὲ τοὺς μύθους

The elements occur in the same order in each clause- 'from' (ἀπό) contrasts 'upon' or 'to' (ἐπί); 'truth' contrasts 'myths'; and both nouns have the

it. This may be more the result of Malherbe's overemphasis on the harshness of the terms used, missing the more positive nuances. Cf. Marshall 1999: 801, for a reading with more of the positive nuance.

151. Marshall 1999: 801.

152. 'With the solemn introduction of the preceding verse, the drumroll of five imperatives in this verse comes as no surprise' (Quinn and Wacker 2000: 769).

153. Marshall 1999: 801.

154. So also, Towner 1989: 293, n. 11.

155. Quinn and Wacker 2000: 772 add a contrast between 'healthy teaching' and 'itching ears.'

article.[156] This creates clear and intentional cohesion. To this point, then, the connections show two sets of tightly cohesive, contrasting clauses (A&B; A'&B') which are in parallel with each other and are joined by καί. Further cementing the connection between the two sets is the repetition of the word ἀκοή, a word which occurs nowhere else in the letter.[157] Thus, 4.3–4 cohere well with strong thematic, lexical, and semantic links.

The next part of this unit is 4.5. This is another list of imperatives which are all second person singular and active. Three out of the four are aorist. Like the similar list of imperatives in v. 2, they stand out due to their similarity with each other. The last two verbs are explicitly linked to ministry, and κακοπαθέω is used elsewhere in the letter in the context of ministry (2.9; not to mention the cognate συγκακοπαθέω, 1.8 and 2.3). In the context νήφω certainly also has this in view. Thus there is unmistakable unity in genre, verb forms, participants, and theme.

The last part is 4.6–8, which even the most stringent critics of the Pastorals consider to be a coherent, well-written piece.[158] These verses cohere around Paul, with eight discrete occurrences of first person referents.[159] Paul is the subject in vv. 6–7, as four out of five verses are in the first person. Then, in v. 8 the verbs become third person and Paul is the object, with objective forms of ἐγώ occurring three times. Additionally, there is a striking similarity in the verb tenses with four of the first five being perfect tense. There is only one other such significant cluster of perfects in the letter (1.12). 4.7 is a list of verbs such as has been seen elsewhere in the letter. Within the list each verb is first person singular perfect indicative. Each clause follows the same order: article, object (noun or adjective + noun), verb. There is also a significant parallelism in v. 8. Quinn and Wacker note parallelism between the verbs and the δικ- root, noting that the verb comes first in both clauses:[160]

ἀπόκειταί ... δικαιοσύνης
ἀποδώσει ... δίκαιος

---

156. G. Bertram also notes that in early Greek, στρέφω and τρέπω (the roots of the two verbs used here) were used alongside one another (*TDNT*, vol. 7, p. 714).

157. In fact, Quinn and Wacker 2000: 755 note that these are the only two occurrences of the word in all of the Pastoral Epistles.

158. Even Miller says vv. 6–8 is 'a well-ordered and coherent statement' (1997: 122). Hanson (1982: 156) says 4.6–8 'represent the author at his finest.' Falconer calls 4.6–8 'Fine contrast and appeal' (1937: 96). One wonders though if this is any finer piece of contrast that what was just seen in 4.3–4.

159. This is one of the most dense collection of first person referents in the letter.

160. Quinn and Wacker 2000: 789. They suggest the placing of the verb first gives 'a Semitic turn to both clauses.'

Additionally it could be noted that both verbs have divine subjects, even though the subject of the first is not made explicit, and that μοι occurs immediately after both verbs. In fact the structure of both is verb + μοι + subject (with article). Marshall also notes that v. 7 and v. 8 are connected by the athletic motif: finishing the course and receiving the prize.[161] Thus, 4:6–8 demonstrates a significant cohesion.

Having shown the high degree of cohesion within the separate parts of 4.1–8, it remains to argue that these pieces cohere with each other, especially that vv. 6–8 belong with the rest. First, it can be argued that vv. 3–4 and vv. 6–8 function well as grounds for the preceding lists of exhortations. This is denoted by the γάρ at the beginning of v. 3 and v. 6. However, not all are convinced by this obvious use of language.

Falconer (followed by Miller) argued that vv. 3–4 are a later editorial insertion because they break the connection between v. 2 and v. 5 and because they contain so many non-Pauline words.[162] This argument assumes exhortation must follow exhortation missing the place of a grounding for such exhortation and apparently missing the movement of this unit suggested above from exhortation to ground to exhortation to ground. The argument based on non-Pauline words fails simply because so much of the letter has words not found in the accepted Paulines.[163] If anything, the presence of such words in these verses would make it more like the rest of the letter rather than different from it! Indeed, there are other links which connect vv. 3–4 to vv. 1–2. First, there is a strong emphasis on teaching in both parts. The imperatives in v. 2 focus on teaching and conclude with διδαχή. Verses 3–4 continue this concern with references to 'sound doctrine' (διδασκαλία), 'teachers' (διδάσκαλοι), 'truth' and the opposites, 'their own desires' and 'myths.' Miller dismisses the connection between διδαχή and διδασκαλία/διδάσκαλοι as merely a formal connection which caused an editor to put these pieces together but the fact that this theme pervades these verses damages his case. Further, there is a lexical link with καιρός in v. 3 linking back to εὐκαίρως ἀκαίρως from v. 2. Mounce also notes that the mention of opposition provides logical reason for the urgency and solemnity of vv. 1–2.[164]

4.6–8 has similar connections to v. 5 and even some of those who separate 4.6–8 in their discussions concede that these verses function as a ground for what precedes.[165] Miller, however, seems to see no connection.[166] First, then, several scholars have noticed a connection between the

161. Marshall 1999: 808.
162. Falconer 1937: 94–95; Miller 1997: 121.
163. The words in view according to Miller are ὑγιαίνω, ἐπισωρεύω, κνήθω, μῦθος, ἐκτρέπω.
164. Mounce 2000: 574.
165. E.g., Bassler 1996: 171; Johnson 1978: 12. Johnson calls the γάρ in v. 6 'striking.'
166. Miller 1997: 122.

emphatic use of the personal pronoun in the initial position of v. 5 (σύ) and
v. 6 (ἐγώ).[167] This marks a thematic and logical connection between the
verses: what Timothy is charged to do, Paul has done. 4.5 closes with the
call to Timothy to 'fulfill your ministry' and vv. 6–8 focus on the fact that
Paul has done this (esp. v. 7). In addition, Timothy is called to engage in
the work because Paul will no longer be around (v. 6).[168] The mention of
Paul's reward for faithfulness is an incentive to Timothy in carrying out his
charge.[169] There is also a semantic connection between κακοπάθησον (v. 5)[170]
and ἀγῶνα ἠγώνισμαι (v. 7) with the idea of suffering.[171] Indeed Pfitzner has
argued that in the earlier Paul the ἀγών motif is used to refer to the
missionary effort.[172] If this is the case, the statements of v. 7 are especially
pertinent for the calls to ministry in v. 5. All of this supports keeping vv.
6–8 with 4.1–5, serving as a basis.

It is also possible to note some parallels between the two sets of
imperatives (vv. 2, 5) and the two sets of grounds (vv. 3–4, 6–8). 4.2, 5, are
both lists of second person singular imperatives (largely aorist tense) and
therefore resemble each other in form and function. The concern of both
verses is Timothy's ministry (though Marshall notes a difference in
emphasis).[173] 'Preach the word' (v. 2) and 'do the work of an evangelist' (v.
5) are quite similar.[174] Similarly, 4.3–4 and 4.6–8 resemble each other with
an opening γάρ and the way they open with connections to the preceding
imperatives. The word καιρός also occurs in both passages, placing both
sets of exhortations in view of an important time which is imminent. Again
Pfitzner is helpful in noting that the fight of the faith (ἀγών) typically
involves the conflict with opponents.[175] If this is so, it suggests a connection
between the opposition in vv. 3–4 and Paul's statement that he has fought
the good fight in v. 7 (τὸν καλὸν ἀγῶνα ἠγώνισμαι). These elements support

---

167. E.g., Marshall 1999: 805; Mounce 2000: 577; Bassler 1996: 171; Smith and Beekman
1981: 98; Guthrie 1990: 181.

168. Johnson 1978: 12.

169. Johnson 1978: 12.

170. This word is omitted by a*, vg[ms]. However, the inclusion of this word has strong
support and is accepted by all commentaries consulted. Marshall 1999: 798 notes Elliot's
acceptance of this reading. Metzger does not discuss it.

171. E. Stauffer writes, 'there seems to belong to the whole concept of ἀγωνίζεσθαι the
thought of obstacles, dangers and catastrophes through which the Christian must find his
way' (*TDNT*, vol 1, 'ἀγών', 138). Pfitzner 1967 also connects this phrase with suffering (e.g.,
161, 193).

172. Pfitzner 1967. For specific statements see, for example, 82f., 183, 193.

173. Marshall 1999: 799, 803.

174. Both lists also have an occurrence of πᾶς. Quinn and Wacker 2000: 781 notes Spicq's
suggestion (1969: 802) of a connection between νήφω and ἕστημι, but it does not seem to be
strong.

175. Pfitzner 1967, e.g., 171, 193.

the idea presented at the beginning of this section that the structure of this unit is:

Exhortation
Ground
Exhortation
Ground

Another piece of evidence for the cohesion of 4.1–8 is the inclusio created by the repetition of words and themes concerning judgment and Christ's appearing at the opening and closing of the unit. Τὴν ἐπιφάνειαν αὐτοῦ occurs in 4.1 amd 8. The noun occurs only once elsewhere in the letter (1.10), and there refers to Christ's first coming rather than to his second as here. 4.1 refers to Christ Jesus judging (κρίνειν) and 4.8 refers to 'the Lord' as 'the righteous judge' (κριτής; neither word appears elsewhere in the letter). Lastly, the unit is enveloped by divine references. Verse 1 refers to God and Christ Jesus. In v. 8 there are references to 'the Lord', 'the righteous Judge,' and ἀπόκειμαι (v. 8) has an implied divine subject.[176] Between v. 1 and v. 8 there are no divine references. Thus, mention of God, and especially Christ, in view of his coming and judgment marks this unit and gives this final appeal an added urgency, power, and sense of solemnity.[177]

Finally, within this inclusio there is a semantic chain running throughout concerning true/false teaching. The verbs of vv. 2 and 5 fit this as well as the references to 'the word' (v. 2), 'teaching' (v. 2), 'sound teaching' (v. 3), 'the truth' (v. 4), 'the good fight' (v. 7), 'the faith' (v. 7), and the contrasting 'myths' (v. 4).[178] All of these elements argue strongly for the tight cohesion of 4.1–8.

4.9–13

Boundaries
There is much disagreement among scholars regarding the boundaries of units from 4.9 to the end of the letter. All note that 4.22 is the epistolary closing; therefore, it can be set to itself. From there, there are at least three proposals. Some argue for keeping all of 4.9–21 together, in keeping with Mounce's arguments that it is difficult and not helpful to try to break up

---

176. Smith and Beekman 1981: 96 also note this as a unifying element.
177. One might also note that ἐφίστημι occurs in v. 2 and v. 6 but nowhere else in the letter. However, a link between these occurrences is not clear, and they are not as close to the boundaries of the unit as one would expect for an 'enveloping' use.
178. Cf. Smith and Beekman 1981: 96.

sections in 2 Timothy into smaller units.[179] Secondly, the most common proposal is to divide 4.9–21 into two units, 4.9–18 and 4.19–21, recognizing the strong concluding function of the doxology in v. 18. Still others break the passage into three units: 4.9–15, 16–18, 19–22.[180] There are cohesive elements which can bind this larger section together (see next chapter), but the goal here is to note shifts and their indications of discrete paragraphs. Indeed, many who keep larger groupings together note that there are smaller paragraphs within their groupings. Therefore, it is argued here that the evidence most clearly supports dividing the passage in this way: 4.9–13, 14–15, 16–18, 19–21.[181]

The beginning boundary of 4.9–13 is marked by the shift to travel plans, a familiar topic in ancient letters. Correspondingly, there is a dramatic shift in participants as many more individuals come into view than has been common previously in the letter, many of them for the first time in the letter. The concern is no longer Timothy's ministry explicitly, but Timothy's journey to Paul.

The final boundary is the more disputed issue. Most scholars keep vv. 14–15 with 4.9–13 in their outlines, but some of these same scholars acknowledge that these verses do not fit easily into the unit with the previous verses.[182] Mounce supports this boundary, keeping vv. 14–15 with vv. 16–18.[183] 4.13 is taken as the end of a unit here because the travel talk which dominates 4.9–13 disappears in 4.14–15. Indeed, the very tight cohesion of 4.9–13 around the travel theme (see below) is itself a reason for excluding vv. 14–15.

Cohesion

The unit coheres around travel language: 'come' (v. 9), 'went' (v. 10), 'with me' (v. 11), 'bring' (v. 11), 'left' (v. 12), 'left' (v. 13), 'coming' (v. 13), 'bring' (v. 13). There is at least one reference to this semantic chain in each verse. The theme of Paul's 'aloneness' is tied up with the travel language and is part of the reason for the call for Timothy to come. In connection with the theme of travel and Paul's companionship, the unit is full of references to people (seven personal names) and places (five specific place names). These references to names and places run from v. 10 to v. 13.

The unit is structured by three second person singular imperatives, each having to do with Timothy coming to Paul: 'be diligent to come' (v. 9), 'bring' (v. 11), 'bring' (v. 13). Each of these imperatives is linked closely with an adjacent non-finite verb form, creating some parallel between the

179. Mounce; Quinn and Wacker.
180. Bassler; Hanson.
181. So also Smith and Beekman 1981: 101–11.
182. E.g., Marshall 1999: 811; Merkel 1991: 85; Fee 1988: 295.
183. Mounce 2000: 587.

commands (Σπούδασον ἐλθεῖν; ἀναλαβὼν ἄγε; ἐρχόμενος φέρε). Also the first two commands are followed by mention of companions who are no longer with Paul. In v. 11b and v. 13 the imperative verbs are virtually synonymous,[184] and both are preceded by a nominative masculine singular participle. Based on the call to come in v. 9, the imperatives in vv. 11b and 13 tell Timothy who/what to bring with him. Finally, the unit is bracketed by two occurrences of ἔρχομαι.[185] These factors argue strongly for a high degree of cohesion in this unit.

4.14–15

Boundaries

The initial boundary of this unit has been discussed above. While the motif of travel occurred in every verse of 4.9–13, it does not appear at all in 4.14–15.[186] There is a shift away from travel talk to discussion of opposition. As Merkel notes, this new topic seems to appear without any transition ('ohne Übergang').[187] Marshall, also, even though he keeps vv. 14–15 with the preceding verses, notes that, 'A fresh motif appears…'[188] The unit then ends at v. 15 because v. 16 introduces a new topic once again. Other distinguishing characteristics of 4.16–18 which support this boundary will be noted below.

Cohesion

4.14–15 cohere around the person of Alexander. After being named, three pronouns refer to him (αὐτῷ, αὐτοῦ, v. 14; ὅν, v. 15), and he is either the subject or object of every verb in this unit. The topic throughout is opposition. As would be expected from such a small unit, there is a high degree of cohesion.

---

184. Louw and Nida (1989) list ἄγω as 15.165 and φέρω as 15.166. Smith and Beekman 1981: 103 also note that the verbs are virtually synonymous.

185. So also, Smith and Beekman 1981: 103.

186. Some have suggested that vv. 14–15 are connected with the preceding verses in that it is suggested that Alexander would be encountered by Timothy on the journey discussed in vv. 9–13 (Marshall 1999: 821 notes this as a possibility; cf. also Easton 1947: 73; Fee 1988: 296; Quinn 1980: 295; Quinn and Wacker 2000: 813.). This is certainly possible and will be considered in the following chapter as connections between units are considered. The issue here focuses more on explicit connection.

187. Merkel 1991: 85.

188. Marshall 1999: 821. He goes on to suggest that the 'new' motif might should be regarded as a development of the abandonment motif of v. 10.

4.16–18

Boundaries
A clear shift in topic is seen as v. 16 opens with a reference to Paul's 'first defense,' a topic which has not been mentioned previously in the letter.[189] This coincides with a shift in topic, from opposition and Timothy's journey, to Paul's situation.[190] While Paul's situation (particularly his 'aloneness') have been in view in the previous verses, vv. 16–18 focus specifically on this situation. Thus, there is a shift away from the focus on Timothy. There are no imperatives and no second person singular references of any sort.[191] Lastly, there is also a shift in genre from warning to testimony.

Cohesion
This unit coheres around the topic of Paul's defense and the Lord's help. This naturally leads to a note of expectant triumph and a closing doxology. As the unit has shifted away from Timothy, it coheres around Paul. Paul is the object of four of the first five verbs (μοι παρεγένετο, με ἐγκατέλιπον, μοι παρέστη, ἐνεδυνάμωσέν με; all but the optative prayer), the agent of the next two verbs (δι' ἐμοῦ ... πληροφορηθῇ καὶ ἀκούσωσῃ), the subject of the next one (ἐρρύσθην), and the object of the last two (ῥύσεταί με ... καὶ σώσει). Thus, the entire unit revolves around Paul, especially 'the Lord' and Paul as κύριος also figures prominently. The idea of trouble for Paul also runs throughout the unit with abandonment (v. 16), the 'lion's mouth' (v. 17), and 'every evil deed' (v. 18). There is a natural movement in the unit from the abandonment by people, to the faithfulness and strengthening of the Lord for ministry, to deliverance (both past and the expected future).[192] Lastly, there is a consistent pattern with each of the main statements consisting of verb doublets:

> 'No one supported me but all deserted me' (v. 16)
> 'The Lord stood with me and strengthened me' (v. 17)
> 'The Lord will deliver me and save [me]' (v. 18)

These elements support the cohesion of this unit.

---

189. Merkel 1991: 86 also notes shift, calling it 'abrupt' ('unvermittelt').
190. So also, Fee 1988: 296, who writes, 'Paul now turns from the request for Timothy to come to a brief explanation about his own situation...'
191. Quinn and Wacker 2000: 820 note the absence of second person singular verbs.
192. In the last three verbs are two occurrences of ῥύομαι and one of σώζω. These verbs are very close in meaning.

4.19–22

The doxology of v. 18 clearly marks the closing of the previous unit and of the body of the letter. 4.19, therefore, begins a new unit. The appearance of the verb ἀσπάζομαι marks this unit as the customary closing greetings.[193] A couple of other statements are placed within the two bracketing occurrences of ἀσπάζομαι, so that the unit opens with Paul giving greetings and closes with Timothy receiving greetings from those with Paul. Some question the coherence of the greetings since the two greetings statements are separated by travel discussion and a repeated command. However, something similar can be seen in other New Testament letters (Col. 4.10–17, 1 Thess. 5.27) and the papyri (e.g. PLond III 893, *c.* 40 AD).[194] The concluding benediction is attached in a customary manner.

Conclusion

This chapter has had two primary goals: (1) to distinguish the boundaries of the discrete units of 2 Timothy and (2) to examine the coherence of each unit. At certain places it has been difficult to decide whether to hold two sets of verses together as one unit or to distinguish them as two units (e.g., 2.1–13; 4.9–18). Each unit has been found to cohere through a variety of linguistic, semantic, and thematic elements. The next issue is discerning how or if these discrete units connect and how that shapes the letter of 2 Timothy.

193.   Quinn and Wacker 2000: 830: 'The attachment of greetings to letters with this verb as a technical term seems to have become progressively more common in the Hellenistic age, and it is particularly characteristic of the Pauline correspondence.' Cf. Exler 1923: 116.
194.   Reproduced in White 1986: 124.

Chapter 5

CONNECTIONS BETWEEN UNITS IN 2 TIMOTHY

The last chapter identified discrete units within 2 Timothy and argued that these units cohered within themselves. Such cohesion is important, but for the entire letter to cohere these units must connect in some way with each other. Examining such interconnection between units is the focus of this chapter.

The analysis will take place in three parts. First, there will be an examination of connections between contiguous units, between each unit and the one which follows. In a cohesive document one will expect there to be some coherent flow from one unit to the next, though the level of connection may vary since discourses do not develop only linearly. Specific attention will be given to conjunctions, transitional devices (e.g. hooked keywords, etc.), and continuities in cohesion fields.

The second part will shift to the macroperspective examining semantic chains which run through significant portions of the letter. These chains consist of recurring elements related to each other lexically or semantically and reveal a common concern throughout the letter. If these chains themselves overlap and are interrelated the cohesive function is even greater.

The third part will focus on how the units may form larger sections and how this effects the shape of the whole. The burden of the argument for cohesion will rest primarily on the first two parts while the third part examines how the various units of the letter interrelate.

Connections Between Contiguous Units

1.3–5 and 1.6–14

It is commonly held by commentators that these two units are closely linked. Indeed, Donald Guthrie sums up the common view stating, 'There is no real break between this section and the last.'[1] Generally this connection is based on two points. First, the conjunction δι' ἣν αἰτίαν

---

1. Guthrie 1990: 138. Kelly 1963: 159, also states, 'The transition from the preceding section is easy and natural.'

suggests a strong connection, presenting vv. 6–14 as based on and growing out of vv. 3–5.[2] Secondly, this connection is considered logical as the admonitions are understood as arising from the belief (or hope) that Timothy's faith is sincere. However, Miller contests this connection. First, he sees no logical connection between the contents of the two units since, in his view, 1.3–5 is about Timothy's heritage and 1.6ff. is about ordination.[3] Quite apart from the issue of whether ordination is the primary or sole issue of 1.6–14, he does not discuss why these two issues could not possibly be related in an argument. In fact commentators commonly note that the calls to action in 1.6ff. grow out of Paul's confidence (or hope) in the sincerity of Timothy's faith.[4] Why this view should be discarded, Miller does not explain. Secondly, based on his perceived lack of logical connection, Miller suggests δι' ἣν αἰτίαν has no real conjunctive function but simply serves as a marker to introduce traditional materials. In support of this he writes, 'this conjecture gains credibility when it is observed that the same phrase introduces a catena of three citations in Heb. 2.11....'[5] However, the credibility of his conjecture is not firmly established. In its other NT uses δι' ἣν αἰτίαν does not serve to introduce traditional material and it is doubtful whether this is actually its function in Heb. 2.11 either. In fact in Heb. 2.11 it functions causally, as traditionally understood here in 2 Timothy 1.6, and is not directly linked to the citations which follow.[6] Thus, Miller's objections do not hold, and the traditional understanding of the connection of these units stands.

In addition to the conjunction, there are a couple of transitional devices in view here as well. First, there is a hooked keyword, or in this case, 'key-root.' As noted in the previous chapter, cognate words for remembrance occur once in each verse of 1.3–5 (μνείαν, v. 3; μεμνημένος, v. 4; ὑπόμνησιν, v. 5). This was shown to be one of the cohesive themes of 1.3–5. 1.6 then opens with ἀναμιμνῄσκω creating a connection with this lexical chain. This root then occurs no more in 1.6–14, thus following the pattern of key words and suggesting the remembrance language is intentionally used at the beginning of this unit to create a link.[7]

---

2. So practically all recent commentators.

3. Miller 1997: 101.

4. E.g., Marshall 1999: 696; Quinn and Wacker 2000: 589–90; Mounce 2000: 474; Bassler 1996: 129; Bernard 1906: 108; Lock 1924: 84; Kelly 1963: 159.

5. Miller 1997: 101.

6. In fact Miller seems to be alone in suggesting this function of δι' ἣν αἰτίαν. Having consulted the commentaries by Ellingworth, Attridge, Bruce and Moffatt no mention of anything close to Miller's view was found.

7. Quinn and Wacker 2000: 589 also note agreement with Spicq in seeing a connection due to repetition of ὁη θέος (vv. 3, 6). However, this word occurs often enough in the letter that a conjunctive function is not clear.

Secondly, the person and number of the verbs create a 'hooked' transition. First person singular dominates 1.3–5, with Paul being the subject of every verb but one (ἐνοικέω, v. 5). Though there have been shown to be significant shifts at 1.6, the first verb continues the chain of first person singular verbs. The following verbs then make the shift to second person. Thus, the maintenance of continuity in this one cohesion field, while the others shift, creates a connection. This is a 'hooked' transition because what was common in the previous unit appears at the beginning of the next unit but does not continue. So, in vv. 3–5, Paul has memory of Timothy, Paul longs to see Timothy, Paul remembers Timothy's tears, Paul receives reminders of Timothy's faith, and Paul is persuaded about Timothy. Paul is the subject and Timothy is the object. This continues in the first verb of 1.6: Paul reminds Timothy. Then there is a shift, however. From 1.7 Timothy is to stir up, Timothy is not to be ashamed, Timothy is to suffer with Paul. This progression can be seen in the participant structure. 1.3 begins with Paul's heritage and state ('clean conscience') and v. 5 ends with the focus on Timothy's heritage and state ('sincere faith'). This move to focus on Timothy prepares the way for 1.6ff.

Third, there is another lexical repetition, with πείθω occurring in 1.5 and 1.12, the only occurrences in the letter. In both instances the confidence is connected with faith. In 1.5 Paul is convinced of the sincerity of Timothy's faith (πίστις). In 1.12 Paul is convinced in the ability of the God in whom he believes (πιστεύω). The conviction concerning the sincerity of Timothy's faith leads Paul to exhort him not to be ashamed and to suffer. Paul suffers and is not ashamed because of his conviction in the power of God.

These linguistic connections show a reasonable progression from one unit to the next. Therefore, they support the common conjunctive understanding of δι' ἣν αἰτίαν and show that 1.3–5 and 1.6–14 cohere.

1.6–14 and 1.15–18

It is clear to all that significant shifts occur at 1.15, and thus it has been considered the initial boundary of a new unit. Even with the significant shifts, most have understood 1.15–18 to be connected with the previous unit because these verses provide positive and negative examples of the call to faithfulness in 1.6–14.[8] So Bassler writes, 'This short passage provides concrete illustrations of what it means to be ashamed, and not ashamed, of Paul and his gospel.'[9] Dibelius and Conzelmann even state, 'The personal references ... are intimately connected with the preceding section.'[10]

---

8.   So for example, Marshall 1999: 716; Wolter 1988: 216; Mounce 2000: 492; Bassler 1996: 136; Knight 1992: 383; Johnson 1996: 60; Dibelius and Conzelmann 1972: 106; Guthrie 1990: 147; Donelson 1986: 107; Läger 1996: 73.

9.   Bassler 1996: 137.

10.   Dibelius and Conzelmann 1972: 106.

Miller, however, disputes any connection, saying the shift at v. 15 is 'sudden and unexpected' and concluding that 1.15–18 is a block of genuine material inserted here without any connection to the surrounding material.[11] Indeed, according to Miller, 'The whole block of personalia distinctively protrudes within its context . . . .'[12] Miller notes the suggestion that 1.15–18 provides examples for 1.6–14 but dismisses this as attributing 'far too much subtlety to the author of the Pastorals.'[13] This does more to reveal his opinion of the writing of the Pastorals than to disprove this connection. Miller claims that there is nothing in the immediate context to prompt the statements of 1.15–18 and that the references to specific individuals in this unit 'contrasts with the general parenetic nature of the materials that precede and follow.'[14] Miller, however, is patently wrong in positing a disjunction between parenesis and reference to specific individuals. In fact it was common to include specific examples in parenesis.[15] The fact that this was a common practice supports the idea that this is exactly what is being done in 1.15–18. What prompts the statements of 1.15–18 is, then, the preceding instruction which can use some concrete illustration. Thus, Miller's criticisms do not hold.

There are also other indications of connection between 1.6–14 and 1.15–18. First there are simply some continuities. For example the topic is still faithfulness to Paul and his gospel. Also 1.16 specifically picks up a key verb from vv. 8 and 12, ἐπαισχύνομαι, and the language of imprisonment. Paul in v. 8 urged Timothy not to be ashamed 'of me, his prisoner' (δέσμιος; Louw and Nida 1989: 37.117) and in v. 16 Onesiphorus is not ashamed of Paul's imprisonment (ἅλυσις; Louw and Nida 1989: 37.115).[16] Additionally, εἰς ἐκείνην τὴν ἡμέραν in v. 12 connects with ἐν ἐκείνῃ τῇ ἡμέρᾳ in v. 18, a phrase which occurs only once more in the letter (4.8). The phrase points to the eschatological outlook common to both 1.6–14 and 1.15–18. These clear lexical and semantic links support the idea that 1.15–18 provides examples for the exhortations in 1.6–14.

Lastly, there is in 1.15 a hooked transition very similar to the one discerned in 1.6. 1.15 opens with a second person singular verb in continuity with the preceding unit which closed with three straight second person singular verbs (vv. 13–14). However, as was noted in the previous chapter, 1.15–18 focus primarily on the third person. As in 1.6, while the genre and other fields shift at the beginning of the verse, the person and number of the verb do not shift until the second verb, creating an overlap,

11. Miller 1997: 105, 106, respectively.
12. Miller 1997: 106.
13. Miller 1997: 105, n. 32.
14. Miller 1997: 106.
15. Cf. Fiore 1986; Malherbe 1986, 136f.
16. So also Bassler 1996: 136.

and therefore a connection. The fact that this occurs in 1.6 and 1.15 supports the idea of understanding this as a transitional technique (whether conscious or subconscious).

Thus, Miller's objections do not hold and additional connections can be seen which support the connection of 1.6–14 and 1.15–18.

1.15–18 and 2.1–13

It is commonly held that σὺ οὖν in 2.1 links what follows with 1.15–18 and perhaps 1.6–14 as well.[17] Johnson states, 'The *su oun teknon mou* of 2.1 must be seen as following directly from these examples [1.15–18].'[18] Miller, however, disputes the idea that σὺ οὖν has any sort of connective function, regarding it instead as merely a marker of traditional material. While this is possible, it is not necessary and is dependent on his view of 2.1ff. as miscellaneous traditional material. The common inferential function of οὖν works well in 2.1. The appeal to Timothy to be steadfast is seen as an inference from the example of Onesiphorus and from the urgency created by the desertion of others.[19]

Furthermore, there are other indications of connections between the units. Faithfulness to Paul and his gospel continues to be the theme in 2.1–13: those in Asia were not faithful, Onesiphorus was, and Timothy should be. The eschatological outlook remains as well. 1.15–18 closes with the reference to Onesiphorus finding mercy on the final day and this perspective is elaborated in 2.1–13 with the mention of reward (vv. 6–7), final salvation (v. 10), and the final verdict in view in the faithful saying (vv. 11b–13). Indeed, it could be said that the diligent search (σπουδαίως ζητεῖν) of Onesiphorus followed by mention of finding peace corresponds to the hardworking (κοπιάω) farmer who receives his reward (v. 6). There is also continuity in Paul's situation. In 1.15–18 he is abandoned (v. 15) and in chains (v. 16) and in 2.9 he is suffering to the point of imprisonment.

Finally, there is another hooked transition based on the person and number of the verbs. Although second person singular verbs are not common in 1.15–18, the final verb (indeed the final word) returns to second person singular. Second person singular then dominates 2.1–13. Indeed there is a clear move in 1.18 reintroducing the second person which creates a transition to the exhortations to Timothy in 2.1–13. This is enhanced by the fact that the second person singular pronoun occurs explicitly as the

---

17. E.g., Marshall 1999: 723; Mounce 2000: 503; Bassler 1996: 138; Knight 1992: 389; Fee 1988: 239. The concern here is only with connections with the immediately preceding unit. Connections with 1.6–14 will be treated later in the chapter.

18. Johnson 1978: 8.

19. Even if one prefers to take οὖν as resumptive (cf. Heckert 1996: 100), this would suggest a connection with 1.6–14 which will be discussed later in this chapter.

subject in both 1.18 and 2.1. Σύ had not occurred since 1.6 and does not occur again until 2.7. It has been placed at the end of one unit and the beginning of another to create a transitional link.[20]

2.1–13 and 2.14–26

The connection between 2.1–13 and 2.14–26 has been questioned more than the other connections considered so far. Barrett represented others when he wrote, 'the connexion with the preceding paragraph is indeed not close.'[21] Thus, Miller says at 2.14 there is 'an abrupt change in subject matter as well as literary style' with 'no clear connection to what precedes.'[22] The most commonly recognized connection is the Ταῦτα which begins the unit in 2.14. If one understands the pronoun to refer to previous material as most agree,[23] then this creates some connection by causing the reader to look back for a referent. Indeed, Oberlinner argues that the backward referring ταῦτα shows that in the mind of the author the exhortations of 2.14–26 were understood as a continuation, deepening and concretizing of 2.8–13.[24] However, Miller contends that ταῦτα is simply a marker of traditional material.[25] The question, then, is whether there are other links between the two units which support the more common understanding of ταῦτα.

2.11–13 (not to mention possibilities of connections further back) does provide a number of points of contact with 2.14. With its structural balance and its identification as a faithful saying, vv. 11–13 carry a certain weight or solemnity which corresponds to the solemn adjuration of v. 14. The concern of vv. 11–13 is reward or judgment before God and the charge in v. 14 is 'in the presence of God.' In light of the promised reward and the reality of judgement, Timothy is to warn people to have nothing to do with the false teachers. These factors show that 2.11–13 are well suited as a referent for Ταῦτα ὑπομίμνησκε, suggesting the admittedly new issues of 2.14–26 flow out of the preceding material.

In addition to the function of ταῦτα in v. 14, there are other points of continuity and connection between the units. First, 2.14–26 continues the

---

20.   Marshall 1999: 721 notes that 1.18b is often regarded as an afterthought (cf. Fee 1988: 237). This strengthens the case for the author adding this apparent afterthought in order to encapsulate the entire unit in references to Timothy (see previous chapter) and to transition back to a focus on Timothy.

21.   Barrett 1963: 105. Similarly Johnson states, 'the transition to this new section of this letter is not smooth' (1996: 70), and Falconer refers to v. 14 as 'An abrupt beginning of a new theme' (1937: 84).

22.   Miller 1997: 111.

23.   See, e.g., Marshall 1999: 745–46; Mounce 2000: 523; Oberlinner 1995: 91; Merkel 1991: 66; Fee 1988: 254; Guthrie 1990: 158–59.

24.   Oberlinner 1995: 91.

25.   Miller 1997: 111.

exhortation from Paul to Timothy in second person singular imperatives as has been common in previous units. Beyond this general similarity, many of the specific commands in 2.14–26 connect back to 2.1–13. The first verb of 2.14, ὑπομίμνησκω, connects back to its cognate, μνημονεύω, in 2.8. There is a logical progression from urging Timothy, himself, to remember and then telling him to remind others. The next imperative in 2.14–26 comes in 2.15 which calls for a diligent pursuit of divine approval. This connects well with the reference in 2.4 to pleasing the commanding officer, who, in light of v. 3, is clearly Christ. The other imperatives in 2.14–26 revolve around avoiding the evils of the opponents which correspond well with the calls in 2.1–13 to strength (2.1), suffering (2.3, 9, 11), and endurance (2.10, 12). 2.14–26 clarify the reason for the calls to endurance. Thus, while opposition and heresy are made explicit for the first time in 2.14–26, they flow logically out of the content of the previous unit.[26] Indeed, the reference to the possibility of apostasy in 2.12 virtually introduces the discussion of opponents in 2.14–26. Thus, the message to Timothy in both units is the same: remain faithful. 2.14–26 merely advances the discourse by introducing explicit discussion of the opposition.

The focus on opponents in 2.14–26 creates contrasting connections also. 2.1–13 is concerned about the Pauline message ('what you heard from me,' 2.2; 'my gospel,' 2.8), but 2.14–26 is concerned with 'their message' (2.17), i.e., the opponents' message. The faithful λόγος appears to stand in contradiction to the opponents' λόγος (2.17).[27] There is a succinct summary of both messages (2.8; 2.18), followed by contrasting results: salvation (2.10) and upsetting of faith (2.18).

Further, the units share a similar evangelistic concern. In 2.10 Paul says he endures hardships so that the elect might obtain salvation. In 2.25–26, Paul calls for gentle correction in hopes that even some of the opponents might be granted repentance. Thus the concern for salvation and the presentation of it in terms of God's sovereignty unite the two units.[28]

Lastly, there is a lexical connection between 2.2 and 2.24. In 2.2 Timothy is to hand down the deposit to men who are 'able to teach others' (ἱκανοὶ ... διδάξαι) and in 2.24 the 'servant of the Lord' must be 'able to teach' (διδακτικός). There is a common concern that the deposit of truth be in the

---

26. So similarly, Oberlinner 1995: 91. Each of these points also connect with 1.6–18.

27. The life and reign envisioned in 2.11–12 appear to be future, whereas the opponents in 2.18 say the resurrection has already occurred.

28. Mounce 2000: 529 also argues that the quote from Num. 16.5 (LXX) in 2.19c connotes election. If so, this is another point of connection in this emphasis on divine sovereignty in salvation.

hands of men capable to teach, particularly because of the threat of the opponents.[29]

Thus, in addition to the backward referring ταῦτα in 2.14, a number of connections and continuities hold 2.1–13 and 2.14–26 together. However, it can be noted that the connections between these units are more general than the connections noted between the previous four units. For example no explicit transitional device was found. There is sufficient connection to affirm the cohesion of the two units, but it may be that 1.3–2.13 cohere more closely with each other than with 2.14–26. This will be taken up later in a discussion of larger sections within 2 Timothy.

2.14–26 and 3.1–9

The connection between 2.14–26 and 3.1–9 is not greatly disputed. First, on the face of it, the introductory δέ suggests a connection between the units, and it has regularly been understood as a contrasting connection. For example Johnson writes, 'The adversative de should be taken at full force here. These characteristics of the false teachers stand in opposition to the ideal sketched in the preceding verses …'[30] The contrast may also be between the hope for conversion of the opponents in 2.25–26 and the reality that people will get worse in 3.1f.,[31] or between the gentleness called for in 2.24–26 and the brutish behavior described in 3.2–4.[32] There is, then, a good basis for interpreting the δέ as marking a contrasting connection.

There is also significant continuity between the two units. The major concern in both units is the opponents. The shift between the units is that the opponents become almost the sole focus in 3.1–9, but the concern with the opponents is the same. The opponents are bad and Timothy is to avoid them and their controversies (2.16, 23; 3.5).[33] In fact the commands to avoid the opponents in 2.23 and 3.5 use verbs (παραιτέομαι and ἀποτρέπομαι respectively) which are synonymous, thus creating a connection.[34] There are several other lexical and semantic connections between the descriptions of the opponents in these two units. Both units open with a verb of cognition + οὗτος. In both units the opponents are quarrelsome and combative (λογομαχεῖν, 2.14; μάχας, 2.23; βλάσφημοι, 3.2; ἄσπονδοι, διάβολοι, ἀνήμεροι, 3.3). In 2.16 their teaching leads to 'ungodliness' (ἀσέβεια) and is

29.   There is also an interesting contrast between the cognitive status of Timothy in 2.7 and the opponents in 2.14–26. God will give Timothy understanding (2.7) but the opponents' teaching is foolish (v. 16), ignorant, and untaught (v. 23).

30.   Johnson 1978: 11. Quinn and Wacker 2000: 713 interprets the δέ as 'a slight contrast to what has preceded.'

31.   So, e.g. Knight 1992: 428.

32.   So, e.g. Bassler 1996: 157.

33.   Cf. Bassler 1996: 149; Johnson 1978: 11.

34.   Louw and Nida list both verbs under the same listing, 1989: 34.41.

characterized as 'worldly.' Similarly in 3.2–5 they are at least connected with a strong vice list, including the charge that they deny the power of 'godliness' (εὐσέβεια).³⁵ In both units the opponents are associated with wrong desires (ἐπιθυμία, 2.22; 3.6).³⁶ The description of the opponents' teaching as foolish (κενοφωνία, 2.16; μωρός, ἀπαίδευτος, 2.23) connects to the references in 3.8–9 to men of depraved minds (νοῦς) and their foolishness (ἄνοια). In 2.18 they have abandoned truth (ἀλήθεια), and in 3.8 they oppose truth (ἀλήθεια). Indeed, the verb for oppose in 3.8 (ἀνθίστημι) is synonymous with the verb used in 2.25 to characterize these people as opponents (ἀντιδιατίθημι).³⁷ The opponents in 2.26 have been captured (ζωγρέω; Louw and Nida 1989: 37.1) by the devil and in 3.6 they are capturing (αἰχμαλωτίζω; Louw and Nida 1989: 37.29) others. In the context of this capture in both units there is a statement of the opponents' lack of knowledge of the truth. The same phrase is used in both 2.25 and 3.7 (εἰς ἐπίγνωσιν ἀληθείας) to say that the opponents are unable themselves to come to the knowledge of the truth.³⁸ Lastly, the sneaking into homes by these opponents (3.6) reminds one of those in 2.17 whose teaching spreads like gangrene, and their capturing of the weak resembles the destruction of the hearers in 2.14 and the upsetting of faith in 2.18.

A further lexical connection is the occurrence of the verb προκόπτω in 2.16 and 3.9. While both occurrences refer to the opponents, one makes a positive assessment of their progress and the other a negative one. Thus, some scholars have found here a contradiction suggesting the incoherence of these two units.³⁹ However, two different things are actually in view. 2.16 says ungodly and foolish talk will progress to further ungodliness, and 3.9 says the opponents will not make further progress in their opposition to the truth. The tension caused by using the same verb in contrasting ways (thus a wordplay),⁴⁰ creates a connection witnessed to by the scholarly discussion on the relation between the two statements.

These lexical and semantic connections show that there is a very significant continuity between 2.14–26 and 3.1–9 in their concern with and response to the opponents. 2.14–26 is structured around the shifting contrast between Timothy and the opponents. 3.1–9 then focuses more

35.   These are the only two occurrences of cognates of εὐσέβεια in 2 Timothy.
36.   The idea of wrong desires also shows in the φιλ- cognates in 3.2, 4 (lovers of self, lovers of money, lovers of pleasure rather than God).
37.   Louw and Nida list both words under the same heading, 1989: 39.1.
38.   In 2.25 they need to be *granted* repentance unto this knowledge and in 3.7 it is simply stated that they are unable.
39.   E.g., Miller 1997: 118; Brox 1969a: 256; Easton 1947: 64; Holtzmann 1880: 430. Hanson 1982: 148 mentions a possible solution to what he sees as a contradiction but does not say he is convinced by the solution.
40.   The rhetorical stylistic device *traductio* (Rowe 1997: 132).

exclusively on the opponents though there is still a contrast made with Timothy (3.5).

3.1–9 and 3.10–17

Commentators have regularly understood 3.10–17 to be connected to 3.1–9 as a contrast marked by the δέ with an emphatic σύ in 3.10.[41] However, some have failed to see or have disputed any such connection. Harrison considered 3.10ff. an authentic fragment, distinct from the preceding material.[42] Hanson appears to see no connection, and Moffatt described 3.10–12 as an 'erratic boulder' interrupting the context.[43] Miller most specifically addresses the issue claiming that the Σὺ δέ in 3.10 is merely a formulaic marker for traditional material, rather than marking a contrast and that 'There is no clear development of thought between 3:6–9 and the unit which follows it (3.10–13).'[44] For Miller the only connection is a formal connection due to the repetition of προκόπτω in 3.9, 13.

In response to Miller and the others, it can first be said that they have not given adequate attention to the Σὺ δέ in 3.10. Miller simply asserts that it is formulaic without considering an actual contextual, conjunctive function. The initial emphatic placement of σύ following a thorough discussion of people who are portrayed as against Timothy, suggests a contrasting shift from the way 'they' (opponents) act to the way 'you' (Timothy) should act. Such a contrast simply follows the pattern already established in 2.14–26.[45] This contrast is further made clear since 3.10 opens with a virtue list in contrast to the vice lists of 3.1–9. Indeed the qualities of these lists are in stark contrast with each other.[46] While the vice list in 3.2–4 is characterized by fierceness and self-centeredness,[47] 3.10 calls for patience and love. Specifically ἄστοργος (3.3), 'lacking in natural affection,' contrasts with ἀγάπη (3.10). While some have misdirected love (loving self, money and pleasure; 3.2, 4), Timothy is to follow Paul's model of love. While violence is a common thread in the vice list, 3.10 refers to a

---

41. So for example, Marshall 1999: 783; Knight 1992: 438; Mounce 2000: 556; Merkel 1991: 73; Fee 1988: 275–76; Bassler 1996: 162–63; Barrett 1963: 112; Easton 1947: 66.

42. Harrison 1921: 124.

43. Hanson 1982: 148; Moffatt 1920: 403. Dibelius and Conzelmann 1972: 118–19, also make no mention of any contrast.

44. Miller 1997: 119.

45. Indeed, Marshall 1999: 783 notes that such a shift from the evil of the opponents to the good which Timothy should follow is a common switch in 2 Timothy and elsewhere in the Pastoral Epistles.

46. Bassler 1996: 163; Fee 1988: 276.

47. Mounce 2000: 543, 'The theme of self-centeredness permeates the list'; Marshall 1999: 772, 'There is a stress on self-centeredness....'

willingness to suffer.[48] In contrast to the 'traitors' (προδότης) of 3.4, Timothy is urged to remain in the tradition he has received from Paul (3.10–11, 14).[49] The Scriptures lead to 'righteousness' (δικαιοσύνη) which stands in global contrast to the vice lists of 3.1–9. 3.1–9 closes with a statement of the opponents' failure to progress and their obvious foolishness, but 3.10–17 closes with a statement of the 'completeness' of the man of God and his preparedness for any good work. There also seems to be a presentation of contrasting models. The opponents are like Jannes and Jambres, while Timothy is to be like Paul.[50] These specific contrasts suggest that Paul's 'teaching' and 'lifestyle' in 3.10 are intended to be understood as in contrast to the wicked lifestyle (3.2–5) and teaching (3.6–9) of the opponents.[51]

Furthermore, there is a specific contrast between 3.7 and 3.14–15 involving two lexical links as well. 3.7 and 3.14 contain all the occurrences of μανθάνω in the letter. The women influenced by the opponents are never able to truly learn (i.e., they learn but never come to knowledge), but Timothy has learned. This is connected with the only two occurrences of δύναμαι (3.7, 15). These women are never 'able' to come to salvation ('the knowledge of the truth'),[52] but Timothy has known the Holy Scriptures which are 'able' to make you wise unto salvation.[53] This knowledge of Timothy would then also contrast with the depraved minds of the opponents (3.8). Thus, these two terms are used in both units with the same connection but contrasting results. This strongly suggests cohesion of the thought behind both units and supports Bassler's claim that 3.10f. 'is clearly meant to be read in conjunction with the preceding description of the opposing teachers.'[54]

The fact that there is such a clear contrast between 3.1–9 and 3.10–17 provides the 'clear development of thought' between the units which Miller denied. Timothy, having been warned of the evil, is urged to follow a different way. Such a progression of thought would be standard parenetic fare.[55] As Marshall states, 'After the description of the character and activities of the opponents, which serves to emphasize the urgency of right

---

48. Violence: ἄσπονδος ('implacable'), ἀνήμερος ('savage, brutal'), προπετής ('rash, reckless'; Marshall 1999: 774 connects it with violence).

49. Marshall 1999: 774 notes that this word is the opposite of πιστός. If πιστός in 3.10 means 'faithfulness' (this is debated) then this would be another strong contrast.

50. So also, Johnson 1978: 11.

51. Bassler 1996: 162–63 also says 3.10f are intended to be a contrasting pattern of behavior.

52. Cf. Towner 1989: 122; Dibelius and Conzelmann 1972: 41; Ho 2000: 180.

53. Marshall 1999: 789 notes that v. 15 may provide a contrast with v. 7.

54. Bassler 1996: 162–63.

55. Cf. Johnson 1978: 14–15. Johnson specifically points out how this is true of Pseudo-Isocrates' *Ad Demonicum*.

living and teaching in the church, it is natural that there is a renewed appeal to Timothy to live in the right way.'[56]

Another point of connection between the units is continuity in the description of the opponents. In the only reference to opponents in 3.10–17, v. 13 refers to 'evil men' (ἄνθρωποι) and 'impostors' (γόητες). Both of these terms link back to the description in 3.1–9, especially the closing description in 3.8. The description of the opponents in 3.1–9 is flanked by occurrences of the plural ἄνθρωποι (vv. 2, 8), causing the reader to connect the reference in 3.13 back to 3.1–9.[57] Specifically, 'men of depraved minds' (v. 8) coincide with 'evil men' (3.13). The 'man of God' in v. 17 would then stand in contrast to these evil men. Also, γόητες can have the connotation of 'sorcerer,' which would link back to Jannes and Jambres in 3.8. Even if the term is meant more generally here (as most agree), the use of a word which commonly had this broader connotation[58] may suggest that a connection is intended.[59] Additionally, there is a direct lexical repetition between v. 9 and v. 13:

v. 9 – ἀλλ' οὐ προκόψουσιν ἐπὶ πλεῖον
v. 13 – προκόψουσιν ἐπὶ τὸ χεῖρον

Both of these statements describe the opponents, though in contrasting ways. Miller and others say this is a contradiction and proves the discontinuity of the two units.[60] However, two different things are in view in these verses. 3.9 refers to success of the opponents, but 3.13 uses the verb ironically to refer to their increasing descent into evil.[61] Thus, the point of 3.13 is very similar to that of 3.1. Therefore, the use of the same verb in both instances appears to be a deliberate play on words, connecting the unit.

Finally, there are two structural indications of cohesion. First, in line with the contrasting connection, the two units appear to be arranged as mirror images of each other. 3.1–9, after the introductory statement ('But know this'), focuses almost exclusively on opponents with only one other statement to Timothy, tucked in the middle (v. 5). 3.10–17 in contrast focuses almost exclusively on Timothy with just one reference to the opponents stuck in the middle (v. 13). Secondly, and more tentatively, 3.1–9 closes with an aorist tense verb though the tense has not been common in the unit (two other instances). 3.10–11 then opens with four

56. Marshall 1999: 781.
57. So, Knight 1992: 441.
58. Cf. G. Delling, 'γόης,' *TDNT* 1, 737–38; BAGD, s.v.
59. Quinn and Wacker 2000: 745 say the word 'almost certainly' refers back to those described in 3.6–8.
60. Miller 1997: 118; Brox 1969a: 256; Easton 1947: 64; Holtzmann 1880: 430.
61. Cf. Marshall 1999: 787.

straight aorist verbs creating (with the verb of 3.9) the most significant cluster of aorist verbs since 1.16–18. It may be that the last verb of 3.9 provides a transition to the verbs of 3.10–11, though this is not as firm as the other connections already noted.[62]

3.10–17 and 4.1–8

It is almost universally agreed that 3.10–17 and 4.1–8 are significantly connected with each other. Even Miller does not raise the issue of incoherence between these units.[63] Indeed, Mounce, Dibelius and Conzelmann, and Hanson all keep 3.10–4.8 together as one unit,[64] and Quinn and Wacker and Bassler keep portions of the units together. Thus, there is wide agreement on the presence of some connection between 3.10–17 and 4.1–8.

One prime element of the cohesion of these units is a significant level of continuity. The previous chapter noted that the shift in cohesion fields between these units is not strong. Second person singular referents, having decreased in 3.1–9 (only two occurrences), came back to prominence in 3.10–17 (seven occurrences) and continue prominently through 4.1–8 (ten occurrences). Even more significantly, first person singular referents had disappeared totally after 2.10, but reappear at 3.10–11 (four times) and then again in 4.1, 6–8 (eight times). As the opponents are also in view in both units (3.13; 4.3–4), this marks a significant continuity in the participants of these units. The interrelation of the participants is the same as well. Timothy is exhorted (3.10, 14; 4.1–2, 5) in the light of Paul's example (3.10–11; 4.6–8) and in contrast to the opponents (3.13, σὺ δέ; 4.3–4, σὺ δέ).[65] This demonstrates significant cohesion.

Furthermore, the example of Paul serves to bind the units together in other ways. First, Bassler and Mounce have noted that the two units are framed by discussions of Paul's experience – past (3.10–11) and future (4.6–8).[66] There are also connections between Paul's example and what Timothy is called to do. As Paul has continued faithfully in spite of hard times (3.10–11) so is Timothy (4.2–4).[67] In 4.2 Timothy's ministry is to be

---

62.   3.1–9 and 3.10–17 also resemble each other in contrast to the other surrounding units in that they have only two and one imperatives, respectively. The other units are marked by several imperatives.

63.   Falconer 1937: 94 is an extreme minority in suggesting that the 'note of urgency [in 4.1] indicates the resumption of the letter, i.3-ii.13.' One shift is not enough basis for arguing incohesiveness and Falconer's view overlooks the urgency in view in 2.14, 3.1, and elsewhere.

64.   Of course, in Hanson's case this need not suggest any opinion of cohesion on his part.

65.   All three occurrences of σὺ δέ in this letter occur in these two units (3.10, 14; 4.5).

66.   Bassler 1996: 163, 170; Mounce 2000: 555. Dibelius and Conzelmann 1972: 118 also connect these verses but on the theme of suffering (cf. Mounce 2000: 555, as well).

67.   Bassler 1996: 169.

marked by patience and teaching (μακροθυμίᾳ καὶ διδαχῇ), both of which are mentioned in Paul's example in 3.10 (μακροθυμία, διδασκαλία).[68] Timothy is urged to 'remain' in what he has learned (3.14) as Paul has in finishing his course and keeping the faith (4.7).

Similarly, there is a direct contrast between the description of the opponents in 4.3–4 and the exhortation to Timothy in 3.10–17. Timothy is to remain in what he has learned but those in 4.3–4 will not tolerate sound teaching and turn their ears away from the truth. Timothy's confidence is grounded in the fact that he knows those who taught him (3.14), but those in 4.3–4 gather teachers according to their own desires. They hold to myths but Timothy from his infancy has known the sacred writings (3.15).

Lastly, 3.16–17 appears to function as a transition between the two units. The word θεός (which has not occurred since 2.25) occurs only once in each of these units – at the end of 3.10–17 and the beginning of 4.1. This resembles the transitional device, 'hook word.' Other connections support this. 3.10–17 focuses on Timothy remaining in the truth. 3.16–17 begin mentioning the ministry of proclaiming this truth (while still focusing primarily on Timothy's preparation, cf. v. 17), which prepares the way for exhortations regarding Timothy's public ministry in 4.1ff. Indeed, 3.17 closes with a reference to readiness for every good work (ἀγαθὸν ἔργον), and 4.1 begins a solemn exhortation to do this work (cf. ἔργον εὐαγγελιστοῦ). The four nouns in 3.16 anticipate the imperatives of 4.2.[69] Specifically, διδαχή (4.2) connects with διδασκαλία (3.16) and ἐλέγχω (4.2) picks up on ἐλεγμός (3.16).[70] Both lists seem to alternate: positive, negative, positive, negative. The combination of teaching and rebuking is clear in both verses. Additionally, the exhortation to preach τὸν λόγον in 4.2 naturally connects with the description of this in 3.15–17. Indeed, the statements of 3.10–17 ('you followed my teaching'; 'remain in what you have learned'; you have known the sacred writings') prepare for the call to preach this message. Thus, 3.16–17 serve as a transition by introducing many of the terms and themes which will be discussed in 4.1–8.

4.1–8 and 4.9–13

That there is a significant shift at 4.9 is easily recognized and commonly noted.[71] The question, however, is whether this is an understandable shift within a letter or such a stark difference as to suggest incoherence. Harrison and others in the past suggested 4.9f. were an original letter

---

68. Quinn and Wacker 2000: 771; Bassler 1996: 169; Johnson 1978: 11.

69. Mounce 2000: 573 says the four main imperatives in 4.2 loosely parallel the four prepositional phrases of 3.16.

70. Marshall 1999: 801; Quinn and Wacker 2000: 770.

71. See previous chapter.

fragment distinct from the preceding material.[72] Others, not following the fragmentary hypotheses, see troublesome differences between 4.9f. and 4.1–8. For example, Miller says the 'tone and mood' of 4.9f. 'differ considerably' from that of the previous unit.[73] It is considered problematic and anti-climactic that the mention of Paul's impending death in 4.6–8 is followed by more mundane matters.[74] Indeed, the call for Timothy to come in v. 9 is considered contradictory to the mention of Paul's impending death.[75]

To address these objections fully would require assessing possible connections between 4.9f. and all of the rest of the letter. What is of concern at this point, however, is any connection specifically with 4.1–8 (other connections will be addressed later in this chapter). A shift in tense and mood is to be expected as the letter shifts to closing matters, including the common discussion of travel plans. Such 'mundane' matters often close New Testament letters.[76] Disappointment of modern readers over the supposed anti-climactic nature of 4.9f. does not argue for incoherence if there are other indicators of cohesion, as will be argued. The mention of Paul's impending death in 4.6–8 does not necessarily conflict with the call for Timothy to come (v. 9). His death is certain and will be forthcoming, but there is not enough information given in the letter to say Timothy could not make it to Paul in time.[77] In fact the impending nature of Paul's death fits with the urgency of v. 9 (Σπούδασον, ταχέως).[78] Indeed, Falconer, who sees incoherence elsewhere, writes, 'Verses 9–12 follow naturally on vv. 6–8.'[79]

There are also other connections between the units. The pattern of second person singular imperatives followed by γάρ which occurred in the previous unit (4.2–3, 5–6) continues in 4.9–10. Also, in 4.6–8 there is a significant return to a focus on Paul (with nine discrete first person referents after just one such referent in the previous 11 verses), and 4.9–13

---

72. Harrison 1921: 122–24; Barrett 1963: 10–12.

73. Miller 1997: 122. Easton 1947: 75 writes, 'the tone of the Epistle changes with startling abruptness'.

74. Miller 1997: 122; Easton 1947: 75; similarly, Hanson 1982: 15.

75. E.g., Barrett 1963: 120.

76. Cf. Rom. 16; Col. 4.7–18; Tit. 3.12–15.

77. Cf. also, Mounce 2000: 588–89; Knight 1992: 464; Kelly 1963: 211–12. The argument here is given within the perspective of the letter, without regard to whether it is regarded as historical or fictional. The concern is whether or not the statements in the letter, taken at face value, can cohere whether as authentic Pauline correspondence or as competent writing of some other sort.

78. Cf. Knight 1992: 463; Marshall 1999: 814, 'the possibility that Paul might die or be put to death at some unspecified date could well lead to the desire that Timothy should visit him before it was too late.'

79. Falconer 1937: 97.

continue this focus (six referents). While 4.1–5 focus specifically on Timothy, 4.6–8 focus on Paul's experience as a ground for the exhortations. Similarly, the exhortation to Timothy in 4.9 is grounded in the experiences of Paul. Thus, the shift to Paul in 4.6–8 prepares for the focus on Paul in 4.9f.[80] Even the experiences of Paul in both units are similar – suffering (v. 6) and abandonment (v. 10).

Lastly, there are two lexical links between the units. First, the only two occurrences of διακονία are found in these units (4.5, 11). Timothy is exhorted to fulfill his ministry and Paul is seen to be concerned about ministry even until the end.[81] Second, and most significantly, is the repetition of the verb ἀγαπάω in 4.9, 10. This repetition, commonly noted by commentators, creates a contrast between those who love Christ's appearing and Demas who loved this age.[82] There is a contrast not only in differing objects of love but also between the temporal frames – present 'age' and future 'coming.'[83] As a result of this contrasting connection, Kelly wrote, 'The presence of this contrast makes it likely, as against some versions of the "fragments hypothesis", that whoever wrote this verse wrote the preceding paragraph also.'[84] One other point strengthens the connecting function of this repetition and is not mentioned by the commentators. This is the fact that these contrasting statements on the object of love appear to function as hook words. The word does not appear elsewhere in the unit (indeed in the letter) and the occurrences are at the end of one unit and the beginning of the next unit. Thus, this fits the normal pattern of a hooked transition suggesting the reference to faithful believers at the end of v. 8 has been intentionally stated in these terms in order to prepare the way for the discussion of Demas, whose desertion has also been intentionally stated in these terms.

Thus, there are significant indicators of cohesion between 4.1–8 and 4.9–13. The arguments for contradiction between the units are overstated and open to different interpretation. Then, there are various links between the units, most importantly the preparatory shift to first person in 4.6–8 and the hooked connection created by the repetition of ἀγαπάω.

---

80. Marshall 1999: 37 suggests something similar in less detail.
81. Marshall 1999: 817, 'Despite his own sense of having finished his course, Paul was still concerned for the work of mission.'
82. Lock 1924: 117; Barrett 1963: 120; Bernard 1906: 145; Kelly 1963: 212; Guthrie 1990: 183; Easton 1947: 72; Bassler 1996: 175; Knight 1992: 464; Marshall 1999: 815; Mounce 2000: 589–90.
83. Guthrie 1990: 183; Kelly 1963: 212.
84. Kelly 1963: 212.

4.9–13 and 4.14–15

A connection between 4.9–13 and 4.14–15 is not usually disputed. Indeed, most commentators keep these verses together as one unit.[85] Neither Miller nor Hanson dispute the connection. However, Merkel does point out that vv. 14–15 appear without any transition ('Ohne Übergang'),[86] and it is clear that commentators have puzzled over the connection here. Mounce even says 'what triggered Paul's memory of Alexander can only be guessed.'[87]

In assessing the situation, it must first be noted that in the sections of 'travel talk' in New Testament letters one expects to find items listed in series with less overt connection than elsewhere in the letter. Some commentators suggest the mention of Alexander at this point suggests Paul expects Timothy to meet him along the journey to Paul.[88] More specifically some suggest that Alexander lived in Troas, since there was known to be a guild of coppersmiths in Troas;[89] thus, he appears following the mention of Troas in 4.13. These points show potential logical connections, but the probability of these is strengthened if there are other linguistic continuities or links between the units.

There are continuities between 4.9–13 and 4.14–15. First, vv. 14–15 continue the list of new individuals begun in vv. 9–13.[90] Additionally, the information given about these new individuals in both units centers around their relationship or actions toward Paul – Demas abandoned 'me'; Luke alone is with 'me'; Mark is useful to 'me'; 'I' sent Tychicus; Alexander did evil to 'me.' Thus, vv. 9–15 concern Paul and 'others.' There is also a connection in the picture of Paul's situation. 4.9 and 4.14–15 present people who were disloyal to Paul (abandonment and opposition), and the opposition of vv. 14–15 fits with the general picture given in vv. 9–13 of Paul being alone.[91] Lastly, vv. 14–15 continue the second person imperative which was common in the previous unit (vv. 9, 11, 13),[92] and

---

85. E.g., Marshall, Oberlinner, Bassler, Brox, Hanson, Spicq, Fee, Kelly, Lock.

86. Merkel 1991: 85.

87. Mounce 2000: 592. Cf. also Kelly 1963: 216, who attributes the connection possibly to 'some association of ideas which we cannot now fathom.' Guthrie 1990: 185 also implicitly confesses the uncertainty when he writes, 'There may be some association of ideas which caused the revival of the memory.'

88. E.g., Barrett 1963: 121.

89. Quinn 1980: 295. Cf. also Marshall 1999: 821.

90. Smith and Beekman 1981: 101 cite as evidence of coherence, 'the fact that individuals are named and their relationships and attitudes toward Paul are revealed.'

91. Marshall 1999: 821 calls v. 14 'a continuation of the motif of disloyalty from v. 10 but now in a stronger form.'

92. Smith and Beekman 1981: 101 say the continuation of imperative verbs from v. 9–15 'is evidence of coherence.'

similar to the construction in vv. 9 and 11, v. 15 has an imperative followed by γάρ.

Thus, while Alexander does appear 'unannounced,' this is not a total surprise in this section of a letter. Further, vv. 14–15 cohere with vv. 9–13 as exhortations from Paul to Timothy concerning third parties, particularly in relation to Paul's current state of aloneness.

4.14–15 and 4.16–18
The connection between 4.14–15 and 4.16–18 is rarely disputed. However, Merkel does appropriately note that v. 16 is an abrupt ('unvermittelt') shift to a remembrance.[93] For this reason, in the previous chapter, vv. 16–18 were considered a distinct unit. Still, there are indicators of cohesion between the two units. The abandonment and opposition just shown to be a common bond between 4.9–13 and 14–15 continue in 4.16–18 with Paul being abandoned (ἐγκαταλείπω, v. 16; cf. v. 10) by all.[94] There is also a connection in Paul's response to the opposition (vv. 14–15) and the abandonment (v. 16). In both places a statement is made concerning the future fate of those involved, presumably at the final judgment (one negative, one positive).[95] Similarly, there is a link between the recurrence of ὁ κύριος in these units (vv. 14, 17, 18), since this term did not occur in the previous unit. As Paul depends on the Lord to repay Alexander who did evil to him, so he depended on the Lord at his first defense and depends on the Lord for future deliverance.

Therefore, in spite of an abrupt shift, 4.14–15 and 4.16–18 cohere with thematic and lexical connections. A focus on Paul's situation follows naturally on the references to Paul's situation in the previous verses.

4.16–18 and 4.19–22
Clear shifts between these units were noted in the previous chapter. While these shifts are commonly recognized, there seems to be no serious contention against connections between these two units. This is no doubt due to the fact that closing greetings of this kind were common in New Testament letters and other ancient letters as well.[96] Significant direct connection with the immediately preceding unit is not expected (connections with the rest of the letter will be considered below). However, a general connection can be noted since the call for Timothy to come in v. 21 fits well with the situation of Paul described in 4.16–18.

93. Merkel 1991: 86.
94. Cf. also Marshall 1999: 822; Mounce 2000: 594.
95. Quinn and Wacker 2000: 824 write, 'As the recollection of Alexander and the arrest was accompanied by a parenthetical prayer (v. 14), so now the recollection of the abandonment is accompanied by a parenthetical prayer.'
96. Cf., e.g., Quinn and Wacker 2000: 830; Exler 1923: 116; White 1971b: 19.

Semantic Chains Running Throughout the Letter

Having shown a connection from unit to unit through the letter it will be helpful to consider the letter from the macroperspective noting themes (with semantic and lexical connections) which occur through significant portions of the letter. Each theme or semantic chain does not necessarily occur in each unit of the letter, but they occur in a significant number of units. Therefore they bind the letter together not as one strand around the whole, but as various adhesive strips across various units overlapping one another.

Eschatological Outlook

A number of scholars have noted that an eschatological outlook is common in 2 Timothy, though they have not developed it as a cohesive chain in the letter.[97] The explicit elements of this chain center around references to 'the last day,' judgment, reward, and appearing/kingdom vs. the present age. Some of these overlap.

First, the 'last day' is mentioned twice in reference to the final judgment (1.12, εἰς ἐκείνην τὴν ἡμέραν; 1:18, ἐν ἐκείνῃ τῇ ἡμέρᾳ). Interestingly, in both instances there is an expectation of positive results in the judgment. These then link to references elsewhere to final reward. 2.4–6 center on what is necessary for finding reward in the end. In 2.10, salvation is accompanied with 'eternal glory' which appears to be part of the final blessing of salvation. In the faithful saying of 2.11–13, the whole point is one's final standing before God. Two statements point to reward: 'if we die we will *live*' (2.11) and 'if we endure we will *reign*' (2.12). The reference to life here may link back to 1.10 where the work of Christ makes available 'life and immortality.' These may be intended to refer to final reward as well. Lastly, 4.8 refers to the Lord, the righteous 'judge' (κριτής) giving (ἀποδίδωμι) a crown of righteousness to certain ones which is obviously final reward. The reference to 'crown' (στέφανος) also links back to the reward in 2.5 (στεφανόω).

There are also two references to negative judgment. Within the faithful saying of 2.11–13, referred to above, one reference is negative: 'if we deny, he will deny us' (2.12). Also, 4.14 refers to the Lord giving to Alexander according to his works, which are clearly evil. The use of ἀποδίδωμι in this verse links in contrast to the use of the same verb in reference to reward in 4.8. Lastly, 4.1 refers to judgment in general with 'Christ Jesus about to judge (κρίνω) the living and the dead.'

These references to judgment then connect to references to Christ's appearing and kingdom. The general reference to judgment in 4.1 is linked

---

97. E.g. Mounce 2000: 542; Fee 1988: 268.

to Christ's appearing and his kingdom. The reward in 4.8 is for those who love his appearing (in contrast to those who love the present age in 4.10). And, lastly, Paul expects, in the future, deliverance into Christ's heavenly kingdom (4.18).

This represents a significant lexical and semantic chain running through the letter creating a consistent eschatological focus to the whole. It may be useful to list the elements in a table in order of their occurrence with the lexical links.

Reference	Semantic	Lexical
1.10	Reward: Life and immortality	ζωή
1.12	Last day	ἐκείνη ἡμέρα
1.18	Last day	ἐκείνη ἡμέρα
2.4–6	Reward	στεφανόω
2.10	Reward: Eternal glory	
2.11	Reward: 'We will live'	συζάω
2.12	Reward: 'We will reign'	
2.12	Judgment: 'He will deny us'	
4.1	Judge the living and dead	κρίνω
4.1	His appearing and kingdom	ἐπιφάνεια, βασιλεία
4.8	Reward: crown of righteousness	στέφανος, ἀποδίδωμι
4.8	Love his appearing	ἀγαπάω, ἐπιφάνεια
4.10	Love this present age	ἀγαπάω
4.14	Judgment	ἀποδίδωμι
4.18	Deliverance into heavenly kingdom	βασιλεία

It can be noted that this chain occurs in units 1.6–2.13 and 4.1–8, 9ff. It basically occurs throughout the letter except 2.14–3.17.

The eschatological chain examined above focuses on the age to come. There are also other elements which are future oriented while still relating to this present age. As they contribute to the overall eschatological outlook it will be good to note them. The most obvious of these are the references to difficult times to come. 3.1 refers to 'last days' (ἐσχάται ἡμέραι) and the 'hard times' (καιροὶ χαλεποί) that will attend them. 4.3 also refers a future 'time' (καιρός) that will be difficult. Both passages have in view a time when people will be unconcerned or opposed to Timothy's message. The general concern about the future occurs elsewhere creating the sense of Paul instructing Timothy in things Timothy will need to remember once Paul is gone. Thus, in 2.2 there is the concern for handing on the message so that the work will be carried on. The references to future evil fit this as well as they seem to warn about things that will have to be faced without Paul.

Salvation

The issue of salvation also permeates the letter with explicit discussions of salvation and more general statements regarding mission. Some of these come up in the discussion of the eschatological outlook as the two issues are linked. There are at least six explicit discussions of salvation, i.e., passages which use σώζω or its cognates or other set terms referring to salvation (e.g., 'knowledge of the truth').[98] 1.9–11 is a full, almost confessional, statement regarding the work of God in providing salvation.[99] 2.10 states that Paul's reason for enduring is so that the elect might obtain salvation. In 2.25–26 Timothy is instructed to act towards the opponents in such a way that they might be granted repentance, and thus salvation. 3.7 refers to some who are unable to come to salvation. 3.15 refers to the Scriptures making Timothy wise unto salvation. Lastly, 4.18 mentions Paul's confidence that the Lord will save him. Thus, these explicit references to salvation occur throughout the letter in almost every unit.[100]

These statements have a cohesive function due simply to the repetition of the theme of salvation. This cohesive function is strengthened, though, by a number of similarities between the statements themselves. In 1.9, 2.10 and 3.15 salvation is specifically rooted 'in Christ' ('in Christ Jesus' in 3.15). Also common to many of the passages is an emphasis on divine sovereignty. In 1.9 one might expect the juxtaposition of 'not by works but by grace'; however, before the mention of grace there is inserted 'according to his own plan.'[101] The divine side of it is also highlighted by the fact that this was done 'from eternity.' Also, the use of the verb καλέω is often understood to emphasize divine initiative.[102] In 2:10, those who are to obtain salvation are 'the elect' (οἱ ἐκλεκτοί). In 2.25 the hope is that God

---

98.   Marshall 1999: 428, 'εἰς ἐπίγνωσιν ἀληθείας ἐλθεῖν is a technical phrase in the PE for coming to faith in Christ.' Cf. also Towner 1989: 122; Quinn and Wacker 2000: 180.

99.   Cf. Lau 1996: 114, 'The christological formulation of 2T1.9–10 is understood to be a clear (but not necessarily complete) summary of the gospel.'

100.   There is within these statements a full scope of salvation history (past, present, future) which develops linearly as one progresses through the letter. The first statement refers to the past (grace given before time) and the present (now revealed). The rest of the letter seems to focus on the future aspect with 'eternal glory' (2.10), his appearing (4.1, 8) and his heavenly kingdom (4.1, 18). Perhaps the emphasis on the future aspect is intended to respond to the assertion that the resurrection has already occurred. Towner 1986: 427–28 makes a similar suggestion regarding the Pastoral Epistles as a whole. Here the observation is squarely rooted in 2 Timothy itself, the only letter which mentions people teaching that the resurrection had already occurred.

101.   Towner 1989: 97 says the whole phrase makes the point that 'salvation is also entirely dependent upon God in that he alone has executed it and made it available on the basis of his grace.' Cf. also Lau 1996: 117–18.

102.   Lau 1996: 115, n. 262, 'The τοῦ καλέσαντος emphasizes God's divine initiative ...' Cf. Schmidt, 'καλέω', *TDNT*, vol. 3, 489.

might grant repentance unto the knowledge of the truth. The need of divine action is emphasized by the immediately following statement of human inability – they are held captive. This human inability also comes out in 3.7, where it is specifically stated that these individuals are not able (δύναμαι) to come to the knowledge of the truth. Though 3.15 is not as explicit as the preceding passages, the ability (δύναμαι) to come to salvation is still located in a divine resource (the Scriptures). This displays a significant theological coherence between these statements located in various parts of the letter.[103]

Another connection between some of the salvation statements is hinted at in the previous discussion. In three of the statements, at least, there is an emphasis on the cognitive side of salvation. Both 2.15 and 3.7 refer to salvation in terms of 'the knowledge of the truth' (εἰς ἐπίγνωσιν ἀληθείας). This cognitive idea is further affirmed in 2.25–26 by the parallel clause which further explains 'repentance into the knowledge of the truth' as coming to one's senses (ἀνανήφω). The same idea appears to be confirmed in 3.7 by the following mention of being depraved in the mind and ignorant (κατεφθαρμένοι τὸν νοῦν, 3.8; ἄνοια, 3.9). Cognition also is highlighted in 3.15 as it refers to making wise (σοφίζω) unto salvation. This similarity binds these passages together suggesting a common viewpoint or concern.

Beyond these explicit salvation statements, there is a general concern for the salvation of people (and hence mission) throughout the letter. 1.12 refers to Paul's confidence in finding final salvation. In 1.16, 18, Paul prays for Onesiphorus's final salvation. 2.10, which was just discussed, shows a concern for the salvation of others ('the elect'). 2.11–13 show the way to perseverance unto salvation.[104] 2.19 ('The Lord knows those who are his') may fit here as a statement on the surety of salvation, emphasizing divine sovereignty and thus connecting with that theme in the explicit salvation statements. 2.24–26, discussed above, is concerned for the salvation even of the opponents. 3.15, also discussed above, refers to the salvation of Timothy. Then, 4.18 refers to Paul's confidence in being saved. Thus, there is throughout the letter a concern for salvation of various people, friend and foe alike. Interestingly, this list opens and concludes (1.12; 4.18) with statements of Paul's confidence in final salvation which will be accomplished by the Lord.

Since the concern for the salvation of others ties into a mission concern a few others passages can be connected to this chain. Paul is referred to as

---

103. Mounce 2000: 529 argues that the quote from Num. 16.5 (LXX) in 2.19c connotes election. If this is so, it then would be another element in this chain.

104. The emphasis here on personal responsibility balances the emphasis on divine sovereignty detailed earlier.

'preacher' (κῆρυξ), apostle, and 'teacher' (διδάσκολος). 2.2, then, refers to an ongoing teaching (διδάσκω) ministry. 4.2, 5 refer explicitly to ongoing mission ('Preach [κήρυξον] the word ... do the work of an evangelist'). 4.17 then also refers to preaching (κήρυγμα) to the nations. These points add links to the semantic chain of 'salvation' further enhancing its cohesive effect as it occurs throughout the letter with a similar concern.

Message/Gospel/Word
Related to the chain concerning salvation is the recurrence of terms related to the basic message which Timothy is to preserve and proclaim. Already in the prescript there is reference to 'the promise of life which is in Christ Jesus,' concerning which Marshall writes, 'the phrase sums up the content of Paul's gospel.'[105] There follows then throughout the letter a stream of words such as gospel, word, teaching, etc., that refer to the Pauline message. The occurrences are shown in the following table.

Reference	Semantic	Lexical
1.2	Promise of life in XI	
1.8	Testimony of our Lord	
1.8	The gospel	εὐαγγέλιον
1.9–11	Summary of message	
1.11	The gospel	εὐαγγέλιον
1.13	Sounds words which you	ὑγιαίνων λόγοι
	heard from me	παρ' ἐμού ἤκουσας
1.14	The deposit	
2.2	What you heard from me	ἤκουσας παρ' ἐμου
2.8	Summary of the message	
2.9	The word of God	ὁ λόγος τοῦ θεοῦ
2.15	The word of truth	ὁ λόγος τῆς ἀληθείας
3.8	The truth	ἡ ἀλήθεια
3.10	My (Paul's) teaching	μου ἡ διδασκαλία
3.14	What you have learned and	
	become convinced of	
3.15	The holy writings	
3.16	Scripture	

105. Marshall 1999: 685. He cites Brox 1969a: 223, in agreement.
106. 'The faith' in 4.7 might also belong in this chain if it refers here to the message believed. It has not been included here since the point is disputed. The occurrences of ἀλήθεια in 2.25 and 3.7 might also be included here. At issue would be whether the phrase 'knowledge of the truth' is a fixed term for salvation or whether the author intended to refer to knowing the 'truth', i.e., the Pauline message. This also shows the interconnectedness of the chains concerning salvation and the Pauline message.

4.2	The word	ὁ λόγος
4.2	Teaching	διδαχή
4.3	Sound teaching	ὑγιαινούσῃ διδασκαλίᾳ
4.4	The truth	ἡ ἀλήθεια
4.17	The preaching	τὸ κήρυγμα[106]

Thus, the concern with the Pauline message permeates the letter providing a cohesive theme. Furthermore, this chain is inextricably bound with the chain concerning salvation. It is the message which tells of and leads to salvation (1.9–11; 3.15).[107] The frequent occurrence of these chains and their interconnection argue strongly for coherence.

Confidence in/Reliance upon God and his Resources
This chain was touched upon in the discussion of salvation. There are six explicit statements of confidence in God. In 1.12 Paul is persuaded that God is able to preserve him on the last day. In 2.13 there is confidence that God is faithful in spite of the unfaithfulness of his people. In 2.19 the fact that the faith of some is being overturned is countered by the assurance that God's foundation stands firm. In spite of the success of the opponents Paul is confident in the stability of God's work. In 4.8 and 4.14 Paul expresses a clear confidence that God will reward those who love him and judge those who have opposed his work. Lastly, in 4.17 Paul expresses confidence that as God has delivered him in the past, so God will one day deliver him into heaven. This confidence then creates a common background to the exhortations.

The explicit statements of confidence in God are also connected to a more extensive chain of references to reliance on divine resources. This reliance implies the confidence mentioned in the other passages. The call to action begins with a call to stir up 'the gift of God' (1.6) suggesting this gift is needed for the work which will commanded. This call to stir up is itself grounded in the fact of a God-given Spirit of power (1.7). In 1.8 Timothy is called to suffer 'according to the power of God.' In 1.9 salvation is accomplished not by human means ('our works') but by divine work ('plan and grace').[108] In 1.14 the deposit is to be guarded 'through the Holy Spirit.' In 2.1 Timothy is to be strong not in his own capacity but 'in the grace which is in Christ Jesus.' In 2.7 Paul is confident that the understanding Timothy needs will be given by the Lord. 2.25 states a clear dependence on the Lord to grant repentance to the opponents. Timothy cannot effect this alone. In 3.16–17 Scripture is the divine

107. The opposite is also true: the rejection of the message prevents salvation (e.g. 3.7–8).
108. Perhaps there is an intentional comparison being made: rely on God's power to endure (1.8) just as you had to rely on God's grace to be saved (1.9).

resource which will equip Timothy. Paul also, in his ordeal (4.16–17), had only the Lord to rely upon.

Thus this theme of reliance upon God and his resources and the confidence that God will come through occurs throughout the letter providing yet another cohesive thread to the whole.

Suffering

Suffering has often been noted as a theme common to 2 Timothy.[109] The semantic chain centers around words for suffering, bondage, endurance, abandonment and persecution. The occurrences of this chain are shown in the following table.

Reference	Semantic	Lexical
1.8	Suffer	συγκακοπαθέω
1.8	Bondage	δέσμιον
1.12	Suffer	πάσχω
1.15	Abandonment (by all)	πᾶς
1.16	Bondage	
2.3	Suffer	συγκακοπαθέω
2.4–6	Hard work – perhaps suffering[110]	
2.9	Suffer	κακοπαθέω
2.9	Bondage	δεσμός
2.10	Endure	ὑπομένω
2.11	Die – persecution?	
2.12	Endure	ὑπομένω
3.10	Endure	ὑπομονή
3.11	Persecution (2x)	διωγμός
3.11	Suffer	παθήμα
3.11	Endure	ὑποφέρω
3.12	Persecution	διώκω
4.5	Suffer	κακοπαθέω
4.7	Suffer?	ἀγών
4.10	Abandonment	ἐγκαταλείπω
4.14	Suffer	
4.16	Abandonment (by all)	ἐγκαταλείπω, πᾶς

109. Mounce 2000: 474, 'The theme of suffering ties almost all of the epistle together.' Dibelius and Conzelmann 1972: 98 also say the exhortation to suffer for the faith 'recurs throughout the epistle.' Cf. also, Johnson 2001: 327.

110. Mounce 2000: 507 connects these metaphors to suffering writing, 'Whatever the three metaphors mean, at a minimum they illustrate Timothy's need to "share in suffering."'

This chain occurs in each main unit of the letter except 2.14–26 and 3.1–9, those units which focus on the opponents. This forms a significant connection between 1.6–2.13 and 3.10–4.18. The links in this chain are even more obviously connected than those in the previous chains, with a significant level of lexical repetition. This chain is then intimately bound up with the chain concerning the Pauline message. In many of the passages the suffering is directly linked to the message (e.g., 1.8, 12; 2.9; 3.11; 4.5). In 1.8 and 2.8–9 it is explicitly stated that the suffering is for the gospel. In 1.12 Paul's suffering is connected to his role as herald of the gospel. 3.11 gives as examples of suffering incidences from Paul's missionary journeys. In 4.5 the call to suffer occurs right alongside the call to do the work of an evangelist and to fulfill your ministry. The tight connection between these two significant chains ('suffering' and 'message') binds much of the letter together.

Opposition

The examination of the theme of suffering leads naturally to an examination of the idea of opposition within 2 Timothy. Opponents are not explicitly mentioned until 2.14–26, but they then occur in practically every other unit of the letter.[111] The main discussions of opposition are in 2.14–26, 3.1–9, 3.13, 4.3–4, and 4.14–15. Thus, the repetition of the idea of opposition provides some connection through the latter two-thirds of the letter. The cohesive function of this repetition is strengthened by a number of other connections between the passages which deal with opposition. In essence there are a number of smaller chains binding together these opposition passages. This is significant since it would suggest a unified, coherent view of the opposition behind these various passages in contrast to what Miller's composite view would expect.

First, there is a significant futuristic cast to much of the discussion of the opponents. Of the 24 occurrences of future verbs in the letter, 14 occur in the discussion of the opponents.[112] Three of these future verb occurrences are the verb προκόπτω, occurring in three of the five passages which deal with the opponents (2.16; 3.9, 13). 3.1–5, 3.13, and 4.3–4 are especially framed as future. Both 3.1 and 4.3 refer to times (καιροί, 3.1; καιρός, 4.3) to come which will be difficult due to the wickedness of people.

These passages are also connected by the repetition of two synonymous verbs of opposition: ἀνθίστημι (3.8 [2x], 4.15) and ἀντιδιατίθημι (2.25).[113] 2.25 uses the verb in an absolute sense for 'those who oppose.' In 3.8 they

---

111. Technically opponents are not explicitly mentioned in 4.16–18 and 4.19–21.
112. 2.16, 17, 21; 3.1, 2, 9 [2x], 13; 4.3 [3x], 4 [2x], 14.
113. Both verbs are listed by Louw and Nida 1989 under heading 39.1.

oppose the truth, and in 4.15 Alexander opposed 'our words.' Thus, this lexical repetition binds three of the passages with reference to opposition to the Pauline message. The opposition to 'truth' in 3.8 connects to the other four occurrences of ἀλήθεια in reference to the opponents.[114] The occurrences and their similarities can be summarized in the following list.

2.18 – abandon truth (ἀστοχέω; Louw and Nida 31.68)
2.25 – devoid of knowledge of truth
3.7 – devoid of knowledge of truth
3.8 – oppose truth
4.4 – turn ears away from truth (ἀποστρέφω; Louw and Nida 31.62)[115]

While one might expect 'opponents' to be characterized as on the wrong side of truth, the significance here is the similarity in the descriptions.

Several of the passages are also connected by the theme of wrong desires. Every occurrence of ἐπιθυμία in the letter is to be found in these passages in reference to the opponents (2.22; 3.6; 4.3). In each case the connotation of the word is negative. The misplaced love in 3.2–4 also fits in this category, as the people described love themselves, money, and pleasure, but not God. Lastly, Demas in 4.10 is also connected to this, as he loved this age (4.10), rather than Christ's appearing (4.8).

There is also a common point of the destructive nature of the opponents' activity. It will be simplest to list these occurrences.

2.14 – useless, leads to ruin of hearers
2.16 – produces further ungodliness
2.17 – spreads like gangrene
2.17 – upsets faith of some
2.23 – begets quarrels
2.26 – held captive by the devil
3.6 – take captive certain women
3.8 – rejected concerning the faith
3.13 – deceptive

The negative results of the opponents' activity then stand in contrast to the message which Timothy is to hold to, which, as has been shown, leads to salvation.

Ignorance is also a common theme in the description of the opponents. Again it will be simplest to list the relevant statements or words.

114. Every occurrence of ἀλήθεια in 2 Timothy occurs in the passages in view here and all but one of these occurrences (2.15) is used in reference to the opponents.
115. Cf. Quinn and Wacker 2000: 755.

Reference	Semantic	Lexical
2.16	foolish talk	κενοφωνία
2.23	foolish and ignorant	μωρός καί ἀπαίδευτος
2.26	need to regain their senses	ἀνανήφω
3.6	'silly women'	
3.7	always learning but never able to come to truth	
3.8	depraved mind	νοῦς
3.9	foolishness	ἄνοια
3.13	deceived	

This stands in contrast to Timothy who is described as having knowledge.

Reference	Semantic	Lexical
1.7	sound mind	σωφρονισμός
1.15	you know	οἶδα
1.18	you know	γινώσκω
2.7	Timothy should 'consider and the Lord will give him 'understanding'	νοέω
2.23	Knowing (Timothy)	οἶδα
2.24	able to teach	
2.25	he is to 'educate' those who hold on to 'uneducated' speculations	παιδεύω
		ἀπαίδευτος
3.1	Know!	γινώσκω
3.14	he has learned and been convinced	
3.15	from his earliest days he has 'known' that which makes one 'wise'	οἶδα
4.5	Be sober-minded	νήφω

Paul also stands in contrast with the opponents as he 'knows' (οἶδα) and is 'persuaded' concerning God. Thus, there is here a semantic chain of knowledge/ignorance which covers much of the letter and places Paul and Timothy in clear contrast with the opponents.

Finally, the five key passages which discuss opposition are typically set in contrast to Timothy in the flow of the letter. For instance, 3.1–9, 3.13, and 4.3–4 all are immediately followed by Σὺ δέ.[116] In 2.14–26 there is a regular shifting contrast between Timothy and the opponents as was shown in the previous chapter. In 4.14–15, after describing Alexander in 4.14, 4.15 tells Timothy to be on guard against him.

The similarities between the passages which discuss the opponents can be laid out as in Table 1, 'Opponents in 2 Timothy'.

Paul as Example
One final theme which occurs throughout the letter is the use of Paul as an example for Timothy. Sometimes Paul is explicitly held up as a model. In other instances, it is less explicit with Paul being presented as having done or currently doing what he calls Timothy to do. 1.3 refers to Paul's spiritual heritage and 1.5 then refers to Timothy's heritage. Paul's heritage is connected to the point that he serves God with a clear conscience. In a similar way Timothy's heritage is brought up in reference to Paul's confidence that Timothy possesses a sincere faith.[117] In 1.4 Paul longs to see Timothy and at the close of the letter (4.9, 21) Timothy is to show a similar longing by being diligent to come to Paul. In 1.6 Paul reminds Timothy, and in 2.14 Timothy is to remind others. Similarly, in 2.2 as Timothy has received from Paul so he is to pass on to others. In 1.8 Timothy is called to be unashamed (ἐπαισχύνομαι) and to suffer. 1.12 says Paul is doing both of these things himself (ἐπαισχύνομαι). In 1.11 Paul calls himself a 'preacher' (κῆρυξ) and in 4.2 Timothy is to 'preach' (κηρύσσω).[118] In 1.12 Paul 'knows' and is 'persuaded' (πείθω); in 3.14 Timothy has 'learned' and 'been convinced' (πιστόω). In 2.1 Timothy is to be strong (ἐνδυναμόω) in divine grace, as in 4.17 Paul was strengthened (ἐνδυναμόω) by the Lord.[119] In 2.3 Timothy is called to suffer (συγκακοπαθέω), and in 2.9 Paul is already suffering (κακοπαθέω). Paul perseveres because he is mindful of God (1.12), so he urges Timothy to be mindful as well (2.8). Paul's endurance is mentioned in 2.10 as an example for the exhortations in 2.1–6. In 2.15 Timothy is to seek divine approval, and in 4.6–8 Paul expects divine approval. 3.10–11 may be the most explicit occurrence with Paul specifically telling Timothy to follow his ways. In 4.2 Timothy is to exercise patience (μακροθυμία), which he has seen in Paul (3.10, μακροθυμία).[120] In 4.5 Timothy is to fulfill (πληροφορέω) his ministry, which Paul in fact has done (πληροφορέω; 4.17). Lastly, Alexander's opposition to

116. These are the only occurrences of σὺ δέ in the letter.
117. Cf. Mounce 2000: 466, 'Throughout the first half of the epistle Paul shows Timothy that their lives and ministries are intertwined and because of this Timothy can draw encouragement from Paul.' Cf. also Dibelius and Conzelmann 1972: 98.
118. Bassler 1996: 169; Johnson 1978: 11.
119. Marshall 1999: 824.
120. Marshall 1999: 824.

Paul is an example with the assumption that he will oppose Timothy as well.

This is a significant chain of example. To this could also be connected the other examples which are held up for Timothy. Timothy is expected to have a sincere faith like Eunice and Lois (1.5). Onesiphorus is an example of not being ashamed (ἐπαισχύνομαι, 1.16; cp. 1.8). Onesiphorus is also an example in that he diligently (σπουδαίως) sought for and found Paul, because in 4.9, 21, Timothy is urged to be diligent (σπουδάζω) in coming to see Paul.

Also connected to the chain of Paul as example are the other statements which connect Timothy's ministry to Paul, showing a dependence on Paul. Timothy's gift came through the laying on of Paul's hands (1.6). What Timothy is not to be ashamed of is not only the message but also Paul himself (1.8). The gospel in view is Paul's gospel (2.8), for which he was appointed (1.13). The message is that which has been heard from Paul (1.13; 2.2). Lastly, Paul is surely at least included among those from whom Timothy has learned in 3.14.

Thus, the centrality of Paul as source and example recurs throughout the letter again creating cohesion. It can also be seen that this chain connects with the chain concerning 'message' as that message comes from Paul. It connects as well with the themes of suffering and mission.

Summary of Chains
It has been shown that there are a number of semantic chains which run through significant portions of 2 Timothy. No doubt others could be added. The fact that these chains are so intimately connected and interrelated argues strongly for cohesion.

Table 1 Opponents in 2 Timothy

2.14–26	3.1–9	3.13	4.3–4	4.14–15
προκόπτω (v. 16)	προκόπτω (v. 9) Hard times (καιροί) in future (v. 1)	προκόπτω	Difficult time (καιρός) in future (v. 3)	
ἀντιδιατίθημι (v. 25)	ἀνθίστημι (v. 8 [2x])			ἀνθίστημι
Abandon truth (v. 18)	Oppose truth (v. 8)		Abandon truth (v. 4)	
Devoid of knowledge of truth (v. 25)	Devoid of knowledge of truth (v. 7)			
Ignorance: κενοφωνία (v. 16)	Ignorance: 'silly women' (v. 6)	Ignorance: Deceived		

μωρός, ἀπαίδευτος (v. 23)	unable to come to truth (v. 7)			
ἀνανήφω (v. 26)	depraved νοῦς (v. 8)			
	ἄνοια (v. 9)			
ἐπιθυμία (v. 22)	ἐπιθυμία (v. 6)			ἐπιθυμία (v. 3)
	Misplaced love (vv. 2–4)			
Negative results:	Negative results:	Negative results:		
Ruin of hearers (v. 14)	Take captive (v. 6)	Deceiving		
Further ungodliness (v. 16)	Unable to come to truth (v. 7)			
Spread like gangrene (v. 17)	Rejected concerning faith (v. 8)			
Upset faith (v. 17)				
Held captive (v. 26)				
Contrast with Timothy:	Contrast with Timothy:	Contrast with Timothy:	Contrast with Timothy:	Contrast with Timothy:
Shifting contrast	Σὺ δέ	Σὺ δέ	Σὺ δέ	Guard against

Grouping Units into Larger Sections

So far it has been argued that there is a cohesive flow from one unit to the next within 2 Timothy and that across these units there are a number of interrelated semantic chains running throughout the letter. On these points rests the primary weight of the argument for cohesion. This last section will examine how the cohesion works, i.e., how the different units fit together to form the whole. It must be asked whether the different units group together in any way to form larger sections. It is entirely possible that a document could consist simply of a series of units, but the varying degrees of connectedness between the various units suggests that some units may cohere especially with one another forming sections. Some commentators do not address any larger groupings (e.g., Hanson, Oberlinner), but most who display any concern with structure do.

The analysis will not move linearly through the letter, but will first take up two potential section groupings which are fairly clear (1.6–2.13; 4.9–21). Then it will turn to the intervening material concerning which there is less unanimity.

1.6–2.13

The analysis of 1.6–14 and 2.1–13 in the previous chapter revealed a number of similarities between these units which suggest 1.6–2.13 may hold together as a section. This initial opinion is shared by a number of scholars though it is debated.[121] Evidence of connection will first be examined and then will be compared with the opinions of those who disagree.

1.6–14 and 2.1–13 have some striking similarities. Both are exhortations from Paul to Timothy primarily concerning Timothy personally. As such both units are built on second person imperatives (or equivalents; five in 1.6–14 and four in 2.1–13) which then have supporting material attached. The similarity between these units in these terms is heightened by the fact that the intervening unit, 1.15–18, is different, focusing more on third person referents and totally lacking in any imperatives. Others have noted some important lexical and thematic connections between 1.6–14 and 2.1–13. There also seems to be a general similarity in the structure and order of the two units. They are not exact but similar enough to be striking. In tracing this structural similarity the lexical connections will be noted.

First, both units open with a call to action (1.6–7; 2.1).[122] Also, what Timothy is to stir up is the χάρισμα of God (1.6), and he is to be strong in the χάρις which is in Christ Jesus (2.1). Both exhortations are rooted in divine resources which are graciously provided. Both exhortations require power (δύναμις, 1.7, 8; ἐνδυναμόω, 2.1) which are again rooted in the divine (the Spirit of power is given by God, 1.7).

2.2 then does not follow on in the same sequence connecting with 1.8, but connects closely with 1.13–14. There are two major lexical connections. First, ἃ ἤκουσας παρ' ἐμοῦ in 2.1 repeats ὧν παρ' ἐμοῦ ἤκουσας from 1.13. Both passages are concerned with Paul's teaching. Second, and commonly noted, the 'deposit' language is repeated with παρατίθημι (2.2; Louw and Nida 1989: 35.47) and παραθήκη (1.12, 14; Louw and Nida 1989: 35.48).[123] Thus, 2.2 advances the thought of 1.13–14 showing that one way the deposit of Paul's message is to be guarded is by entrusting it to a new generation of faithful men.

121. Those who support this collection of units include some who also would keep 1.3–5 with these units. Advocates of this view include Mounce 2000: 500; Bassler 1996: 127; Wolter 1988: 215–16; Spicq 1969: 700; Bernard 1906: 105. Mounce 2000: 475 writes, 'It is difficult to break 1:3–2:13 into divisions. It is a consistent discussion with multiple themes and word plays woven throughout.' However, Marshall (1999: 33f.) and Quinn and Wacker (cf. 2000: 565) disagree.

122. Oberlinner 1995: 66 says 2.1 reminds one of 1.6.

123. So also Marshall 1999: 722; Wolter 1988: 216; Johnson 1978: 8; Barrett 1963: 100;

2.3 picks back up with 1.8 with the call for Timothy to suffer using the same verb and same parsing (συγκακοπαθέω).[124] This verb occurs nowhere else in the letter. The suffering in 1.8 is to be done according to the power (δύναμις) of God, and the suffering in 2.3 follows the call to be strong (ἐνδυναμόω). There also seems to be a similar flow of thought here. In 1.8 Timothy is not to be ashamed of the message but suffer. In 2.1–3, Timothy is to be strong (the opposite of ashamed?), pass on the message, and suffer. The suffering in both instances is connected to faithfulness to the message.

Following the call to mutual suffering, both units support the argument so far with traditional or proverbial material (1.9–11; 2.4–7). In both pieces the support is, at least partially, based on eschatological reward. 1.9–11 climaxes with the note of Christ Jesus destroying death and bringing to light life and immortality (1.10). 2.5–6 focus on being crowned and receiving the first fruits, obviously in the sense of eschatological reward. As a 'gospel statement' 2.8 also connects with 1.9–11 (though the flow of the units is admittedly different here). The mention of the resurrection in 2.8 reminds of the reference to the destruction of death and manifestation of immortality in 1.10. The gospel statements in both units are followed by statements which connect them with Paul's gospel:

1.10–11 – 'the gospel (εὐαγγέλιον) unto which I was appointed preacher, apostle, and teacher'
2.8 – 'according to my gospel (εὐαγγέλιον)'

The repetition of εὐαγγέλιον as well as the first person pronoun bind these statements.

Next in both units comes a reference to Paul's own suffering which seem to grow out of his association with the gospel (πάσχω, 1.12; κακοπαθέω, 2.9). In both places the suffering of Paul serves as a model for the suffering to which he calls Timothy.[125] Also, in both places the mention of suffering is followed by a note of triumph or assurance introduced by ἀλλά: 'but I am not ashamed for I know whom I have believed'; 'but the word of God is not bound.' This confident endurance is then connected to salvation, for Paul in 1.12 and for the elect in 2.10.

There is nothing in 1.6–14 to correspond to 2.11–13 so the units are not exact parallels, but there is significant similarity in the order of the units. The links lexically, semantically, and thematically are also impressive.[126] One can add to these links others which do not necessarily correspond in the order of the argument. The theme of faithful endurance runs straight

124. Also, Wolter 1988: 216; Johnson 1978: 8.
125. So most.
126. Thus, Marshall 1999: 37, without noting the similarity in order, states 'there are strong verbal and contextual links between the two sections.'

through both units:[127] with the calls to stir up the divine gift (1.6), not to be ashamed (1.8, 12), to suffer (1.8, 12; 2.3, 9), to be strong (2.1), and endure (2.10). Throughout both units, the endurance called for is made possible by reliance on divine resources.[128] The previous chapter noted how this was common in each unit individually. 1.6–14 was seen to be bracketed by references to the Spirit as the one would enable the faithful perseverance in the truth (1.6, 7, 14). The suffering in 1.8 is explicitly said to be done 'according to the power of God.' Then, the empowerment called for in 2.1 is to be found in 'the grace which is in Christ Jesus.'[129] In 2.7, also, Timothy is to rely on the Lord to give him insight into what Paul writes. There is also an eschatological focus common to both units. The gospel statement of 1.9–11 closes with a reference to Christ making available immortality. 1.12 refers to the final judgement with 'that day.' 2.5–6 have in view the eschatological reward. The reference to salvation in 2.10 mentions 'eternal glory' as an accompaniment, and finally 2.11–13 focuses clearly on eschatological judgment. Lastly, there is a reference to Paul's chains in both units (δεσμός, 2.9; δέσμιος, 1.8). The fact that it is not paralleled in 1.6–14 when so much else is and its status as a faithful saying may support viewing 2.11–13 as a powerful conclusion to all of 1.6–2.10. These links, some stronger than others, bind these units closely.

Having argued for the cohesion of 1.6–14 and 2.1–13, 1.15–18 stands out since it contains no imperatives, is not explicit exhortation, and shifts to an interest in third parties rather than Timothy specifically. However, it has been argued above that 1.15–18 connects to the units on either side of it in spite of the criticisms against the unit. What is of interest here is that 1.15–18 appears to be crafted in such a way as to connect between the two units as perhaps an illustrative pause.[130] 1.15–18 stands out from the other two units in that it has only two second person referents; however, these two second person verbs are placed as the very first and very last words of the unit thus connecting to the second person address on either side.

By introducing and concluding 1.15–18 with references to Timothy, the author connects this 'report' on 'others' to the admonitions to Timothy.

---

127. So many, e.g., Marshall 1999: 723; Mounce 2000: 503; Fee 1988: 239; Merkel 1991: 62.

128. Mounce 2000: 503, and Bassler 1996: 139, also note this continuity in similar ways.

129. 2.1 has lexical connections to 1.9 as well. 2.1 refers to grace which is in Christ Jesus (τῇ χάριτι τῇ ἐν Χριστῷ Ἰησοῦ), and 1.9 refers to grace given to us in Christ Jesus (χάριν τὴν δοθεῖσαν ἡμῖν ἐν Χριστῷ Ἰησοῦ). These are the only two uses of χάρις in this sense apart from the salutation and closing (1.2; 4.22. The word does also occur in 1.3 but it has an obviously different shade of connotation there).

130. Marshall 1999: 36, notes '1.15–18 ... appears to act as a bridge between the preceding and following units,' though he does not refer to the connective function of the personal referents.

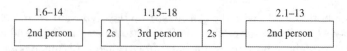

1.15–18 also fits within the exhortations as an example which was common in ancient exhortatory discourse as was noted earlier.[131] The eschatological perspective of the other two units is found in 1.15–18 as well with the concern for the Lord's verdict 'on that day' (1.18). The ideas of abandonment and shame (1.15, 16) cohere with the theme of faithful endurance and the thread of Paul's imprisonment runs through this unit as well as the other two (δέσμιος, 1.8; ἅλυσις, 1.16; δεσμός, 2.9).

This argumentation contradicts the view of Dibelius and Conzelmann, Barrett, Lohfink,[132] and others who argue that 2.1 begins the actual parenesis of the letter with Ch. 1 being introductory. These views fail to account for the significant cohesion between 1.6–14 and 2.1–13. For example, Dibelius and Conzelmann write, 'After "Paul" has introduced himself as an example in the first section [1.3–14], the next section of 2 Timothy presents the actual parenesis (extending to 2 Tim 4:8).'[133] In fact, however, as has been shown, 1.6–14 is as parenetic as 2.1–13, and Paul still functions as an example in 2.9–10. The sectional division between the units then is unnecessary. This view also misses the serious shift at 2.14, keeping 2.1–13 with 2.14–4.8.[134] Whereas the emphasis in 1.6–2.13 has been on Timothy's own behavior (with 1.15–18 being examples to Timothy), 2.14 marks a shift as the concern for the congregation comes to the fore. The relational setting shifts as well. While 1.6–2.13 had been in the form of Paul to Timothy, with first person singular verbs common, in 2.14–26, first person singular verbs disappear and the relational setting is 'Timothy, the church and the opponents.'[135] The opponents become explicit for the first time in 2.14ff. This is a significant shift in the letter as the calls to faithful endurance in 1.6–2.13 are unpacked in light of the threat of the opponents.[136]

131. Cf. Fiore 1986: 26–163; Donelson 1986: 94.

132. Lohfink 1981: 89–91. Wolter 1988: 215–16, esp. interacts and counters Lohfink.

133. Dibelius and Conzelmann 1972: 107.

134. Barrett 1963: 100 also does this. The shift at 2.14 is discussed in more detail in the previous chapter.

135. For similar observations see Marshall 1999: 745; Bassler 1996: 150; Knight 1992: 409.

136. Johnson 2001: 389, also says that at 2.14 there is a shift 'from the memory and imitation of models to a more direct from of moral instruction through maxims.'

Therefore, the significant connections within 1.6–2.13 and the shift which occurs at 2.14 combine to suggest that 1.6–2.13 should be seen as a coherent larger section.[137]

4.9–22

This section is often held together by scholars, with many even deciding against breaking it down into smaller units. Even Miller does not contest their coherence. However, some do suggest there is incoherence within these verses, primarily because they see a contradiction between the statement 'only Luke is with me' (4.11) and the greetings from some who are indeed with Paul in 4.21.[138] This does appear, on the face of it, to be a contradiction. However, the discussion in 4.9–12, concerning who is away, deals with names who are known members of Paul's missionary group (note esp. Col. 4.7ff.) while those who are yet with Paul in 4.21 are all new names.[139] Thus, the point in 4.11 is that, *of Paul's co-workers*, only Luke is left with him. The new names in 4.21, especially with the inclusive 'all the brothers,' most likely refer to the local Christians.[140] This is a plausible reading which requires no contradiction.

On a positive note, there are a number of indications of connection within 4.9–21. First, and most commonly adduced, is the repetition of Σπούδασον ἐλθεῖν (4.9, 21).[141] This creates an inclusio around the section highlighting the main issue of calling Timothy to Paul. This also sets the context for the rest of the section. The other travel discussions (4.10–13, 20) show why Timothy's visit is important and give him instructions for his travel. Even the discussion of Paul's situation (4.16–18) serves to heighten the call for Timothy to come. The identification of this repetition as an inclusio is strengthened by the fact that travel language in general is restricted to 4.9–13 and 19–21, with ἀπολείπω also being repeated (4.13, 20).

Second, in addition to travel language and lexical repetition, 4.9–15 and 19–21 are strongly bound by their high concentration of personal names.[142] Setting aside the names of Paul, Timothy, and divine names, there are only ten personal names in 1.1–4.8 (1044 words), but there are 17 names in 4.9–15, 19–21 (130 words). So, personal names are almost 14 times more

---

137. Mounce 2000: 475, 'It is difficult to break 1:3–2:13 into divisions. It is a consistent discussion with multiple themes and wordplays throughout.'

138. E.g., Merkel 1991: 83; Dibelius and Conzelmann 1972: 122.

139. Marshall 1999: 812–13; Quinn and Wacker 2000: 800, 834–35.

140. Ibid.

141. Quinn and Wacker 2000: 834, 'This sentence [4.21a] should almost certainly be read with the material from verse 9 on, with which it forms parentheses around the whole section.' Cf. also Merkel 1991: 82.

142. Cf. also, Bassler 1996: 175; Dibelius and Conzelmann 1972: 122.

common in 4.9–15, 19–21, than in the rest of the letter. While this is to be expected in the closing of letters, that simply proves the point that these verses read as a natural letter closing with a significant degree of cohesion from the concentration of personal names.

Third, 4.16–18 fits within the 'bookends' of 4.9–15 and 4.19–21. 4.16–18 develop the theme of abandonment from the preceding verses, supporting the repeated call for Timothy to come. The action of Demas in v. 10 (με ἐγκατέλιπεν) corresponds to the action of those in view in v. 16 (με ἐγκατέλιπον). Both statements of abandonment also have a statement of Paul's 'aloneness.' In 4.11 only Luke is with him (μετ' ἐμοῦ) while at his first defense no one stood with him (μοι). There is even a contrast between Demas who turned away because he loved this world and Paul who remains faithful having placed his hope in being saved into the Lord's heavenly kingdom (v. 18).

Fourth, all of 4.9–21 is united around a focus on Paul.[143] There are 17 occurrences of first person references, at least one in every verse but vv. 15, 19, and 21. This section accounts for over one-third of the first person pronoun occurrences in the letter (11 out of 30). Timothy is to come to Paul; Mark is useful to Paul; Paul is abandoned, sends, and leaves. The Lord stands by, strengthens, and delivers Paul and will save Paul. Paul is the focal point of this section.[144]

These factors show that 4.9–21 cohere well and function as a unit closing the letter.

The Remaining Portion (2.14–4.8)

While there is by no means unanimity among scholars on the previous sections, in this portion of the letter, agreement is even scarcer. Most agree that there is a significant shift at 2.14 and that 2.14–26 and 3.1–9 are closely connected. Based on the strong connections between 2.14–26 and 3.1–9 noted previously in this chapter (especially the focus on opposition), 2.14–3.9 can be held together. 3.10–17 could also be included in this section. It was noted above that 3.1–9 and 3.10–17 function well together as mirror images even in structure. Following the description of the ideal 'servant of the Lord' in 2.24–26, 3.1 begins with a contrast describing the opponents. 3.10 then picks up with another contrast describing Timothy. 3.1–9 focuses on the opponents with one contrasting statement about Timothy in the middle (3.5b); and, 3.10–17 focuses on Timothy with one contrasting statement about the opponents in the middle (3.13). These two

---

143. Cf. Mounce 2000: 587.

144. There is also a fair degree of cohesion in the verb tenses of the unit. The verbs in 4.9–22 are overwhelmingly aorist (23 out of 34) a percentage which is higher than any other part of the letter except 1.15–18.

units flow naturally out of 2.14–26. 2.14–26 contrasts Timothy and the opponents shifting back and forth between them. 3.1–17 then develops this by focusing a unit on each 'character' and placing the two units in contrast. There is then some basis for considering 2.14–3.17 as one section.

However, there are also strong considerations for considering 3.10–4.8 as a section. The strong connections between 3.10–17 and 4.1–8 have been detailed above. The argument for considering 3.10–4.8 as a section rest on these connections and the fact that 3.10–4.8 shares striking similarities with 1.6–2.13 in contradistinction from 2.14–3.9. First, and perhaps most striking, is the use of first person singular referents. These are common in 1.3–2.13, disappear completely in 2.14–3.9, and appear again prominently from 3.10 onwards. This marks a significant similarity between 1.3–2.13 and 3.10–4.8 which separates them from 2.14–3.9. In 1.3–2.13 and 3.10–4.8 the principal characters are Paul and Timothy. In 2.14–3.9 the principal characters are Timothy and the opponents. Accordingly, the explicit references to Paul's experience (and its exemplary nature) are found in 1.3–2.13 and 3.10ff. but not at all in 2.14–3.9.[145] Also, the semantic chain of 'suffering' noted above was shown to be common in 1.6–2.13 but absent from 2.14–3.9. It then reappears with a flurry of referents in 3.10–12.[146] Of course the opponents in view in 2.14–3.9 are logically connected to this suffering but it is interesting that explicit reference to suffering is missing from 2.14–3.9.

There are also some connections between 3.10–17 and 1.3–5. The concern with Timothy's spiritual beginnings in 1.5 is well known. However, this is also a prominent issue in 3.10–17.[147] Lystra in 3.11 is Timothy's home town and, according to the Acts account, Paul's persecution there precedes Timothy's joining Paul's entourage. Several scholars interpret the statement as stating that from the first time Timothy heard of Paul, suffering was involved.[148] This is then a reference to his beginnings. 3.15 also refers to Timothy's childhood in connection with the Scriptures. The reference to those from whom he learned in 3.14 might refer back to Eunice and Lois. So, there is a common interest in Timothy's spiritual beginnings in both 1.3–5 and 3.10–17.

Thus, there are two blocks of material (1.3–2.13 and 3.10–4.8) which focus on the interaction between Paul and Timothy, Paul's example, and the call to suffer. Additionally, at the beginning of both sections there are references to Timothy's spiritual heritage. These are significant connections and suggest the following basic structure.

---

145. So also, Fee 1988: 275; followed by Mounce 2000: 555.
146. So also, Fee 1988: 275; Knight 1992: 438; Karris 1979: 34; Mounce 2000: 555.
147. So also, Fee 1988: 275; followed by Mounce 2000: 555.
148. Fee 1988: 277; Knight 1992: 440; Marshall 1999: 785; Mounce 2000: 558.

1.3–2.13 – Paul and Timothy – 'Hold Fast'
   2.14–3.9 – Timothy and Opponents – 'Avoid Them'
3.10–4.8 – Paul and Timothy – 'Do the Ministry'

However, the connections between 3.10–17 and 2.14–3.9 should not be discounted. It seems that 3.10–17 serves as a hinge with significant connections to both the preceding and following material. It would be difficult to represent this well in an outline, but it might look like the following.

1.3–2.13 – Paul and Timothy – 'Hold Fast'
   2.14–3.9 – Timothy and Opponents – 'Avoid Them'
                        ⋮
   [HINGE]: 3.10–17
                        ⋮
4.1–8 – Paul and Timothy – 'Do the Ministry'

The fact that 3.10–17 has such strong connections in both directions only enhances the cohesion of the letter, though it may make outlining more difficult.

Conclusion

The letter then begins with a call for Timothy to hold fast to the message and endure (1.3–2.13). There is only one explicit call to actual teaching. The discussion then turns to the presence of opposition, no doubt the reason why a call to endurance is necessary (2.14–3.9). The focus of the exhortations in this section is avoidance. Then, as the focus returns to Paul and Timothy, the hinge unit (3.10–17) contrasts the opponents, and the exhortation is again to endure (3.15). 4.1–8 continues in the focus on Paul but takes the argument a step further with the exhortations focusing on proclamation. 4.1–8 then is the climax of the letter.[149] 4.9–22 is then the closing of the letter with the customary discussion of travel and personnel with connections to the rest of the letter.

Thus, 2 Timothy displays a high degree of cohesion. Various devices were found creating links between units including hook words, hooked keywords (or roots), parallel introductions, plays on words, and a 'hooked' device based on participants. There was significant connection unit by unit throughout the letter. Also the interweaving of various semantic chains further substantiated the cohesion of the letter. The identification of a significant semantic chain concerning an 'eschatological outlook' supports the growing critique of the bourgeois view of the Pastorals.

149.   So also, Marshall 1999: 797; Bassler 1996: 169.

There has been very little work done on the macrostructure of 2 Timothy so the analysis here fills a gap. The structure argued for differs from that given in the few commentaries which actually present a detailed structure (cf. e.g., Mounce, Marshall, Quinn and Wacker). The commentaries do not (at least explicitly) note in their structural outlines the movement in the letter from 'Paul and Timothy' to 'Timothy and Opponents' and back to 'Paul and Timothy' as has been shown here. However, the first structural outline listed above is quite similar to the structure presented by Bassler. She does not go on to seek to symbolize the hinge function of 3.10–17 though she does seem to recognize the connections of the unit in both directions.[150]

150. Cf. Bassler 1996: 162–63.

Chapter 6

THE TEXTUAL UNITS OF TITUS

This chapter will undertake the first two steps in the analysis of cohesion in Titus. The first step is the demarcation of the basic communicative units of the letter, the discrete 'units' or paragraphs. It is important to identify these units so the following chapter can analyze the level of cohesion between these units. However, before examining possible connections between units, one must ascertain whether or not these units are themselves unified. Miller contends that most are not. Thus, the second and most crucial step in this chapter is the analysis of the cohesion of each unit.

Units will be taken up consecutively through the letter. For each one an analysis of their boundaries will be given first, followed by a more extensive analysis of cohesion within the unit.

1.1–4

Boundaries
Titus 1.1–4 is clearly marked as the epistolary prescript ('A to B') and salutation, or the opening of the letter, and is therefore the first unit. The close of the salutation in 1.4 marks the close of the unit.

Cohesion
Miller is especially critical of this unit saying the grammatical structure is 'notoriously complicated and confusing,' and 'The sentence, with its compact phrases and rough transitions, does not read well as a whole.'[1] The inherent subjectivity of this assessment can be seen by the fact that Johnson can say of the same unit, 'The entire greeting is a single, long sentence, which works both logically and rhetorically in Greek . . .'[2] Miller lists three 'difficulties inherent in the salutation' which lead him to suggest that 1.1–4 has been expanded by later editors: (1) overloaded style, (2)

---

1. Miller 1997: 124. Scott 1936: 149 says it is 'so complicated in structure that the thought is difficult to follow.'
2. Johnson 1996: 215.

confusing grammar, (3) unusual content (creedal material, apostolic credentials).[3] While it is true that the grammar is not entirely clear, especially in the prepositional phrases at the beginning, this is due to the fact that this is not straightforward prose with full sentences but a listing of items to further describe the sender, as was common in ancient letters in general and in Pauline letters especially (e.g., esp. Romans and Galatians).[4] The evaluation of overloaded style and unusual content is based on Miller's overall view of the letter. There is nothing objectionable about an ancient letter incorporating creedal-like material into a salutation since the letter form was incredibly elastic. The mention of credentials of the sender was also common.

Quinn says that at 1.3 'the carefully spun out thread of thought snaps.'[5] He expected a 'second contrasting (*de*) adjectival clause that would have described the revelation of life eternal in the historical order.'[6] To answer Quinn's objection it will be useful to trace the flow of thought in 1.1–3. In 1.1 Paul identifies himself as 'slave' and 'apostle.' He further expounds his apostleship with three prepositional phrases which all have to do with salvation: κατὰ πίστιν, κατὰ ... ἐπίγνωσιν ἀληθείας, ἐπ᾽ ἐλπίδι ζωῆς αἰωνίου.[7] The thought then moves to the activity of God in providing this salvation: it was promised in the past, but now has been revealed. Apparently what bothered Quinn is that v. 3 does not refer to the revealing of eternal life but of 'his word.' The change of object is a bit surprising, but the schema of promise and fulfillment is still there.[8] It seems that at least one reason the revelation of salvation has been specifically linked to the message is in order to set up the statement of Paul being entrusted with this message. Thus, the identification of the sender finishes on the same point with which it began: Paul appointed by God. There is then a clear and logical flow to the thought: Paul has a divinely authorized position, for the cause of salvation, which has been promised in the past and now revealed in a message which has been entrusted to Paul.

Lastly, there is significant continuity in a concern about salvation throughout the unit.[9] It was just mentioned that the three prepositional phrases in 1.1 are concerned with salvation and that 1.2–3 are concerned with the revelation of salvation. Then, in 1.3 God is referred to as our

---

3. Miller 1997: 124.
4. Reed 1993b: 182 says such expansion of the prescript is a distinguishing feature of Paul's letters and 'was practiced by many.' He gives several papyri examples (182–83). E. M. Pease also says this is common in Cicero's letters (1902: 396).
5. Quinn 1990: 67.
6. Quinn 1990: 67.
7. Cf. Towner 1989: 127.
8. Cf. Mounce 2000: 381. Mounce explicitly sets his argument in contrast with Quinn.
9. Cf. Marshall 1999: 112, 'The stress is particularly upon the doctrine of salvation.'

savior and in 1.4 Christ Jesus is referred to as 'our savior' (the last words of the unit).

1.5–9

Boundaries
Commentators widely agree that 1.5–9 form a discrete unit. The initial boundary is clearly marked by the close of the epistolary salutation at the end of 1.4. Also, 1.5 opens with a reference to previous instruction which was a known way in the papyri to transition to the body of a letter.[10] The unit closes at 1.9 since a new topic (see below) emerges at 1.10.

Cohesion
The cohesion of this unit has been widely attacked, and its syntax is admittedly rough in places. Miller writes, 'Although a thematic unity (on the qualities of a good leader) serves to tie this material together, there are clear signs that originally it was not the composition of one author.'[11] Seams or breaks in the flow of thought have been detected by various scholars following 1.5, 6, and 7a. These will be addressed in order.

Miller separates 1.5 as the 'Epistolary motive' but provides no argumentation for the division.[12] Quinn suggests that at v. 6 material from a different source is being incorporated.[13] Quinn's suggestion arises from the fact that at v. 6 an εἴ τις clause occurs without an apodosis.[14] While the syntax is slightly obscure, the thought is fairly clear. Thus, several scholars suggest the apodosis, 'let him be appointed,' is implied.[15] Also, 'as I commanded you' at the close of 1.5 may serve to introduce 1.6

---

10.   White 1972a: 40–42; also White 1984: 1730–56. White refers to 'compliance statements' in which 'The body of the letter is introduced in some letters by reference to previous instruction' (1972a: 41). In addition to the five examples given by White (1972a: 42), the same phenomenon can be observed in the following papyri letters:
Referring to instruction from recipient to the author – P. Cairo Zen. 59060; P. S. I. 333; P. Cairo Zen. 59021; P. Gren f. ii.14(b)
Referring to instruction from author to recipient – P. Mich 217
Referring to instruction from a third party to the recipient – P.S.I. 328
Referring to previous communication, not necessarily instruction – P. Cairo Zen. 59036; P. Mich. 205
Although White states that the verb used in such introductions is commonly ἐντέλλω (41, n. 36), several examples from the papyri do not use this verb (for e.g., P. Mich. 202; P. Mich. 205). Therefore, it is not problematic that ἐντέλλω is not used in Tit. 1.5.
11.   Miller 1997: 126.
12.   Miller 1997: 126.
13.   Quinn 1990: 84–85.
14.   Johnson 1996: 221, also notes 'lack of syntactical transition' at the beginning of v. 6.
15.   E.g. Marshall 1999: 154 (a possibility); Mounce 2000: 388; Knight 1992: 289.

as a quotation or summary of what Paul said to Titus when he had left him in Crete. This would fit the common practice in ancient letter writing of beginning a letter with a reference to previous communication or instruction. The use of such a quotation could explain why it was unnecessary to make explicit the apodosis – having restated the command to appoint elders, he simply recites a portion of the qualification list which had previously been given. 1.7f. then expound and further develop these original instructions.

Banker also isolates 1.5 as the heading for the entire letter.[16] His argument for this division relies primarily on his view of the macro-structure of the letter and, therefore, will be dealt with more fully in the following chapter. However, some problems with his position can be noted here. First, it is grammatically difficult to separate 1.5 from 1.6 since 1.6 does not have a finite verb and at least appears to be dependent on the verb in 1.5. Banker recognizes this and suggests that though 1.5 is connected syntactically to 1.6, semantically it functions as an independent unit. Why this is so, however, is not clear. Banker relies largely on the fact that the call to 'set in order what remains' summarizes the rest of the letter body. While that is generally true, it does not require or even suggest that 1.5 should be isolated. It is in fact common among the papyri letters for the body opening to introduce the key issues of the letter. As White writes:

> The body-opening is the point at which the principal occasion for the letter is usually indicated ... The body-opening lays the foundation ... from which the superstructure may grow.[17]

Thus, the fact that the beginning of the first unit anticipates the rest of the letter does not suggest that 1.5 should be isolated especially since it is so integrally connected with what follows on a syntactical level.[18]

Quite a few scholars have argued that there is a significant break between vv. 6 and 7. Some have argued that vv. 7–9 are a later interpolation,[19] and Miller says 1.5–6 and 1.7–9 were simply previously independent pieces.[20] There are four primary bases for this view.[21]

1. 1.7–9 breaks the connection between 1.6 and 1.10, both of which refer to disobedience

---

16. Banker 1987: 30–33.
17. White 1972a: 33.
18. Cf. Marshall 1999: 20–21.
19. E.g., Falconer 1937: 142; Moffatt 1918: 402. Miller also cites A. von Harnack and O. Ritschl as proponents of this view.
20. Miller 1997: 127. Cf. Oberlinner 1996: 17.
21. The first three are summarized in Miller 1997: 126–27. The fourth can be seen, e.g., in Moffatt 1918: 402.

2. the 'abrupt and unexpected' shift from the plural πρεσβυτέροι to the singular ἐπίσκοπος
3. the presence of a different list of requirements for the πρεσβυτέροι and the ἐπίσκοπος
4. the significant difference in form between the two lists

In response, the first point assumes that material must develop only in a linear manner and does not take into account the various ways in which repetition is used in discourse. It simply does not follow that the references to disobedience must occur back to back. Second, the shift from plural to singular in the terms is overplayed. Πρεσβυτέροι is plural because in the context a number of people are in view.[22] However, the focus shifts in verse 6 with the use of the singular τίς (before ἐπίσκοπος is ever mentioned).[23] Now the focus is on any individual who may be qualified for this position. Verse 7 then simply continues this generic singular usage which demonstrates continuity with v. 6 rather than discontinuity. Though there is a shift in the word used, there is no compelling evidence that the words could not be used synonymously or at least with significant semantic overlap.[24] Third, the differences in the lists of requirements are not troublesome (they are complementary) especially if 1.6 is a summary of what Titus was told previously. 1.6 references the previous instruction and 1.7–9 expound and amplify the previous statement. This arrangement could also answer the difference in form. Since lists occurred in various forms in ancient writing there is no reason to expect the form of 1.7–9 to match exactly the form of 1:6.[25] Thus, the view of 1.7–9 as an interpolation has lost favor among scholars with even Houlden and Hanson (who often see incoherence) rejecting it.[26]

The third supposed seam is found by Miller who suggests 1.7b–8 was inserted between 1.7a and 9.[27] Miller basis this argument on a difference in form since 1.7b–8 is a list of individual terms whereas 1.7a and 1.9 are not

22. It is also significant to note that πρεσβυτέρος usually occurs in the plural and ἐπίσκοπος is consistently found in the singular (Young 1994: 104–105; Bornkam, 'πρέσβυς,' *TDNT*, vol. 6).

23. Cf. the same conclusion by Meier 1973: 338, 'the switch from plural to singular takes place in vs. 6, with *tis*, so that there is nothing at all surprising about the singular *ton episkopon* in vs. 7.'

24. Cf. Marshall 1999: 159, 'The identity of the elder with the overseer is patent …' Also, Mounce 2000: 390; Fee 1988: 174; Meier 1973: 338; Barrett 1963: 129; Ellicott 1856: 171; Kelly 1963: 231–32.

25. Cf. Fitzgerald 1997: 282–84.

26. Houlden 1976: 142; Hanson 1982: 173. Houlden calls the interpolation theory 'a last resort.' Marshall 1999: 154, n. 19, states, 'The theory that there has been a later interpolation into the letter in the interests of the monarchical episcopate is no longer seriously considered by scholars.'

27. Miller 1997: 127–28.

simple lists. However, this is a failure to understand how lists were used in the ancient world. Fitzgerald, in his analysis of catalogues, or lists, in the ancient world, has shown that the items in a list are often not homogenous in form and that it is very common for the final element to be expanded for emphasis.[28] Thus, there is no basis for Miller's division of 1.7–9.

Beyond answering the criticisms of this unit some other cohesive factors can be noted. There is a continuity of topic as the concern throughout is the appointment of church leaders. Also, there is an authoritative tone throughout. Paul recaps instruction to Titus and 'commands' (διατάσσω) him.[29] The 'necessity' of certain characteristics of leaders is mentioned (δεῖ, 1.7), and these leaders are to demonstrate authority in relation to the community, especially those who dispute (1.9). Lastly, there is a continuity in a concern for ethics as most of the unit is take up with a virtue list.

1.10–16

Boundaries
1.10–16 is commonly considered a unit in the commentaries. At 1.10 there is a shift from a focus on church leaders to a focus on opposition. Correspondingly, there is a shift from positive ethical qualities to negative ones. All the verb forms in 1.5–9 were single in number, but at 1.10 third person plural verbs appear (for the first time in the letter) and are prominent throughout the unit. The focus on opponents continues through 1.16 but is not found in 2.1. Therefore, 1.16 will be considered the final boundary.[30]

Cohesion
These verses are generally considered to be unified by their focus on false teachers. However, Miller, while acknowledging the unifying effect of the polemical concern, argues that the unit is composed of diverse elements between which logical connections are 'often strained and obscure' and 'real movement of thought' is lacking.[31] Therefore, he breaks the unit into four pieces: vv. 10–11, 12–13a, 13b–14, 15–16. He substantiates a break in thought only at 1.11/12, where he, like Barrett and others,[32] note a problem

---

28. Fitzgerald 1997: 290–91.
29. Marshall 1999: 153, notes that διατάσσω is 'one of the group of terms used in the PE to express authoritative instructions.' Cf. Quinn 1990: 84.
30. E. E. Ellis appears to be alone in keeping 2.1 with 1.10–16 (1993: 665). The article only lists an outline without discussion so there is no defense of the division. Since 2.1 provides the main verb on which 2.2–5 depend, it is not convincing to make a break between 2.1 and 2.2.
31. Miller 1997: 128–29.
32. Barrett 1963: 131. Barrett suggests the problem may be that 'the author has not fully thought through his material.'

since the context leads one to suspect that a Jew is being quoted. It is true that τις in 1.12 would be expected to refer back to the opponents in 1.10–11 who have been characterized as Jewish. However, the force of the quotation in 1.12 makes it clear that what is in view is a self-description, and therefore the reference is to Cretans.[33] The apparent discrepancy is solved if οι has in view Judaizing Cretans.[34] There is, then, no need to posit a seam at 1.12.

Miller also argues that οἱ ἐκ τῆς περιτομῆς is out of place since the rest of 1.10–11 is very general and goes on to suggest that the Jewish references in vv. 10, 14, are simply anti-Jewish glosses inserted later.[35] However, Miller misses the force of μάλιστα which is a specifying word whether it is understood as 'especially' (designating part of a larger whole) or 'namely' (making a general statement more specific).[36] Thus, in a very logical manner the close of the list introduces a more specific designation of the opposition. Furthermore, other elements in the unit can be understood against a Jewish background like 'commands of men' (1.14) and the discussion of ritual purity in 1.15.[37] Thus, most scholars find an emphasis on the Jewish character of the opposition to be integral to the picture given here.

In general there is a fairly clear flow of thought to the unit. 1.10–11 state the problem of the opponents (both morally and doctrinally). 1.12 further grounds this description in a well-known saying. This description leads naturally to the call for stiff rebuke in vv. 13a–14. 1.15–16 further describe the opponents taking up specific points and apparently refuting their claims to purity and knowledge of God. The comprehensiveness and finality of 1.16 serves well as a conclusion.[38] The continuity of focus on false teachers, with doctrine and ethics, is significant. Also, the picture of the opponents progresses sensibly. The characterization as deceivers in 1.10 corresponds to the mention of liars in the quotation in 1.12. Their wrong teaching in 1.11 is further explained by the Jewish myths and commands of men in 1.14. The general moral description of 1.10–12 is applied specifically in 1.15–16. Indeed the unit is bracketed by references to

---

33. Marshall 1999: 199, 'the connection is loose and most commentators assume that the reference of αὐτῶν is determined by the following plural Κρῆτες.'

34. Marshall 1999: 192, and Dibelius and Conzelmann 1972: 135, cite ancient sources showing a significant Jewish community on Crete.

35. Miller 1997: 129.

36. Cf. BAGD, s.v.; Skeat 1979: 173–77.

37. So e.g. Marshall 1999: 208; Mounce 2000: 401; Quinn 1990: 113f.

38. Cf. Quinn 1990: 115, 'The indictment reaches its climax in the expansive third member ... where those who pride themselves on their superfluity of good works are radically deprived of every one of them.'

rebellion using synonymous words (ἀνυπότακτοι, 1.10; ἀπειθής, 1.16). Thus, 1.10–16 holds together well as an indicting discussion of the opposition.[39]

2.1–10

Boundaries

Scholars almost universally consider 2.1–10 to be a unit. The use of the vocative commonly denoted a transition in papyri letters,[40] and here its use (Σύ) with δέ marks a shift in subject from the opponents to Titus himself.[41] 2.1–10, like 1.10–16, consists largely of ethical lists, but the lists in 2.1–10 refer to positive rather than negative characteristics. Various groups within the church are now taken up for the first time in the letter. Significant shifts at 2.11 (see below) mark 2.10 as the final boundary of this unit.

Cohesion

The inner cohesion of this unit is not significantly contested. Miller raises no objections to its inner coherence. Quinn and Hanson do note a harsh transition and loose grammar in 2.7–8.[42] Quinn is troubled with the way in which Titus is introduced in v. 7, but the connection is sensible since there is an assumption that Titus is to be numbered amongst the younger men.[43] The grammatical connection between ἐν τῇ διδασκαλίᾳ ἀφθορίαν, σεμνότητα and the participle, παρεχόμενος, is loose, but the general point is clear.[44]

The unit hangs together as a domestic code (genre) with the pervasive concern for behavior (topic).[45] Lists of ethical terms dominate the unit creating a formal and semantic coherence. The lists consist of nouns dependent on infinitives (2.2, 4, 6, 9 [twice]) which are dependent on the two imperatives of the unit (λάλει, 2.1; παρακάλει, 2.6).[46] There are six basic parts of the unit:

---

39. The chiastic structure proposed by E. Wendland for this unit is not convincing as it is not based on any lexical (or even strong semantic) repetition. The connections are strained and too subjective (1999: 347).

40. White 1972a: 29, 'The vocative is employed intermittently, during the Roman period, as a means of making major transitions in all three body-sections.'

41. Cf. the similar conclusion of Quinn 1990: 128, 'The singular address, reinforced by the pronoun, clearly marks a new stage in the exposition ...' See also Weiser 1989: 400.

42. Quinn 1990: 139; Hanson 1982: 181.

43. So most commentators.

44. Cf. the discussion in Marshall 1999: 254f.

45. Quinn 1990: 137, 'This whole section (2.2–10) reveals a concept of and a concern for order in the Christian home and in the lives of the individuals who constitute that household.'

46. Cf. esp. Weiser 1989: 401–402; also Johnson 1996: 232.

2.1 – heading[47]
2.2 – instruction to older men
2.3 – instruction to older women
2.4–5 – instruction to younger women
2.6–8 – instruction to younger men (including Titus)
2.9–10 – instruction to slaves

The heading introduces the behaviors which follow as that which is fitting for 'sound doctrine' (ὑγιαίνουσα διδασκαλία). This connection between behavior and doctrine continues as the proper behavior of the young women will prevent 'the word of God' from being blasphemed (v. 5), and the proper behavior of slaves will adorn the doctrine (διδασκαλία) of God our Savior (v.10).[48] Titus also is to be an example in 'doctrine' (διδασκαλία). There is also a connection with the concern for older men to be 'sound' (ὑγιαίνω) in faith, love, and endurance.

The structure of the instructions themselves follow a reasonable form being structured along familial lines (similar to 1 Tim. 5.1–2).[49] Since the instruction to younger women is to be done by the older women, the instruction to younger women is contained within the instruction to older women resulting in a basic chiastic arrangement.[50] In v. 6 there is a return to an explicit imperative (παρακάλει) which might seem to disrupt the structure. However, it is sensible to return to an explicit imperative at this point since the previous group's discussion (to young women) had moved to a more indirect form, being dependent on a ἵνα clause rather than the initial imperative. Thus, v. 6 returns to a clear imperative.[51] The instructions to each of the first four groups contains a reference to σώφρων/σωφρονίζω (vv. 2, 4, 5, 6).[52] In fact all of the instructions share a common concern for respectability.[53] Throughout the unit the rules are justified with purpose clauses (vv. 4, 5, 8, 10),[54] and three of these focus on

47. Cf. Weiser 1989: 400; Marshall 1999: 237.
48. The unit then opens and closes with statements about the proper correlation between belief and behavior. Wendland 1999: 340 suggests the occurrences of διδασκαλία in 2.1, 10, create an inclusio. However, the fact that διδασκαλία also occurs in 2.7 argues against this. διδασκαλία binds the unit as a keyword and the inclusio effect is created by the connection of teaching and behavior in 2.1 and 2.10.
49. As several scholars note, it is reminiscent of 1 Tim. 5.1–2 with 6.1–2. This is not intended to suggest that the passage is *Haustafel* rather than *Gemeindeparänese*, but that the categories are common.
50. Quinn 1990: 129.
51. Weiser 1989: 403 also notes that παρακάλει occurs in the direct center of the argument with three groups discussed before and three groups afterward.
52. So also, Quinn 1990: 129; Marshall 1999: 231; Mounce 2000: 407.
53. Cf. Towner 1989: 192, 'If the ethical instructions of 2.2–10 share one thing in common, it is that each group is called to pursue a lifestyle that is respectable.'
54. Marshall 1999: 231; Weiser 1989: 402.

a concern for how behavior will effect outsiders (vv. 5, 8, 10).[55] The various instructions then share common concerns as well as structures.[56] Thus, these instructions hold together as a coherent whole.[57]

2.11–14

Boundaries

Several shifts occur at 2.11 suggesting, as most scholars agree, that a new unit begins at 2.11. There is a shift in genre from a domestic code to a theological statement.[58] Thus, imperatives, which were the backbone of 2.1–10, do not occur in 2.11–14. Whereas the verbs in 2.1–10 were predominantly present tense, most of the verbs in 2.11–14 are aorists.[59] There is also a significant shift in actors. Whereas in 2.1–10 it was Paul exhorting Titus concerning various groups within the church, in 2.1–10 the actors are God/Jesus and 'us.' Correspondingly the verb forms shift from second person singular with Titus as subject to third person singular with divine subjects. Also first person plural becomes frequent (five occurrences) in this unit, though it had only appeared in passing in the previous unit (2.8, 10). Indeed, a first person plural verb occurs for the first time (ζήσωμεν, 2.12). Thus, it is clear that a new thought begins in 2.11.

Concerning the final boundary there is less apparent agreement. Some commentators end the unit at v. 14 while others include v. 15.[60] However, even many of those who include v. 15 with this unit note that it shifts to a different point.[61] Significant shifts which occur at 2.15 suggest v. 14 should be considered the final boundary of this unit. These shifts will be discussed below.

Cohesion

There does not seem to be any dispute of the coherence of this unit, even from Miller. Quinn does state that the 'terminology and style' change

---

55. Commonly noted. E.g., Barrett 1963: 134; Mounce 2000: 407. Alan Padgett suggests this feature is more prominent here than in other similar NT passages (1987a: 47–48).

56. Note also the common concern for submission for young women and slaves (2.4, 9). In both instances the submission is explicitly linked to 'their own' (ἴδιος) husbands or masters. Johnson 1996: 232, suggests this may hint at a problem with others encroaching on rightful authority.

57. Cf. Weiser 1989: 403, who attributes to the unit, 'Kohärenz und Ausgeglichenheit.' Johnson 1996: 232, writes, 'The passage [2.1–10] is well constructed.' Padgett 1987a: 49, says the passage has 'a fairly obvious structure.'

58. Cf. also Miller 1997: 132.

59. In 2.1–10, 15/16 verbs are in present tense. In 2.11–14, 5/8 are aorists.

60. For the former, see Marshall 1999: 261f. Quinn 1990: 178; Easton 1947: 93f. For the latter, cf. Knight 1992: 318f.; Fee 1988: 193f.

61. E.g. Fee 1988: 197; Mounce 2000: 432.

'abruptly' at v. 14, but he goes on to say, 'Yet the whole clause is so nicely joined to the preceding verse that, if in fact it is the citation of an archaic Christian hymn, it must have been made by those who originally composed the confession [2.11–13].'[62] Thus, there are no serious attacks on the cohesion of this unit.

Positively, 2.11–14 cohere grammatically as one sentence. Salvation terminology running throughout (χάρις, σωτήριος, ἡ μακάρια ἐλπίς, σωτήρ, ἔδωκεν ἑαυτὸν ὑπὲρ ἡμῶν) further unites the sentence. The sentence is then composed of two parts: vv. 11–13 and v. 14, as is commonly noted. 2.11–13 are bracketed by the only occurrences of 'epiphany' language (ἐπιφαίνω, v. 11; ἐπιφάνεια, v. 13), the σωτηρ- root (σωτήριος, v. 11; σωτήρ, v. 13), and explicit mention of θέος (v. 11, 13). This binds vv. 11–13 together linguistically. Logically, the verses progress from the past manifestation of salvation (v. 11) to the present effects ('in the present age,' v. 12), and to the future manifestation of the savior (v. 13). The explicit naming of the savior as Jesus Christ at the end of v. 13 serves to introduce the further statement in v. 14.[63] 2.14 returns to the past historical work of Christ, as in v. 11, and in essence further expounds v. 11.[64] This creates symmetry within the unit which has been noticed by Lau.[65] 2.11 and 2.14 refer to the incarnate ministry of Christ in the past. Then, both statements have ἵνα-clauses describing the goal/purpose of the event (vv. 12, 14). Though Lau did not mention it, both purpose statements also describe the negative (removal of sin) and then the positive (proper living) results of Christ's work.[66] Then, between these parallel statements is a reference to the future parousia (v. 13). This could be represented as follows:

A Past work of Christ – appearing of saving grace
B   Goal – Negative – deny sin, etc.
      Positive – live soberly, etc.
C   Parousia – the blessed hope
A' Past work of Christ – he gave himself for us
B'   Goal – Negative – redeem us from lawlessness
      Positive – cleanse, good deeds

---

62.   Quinn 1990: 171. Cf. also Marshall 1999: 282, who also notes that v. 14 is 'a somewhat loosely attached addition to the sentence.'

63.   Fee 1988: 196, 'In order to make his present point Paul would not has had to use the name of Christ at all … But he then adds the personal name, **Jesus Christ**, because he has some more things he wants to say about him (as in Col. 2.2), which leads to verse 14.' Cf. also Lau 1996: 157, n. 443.

64.   Lau 1996: 155; Bassler 1996: 201. Marshall 1999: 282 says v. 14 is 'broadly parallel' with vv. 11f.

65.   Lau 1996: 155–56.

66.   So also Mounce 2000: 421.

The temporal frame moves in the same way: past, present, future, past, present. There is then a flow to the progression of thought. This in conjunction with the coherence of theme and actors grounds the cohesion of this unit.

2.15

Boundaries

As noted above 2.15 is commonly connected with 2.11–14. However, there are clear shifts between 2.11–14 and 2.15. The genre shifts from a doctrinal exposition to exhortation. Correspondingly, imperatives, which were absent in 2.11–14, come back in a flurry (four occurrences) in v. 15. Also, 2.15 returns to second person singular referents which were absent in 2.11–14. Thus, there is a shift in subjects from 'Christ and us' back to 'Paul to Titus concerning the church.' Lastly, while the main verbs of 2.11–14 were predominately aorist, all the verbs in 2.15 are present tense.[67] Without disputing connections on a larger scale, 2.15 clearly marks a shift in thought and will be considered a new unit.

The next issue is the final boundary, whether 2.15 is to be considered alone or connected with 3.1f. Quinn and Easton combine 2.15 with 3.1f.[68] Quinn properly notes significant continuity between 2.15 and 3.1–2 such as direct address to Titus which is absent in 2.11–14 but common to 2.15–3.2. One could also note the continuity of imperatives and the genre of exhortation. However, other factors suggest 2.15 should not be simply connected with 3.1–2. 2.15 appears to be a summarizing statement and ταῦτα usually refers backward in the Pastoral Epistles.[69] Then, there is a slight difference in that 2.15 concerns the manner of teaching whereas 3.1–2 returns to specific content. In connection with this observation, it is in 3.1–2, and not 2.15, that the ethical description of life continues with the list of infinitives dependent on the imperatives. Thus, while the shifts between 2.15 and 3.1 are not drastic, there does appear to be some shift so 2.15 will be considered alone.[70] Later discussion will further analyze the relation of 2.15 to the rest of the letter.

67. Banker 1987: 89 also notes the shifts to imperatives, aorists, and second person singular. Wendland 1999: 339, n. 11, also notes several of these shifts.

68. Quinn 1990: 181–82; Easton 1947: 98.

69. So most. Quinn 1990: 178 cites examples of ταῦτα pointing forward and introducing a new step in the argument but his examples are not convincing.

70. So also Marshall 1999: 296; Banker 1987: 105; Bernard 1906: 174–75. Mounce 2000: 421 writes, 'V 15 is a transitional verse that could be placed with 2.11–14, by itself, or with 3.1–11.'

Cohesion
The cohesion of this verse is unquestioned. All four verbs are present active imperatives, and the first three are second person singular. The verse coheres around the topic of Titus' authority in teaching, stated positively 'with all authority' and negatively 'let no one despise you.'

3.1–2

Boundaries
The reasons for beginning a new unit at 3.1 have been argued above. At 3.3 further shifts suggest 3.2 is the final boundary of this unit. The shifts at 3.2/3 will be detailed in the discussion of the next unit.

Cohesion
There seems to be no objection to the coherence of this unit, and for good reason. It coheres as one sentence, one imperative with five dependent infinitives and a concluding participial phrase. Every verb form is present tense. The genre is exhortation throughout and the topic is proper behavior. Obedience, gentleness, and general goodness unite as the common themes.[71] The closing participial phrase is particularly suited for a conclusion and thus enhances the sense of cohesion. After a series of more 'passive' qualities, the participial phrase calls for the people to take initiative in 'showing' gentleness.[72] Then, the double use of πᾶς ('all gentleness to all people') creates a climactic sense of completion, which was common at the end of lists like this one in ancient literature.[73] Thus, 3.1–2 coheres well as an exhortative list with significant continuity in several areas and following normal patterns for such lists.

3.3–7

Boundaries
There is a strong shift in cohesion fields at 3.3 marking it as the beginning of a new unit. The verbs shift from entirely present tense to an imperfect and aorists, from second person singular to first person plural,[74] from

---

71.   The list actually begins with two semantically similar verbs (ὑποτάσσω, πειθαρχέω) and two roughly synonymous nouns (ἀρχή, ἐξουσία). Marshall 1999: 301 says the combination of the two nouns 'was something of a cliché.' Quinn 1990: 185 also notes the shared root between ἀρχή and πειθαρχέω.

72.   Marshall 1999: 304; Spicq 1969: 647.

73.   Fitzgerald 1997: 288; cf. also, 285. Mounce 2000: 445, also says the repeated πᾶς creates a sense of completeness.

74.   Quinn 1990: 200, also notes the shift in person and number.

imperative to indicative. Accordingly the subject shifts from Titus to 'we,' presumably Christians in general.[75] There is a shift as well from ethical exhortation to theological exposition, as the theme of salvation comes to the fore again. Thus, 3.3 clearly marks the beginning of a new unit. Most commentaries note this,[76] but several do not make any division between 3.2 and 3.3.[77] However, those who do not make a division here still note the shift to theological grounding at 3.3.

The final boundary of this unit is understood quite differently among commentators. Some conclude the unit at the end of v. 7,[78] others after v. 8a (Πιστὸς ὁ λόγος),[79] and others at the end of v. 8.[80] It will be argued below that significant shifts require 3.8b onwards to be considered as a new unit. What remains here then is the place of v. 8a (Πιστὸς ὁ λόγος). The phrase refers to preceding material as scholars almost unanimously affirm.[81] As a confirmation of the preceding material it can be viewed as a conclusion or as a transition introducing a shift. The difference in understanding is not great, but since the phrase is joined by καί with v. 8b it will be considered with the following unit. Therefore, 3.7 will be considered the final boundary of the unit beginning at 3.3.

Cohesion

Scholars do not demonstrate any concern about the cohesion of this unit. The actors throughout are God, Jesus, Holy Spirit, and 'we.' Every verb is in aorist tense except the initial εἰμί (for which there is no aorist form). The topic throughout is salvation as seen in the use of terms like σωτήρ (vv. 4, 6), σῴζω (v. 5), δικαιόω (v. 7), ἐλπίς ζωῆς αἰωνίου (v. 7), among others.[82]

---

75. C. E. B. Cranfield notes that Paul commonly used the first person plural in 'general doctrinal statements concerning all Christians.' He suggests that in such passages in the accepted Pauline letters 'the "we" most probably means Christians generally' (1982: 285). The same appears to be true here.

76. E.g. Knight 1992: 335; Quinn 1990: 187; Marshall 1999: 304; Bassler 1996: 206; Hanson 1982: 189; Guthrie 1990: 215; Bernard 1906: 177; Barrett 1963: 140.

77. Mounce 2000: 438; Oberlinner 1996: 160; Merkel 1991: 100; Brox 1969a: 303; Fee 1988: 200f.; Dibelius and Conzelmann 1972: 147. It is interesting to note, however, that each of these commentators does make a division between 2.1–10 and 2.11–14(15). The shift at 3.3 seems to be just as clear as the one at 2.11.

78. E.g. Marshall 1999: 304f.; Oberlinner 1996: 161; Hanson 1982: 193; Brox 1969a: 303f.; cf. NA 26.

79. E.g. Quinn 1990: 187; Dibelius and Conzelmann 1972: 147f.; Falconer 1937: 114f.

80. E.g. Knight 1992: 347.

81. Marshall 1999: 328, 'There should be no dispute that the reference ... is backwards in Tit 3.8.' So also, e.g., Knight 1992: 347; Mounce 2000: 451; Oberlinner 1996: 181; Merkel 1991: 105; Towner 1989: 112; Hanson 1982: 193; Dibelius and Conzelmann 1972: 150.

82. Cf. Marshall 1999: 307, 'The statement is entirely concerned with soteriology.'

There is a chronological, salvation-historical development as well, from the former state (v. 3), to God's act to save (vv. 4–6), to the future hope (v. 7).[83] Thus the unit displays significant continuity and logical development.

Miller does consider the possibility that 3.3 and 3.4–7 were originally separate pieces since 'a striking change in literary style occurs' between them.[84] However, he concedes that it would be difficult the separate the verses. The ποτε καὶ ... ὅτε δὲ construction binds verses 3 and 4 together as one anticipates the other.[85] The temporal contrast is then anchored in an ethical contrast as the vices of v. 3 contrast the transformation in view in 3.4f. This is seen perhaps most clearly in the closing of v. 3 with 'hateful and hating one another' (στυγητοί, μισοῦντες ἀλλήλους) and opening v. 4 with reference to God's 'mercy and lovingkindness' (ἡ χρηστότης καὶ ἡ φιλανθρωπία).[86] Secondly, the first person plural referents which are introduced in 3.3 continue straight through v. 7. Just as in vv. 3 and 4 there was a contrast between 'then' and 'now', in v. 5 a deliberate contrast is set up between what 'we' have done (ἐποιήσαμεν) and what 'God' has done (ἔσωσεν). Where the 'we' is the actor, there is only a list of negatives; but, when the actor shifts to 'God,' salvation and its benefits become the topic of discussion. The first person plural continues to appear in the rest of the section but now as the recipient rather than the actor.[87] Thus the two subjects occurring in vv. 4–7 are integrally related, and the verses cohere around a discussion of salvation.[88]

3.8

Boundaries
Significant shifts require the start of a new unit at 3.8. Whereas the verbs in 3.3–7 were almost entirely aorist, the verbs in 3.8 return to present tense. Also, at 3.8 there is a shift to first person singular, a shift which is all the more significant since the author alone has not been the subject of a verb since 1.5.[89] There is also a return of the second person referent (absent in

83. Towner 1989: 112.
84. Miller 1997: 135.
85. Cf. Läger 1996: 99.
86. Cf. Bassler 1996: 206–207.
87. In v. 5, ἡμᾶς is the recipient of the saving action and the implied recipient of the washing and renewal. In v. 6, the Spirit is poured out ἐφ' ἡμᾶς, and Jesus Christ is 'our' (ἡμῶν) savior. In v. 7, it is 'we' who are justified (δικαιωθέντες) and made heirs (κληρονόμοι).
88. The chiastic shift between 3.4–5 and 3.6–7 proposed by Wendland (1999: 348) is not convincing. The general connections are noted above but the chiastic ordering of each element as he proposes is strained.
89. Quinn 1990: 241 also notes that first person singular referents have not occurred since 1.5.

vv. 3–7) and the congregation returns to view (e.g., 'those who have believed in God'). Lastly, v. 8 returns to exhortation rather than theological exposition.[90]

The final boundary is not as clear and is in many way analogous to 2.15. 3.9–11 continue the predominant present tense and exhortation. Second person singular referents continue in vv. 9–11. However, there seems to be a shift in topic.[91] 3.8 refers to Titus' teaching and looks back to what was just previously stated (περί τούτων, ταῦτα). 3.9–11 moves on to the issue of opposition. In 3.8 the congregation as a whole is in view, but in 3.9–11 only the opponents are in view. Also Towner notes that while in 3.8 the verbs are positive and the 'things' in view are commended, in 3.9–11 the verbs connote avoidance and the things in view are negative.[92] While these are not drastic shifts, they do represent some difference, and in line with what was argued at 2.15, 3.8 will be considered separately.[93] Connections with 3.9–11 are not disputed and will be examined further in the following chapter.[94]

Cohesion

This verse coheres well. Having affirmed the previous material (v. 8a), it calls for confident teaching, states the purpose of the teaching (ἵνα), and closes with a clause which appears to provide a grounding or rationale for the exhortation (v. 8c, 'these things are good and profitable for people'). However, Miller says 3.8c 'seems rather pointless' and Falconer calls it an 'editorial platitude,' suggesting it has been inserted later.[95] In response, 3.8c fits well and meaningfully into the argument by affirming the usefulness of the things being urged. This summary statement then opens with an affirmation of reliability (3.8a) and closes with an affirmation of profitability (3.8c).

---

90. Cf. Marshall 1999: 22.
91. Oberlinner 1996: 180 calls it a shift in emphasis.
92. Towner 1994: 3.
93. Hanson 1982: 193 also considers 3.8 separately.
94. Banker 1987: 111 summarizes well the situation at this point: 'Finally, it must be said that some boundaries are not as distinct as we would like them to be. Where there is definite semantic relationship, sometimes the two constituents blend into each other at the borders, and it is difficult to make an exact cut.' Cf. Bassler 1996: 210, who also posits a unit break at 3.9: 'The argument flows so smoothly from 3.8 into these verses that they barely constitute a new section, even though the content changes significantly.'
95. Miller 1997: 136; Falconer 1937: 116. Hanson 1982: 194 also criticizes this statement saying 'nowhere does the author descend lower in mere banality then here. Perhaps he was running out of material' (cf. Quinn 1990: 243). However, Hanson's criticism here is not concerning cohesion.

3.9–11

Boundaries

The reasons for regarding 3.9 as the initial boundary of a new unit have been given above. The δέ marks a contrasting shift as has happened elsewhere in the letter (e.g., 2.1).[96] Significant shifts at 3.12 suggest 3.11 is the final boundary of this unit.

Cohesion

The cohesion of these two sentences is not disputed. They cohere as exhortation to Titus built on two second person singular imperatives (περιΐστασο, v. 9; παραιτοῦ, v. 10). The topic throughout is the opponents – avoiding their activities (v. 9) and dealing with those of their number (vv. 10–11). Terms for strife and division feature prominently (ζήτησις, ἔρις, μαχή, v. 9; αἱρετικός, v. 10).[97] Following that description, words with a nuance of judgment characterize the response (νουθεσία, παραιτέομαι, v. 10;[98] αὐτοκατάκριτος, v. 11). The connotations of the two imperatives are similar as well: avoid and reject. Both imperatives are justified by a description which employs doublets. Avoid their ways because they are 'useless and meaningless' (ἀνωφελεῖς καὶ μάταιοι); reject the divisive man because he is 'depraved and sinning' (ἐξέστραπται ... ἁμαρτάνει). Thus, there is continuity in topic as well as semantic and stylistic cohesion.

3.12–14

Boundaries

Significant shifts at 3.12 show a new unit begins there as practically all the commentators agree. The verbs shift from primarily present tense to primarily aorist. First person singular referents return.[99] Most importantly the opponents fade from view and the topic shifts to travel plans. Similar travelogues occur near the end of letters attributed to Paul (e.g., Rom. 15.14–33; 1 Cor. 16.1–11; Phlm. 21–22), other New Testament letters (Heb. 13. 18–19, 22–23; 2 Jn 12; 3 Jn 13–14),[100] and of the papyri letters.[101] Thus,

---

96. Scholars who begin a new unit at 3.9 include Knight 1992: 353; Bassler 1996: 210; Fee 1988: 210.

97. The Louw and Nida (1989) domain classification of the last three terms are very close. Respectively they are: 39.22, 39.23, 39.17.

98. Cf. G. Stählin, 'αἰτέω', *TDNT*, vol. 1. Concerning παραιτέομαι he writes, 'In the NT the word is used in this sense ['to reject or repudiate'] in relation to different actions in the supervision of doctrine and the exercise of congregational discipline' (195).

99. So also Quinn 1990: 260.

100. See Funk 1967: 249–68; Mitchell 1992: 641f.

101. White 1972a: 49–51.

3.12–14 fit a common form found in ancient letters, and this further suggests these verses should be considered a unit.

Cohesion

This unit coheres around the idea of travel plans with its dense concentration of verbs for travel (πέμπω, ἔρχομαι, παραχειμάζω, προπέμπω), a place name (Νικόπολις), and names of co-workers who are travelling ('Αρτεμᾶς, Τυχικός, Ζηνᾶς, 'Απολλῶς). The concentration of such terms both distinguishes these verses as a distinct unit and creates cohesion within the unit. The use of σπουδάζω (v. 12) and σπουδαίως (v. 13) links the two verses and creates a continuity in tone. The unit follows the typical pattern of closings found in Pauline letters.[102] Even Miller does not dispute the cohesion of this unit.[103]

Summary

This chapter has had two primary goals: (1) to distinguish the boundaries of the discrete units of Titus and (2) to examine the coherence of each unit. At certain places it has been difficult to decide whether to hold two sets of verses together as one unit or to distinguish them as two units (e.g., 3.8 and 3.9–11). Each unit has been found to cohere through a variety of linguistic, semantic, and thematic elements. The next issue is discerning how or if these discrete units connect and how that shapes the letter to Titus.

---

102.   Merkel 1990: 106; Marshall 1999: 340. Marshall also notes similarity in Hebrews 13. The point here has nothing to do with authorship, but that 3.12–14 follows a common pattern as found in similar literature.

103.   Miller 1997: 137, 'The passage reads well as a unit...'

Chapter 7

CONNECTIONS BETWEEN UNITS IN TITUS

The last chapter identified discrete units within Titus and argued that these units cohered within themselves. Such cohesion is important, but for the entire letter to cohere these units must connect in some way with each other. Examining such interconnection between units is the focus of this chapter.

The analysis will take place in three parts. First, there will be an examination of connections between contiguous units, between each unit and the one which follows. In a cohesive document one will expect there to be some coherent flow from one unit to the next, though the level of connection may vary since discourses do not develop only linearly. Specific attention will be given to conjunctions, transitional devices (e.g. hooked keywords, etc.), and continuities in cohesion fields.

The second part will shift to the macroperspective examining semantic chains which run through significant portions of the letter. These chains consist of recurring elements related to each other lexically or semantically and reveal a common concern throughout the letter. If these chains themselves overlap and are interrelated, the cohesive effect is even greater.

The third part will focus on how the units may form larger sections and how this effects the shape of the whole. Any symmetrical arrangement in the letter's macrostructure can enhance the overall cohesive effect.

Connections Between Contiguous Units

1.1–4 and 1.5–9

Normally there would be no need to discuss direct connections from the epistolary opening (prescript and salutation) and the beginning of the letter body since direct connections would not necessarily be expected. However, the expansion of the epistolary opening in Titus 1.1–4 makes it possible to note a few general connections.

The connection is not disputed since little is expected of it. The connections are primarily continuities of concern. In both units the Pauline message (ἀλήθεια, 1.1; ὁ λόγος θεοῦ, 1.3; ἡ διδασκαλία ἡ ὑγιαίνουσα, 1.9) stands out as a prominent concern. Also, the connection of the message with 'godliness' (εὐσέβεια) in 1.1 may anticipate the string of ethical terms in 1.5–9. Lastly, and probably most significantly, both units are concerned with authority and appointment to ministry. 1.3 refers to Paul being entrusted with God's message. Then, 1.4 shows Titus to be Paul's 'genuine' child in this common faith, suggesting his involvement with Paul in ministry.[1] In 1.5 Titus is indeed involved in ministry under Paul's direction. 1.5–9 then shows Titus delegating authority to others. There is then a continuous chain of authority through these two units: God–Paul–Titus–local elders.[2]

1.5–9 and 1.10–16

Miller says the discussion of 'unspecified opponents' in 1.10–16 interrupts 'instructions regarding church order (cf. 1:6–9, 2:1ff.).'[3] However, most scholars have seen a tight connection between these two units with even Easton saying 'There is no break in the argument' at 1.10.[4] The primary connection that is noticed is the use of γάρ in 1.10 which suggests the presence of 'many' opponents is the reason why such leaders as described in 1.5–9 are needed.[5] The logical flow between the two units is considered by most to be clear. Thus, Miller suggests that 1.10–16 'may have been intentionally placed here by a compiler who wished to underscore the need for care to exercised in the selection of church leaders.'[6] Recognition of such care and logic in the argumentation undermines the case for incoherence.

There are several other connections between these two units. First, there are several continuities. Both units are exhortation directed to Titus. Titus is the one called upon to appoint elders (1.5) and refute opponents (1.13), and he is to be involved in the silencing of 1.11. There is also a continuity of ethical concern as both units are dominated by ethical lists.

Second, there are numerous lexical connections between the units which set the church leaders and opponents in direct contrast,[7] further showing that the presence of the opponents is a reason for the urgent need of leadership. The following table contains the primary lexical links.

---

1. Cf. Marshall 1999: 112.
2. This is not intended to suggest a concern here for apostolic succession, but simply to show a continuous flow of thought in the argument and a concern for legitimate leadership.
3. Miller 1997: 128.
4. Easton 1947: 86.
5. E.g., Marshall 1999: 191; Oberlinner 1996: 33; Mounce 2000: 395–96; Knight 1992: 295; Fee 1988: 177.
6. Miller 1997: 128.
7. Cf. Merkel 1991: 93.

Church Leaders (1.5–9)	**Opponents** (1.10–16)
μὴ ... ἀνυπότακτος (v. 6)	ἀνυπότακτος (v. 10)
πιστός (v. 6)	ἄπιστος (v. 15)
μὴ αἰσχροκερδής (v. 7)	αἰσχρός κέρδος (v. 11)
ἀντεχόμενον 'faithful word' (v. 9)	προσέχοντες myths and commands of men (v. 14)

In 1.6, elders are to have children who are not characterized by disobedience (ἀνυπότακτος), but the first adjective describing the opponents is ἀνυπότακτος (1.10).[8] Also in 1.6, elders are to have children who are characterized by πιστός but the opponents are described as ἄπιστος (1.15).[9] A bishop must be αἰσχροκερδής (1.7) but the opponents are motivated by αἰσχρός κέρδος (1.11).[10] A bishop must 'hold fast' (ἀντεχόμενον, 1.9) to the truth, but the opponents 'pay attention to' (προσέχοντες, 1.14) Jewish myths and the commands of men. Furthermore, the opponents teach 'what they ought not' (διδάσκω, v. 11), but the elders are to be able to exhort in 'sound teaching' (διδασκαλία, v. 9).[11] Thus, the elders hold to 'sound' (ὑγιαίνω, v. 9) doctrine, but the opponents need to be rebuked so that they may be 'sound' (ὑγιαίνω, v. 13) in the faith.[12] There are also more general contrasts without direct verbal links, such as:

Just and devout (v. 8) vs. defiled and detestable (v. 15, 16)
Love what is good (v. 8) vs. worthless for any good deed (v. 16)
Holding fast to the truth (v. 9) vs. turning away from the truth (v. 14)

Thus, there are significant contrasting lexical and semantic links between 1.5–9 and 1.10–16.

Miller concedes that ἀνυπότακτοι serves as a 'link-word' connecting 1.5–9 and 1.10–16 (though he does not note the other lexical connections); however, he suggests this is not the result of a deliberate author but a haphazard compiler since the word refers to the children of elders in 1.6 but seditious opponents in 1.10. Miller writes, 'It is hard to imagine an

8. So also Marshall 1999: 193–94; Quinn 1990: 105–106; Brox 1969a: 287; Merkel 1991: 93; Bassler 1996: 186.
9. Bassler 1996: 186 comments, 'The requirements concerning the elders' children are framed with the presence of the "rebellious people" in mind.'
10. Marshall 1999: 198; Quinn 1990: 106. Karris 1979: 109 also notes this connection along with the connections with the elder's children. Karris also suggests a lexical link between οἰκονόμον (1.7) and οἴκους (1.11), but this is not as strong as the other links mentioned.
11. Marshall 1999: 197.
12. There is some debate concerning the object of the rebuke in 1.13. The options are: (1) only the leaders (e.g. Quinn 1990: 109), (2) only those deceived by the leaders (e.g. Knight 1992: 299f.), or (3) leaders and adherents (Fee 1988: 180; Marshall 1999: 204). It seems best not to posit a strong distinction between leaders and adherents, so option 3 is followed here (cf. Marshall 1999: 204–205).

author using, in such close proximity, the same word to label two very different groups.'[13] However, such repetition is not that hard to imagine. 1.11 states that these 'rebellious' opponents were upsetting whole households, so 1.6 has made it clear that the elder's house is to be free from such 'rebelliousness.'[14] Bassler, in agreement with the view taken here, writes, 'The author's point is that an elder's ability to prevent rebellion and debauchery in his household held promise for success in dealing with instances of it in the church.'[15]

Lastly, the two units are connected by a variation of the transitional device, hooked keyword. The discussion in 1.5–9 focused on the ethical qualities required of church leaders until the final and most elaborate item in 1.9 which ended with the mention of opponents (τοὺς ἀντιλέγοντας) who must be rebuked (ἐλέγχειν). Immediately following this is 1.10–16 which, although it does not use the word ἀντιλέγω,[16] focuses on the existence of opponents and calls for them to be rebuked (ἔλεγχε, v. 13).[17] This strongly suggests that 1.5–9 has been shaped in such a way as to introduce 1.10–16.[18]

1.10–16 and 2.1–10

Miller finds little connection between these two units, saying 2.1–10 'is tied only loosely to the surrounding context' and is probably 'a preformed independent unit.'[19] Hanson is not so strong but does say that 2.1 is purely transitional, apparently implying it has no significant connection to what precedes or follows.[20] At a lesser degree some merely find at 2.1 a shift to a new point with little connection to what has preceded.[21]

However, most have found at 2.1 a contrast between the behavior of the opponents and that expected of church members.[22] While δέ itself does not

13. Miller 1997: 129.
14. Also the elder's house is to be marked by those who have faith (πιστός, 1.6) in contrast to the faithless (ἄπιστος) opponents (1.15).
15. Bassler 1996: 186–87.
16. Guthrie 1990: 199, captures the basic idea stating, 'The apostle proceeds to describe those who contradict.'
17. The following also note the repetition of this verb: Marshall 1999: 704; Oberlinner 1996: 32; Bassler 1996: 191.
18. Cf. Bassler 1996: 191, 'The discussion of church leaders in 1.5–9 serves in large part to introduce the problem of the rebellious people these leaders are charged to refute.'
19. Miller 1997: 130.
20. Hanson 1982: 179.
21. E.g., Quinn 1990: 117; Dibelius and Conzelmann 1972: 139. The NIV seems to follow this reasoning since it leaves δέ untranslated.
22. E.g. Falconer 1937: 108; Easton 1947: 90; Barrett 1963: 133; Guthrie 1990: 203; Fee 1988: 184; Bassler 1996: 193; Oberlinner 1996: 101; Mounce 2000: 408; Marshall 1999: 230. Marshall notes, 'The progression from discussing how heretics behave to how Christians/ leaders should behave is common in the PE.' He cites 1 Tim. 6.11; 2 Tim. 2.1; 3.10; 4.5.

automatically signal a sharp contrast,[23] lexical and semantic connections between the units show that the lifestyles prescribed in 2.1–10 are formed in intentional, direct contrast to the description of the opponents in 1.10–16.[24] The primary thematic contrast is seen between 1.16 and 2.1. The description of the opponents closes with a climactic statement that their actions (ἔργα) belie any claim to know God. In contrast, Titus is to teach the lifestyles which are fitting (ἃ πρέπει) for sound doctrine.[25] While there is a way of life which denies God, there is also a way of life which 'adorns the doctrine of God our Savior' (2.10). This correlation between the end of one unit and the beginning of the next creates significant cohesion and suggests intentionality.[26]

Further, there are a number of specific connections between elements in the lists of the two units as shown in the following table.

Opponents (1.10–16)	**Church** (2.1–10)
ἀνυπότακτος (1.10)	ὑποτάσσω (2.5, 9)
[not] ὑγιαινεῖν ἐν πίστει (1.13)	ὑγιαινεῖν ἐν τῇ πίστει (2.2)
Defiled (1.15)	Pure (young women, 2.5)
Detestable (1.16)	Well-pleasing (slaves, 2.9)
Worthless for any good deed (1.16)	Example of good deeds (Titus, 2.7)[27]

The submissiveness enjoined upon the young women and slaves contrasts the rebelliousness of the opponents.[28] Older men are to be 'sound in the faith' (2.2), but the opponents obviously are not since they must be rebuked so that they become sound (1.13).[29] The general evil of the opponents contrasts especially the pleasing qualities urged for slaves and young women. Furthermore, the self-control called for in 2.2, 4, 5, and 6 (σώφρων, σωφρονίζω) contrasts the depiction of the opponents as 'evil beasts' and 'lazy gluttons' (1.12).[30] The older women are to be 'teachers of good' (καλοδιδάσκαλος, 2.3) and Titus is to be 'incorrupt in doctrine' (ἐν τῇ διδασκαλίᾳ ἀφθορίαν, 2.7), but the opponents teach things they ought not

23. Cf. Heckert 1996: 37–57; BDF §447; Turner 1963: 331–32.
24. Cf. esp. Weiser 1989: 405–406.
25. The referent of ἃ is not given in 2.1 but from what follows it becomes apparent that behavior is in view.
26. Cf. Barrett 1963: 134, 'Others may by their actions deny the God whom they profess to know; Titus must not do so.'
27. Cf. Weiser 1989: 406.
28. Cf. Weiser 1989: 406; Marshall 1999: 231.
29. Cf. Mounce 2000: 407.
30. Lock 1924: 138.

(διδάσκοντες ἃ μὴ δεῖ, 1.11).[31] Additionally, the teaching of the older women (as well as the teaching of 2.2–10 in general) will serve to build up households, while the opponents upset them (1.11).[32]

This wide range of lexical and semantic connections argue for a significant, contrasting connection between 1.10–16 and 2.1–10. This supports Marshall's conclusion that,

> In view of the contrast thus created and the repetition of key ethical themes, it is extremely unlikely that the teaching was adopted in a haphazard manner. The writer enjoins believers in their respective household and community positions to conduct themselves in ways that will neutralise the deleterious effects of the heresy.[33]

2.1–10 and 2.11–14

Hanson and Miller find little connection between these two units. Hanson considers 2.11–14 a liturgical fragment that has simply been placed within the composition.[34] Miller argues that 2.11–14 interrupts the catalogues of rules which appear in 2.2–10 and continue in 3.1–2, saying, 'the transition [from 2.1–10 to 2.11–4] is not smooth and the logical links are not readily apparent.'[35] Miller concludes that 'the two units (2.1–10, 2.11–14) are not the products of a single hand.'[36]

In response, Miller's assumption that the exhortations to virtue must follow each other is a groundless assumption. Alternation of material is valid. Then, concerning transition and logical links, most scholars are not as skeptical. Most understand the γάρ in 2.11 to show that 2.11–14 is the theological grounding of the ethical commands in 2.1–10.[37] Miller, however, criticizes the idea that 2.11–14 serves as the theological ground for 2.1–10 since, as he says, 2.11–14 contains no explicit reference to the rules of 2.1–10 or the concerns which may have prompted them.[38] However, there are explicit links in 2.11–14 to the ethical concern of the

---

31. Cf. Weiser 1989: 406.
32. Lock 1924: 138; Marshal 1999: 231.
33. Marshall 1999: 231. Cf. also Dibelius and Conzelmann 1972: 141, 'The entire list of duties here [2.2–10] is written in view of the opponents.'
34. Hanson 1982: 183.
35. Miller 1997: 132.
36. Miller 1997: 132.
37. E.g., Marshall 1999: 266; Mounce 2000: 420; Oberlinner 1996: 127; Quinn 1990: 162; Läger 1996: 93; Merkel 1991: 98; Bassler 1996: 198; Towner 1989: 108; Johnson 1996: 240; Fee 1988: 194; Weiser 1989: 400, 402; Dibelius and Conzelmann 1972: 142; Lock 1924: 143; Bernard 1906: 170.
38. Miller 1997: 132. Miller cites Barrett's characterization of 2.11–14 as a digression (136) in a manner such as to suggest that Barrett saw little or no connection between 2.1–10 and 2.11–14. However, this is clearly not what Barrett intended as he notes the strong connection with 2.10.

'rules' in 2.1–10.[39] Indeed, the whole discussion of salvation is presented in terms of its ethical implications.[40] The grace of God which saves (σωτήριος) also teaches its pupils to deny ungodliness and worldly lusts which undoubtedly can include gossiping (2.3), being enslaved to wine (2.3), and pilfering (2.10). This same grace teaches people to pursue ethical qualities most notably σωφρόνως (2.12), a quality which, as was noted above, was urged on each of the age groups in 2.1–10. The sacrifice of Christ is also stated in ethical terms: in order to redeem people from 'lawlessness' (ἀνομία) and to cleanse them so that they might be 'zealots for good deeds' (καλά ἔργα, 2.14). This connects as well with the call for Titus to be an example of good deeds (καλά ἔργα, 2.7).[41] Thus, there is a clear reference to the ethical concerns behind 2.1–10 in spite of Miller's contention otherwise.[42] Explicit reference to specific commands in 2.1–10 is not necessary. The command to teach believers how to live (2.1f.) is backed up by a statement that God's saving grace also teaches us to live in a godly manner.[43]

Lastly, 2.1–10 and 2.11–14 are also connected by the transitional device, 'hooked keyword,' wherein a word or phrase appears at the end of one unit (though not common previously in the unit) and becomes a prominent phrase in the following unit. In 2.10 the term τοῦ σωτῆρος ἡμῶν θεοῦ appears for the first time in the body of the letter, introducing salvation language for the first time in the unit.[44] In 2.5 there is a ἵνα- clause very similar to the one here in 2.10, but there is no reference to the σωτήρ word group in 2.5. Immediately following the reference to 'God our Savior' in 2.10, a discussion of salvation ensues beginning with the occurrence of τοῦ θεοῦ σωτήριος in 2.11.[45] This recurs again in an expanded form in 2.13, τοῦ μεγάλου θεοῦ καὶ **σωτῆρος ἡμῶν** Ἰησοῦ Χριστοῦ. Thus, the mention of 'God our Savior' in 2.10 serves to introduce the discussion of God's saving work in 2.11–14.[46] The recurrence of θεός and the σωτηρ- root serve to bind 2.11–14 to 2.10.[47] Thus, even Easton says 'There is no break after v. 10'

---

39. Marshall 1999: 262–63. notes the general connection of ethical concern.

40. Cf. Towner 1989: 111, who says 'in keeping with the context' 2.11–14 'considers salvation largely from the perspective of the life it produces.' Cf. also Lau 1996: 150ff.

41. Cf. Lau 1996: 155.

42. Cf. Bassler 1996: 199–200, who says the description of the life which grace teaches 'aptly summarizes the specific exhortations of verses 2–10.'

43. Marshall 1999: 262; Lock 1924: 143.

44. The exact phrase does occur in the salutation (1.3).

45. Classen 1997: 438 also notes the use of πᾶς in 2.10 and 2.11 suggesting that this is also part of the link between the two verses.

46. Cf. Marshall 1999: 21, '2.10b forms the hook on which vs. 11–14 hang.'

47. Marshall 1999: 262; Quinn 1990: 162; and Lau 1996: 155 note the play on σωτήρ/ σωτήριος.

because of the continuation of salvation language.[48] Also, it was shown in the previous chapter that 2.1–10 was bracketed by references to the true teaching (διδασκαλία, 2.1, 10). 2.11–14 then serves to expound this teaching, showing both its salvific impact ('teaching of God our Savior,' 2.10) and the healthy living it produces ('healthy teaching,' 2.1).[49]

Thus, in spite of the proponents of incoherence, Johnson is right in his assessment that, 'The placement of this magnificent kerygmatic statement is not accidental .... The position and wording of this statement are alike carefully constructed.'[50]

2.11–14 and 2.15

When positing a break at 2.15 in the previous chapter, several shifts in cohesion fields were noted. Some scholars find the difference between 2.11–14 and 2.15 so stark that they suggest it is a later insertion[51] or a mere literary marker with no real connection in the context.[52] Falconer says 2.15 breaks the connection between the mention of 'good works' in 2.14 and the description of such works in 3.1f. Hanson and Miller say the charge to 'speak these things' is inappropriate in its present context since it follows verses which are 'liturgical rather than parenetic.'[53]

However, this skepticism is open to some question. Falconer assumes, as has been noted previously, that similar materials must follow each other. This need not be so. A summarizing statement (as 2.15 clearly is) is appropriate. Further, a charge to teach is sensible after a doctrinal section, though 'exhort' and 'rebuke' would seem to imply parenesis. However, if 2.1–10 and 2.11–14 are as closely bound as has just been argued, there is no reason why the backward referring ταῦτα could not refer to 2.1–10 as well as 2.11–14.[54] Such larger connections will be examined later in the discussion of larger section groupings. While a more complete answer will have to wait until that discussion, it can be seen that though there are not as many links between 2.15 and the immediately preceding unit, there is no need to posit a radical disjunction.

---

48. Easton 1947: 93.
49. Marshall 1999: 262.
50. Johnson 1996: 240.
51. Falconer 1937: 113.
52. Hanson 1982: 188; Miller 1997: 133.
53. Hanson 1982: 188; Miller 1997: 133. The wording quoted is found in both books.
54. Most agree that ταῦτα refers backward, as it usually does in the Pastoral Epistles. The case for a backward reference will be strengthened in the discussion of larger section groupings later in this chapter.

2.15 and 3.1–2
The connection between 3.1–2 and what precedes has been significantly criticized. For some 3.1 appears to be an odd resumption after what appeared to be a conclusion.[55] Miller says there is no logical connection between the two units.[56] Several scholars have drawn particular attention to the apparent ambiguity of the use of αὐτός in 3.1 since it does not have an obvious antecedent. This ambiguity is so puzzling to Hanson and Houlden that they argue 3.1–2 must have been lifted from a preexisting source and inserted rather clumsily into the present document.[57]

Each of these arguments fails to see the transitional value of 2.15 and its links to 3.1–2. While 2.15 acts as a summary it also reintroduces key components which continue in 3.1–2. Titus comes back explicitly to the fore in 2.15 with second person singular referents and these continue in 3.1.[58] The four imperatives of 2.15 lead naturally to the imperative in 3.1.[59] Indeed the three second person singular imperatives of 2.15 concern teaching (λαλέω, παρακαλέω, ἐλέγχω) as does the second person imperative of 3.1 (ὑπομιμνῄσκω).[60] This connection also solves the supposed problem of the referent of αὐτός in 3.1. While the audience of the teaching is not made explicit in 2.15 one would logically assume the church, those who are the objects of the saving work described in 2.11–14. If these people are in view in 2.15 when teaching is discussed, it would be logical to assume they are the αὐτούς of 3.1.[61] Thus, 2.15 connects well with 3.1–2.[62]

3.1–2 and 3.3–7
Most scholars believe that 3.3–7 serves as the theological basis (γάρ) for the commands of 3.1–2.[63] However, Hanson and Miller see little connection between the two units.[64] Miller specifically argues that 3.3f. 'shows no signs of being adapted to its present context' and that there is no 'explicit link' between these two units. Miller concludes that the entire unit (3.3–8)

55. Leaney 1960: 125, says that at 2.15 'the author appeared to close, and now seems to resume his task after reflection.' Miller 1997: 133–34 appears to agree.
56. Miller 1997: 135.
57. Houlden 1976: 152; Hanson 1982: 189. Cf. Miller 1997: 134.
58. Cf. Lau 1996: 155, n. 436.
59. Fee 1988: 200 says the first verb of 3.1 'flows naturally out of 2.15.'
60. Mounce 2000: 421, '2.15 moves the reader smoothly into the instructions of chap. 3, the imperative ὑπομίμνῃσκε, "remind," of 3.1 continuing the flow of thought and style from the four imperatives in 2.15.'
61. Marshall 1999: 300, 'αὐτούς must refer in context to all the members of the church (cf. 2.15).'
62. Cf. also Oberlinner 1996: 160.
63. E.g., Bassler 1996: 206; Marshall 1999: 308; Fee 1988: 200; Mounce 2000: 446; Knight 1992: 335; Oberlinner 1996: 166; Spicq 1969: 649.
64. Hanson 1982: 189f.; Miller 1997: 136.

'protrudes distinctly from the surrounding context in a way that suggests it was placed there as a preformed piece, without modification or adaptation.'[65]

In response, while there are significant shifts at 3.3, there is a continuation of ethical vocabulary – in fact contrasting ethical vocabulary. The seven-part virtue list of 3.1–2 is followed by a seven-part vice list in 3.3.[66] The general contrast is augmented by the lexical connection between πειθαρχεῖν in 3.1 and ἀπειθεῖς in 3.3.[67] The discussion of salvation then stresses ethical change. The ποτε ... ὅτε construction here highlights the fact that while believers 'once' fit this evil description, they do so no longer.[68] Salvation is characterized as involving 'washing' (λουτρόν), 'regeneration' (παλιγγενεσία), and 'renewal' (ἀνακαίνωσις). While the exact referents and interrelation of these words are matters of debate, they clearly refer to an ethical change effected in salvation – spiritual cleansing and a new way of life.[69] Thus, the ethical concern of 3.3–7 fits well with the ethical injunctions of 3.1–2. Logically, 3.3–7 shows why 'we' are able to live the way described in 3.1–2 (not by human effort but because of the change effected in salvation).[70] It may also specifically ground the call to demonstrate kindness in 3.2: 'since we once were what they still are, but were delivered through the kindness of God, so we ought to show kindness to those whom we once resembled.'[71] Thus, 3.3–7 fits well with 3.1–2.

3.3–7 and 3.8

While the previous chapter noted significant shifts at 3.8, it was also seen that the break was not easy to make. Since, as is largely agreed, πιστὸς ὁ λόγος refers to the preceding unit there is a significant connection, and many connect it with vv. 3–7 making a break *after* the phrase.[72] 3.8b, however, is connected to 3.8a with καί, suggesting it flows out of 3.8a and

---

65. Miller 1997: 136. Miller continues, 'The transitions are not tightly drawn.'

66. Spicq 1969: 649; Quinn 1990: 200; Marshall 1999: 309.

67. Bassler 1996: 206; Marshall 1999: 309. It could also be noted that both of these words occur as the second item in their respective lists.

68. Cf. Towner 1989: 63, 'This particular formula has an ethical formulation in that it consistently contrasts pre-Christian and Christian conduct, the Christ-event forming the turning point.'

69. Marshall 1999: 318–22; Mounce 2000: 448–50; Towner 1989: 116f.; Fee 1994: 780–84. Whether or not λουτρόν refers to baptism directly (and I think it probably does not), it does refer to spiritual cleansing.

70. Cf. Marshall 1999: 305; Barrett 1963: 140.

71. Marshall 1999: 305, translating Holtzmann 1880: 494. Cf. Lau 1996: 173. Knight 1992: 335, and Brox 1969a: 305, see this connection in a slightly stronger form.

72. E.g., Quinn 1990: 187; Dibelius and Conzelmann 1972: 150.

making a break at that point difficult.[73] It seems that the fact that the previous 'saying' is reliable is one reason it (and quite probably the exhortations it grounded) should be insisted upon. Also, 'these things' which are to be emphasized in v. 8b certainly include vv. 3–7. Thus, while a basic unit division has been placed at 3.8 there are significant connections between 3.3–7 and 3.8.[74] The summarizing use of ταῦτα with a verb for teaching (διαβεβαιοῦσθαι), frames 3.8 (like 2.15) as a fitting summary statement.[75] These connections speak against Miller and Hanson who argue that 3.8 is a mere literary marker devoid of any value.[76]

3.8 and 3.9–11

The connection between these units is rarely disputed since, as was noted in the previous chapter, the shift between v. 8 and v. 9 is not great. However, Miller finds no connection saying, 'The appearance of this unit in its present context is sudden and unexpected.'[77] In fact there are a number of connections between the units.

First, the setting of exhortation to Titus which reappears in 3.8 continues through vv. 9–11. The main verb of v. 8 (βούλομαι ... διαβεβαιοῦσθαι) is functionally imperatival and the two main verbs of vv. 9–11 are also imperatives (περιΐστασο, παραιτοῦ). All three verbs are explicitly addressed to Titus.[78] These main verbs, as well as most of the other verbs in vv. 8–11, are also present tense – in contrast to the units preceding and following these two. This is a significant continuity. Second, it is commonly noted that v. 8 and v. 9 are connected as contrasts (δέ), a common feature in this letter.[79] The contrast is anchored by the use of ὠφέλιμος (v. 8) and ἀνωφελής (v. 9) in what is almost certainly a deliberate word play.[80] The key contrast in this context between the two ways is that one is profitable and the other is not. Furthermore, there seems to be a play on words in the verbs used for the approach to these profitable and unprofitable

---

73.   Levinsohn 1999: 327, writes, 'As far as discourse development is concerned, however, the implications of starting a sentence with καί are very similar, whether it is conjunctive or adverbial; in either case, the material it introduces is to be associated with previous material, rather than representing a new development in the argument.' Cf. Marshall 1999: 330; Johnson 1996: 250.

74.   Oberlinner 1996: 180 says there is a flowing transition from 3.1–7 to 3.8.

75.   Cf. Marshall 1999: 22.

76.   Miller 1997: 136; Hanson 1982: 193.

77.   Miller 1997: 137.

78.   In v. 8 this is made clear by the direct object σε. In vv. 9–10 it is seen in the person and number (2s) of the verbs.

79.   E.g., Oberlinner 1996: 180; Mounce 2000: 438, 453; Fee 1988: 210; Quinn 1990: 244.

80.   Cf. Barrett 1963: 145; Bassler 1996: 210; Fee 1988: 210; Quinn 1990: 248; Marshall 1999: 337; Lau 1996: 173.

things (προΐστημι, v. 8; περιΐστημι, v. 9). Thus, v. 8 prepares the way for v. 9 and the introduction of the opponents is not as 'sudden and unexpected' as Miller suggests. Indeed, Bassler is correct in concluding, 'The argument flows so smoothly from 3.8 into these verses that they barely constitute a new section, even though the content changes significantly.'[81]

3.9–11 and 3.12–14

The travelogue in 3.12–14 begins somewhat abruptly, without any transition.[82] Miller and Easton surmise that 3.12–14 may be an authentic Pauline fragment appended to the end of the text we have, suggesting it has little real connection to the rest of the letter.[83] However, the abrupt transition at this point is not uncommon,[84] and 3.12–14 fits well the typical function of a 'body-closing.' Two common aspects of body-closings in ancient papyri letters, according to J. L. White, are the urging of responsibility and the notification of a visit.[85] Both are found in 3.12–14 as Titus is urged (and through him the congregation) to take responsibility for visiting teachers whose upcoming visit is announced. Also one of the common functions of the body-closing was 'finalizing the principal motivation for writing (by accentuating or reiterating what was stated earlier in the body).'[86] This is exactly what occurs in 3.14 as the theme of 'good works' is restated with an exact repetition of the phrase from 3.8 (καλῶν ἔργων προΐστασθαι).[87] Thus, 3.12–14 functions well as the body-closing, and therefore coheres with the preceding unit.

More specifically there are some contrasts which connect 3.12–14 specifically with 3.9–11. After discussing the opponents whose talk is unhelpful in 3.9–11, authorized teachers who will be coming are mentioned in 3.12–13. In contrast to the 'uselessness' (ἀνωφελής) of the opponents the Cretan church is to engage in the meeting of practical needs so as not to be 'unfruitful' (ἄκαρπος). Lastly, there would appear to be a connection in the repetition of νομικός in v. 9 and v. 13.[88] While it is largely agreed that the 'Law' in view in v. 9 is the Torah, most commentators think 'lawyer' in

---

81. Bassler 1996: 210.
82. Cf. Quinn 1990: 260; Marshall 1999: 340.
83. Miller 1997: 137; Easton 1947: 106, though Easton is hesitant.
84. Cf. Marshall 1999: 340, 'There is the usual abrupt transition from the preceding "body" material.'
85. White 1972a: 46–51.
86. White 1972a: 42.
87. This repetition is noted by several commentators including Marshall 1999: 345; Mounce 2000: 459; Bassler 1996: 213; Fee 1988: 215.
88. So also, Lock 1924: 158.

v. 13 refers to a jurist, not an expert in Torah.[89] In light of the use of lexical connections elsewhere, it is possible that Jewish law may be in view in spite of the Gentile name.[90] Whether or not there is an intentional connection in the repetition of νομικός, the other links create cohesion between 3.9–11 and 3.12–14.

Semantic Chains Running Throughout the Letter

Having shown a connection from unit to unit through the letter it will be helpful to consider the letter from the macroperspective noting themes (with semantic and lexical connections) which occur through significant portions of the letter. Each theme or semantic chain does not necessarily occur in each unit of the letter, but they occur in a significant number of units. Therefore they bind the letter together not as one strand around the whole, but as various adhesive strips across various units overlapping one another.

Virtue and Vice

A concern for the inculcation of virtue and the avoidance of vice unites the whole letter with related terms and phrases occurring in practically every unit. Indeed, lists of virtue or vice occur in 1.5–9, 1.10–16, 2.1–10, 2.11–14, 3.1–2, 3.3, and 3.9–11. Such lists are a characteristic feature of the letter. The following table lists the occurrences of the primary items in this semantic chain and illustrates the pervasiveness of the chain.[91]

Reference	Virtue	Vice
1.1	εὐσέβεια	
1.2	ἀψευδής	
1.6	ἀνέγκλητος	
	μιᾶς γυναικὸς ἀνήρ	
	πιστός	
	μὴ κατηγορία	
	(μὴ) ἀσωτία	
	(μὴ) ἀνυπότακτος	

---

89. Cf. e.g., Marshall 1999: 343; Knight 1992: 357; Fee 1988: 215; Kelly 1963: 258; Guthrie 1990: 222. Mounce 2000: 458 simply lists both options. Bernard 1906: 182 is uncertain.

90. Cf. Lock 1924: 158; Quinn 1990: 265; Ellicott 1856: 200 says expert in Jewish law is 'slightly more probable' and says this was the view of Chrysostom, Jerome, and Theophilus.

91. Malherbe notes the prevalence of 'moral language' in Titus (1998: 3).

1.7	ἀνέγκλητος	
	μὴ αὐθάδης	
	μὴ ὀργίλος	
	μὴ πάροινος	
	μὴ πλήκτης	
	μὴ αἰσχροκερδής	
1.8	φιλόξενος	
	φιλάγαθος	
	σώφρων	
	δίκαιος	
	ὅσιος	
	ἐγκρατής	
1.10		ἀνυπότακτος
		ματαιολόγος
		φρεναπάτης
1.11		αἰσχροῦ κέρδους χάριν
1.12		ψεύσται
		κακὰ θηρία
		γαστέρες ἀργαί
1.15	καθαρός	μιαίνω
	καθαρός	ἄπιστος
	καθαρός	μιαίνω
1.16		βδελυκτός
		απειθής
		πρὸς πᾶν ἔργον ἀγαθὸν ἀδόκιμοι
2.2	νηφάλιος	
	σεμνός	
	σώφρων	
	ὑγιαίνοντες τῇ πίστει, τῇ	
	ἀγάπῃ, τῇ ὑπομονῇ[92]	
2.3	καταστῆμα ἱεροπρεπής	
	μὴ διάβολος	
	μὴ οἴνῳ πολλῷ δεδουλωμένας	

---

92.   The distinction between ethical and doctrinal referent here is not clear and is probably not sharply distinguished. The phrase is included since it surely has some intended ethical connotation (at least with ἀγάπη). Marshall 1999: 240 says the triad 'is an abbreviated way of referring to the whole of the Christian life.'

2.4–5	φίλανδρος	
	φιλότεκνος	
	σώφρων	
	ἀγνός	
	οἰκουργός	
	ἀγαθός	
	ὑποτάσσω	
2.6	σωφρονέω	
2.7–8	τύπος καλῶν ἔργων	
	σεμνότης	
	ἀκαταγνωστός	
	(μὴ) φαῦλος	
2.9–10	ὑποτάσσω	
	εὐάρεστος	
	μὴ ἀντιλέγω	
	μὴ νοσζομαί	
	πᾶς πίστις ἀγαθή	
2.12	σωφρόνως	ἀσέβεια
	δικαίως	κοσμική ἐπιθυμία
	εὐσεβῶς	
2.14	καθαρίζω	ἀνομία
	ζηλωτὴς καλῶν ἔργων	
3.1–2	ὑποτάσσω	
	πειθαρχέω	
	πρὸς πᾶν ἔργον ἀγαθὸν ἕτοιμος	
	μηδένα βλασφημεῖν	
	ἄμαχος	
	ἐπιεικής	
	πᾶς πραΰτης	
3.3		ἀνόητος
		ἀπειθής
		πλανάω
		δουλεύοντες ἐπιθυμίαις καὶ
		ἡδοναῖς
		κακία
		φθόνος
		στυγητός
		μισέω
3.4–5	χρηστότης	
	φιλανθρωπία	
	ἔλεος	
3.8	καλά ἔργα	
	καλός	
	ὠφέλιμος	

3.9–11   ἔρις
                                                μάχη
                                                ἀνωφελής
                                                μάταιος
                                                αἱρετικός
                                                ἐκστρέφω
                                                ἁμαρτάνω
                                                αὐτωκατάκριτος

3.14   καλά ἔργα
              μὴ ἄκαρπος

These terms are interconnected first by the natural and deliberate contrasting of virtue and vice (e.g., repugnant, 1.16, vs. pleasant, 2.9–10). Furthermore there are clusters of specific ethical concerns within the chain.

One key aspect in the virtue encouraged is propriety and being above criticism. The numerous occurrences of σώφρων (and cognates; 1.8; 2.2, 4, 5, 6, 12) and σεμνός/σεμνότης (2.2, 7) illustrate this concern for propriety. There are also terms for being above criticism such as ἀνέγκλητος (1.6, 7), μὴ κατηγορία (1.6), and ἀκαταγνωστός (2.8). This point is made especially by the ἵνα clauses in 2.5, 8, and 10 where there is a clear concern for avoiding undue criticism, like ensuring opponents have nothing 'bad' (φαῦλος) to say about 'us.'

Submission and obedience are also prominent features in this chain. The opponents are rebellious (ἀνυπότακτος, 1.10) and disobedient (ἀπειθής, 1.16). Disobedience is also a characteristic of life before conversion (ἀπειθής, 3.3). However, this ought not to be so of believers. Children of elders ([μὴ] ἀνυπότακτος, 1.6), young wives (ὑποτάσσω, 2.5), and slaves (ὑποτάσσω, 2.9) are all urged to be submissive to proper authority. Indeed, the whole congregation is to submit to and obey the government (ὑποτάσσω, 3.1).

Purity also seems to be a particular concern. While one would expect general statements regarding purity such as the marital faithfulness of church leaders (μιᾶς γυναικὸς ἀνήρ, 1.6)[93] and the purity of the young women (ἁγνός, 2.5), there seems to be a particular concern vis-à-vis the opponents. In 1.15 the word καθαρός occurs three times in a discussion of ritual purity presumably refuting some of the opponents' claims.[94] 2.14 then describes the work of Christ as 'cleansing' (καθαρίζω). Whereas the

---

93. While the precise meaning of this phrase is disputed, moral purity is in view in each option.

94. Cf. Marshall 1999: 208, 'Clearly, then, the tradition [1.15] is about ritual purity...' So also Mounce 2000: 401–402.

opponents are concerned with ritual purity the true message points to
salvation which brings true, moral cleansing.[95]

Lastly, there is within this chain a clear emphasis on 'good works,' a
theme which is often noted by scholars.[96] Titus is to be an example of
'good works' (καλά ἔργα, 2.7), and believers in general are to be zealots
for 'good works' (καλά ἔργα, 2.14). The church specifically is to be ready
for every good work (ἔργον αγαθόν, 3.1), to be careful to engage in
'good works' (καλά ἔργα, 3.8), and to learn to engage in 'good works'
(καλά ἔργα, 3.14). This is a key theme of the parenesis, occurring in both
parenetic sections, one of the doctrinal groundings, and the closing of
the letter. It also forms one of the key polemical contrasts with the
opponents being described as πρὸς πᾶν ἔργον ἀγαθὸν ἀδόκιμοι (1.16), but
the church being urged to be πρὸς πᾶν ἔργον ἀγαθὸν ἑτοίμους (3.1). The
exact repetition of words except for the final climactic and contrasting
element suggests deliberate contrast in a coherent argument.[97] 3.1 was
formed so as to link back to 1.16.

Thus, there is throughout the letter a continuity in concern over the
behavior of those in view. Within the semantic chain of virtue and vice
there are more specific lexical and semantic clusters which hold together
significant portions of the letter suggesting common concerns and the hand
of a deliberate and coherent writer.

Salvation

Salvation appears as a prominent theme though largely confined to three
units (1.1–4; 2.11–14; 3.3–7). The key items in this chain are represented in
the following table.

Reference	Semantic	Lexical
1.1	Knowledge of truth	
1.1	Chosen	ἐκλεκτός
1.2	Hope, Life	ἐλπίς ζωῆς αἰωνίου
1.3	Savior	σωτήρ
1.4	Savior	σωτήρ
2.10	Savior	σωτήρ
2.12	Life	ζάω
2.13	Hope	ἐλπίς
2.13	Savior	σωτήρ

95. Cf. Schlarb 1990: 84f.
96. Fee 1988: 215, says 'good works' 'is the recurring theme of the entire letter.'
97. These are also the only two places in the letter where the phrase is singular and uses
ἀγαθός rather than καλός.

3.4	Savior	σωτήρ
3.5	Savior	σῴζω
3.6	Savior	σωτήρ
3.7	Hope, Life	ἐλπίς ζωῆς αἰωνίου

If one can include the 'hook' at 2.10 which introduces 2.11–14, then all of the occurrences shown occur within the three 'doctrinal' units just mentioned. Indeed, these three units contain all the occurrences of ζωή/ ζάω, σωτήρ/σῴζω, and ἐλπίς. Thus, the explicit discussion of salvation is quite focused and occurs in key places within the letter – the introduction and the grounding of the parenesis. Cohesion then in these units would be very significant; and, in fact, the three units are very similar, as the following table shows.

1.1–4	2.11–14	3.3–7
ἐφανέρωσεν God's message τοῦ σωτῆρος ἡμῶν θεοῦ	God's grace Ἐπεφάνη τοῦ σωτῆρος ἡμῶν θεοῦ (v.10)	God's mercy ἐπεφάνη τοῦ σωτῆρος ἡμῶν θεοῦ
Χριστοῦ Ἰησοῦ τοῦ σωτῆρος ἡμῶν ἐπ᾽ ἐλπίδι ζωῆς αἰωνίου	τοῦ ... σωτῆρος ἡμῶν Ἰησοῦ Χριστοῦ τήν μακαρίαν ἐλπίδα	Ἰησοῦ Χριστοῦ τοῦ σωτῆρος ἡμῶν κατ᾽ ἐλπίδα ζωῆς αἰωνίου

The significance of these repetitions is heightened by the fact that several of these words do not occur elsewhere in the letter. This table shows all the occurrences of ζωή/ζάω, σωτήρ/σῴζω, ἐλπίς, and the epiphany language (φανερόω/ἐπιφαίνω). These three units are also bound by the fact that they are dominated by aorist tense verbs though the aorist tense is not common in the other units of the letter.[98] First person plurals occur commonly in these sections, but are infrequent in the rest of the letter (2.8, 10; 3.15). Indeed, all first person plural verbs occur in these three units. Third person singular referents occur more frequently here and always refer to God or Jesus. These are the only sections of the letter in which God or Jesus are the actors. Thus, this semantic chain is largely contained within three units which are closely bound to each other by lexical repetition and continuity

98. There are clusters of aorist verbs also at 1.5 and at 3.12f.

in verbal tense, person/number, and participants. All of this suggests these doctrinal pieces were deliberately formed to cohere with one another.[99]

These units also cohere in their presentation of salvation. Each unit traces part of the flow of salvation history. 1.1–4 moves from the promise of God before time to the historical manifestation of his message. 2.11–14 moves from the historical manifestation to its current relevance to the future hope. 3.3–7 moves from the past state of believers to the manifestation of salvation, to the future hope.

The semantic chain concerning salvation also interconnects with the chain on virtue/vice. This is apparent, first, in the fact that the two parenetic units (2.1–10; 3.1–2) are grounded in these statements regarding salvation. Furthermore, as argued above, the exposition of salvation in 2.11–14 and 3.3–7 emphasizes the ethical outcome of salvation. A strong link is forged between salvation and virtue. Indeed, in 2.12 saving grace teaches its pupils to say no to worldly desires (ἐπιθυμία), but before salvation people are slaves to their desires (ἐπιθυμία).[100] Lastly, sinful deeds can even deny one's claim to know God (1.16), thus showing that lack of a proper ethic proves a lack of salvation. These chains are intimately bound in this letter. In fact the entire letter can be traced on the lines of salvation/message (see next chain), positive ethics, and negative ethics.

1.1–4	Salvation
1.5–9	Positive Ethics
1.10–16	Negative Ethics
2.1–10	Positive Ethics
2.11–15	Salvation
3.1–2	Positive Ethics
3.3	Negative Ethics
3.4–8	Salvation
3.9–11	Negative Ethics
3.12–14	Positive Ethics

99.   Contra, for example, Miller 1997: 132–33, 135–36. The close connection between these three units also shows the error in only considering 2.11–14 and 3.3–7 as the more theological portions of the letter. One example of this approach is Donald A. Hagner who in an analysis of the theology of the letter wrote, 'There are two passages in Titus that are especially theological in nature' and then focused on 2.11–14 and 3.4–8 (1998: 4). This seems to stem from a failure to appreciate the way the letter works as a whole.

100.   These are the only two occurrences of ἐπιθυμία in the letter.

One cannot, of course, draw these distinctions so neatly,[101] but the contrasting flow and interrelation of virtue/vice and salvation throughout the letter is clearly represented.

Message

Related to the chain concerning salvation is the recurrence of terms related to the basic message proclaimed by Paul, Titus, and the church leaders. The message is referred to in the first verse of the letter (ἀλήθεια),[102] and the chain continues through most of the letter, as seen in the following table.

Reference	Semantic	Lexical
1.1	Knowledge of the truth	ἀλήθεια
1.3	His (God's) word	λόγος
1.3	Preaching (of Paul)	κήρυγμα
1.9		διδαχή
1.9	Faithful word	λόγος
1.9	Sound doctrine	διδασκαλία
1.14	Truth	ἀλήθεια
2.1	Sound doctrine	διδασκαλία
2.5	God's word	λόγος
2.7		διδασκαλία
2.8	(?) Sound speech	λόγος
2.10	Of God our savior	διδασκαλία
3.8	Faithful word	λόγος

The chain is largely dependent on recurrences of λόγος and διδασκαλία which creates a significant degree of lexical cohesion.[103] Frequently the message is explicitly linked to God or Jesus, showing its validity and authority. Also, it is often described as 'healthy' (1.9; 2.1, 8) or 'faithful' (1.9; 3.8).

In contrast to this true message there is an anti-message, though it is not mentioned as frequently.

---

101. The boundaries do not exactly match those argued for unit boundaries in the previous chapter because the point is simply to note the existence of virtue or vice lists and expositions of salvation.

102. Cf. Marshall 1999: 122, 'In the PE ἀλήθεια refers to the authentic revelation of God bringing salvation.' Cf. Towner 1989: 122.

103. Interestingly, εὐαγγέλιον does not occur in Titus.

Reference	Semantic	Lexical
1.11		ἃ μὴ δεῖ
1.14	Jewish myths	
	Commands of men	
3.9	Speculations	
	Genealogies	
	Disputes about the Law	

The anti-message comes from those who oppose (1.9), rebel against (1.10) the Pauline message and have rejected the 'truth' (1.14). Thus, these two messages are set in opposition.

In addition to references to these messages, there are references to the propagation of them. Titus and the church leaders are called upon to propagate the Pauline message (παρακαλέω – 1.9; 2.15; λαλέω – 2.1, 15; διαβεβαιόομαι – 3.8),[104] while the opponents propagate their message (ἀντιλέγω – 1.9; φρεναπάτης – 1.10; διδάσκω – 1.11). The clash between the two is then seen in the activity of Titus and the church leaders in opposing the spread of the anti-message (ἐλέγχω – 1.9, 13; 2.15; ἐπιστομίζω – 1.11; παραιτέομαι – 3.10; νουθεσία – 3.10).

This chain regarding the Pauline message obviously connects with the chain regarding salvation. The exposition of salvation in 2.11–14 appears to be an explanation of 'the doctrine of God our Savior' in 2.10. Indeed saving grace itself teaches (2.12) even as Titus is to do (e.g., 2.1, 15).

Even more explicitly in this letter, the message is connected with the chain on virtue/vice. In the first verse of the letter, the Pauline message (ἀλήθεια) is directly related to εὐσέβεια, 'godliness,' 'the all-embracing term for genuine Christianity.'[105] The lifestyles urged in 2.2–10 are described as being that which is fitting for 'sound doctrine' (ὑγιαίνουσα διδασκαλία). Thus, there is proper relation between the message and ethics. Also, behavior can either slander the message (2.5) or beautify the message (2.10).

Thus, there is throughout the letter a chain of items related to teaching (proper and improper; its content and the activity of proclaiming it). This

104. The activity of the older women could be included here (καλαδιδάσκαλος – 2.3; σωφρονίζω – 2.4), but the context suggests that what is in view in 2.3–4 has more to do with the inculcation of virtue than the passing on of doctrine, though as argued here, the two cannot be too neatly distinguished.

105. Marshall 1999: 123. Though the exact nature of the relationship between the two terms denoted by κάτα is debated, it is clear that they are closely connected.

chain, then, units much of the letter and interconnects with the other chains identified so far.

Authority

Lastly, there is running through the letter a concern with authority. The elaborate introduction centers on the identification of Paul and his authority.[106] His identity as an apostle and servant of God shows his authority. Further, his commission comes by the command (ἐπιταγή) of God. The body of the letter is bracketed by instances of Paul giving orders to Titus (διατάσσω, 1.5; βούλομαι, 3.8). Titus, then, as Paul's 'true child in the common faith' (1.4) is to act as the delegate of Paul's authority. Titus is also to set up proper leadership within the church who will act with authority in relation to the opponents (1.9). Titus, in faithfulness to Paul's command is to act authoritatively against the opponents, rebuking (1.13), warning, and even rejecting (3.10). He is also to teach the congregation with authority. 2.15 and 3.8 emphasize this point. In 2.15 Titus is to 'rebuke with full authority' (ἔλεγχε μετὰ πάσης ἐπιταγῆς) using the same word as found in 1.3 to describe Paul's commission from God (ἐπιταγή).[107] Followed with a command not to let anyone despise him, this is a strong call to authoritative action. 3.8 also uses a strong word to characterize Titus' teaching (διαβεβαιόομαι). All of this is in contrast to those opponents who reject the proper authority (1.10). Probably the divisiveness in view in 3.9–10 has to do with the rejection of the true message and the authority of the authenticated leaders.

Summary of Chains

It has been shown that there are a number of semantic chains which run through significant portions of Titus. No doubt others could be added. The fact that these chains are so intimately connected and interrelated argues strongly for cohesion.

Grouping into Larger Sections

So far it has been argued that there is generally a cohesive flow from one unit to the next within Titus and that across these units there are a number of interrelated semantic chains running throughout the letter. This last section will examine how the cohesion works, i.e., how the different units fit together to form the whole. It will also address connections beyond those between contiguous units. It must be asked whether the different units group together in any way to form larger sections. It is entirely

---

106. Cf. Mounce 2000: 377; Marshall 1999: 112; Classen 1997: 432.
107. Wendland 1999: 338–39 notes some of the importance of 'authority' for the letter.

possible that a document could consist simply of a series of units, but the varying degrees of connectedness between the various units suggests that some units may cohere especially with one another forming sections.

The analysis will not move linearly through the letter but will take up clear connections and then move to a suggested macrostructure for the entire letter.

2.1–15

2.1–15 is often identified as a cohesive section and a number of linguistic factors favor this.[108] It has already been argued that 2.11–14 serves as the theological basis for the commands of 2.1–10. Now it can be argued that 2.15 functions as an inclusio and thus as the conclusion of this section.[109] As shown earlier, 2.15 stands apart from 2.11–14 in its return to present tense verbs, second person imperatives, and a concern with Titus' teaching. These very points connect with 2.1–10. Additionally, the only two main verbs in 2.1–10 are λάλει and παρακάλει, and they both recur in 2.15.[110] Thus, 2.15 marks a clear return to the setting and verbs of 2.1–10.[111] This explains why there was not a strong connection between 2.15 and 2.11–14. The primary connection went back to the previous unit, enveloping 2.11–14. Thus the section flows as exhortation, doctrinal grounding, summary exhortation. Weiser suggests that the inclusio between 2.1 and 2.15 is evidence of artistic crafting ('kunstvoller Gestaltung').[112]

3.1–8

3.1–8 can be seen to cohere in a manner very similar to that of 2.1–15. Already it has been argued that 3.3–7 functions as the doctrinal grounding of 3.1–2. Now it can be noted that 3.8 marks a return to 3.1–2. 3.8 returns to exhortation to Titus, present tense verbs, and the topic of 'good works' (3.1, 8). Also 3.1 and 3.8 are concerned with Titus' teaching (ὑπομιμνῄσκω, 3.1; διαβεβαιόομαι, 3.8).[113] 3.1 and 3.8 then function as inclusio around

---

108. Those who identify 2.1–15 as a section include Mounce 2000: 420; Marshall 1999: 24; Bassler 1996: 191f.; Knight 1992: 305; Lock 1924: 137; Bernard 1906: 153. Several, however, have argued otherwise, including Quinn and Guthrie.

109. So also Marshall 1999: 297.

110. Several scholars note the repetition of λάλει (e.g. Marshall 1999: 297; Oberlinner 1996: 139; Bassler 1996: 201; Weiser 1989: 400f.), but the importance of the repetition of παρακάλει is not often noted. Classen 1997: 440 acknowledges the repetition of all three verbs.

111. Cf. Holmstrand 1997: 28, 'Any expression containing a suggestion of a summary, onclusion or consequence and entailing some kind of a recurrence of the opening or starting-point of the section can thus serve as a closing marker.'

112. Weiser 1989: 403.

113. So also, Wendland 1999: 340–41.

3.1–8. Thus, in this section, as in the previous one, there is exhortation, doctrinal grounding, and a summary exhortation.[114]

2.1–3.8

Having argued that 2.1–15 and 3.1–8 are cohesive sections, it can now be argued that they cohere together as one larger section. This will, then, unite a significant portion of the letter.

2.1–15 and 3.1–8 cohere as parallels of one another as a several factors show. First, 2.1–10 and 3.1–2 are both exhortations focusing on ethical living formed on an introductory command. In both sections this command is stated in present active second person masculine singular imperatives. The instruction that follows in both sections is presented as infinitives dependent on the introductory command. Both sections also conclude with an occurrence of ἐνδεικνυμένους with a form of πᾶς (2.10; 3.2). Both sections are concerned with submission to the authority structures (ὑποτασσομένας, 2.5; ὑποτάσσεσθαι, 2.9; ὑποτάσσεσθαι, 3.1). Secondly, both exhortation sections are followed by doctrinal sections (2.11–14 and 3.3–7) which are introduced by γάρ. It was noted above that there are significant lexical parallels between these two doctrinal sections. There is significant parallel in their content as well. Both sections describe a turning away from sin (2.12, 3.3–4) and the ethical dimensions of salvation. Both sections see sinful desires (ἐπιθυμία, 2.12 and 3.3) as contrary to the new life of salvation. Both sections also mention an expectant waiting for the consummation of hope (2.13, 3.7). Thirdly, both doctrinal sections are followed by a shift back to the present tense with an exhortation to Titus to authoritatively teach the material being discussed in the letter (2.15 and 3.8). In both instances, the material to be taught is referred to with a neuter plural form of οὗτος.[115] Thus there are two parallel sections calling for proper behavior based on proper doctrine.[116]

In addition, 2.1–15 has a more complete introduction and 3.1–8 has a more complete conclusion possibly suggesting that the two sections are to be seen as one unit. 2.1 indicates a contrasting transition from the previous discussion (Σὺ δὲ) and gives a description of the teaching to follow (ἃ πρέπει τῇ ὑγιαινούσῃ διδασκαλίᾳ).[117] 3.1 has no transitional statement or descriptive phrase but merely continues the exhortation. On the other hand, though both 2.15 and 3.8 act as summary statements, only 3.8 includes a ἵνα clause

114. So also Bassler 1996: 205,

115. 3.8 has περὶ τούτων rather than ταῦτα as in 2.15, and rather than a second person imperative, 3.8 accomplishes the same semantic idea using βούλομαι plus an infinitive.

116. Several scholars note the general parallel of exhortation, ground, summary but without the detail given here (e.g. Wendland 1999: 341; Bassler 1996: 205; Merkel 1991: 101).

117. Cf. Marshall 1999: 22: '2.1 could well function as a theme for the whole of chs. 2–3.'

denoting the overall purpose of the section.[118] Thus, 2.1–3.8 can be seen as a unified section with two parallel parts.[119] This, then unites a large portion of the letter symmetrically, linguistically, and logically.

1.10–16 and 3.9–11

Once 2.1–3.8 is connected as a larger section, it becomes apparent that this central section of the letter is flanked by the only discussions of the opponents in the letter – 1.10–16 and 3.9–11. These two units which discuss the opposition cohere well. The 'empty talkers' (ματαιολόγος) of 1.10 correspond well with those who are into 'worthless' (μάταιος) disputes in 3.9. Both units mention the Jewishness of the opposition. In 1.10–16 they are 'of the circumcision' (1.10), adhere to Jewish myths (1.14), and seem to have a concern for ritual purity (1.15). In 3.9 they are involved in disputes about the Law, almost certainly Torah.[120] In both units they are causing disruption in the church, as they rebel (1.10), upset whole households (1.11), and can be characterized as 'divisive' (αἱρετικός, 3.10). Both units describe them as generally sinful and close with a reference to their rejection (1.16; 3.10–11).[121] Lastly, both units follow a reference to the 'faithful word' (πιστός λόγος, 1.9; Πιστὸς ὁ λόγος, 3.8).[122]

However, Quinn argues that there are significant differences between 1.10–16 and 3.9–11 leading him to surmise, 'It is conceivable that two different sources have been reproduced but not brought into harmony.'[123] Whereas in 1.10–16 the strategy is to silence and refute the opponents, in 3.9–11 Titus is to avoid them. Further, Quinn says, the atmosphere of the two units is 'markedly different.' 1.10–16 contains 'overheated polemic of personal confrontation and denunciation,' but 3.9–11 demonstrates 'a chillier attitude of contempt for and avoidance of' the opponents. However, the magnitude of these differences is exaggerated and even Quinn is forced to admit that the two units are not in 'formal contradiction' and 'the opposition [between units] is only apparent.'[124]

---

118. Bassler 1996: 208 also says the ἵνα clause provides the purpose for all of 2.1–3.8.

119. Cf. Marshall 1999: 23, 'the general similarity in theme between chs. 2 and 3 may rather indicate that they are two parts of one major section.' The further detail given here provides support for his suggestion.

120. This further damages Miller's argument (1997: 130) that the Jewish elements in 1.10–16 are later glosses.

121. Wendland 1999: 341 says of 3.9–11, 'This summary unit corresponds to its more detailed development in 1.10–16 ...'

122. Wendland 1999: 341.

123. Quinn 1990: 244. Quinn appears to be alone in positing a disjunction between 1.10–16 and 3.9–11.

124. Quin 1990: 244. He does not, however, retract his suggestion of sources which have not been harmonized. Indeed, he goes on to argue other 'marked' differences (like atmosphere noted above).

What is to be avoided in 3.9 is the useless discussion of the opponents. This is in no way inconsistent with silencing them but may indeed be effective in silencing them. Further, 3.10 refers to up to two warnings which (as just argued above) is consistent with the call to rebuke (1.13).[125] The final rejection in 3.10 (παραιτέομαι) is just as confrontational as what is urged in 1.10–16.[126] Thus, the proposed difference in atmosphere is strained at best. 3.9–11 does advance the discussion containing new information (as expected in a discourse), but it coheres well with 1.10–16.

Thus, the two parallel exhortations to Titus and the Cretan church are bracketed by discussion of the opponents. As Fee has noted, this results in a chiastic structure.[127]

A Opponents (1.10–16)
  B Proper living based on the gospel (2.1–15)
  B' Proper living based on the gospel (3.1–8)
A' Opponents (3.9–11)

The contrasts already noted between the description of the opponents and the parenesis to the church suggests this symmetry is intentional and that the parenesis is intentionally shaped in contrast to the opponents. Deliberate contrast with lexical repetition was shown above in the connection between 1.10–16 and 2.1–10. There are similar, perhaps even stronger, lexical connections between 1.10–16 and the renewed parenesis in 3.1–2. The first three items in 3.1–2 directly connect with the first item and the last two items in 1.10–16.

Opponents (1.10–16)	Cretan Church (3.1–2)
ἀνυπότακτοι (1.10)	ὑποτάσσω (3.1)
ἀπειθής (1.16)	πειθαρχέω (3.1)
πρὸς πᾶν ἔργον ἀγαθὸν ἀδόκιμοι (1.16)	πρὸς πᾶν ἔργον ἀγαθὸν ἑτοίμους (3.1)

Thus, 3.1 seems to sum up 1.10–16 in contrast and appears to be written in deliberate contrast to the description of the opponents. 3.2 also contrasts with 3.9–11 as the Cretan believers are to be 'uncontentious' (ἄμαχος) but the opponents are into 'quarrels' (μάχη). Lastly, the strongest rebuke of the

---

125. Stählin, *TDNT*, 'αἰτέω', 195, concerning παραιτέομαι writes, 'In the NT the word is used in this sense ['to reject or repudiate'] in relation to different actions in the supervision of doctrine and the exercise of congregational discipline.'

126. The exact force of the verb here is debated but it seems best to understand it as involving disciplinary exclusion from the congregation (Cf. Oberlinner 1996: 188; Marshall 1999: 338–39).

127. Fee 1988: 210; followed by Marshall 1999: 333, n. 105. In section B Fee lists 2.1–14, omitting 2.15. This appears to be an unintentional omission. Interestingly, J. W. Welch, who finds chiasm in most places, says that the letter to Titus is not chiastic (1981: 228).

opponents is that their way of living belies any claim to know God (1.16), and the doctrinal groundings seek to demonstrate that true salvation results in godly living. Thus, the discussion of the opponents frame the intervening discussion, not merely occurring at both ends as if by chance but framing the issues which 2.1–3.8 address. This creates strong cohesion in all of 1.10–3.11.

The Role of 1.5–9

The previous discussion unites all of the letter body except 1.5–9. It will be argued that 1.5–9 function to introduce the rest of the letter body. First, however, the competing view of J. Banker must be analyzed.

In the previous chapter mention was made of Banker's argument that 1.5 stood apart from 1.6–9 as the theme statement for the entire letter. In 1.5 he distinguishes sharply between the two parts of the ἵνα clause (τὰ λείποντα ἐπιδιορθώσῃ and καταστήσῃς κατὰ πόλιν πρεσβυτέρους). He then finds in these two elements a summary of the rest of the letter and a chiastic structure of the whole.[128]

(a) 1.5b – correct what needs to be corrected
  (b) 1.5c – appoint elders
  (b') 1.6–9 – appoint elders
(a') 1.10–3.11 – correct the situation

Banker's argument can be summarized as follows. First, he argues that understanding τὰ λείποντα ἐπιδιορθώσῃ and καταστήσῃς κατὰ πόλιν πρεσβυτέρους as two clearly distinct issues allows one to take καί 'in its most common sense of "and."'[129] Second, Banker argues for a specific understanding of τὰ λείποντα ἐπιδιορθώσῃ arguing that it refers to correcting defects rather than simply setting in order things left undone. Third, this more pejorative meaning of τὰ λείποντα ἐπιδιορθώσῃ allows him to make a connection between this phrase and the problem of the opponents, thus setting up his chiasm.

Banker's analysis is open to criticism at several points. Already his separation of 1.5 as distinct from 1.6–9 has been questioned. Second, his appeal to 'and' as the 'basic' meaning of καί is far too simplistic. Καί is the most widely used particle and conjunction in the Greek of the New Testament,[130] and occurs with a wide range of common uses.[131] The presence of καί simply does not *require* one to understand the two phrases

---

128. Banker 1987: 26–27.
129. Banker 1987: 31, 'This analysis retains the meaning of *kai* as "and," its primary and by far its most commonly used meaning' (p. 32).
130. Stanley E. Porter, *Idioms of the Greek New Testament* (2nd edn.; Sheffield: JSOT Press, 1994): 211; Dana and Mantey 1957: 249.
131. Cf. BDF § 442; Dana and Mantey 1957: 249–52.

as mutually exclusive nor does it suggest that such an understanding is the more likely reading.[132] Without this division between the two phrases Banker's argument, and thus his chiasm, does not work.

Third, Banker's arguments for the meaning of τὰ λείποντα ἐπιδιορθώσῃ are not convincing. He argues strenuously for the sense of 'correction' in ἐπιδιορθώσῃ, but few would dispute that correction is involved in this phrase. The problem is his connecting τὰ λείποντα ἐπιδιορθώσῃ directly with the refuting of the opponents in 1.10–16 and the proper teaching in 2.1–3.11. Banker depends on a similarity in meaning between the verb for correcting in 1.5b (ἐπιδιορθώσῃ) and the verb for correcting in 1.10–16 (ἔλεγχε).[133] Without this connection, 1.5 cannot serve as a heading because it would not foreshadow 1.10–16. One might first raise an objection against basing so much on the nuance of meaning in a word (ἐπιδιορθώσῃ) which appears only here in the New Testament and nowhere in the LXX or the Apostolic Fathers. Secondly, though the semantic range of ἐπιδιορθόω does include 'correct' it seems to be significantly different from ἐλέγχω. This is verified by the listings of possible glosses in the standard lexicons. A more pejorative sense is often associated with ἐλέγχω,[134] and the use of ἀποτόμως with ἐλέγχω in Titus 1.13 suggests that this harshness is intended here. Ἐπιδιορθόω, however, does not seem to convey this same sternness. The only known use of the word prior to New Testament times is a second-century BC inscription from Hierapytna on the southeast coast of Crete.[135] The inscription discussed a treaty between two groups, and ἐπιδιορθόω occurs in a section which states that if anyone in the future alters the conditions of the treaty, these later additions will not be considered part of the binding agreement. The inscription refers to this hypothetical activity of revision with three infinitives in parallel connected by ἄ. The infinitives (in order) are ἐπιδιορθῶσαι, ἐξελέν, and ἐνβαλέν. The last two are clearly antithetical (taking out and inserting). Here ἐπιδιορθῶσαι does not seem to mean correct but something more like alter, revise, or amend. The cognate διορθόω also occurs in inscriptions about laws and treaties from this time period and refers to the revising of treaties and laws in a similar way.[136]

---

132. Even the English gloss 'and' can join two items which, though different, are not mutually exclusive.

133. There is actually another verb in 1.10–16 which describes the correcting of the opponents, ἐπιστομίζειν (v. 11), but Banker makes his connection to ἔλεγχε so that is the verb discussed here.

134. BAGD s.v., includes 'expose,' 'convict,' 'reprove,' and even 'punish.' Liddell and Scott include 'put to shame,' 'cross examine,' 'refute.'

135. Boeckhius, 'Inscriptiones Insularum Aegaei Maris cum Rhodo, Creta, Cypro,' (1843), inscription 2555.

136. Two examples are found in Dittenberger 1942. Item 283 in vol. 1 is a fourth-century BC inscription from Chios and refers to lawgivers (νομογράφους) who write (γράφουσι) and

Thus, there does not appear to be much of a semantic overlap between ἐπιδιορθόω and ἐλέγχω, and this undermines Banker's position.

Lastly, Banker's suggested chiasm is extremely unbalanced with a and b covering two-thirds of one verse and a' and b' covering the rest of the letter body (42 verses)! The value or purpose of such a chiasm is unclear and it does not significantly connect the appointing of elders with the rest of the letter.

While Banker's suggested chiasm, then, does not persuade, the dual ἵνα clause of 1.9 can be seen to introduce the rest of the letter. In the previous chapter, it was already shown that 1.9 stands out as the climax of the list of qualifications in 1.5–9. 1.9 is the most syntactically complex item in the entire list. While the rest of the list is primarily a simple listing of terms (with one small participial phrase, τέκνα ἔχων πιστά, 1.6), 1.9 is framed as a participial phrase with a direct object further explicated by a dual ἵνα clause. These shifts set 1.9 apart and make it particularly suited for marking a transition.[137] Earlier in this chapter it was argued that the second half of the ἵνα clause (τοὺς ἀντιλέγοντας ἐλέγχειν) served as a hook transition introducing the discussion of the opponents in 1.10–16. Now, it can be observed that this reference to opposition in effect introduces not only 1.10–16 but also 3.9–11 since 1.10–16 and 3.9–11 have been closely identified as enveloping the rest of the letter. 3.9–11 also bears semantic similarity to the 'hook' in 1.9. Those who 'speak against' (ἀντιλέγω) proper teaching correspond well with one who is 'divisive' (αἱρετικός). The call to 'rebuke' (ἐλέγχω, 1.9) and to 'warn' (νουθεσία, 3.10), followed by shunning, are similar. Thus, the second half of the ἵνα clause in 1.9 serves to introduce one of the two main parts of the letter (1.10–16; 3.9–11).

Now it can also be argued that the first part of the ἵνα clause in 1.9 (παρακαλεῖν ἐν τῇ διδασκαλίᾳ τῇ ὑγιαινούσῃ) functions as a 'distant hook' introducing 2.1ff. Several lexical links support this. First, παρακαλέω recurs in 2.1–10 as one of only two main verbs and then occurs again in the summary in 2.15. These are the only occurrences of the verb in the letter. Second, the exhortations of 2.1–10 are introduced as that which is fitting for 'sound doctrine' (τῇ ὑγιαινούσῃ διδασκαλίᾳ), an exact repetition of the phrase from 1.9. In fact, there are only three occurrences of διδασκαλία in the letter other than 1.9 and all are found within 2.1–10 (vv. 1, 7, 10). 2.1ff. is a description of exhortation in accordance with sound doctrine as was referenced in 1.9. Furthermore, since it has been argued that 2.1 introduces

revise (διορθώσουσι) laws (lines 6–7). Item 581 in vol. 2 is a second-century BC inscription discussing a treaty between Rhodes and Hierapytna (on Crete). This inscription calls for an allowance for the treaty to be 'revised' or 'amended' (διορθώσασθαι, line 86).

137. The greater complexity may also mark the qualifications listed in 1.9 as particularly important. So also Bassler, 'The final item in the list of qualifications is defined most expansively, marking it as particularly important' (1996: 187).

all of 2.1–3.8, the hook in 1.9 introduces this entire larger section. Thus, the two parts of the ἵνα clause introduce the rest of the letter body. This leads to an analysis of the letter structure as follows:[138]

Salutation – 1.1–4
Body – 1.5–3.14
  1.5–9 – Body Opening –
The need for elders to (a) exhort in sound doctrine and (b) refute opponents.
  (b)   1.10–16 – The problem of opponents
  (a)   2.1–3.8 – Sound doctrine which necessarily includes lifestyles
         2.1–10 – Lifestyles which correspond to sound doctrine
         2.11–14 – Doctrinal basis
         2.15 – Summary exhortation
         3.1–2 – Lifestyles which correspond to sound doctrine
         3.3–7 – Doctrinal basis
         3.8 – Summary exhortation
  (b') 3.9–11 – The problem of opponents
  3.12–14 – Body Closing – Travel plans with concluding exhortation
Closing – 3.15

This representation of the letter structure captures most of the symmetry and lexical connections within the letter – the double hook in 1.9, the inclusio created by 1.10–16 and 3.9–11, the parallels between 2.1–15 and 3.1–8, and the movement within both 2.1–15 and 3.1–8. However, no display can do full justice to the nuance of a discourse. Thus, the transitional nature of 2.15 and 3.8 (not only summarizing the preceding but introducing what follows) which has been argued previously is not emphasized here. Also the strong connections between 1.1–4, 2.11–14, and 3.3–7 cannot be made explicit in this structural outline. Still, this structure demonstrates the high degree of symmetry and therefore cohesion found in this letter. This structure also improves on what is found in most commentaries. Most commentaries simply list the units, but those who do try to present the relations between the units do not usually capture in their structural outlines either the parallels between 2.1–15 and 3.1–11 or the connections between the discussions of the opponents in 1.10–16 and 3.9–11 (cf. Mounce and Marshall). Among the commentaries, Bassler does the most in displaying the parallels between Chapters 2 and 3, though she does not make all the connections argued for here. The analysis of

---

138. Bassler 1996: 9 comes closest to the structure suggested here though without explicating all the connections, esp. the introductory role of 1.9.

Wendland is the closest to the structure argued for here.[139] Wendland notes clearly the movement within 2.1–15 and 3.1–8 and the parallels between these sections. This analysis, however, differs from Wendland in its view of 1.5–9.[140] The introductory function of 1.5–9 as argued here is particularly unique to this analysis.

Summary

In the first section of this chapter it was shown that there are significant connections between contiguous units in this letter, though the connections between some units were stronger than the connections between others. In the second section semantic chains were isolated which occurred through the letter and then were significantly bound up with one another. This creates a high degree of cohesion. Lastly, a high degree of semantic and lexical parallelism was shown in support of a symmetric pattern for the whole of the letter introduced by a 'double hook.' All of these elements suggest a high degree of cohesion in the letter to Titus. Thus, Wendland is correct is his assessment of Titus when he describes it as 'a very carefully constructed and cohesive text in which the author has utilized certain features of style and structure to accentuate his essential message and to facilitate the attainment of his rhetorical objectives.'[141] Furthermore, a new picture of the macrostructure of the letter is argued for which illustrates more of the internal connections in the letter than the outlines commonly given.

---

139. Wendland 1999: 345. Classen 1997: 444 simply lists the units without indication of their interrelation.

140. Wendland also concludes that 2.15 is the central point of the letter. However, the parallel of 2.15 with 3.8 makes this unlikely, and isolating one verse as the central point is as unlikely as isolating one verse as the theme statement (e.g. Banker). Wendland also seems to stretch too far for connections between the epistolary opening and closing.

141. Wendland 1999: 336.

CONCLUSION

The coherence of the Pastoral Epistles has been a debated topic and while the mood of scholarship has swung towards more coherence the debate has not been settled. Therefore, this study has sought to further the discussion by examining 1 Timothy, 2 Timothy, and Titus, individually, discerning the boundaries of the discrete units of each letter, the cohesion of each unit and the cohesion of the various units within the entire discourse. Previous examinations of the coherence of these letters have argued for connections in the theology of the letters (as a corpus) or a credible historical setting. While the coherence of specific units or sections was dealt with, there was no analysis of an entire letter (in the Pastoral Epistles) examining each unit and the letter as a whole. This study is then the most thorough examination of the cohesiveness and structure of the Pastoral Epistles to date.

Chapters 2, 4, and 6 have argued for the boundaries of specific units (paragraphs) in each letter using cohesion shift analysis with an awareness of ancient epistolary transition techniques. While there was ambiguity in some places, the boundaries of most units were fairly well defined. Difficulty deciding whether a certain passage was one unit composed of two parts or two units connected at a higher level (section) is only indicative of a significant level of cohesion in the letter and further supports the conclusion of the thesis. Each unit was found to be cohesive, united often by literary form, keywords, continuity in cohesion fields, and symmetrical arrangement. This, of course, did not resolve every question of flow of thought in units (e.g., the switch from men to women and back to men in 1 Timothy 3.8–13) but there was enough evidence of cohesion that further discussion of such difficulties is warranted in working from an assumption of coherence.

Chapters 3, 5, and 7 have traced the ways in which these various units interrelate. First, connections between contiguous units were examined and significant (perhaps even at times 'artistic') connections were found between most contiguous units though the degree of connection fluctuated (as would be expected). The connecting devices were largely similar in each letter including hook words, hooked keywords (or key roots), plays on words, parallel introductions and conclusions, and hinges as described in the methodology chapter. There were also several instances of a 'hooked' construction based on the participant field where the person and number of the first verb of a unit remained in continuity with the verbs of the previous unit but the following verbs shifted to a different person and number which continued through the rest of the unit. This also occurred with the reintroduction of a key figure (e.g., Paul or Timothy) at the end of a unit where he had been unmentioned followed by a unit which focused on this key figure. This device was not referred to in the methodological works referenced in this study. Thus, if the identification of this device is convincing, the identification of the device will itself be a contribution.

Second, semantic chains were traced through each letter. The fact that there was running through each letter a 'common thread' creates some level of cohesion. Even more importantly, these different chains were intricately bound with each other, again making separation difficult at times. According to J. T. Reed, who has done the most sophisticated study of cohesion in New Testament studies, such interaction between chains is the chief indicator of cohesion in a discourse.[1] The strong connection between semantic chains involving ethics and semantic chains concerning theology demonstrate a thorough integration of theology and ethics contrary to what some scholars have argued and in support of, for example, the work of Towner. Additionally, the identification of a prominent semantic chains regarding salvation in each of the letters (as well as a chain concerning the message) confirms Towner's argument that salvation is a central element of the message of the letters.[2]

Third, the arrangement of the different units was considered to look for larger connections and the structure of the letter as a whole. Here differences between the letters were most apparent. 1 Timothy and Titus seemed to have more clearly symmetrical arrangements than 2 Timothy. 2 Timothy had had clear connections unit by unit through almost the entire letter, supporting the fairly common view of that letter as flowing from one thought right into the next. 1 Timothy and Titus had more clear-cut sections which then related to each other in symmetrical fashions. 1 Timothy, being considerably longer than Titus, had a more intricate and complicated structure. In the end two (complementary) views of 1 Timothy's macrostructure were proposed, one of which was fairly novel. Both suggest care in composition of the discourse. Titus had the clearest symmetrical structure probably due in part to its brevity. Indeed, the symmetry of Titus proposed here suggests the structure of the letter was

---

1. Cf. Reed 1997b: 100.
2. Cf. Chapter 5, 'Salvation: The Centerpoint of the Message,' in Towner 1989: 75–119,.

not only due to the ordered mind of an author (contra Miller) but also the result of a preconceived plan of writing.

Thus, the analysis of this study finds evidence of a high level of cohesion in each of the Pastoral Epistles. All three letters show evidence of care in their design. Throughout the thesis specific arguments for incoherence have been refuted, particularly those of Miller, since he has provided the most thoroughgoing argument for incohesiveness. Often it has been shown that advocates of incoherence failed to understand the Pastorals according to standards of their own time. In other words, they seem to follow the reasoning that since the Pastorals do not develop in the way expected today, they must be incoherent. However, analysis in light of ancient standards is much more favorable. It is not claimed that this proves all the material was originally composed by the author since an editor can skillfully arrange borrowed material. The point, however, is that the letters as we have them cohere, and rather than giving evidence of thoughtless collating or inept editing they demonstrate significant concern for the structuring of the letters. This is yet another blow to the once common view of the incoherence of the Pastorals. If Miller's monograph is the last rally of this view, perhaps this thesis will serve as the *coup de grâce*.

However, the thesis has not merely been a refutation of Miller or other advocates of incoherence. Indeed, cohesive elements have been analyzed in places which have not been questioned, and, even in places which have been disputed, the analysis of cohesive elements often went beyond the contrary arguments. As a result previous assumption of coherence in some places has been given an analytical basis and the cohesion of the letters is traced more thoroughly than has been done before. Furthermore, greater insight has been made available into how the mind of this author works, providing the basis for further comparison (see below). Also, this extensive analysis of the ways words, sentences, and paragraphs connect and how the discourse as a whole coheres provides a sounder basis for further detailed exegesis of the text. Thus, the thesis has both a negative and positive component (in the spirit of Titus 1.9!).

This has been a technical and detailed study which has not allowed space for as much comparison and reflection on further implications. Thus, there is significant room for work to follow the results argued here. First, while the analysis of cohesive devices has aimed at comprehensiveness, the analysis of semantic chains can make no such claim. Further work could be done isolating other semantic chains and their interrelations. Second, while this work has taken up key aspects of the cohesive theory developed by Halliday and Hasan and Reed, it has not specifically dealt with the area they refer to as 'information flow' as it went beyond the scope of the thesis. Further work here could be very useful. Third, having analyzed the way each of these letters cohere and how the letter develops its argument, further work could be done comparing and contrasting the three letters.

Fourth, and building on the previous statement, this analysis provides a sound basis for a more detailed comparison between the Pastoral Epistles and the accepted Pauline letters. Howard Marshall has written,

> An analysis of the structure of the [Pastoral] letters shows that they are constructed in a different manner from the acknowledged letters of Paul. ... Less has been done in the way of analysis here, and therefore one is perhaps reduced more to subjective impressions.[3]

Now more has been done on the structure (both macro- and micro-) of the Pastoral Epistles and this can be used as a basis for comparison with other letters.[4] Lastly, it is hoped that this detailed work may provide useful data and bases for further exegesis of these letters and further work on their theology. It has already been mentioned that further support has been given for the interrelation of theology and ethics in the Pastorals. That attention to structure is important to examinations of the theology of the letters is clear from the attention given to structure in certain places in previous works.[5] While they were able only to treat structural issues as an aside, perhaps this detailed study of structure will clear the way for more work in theology by clarifying the interrelation of the various units. Indeed, Frances Young in *The Theology of the Pastoral Epistles* has stated:

> The project of writing a 'theology of' any particular writing is hampered by an inherent problem, namely the difficulty of avoiding an amalgam of salient features abstracted from their immediate context and organized according to categories in which the reader has an interest.[6]

This analysis of the structure of the letters can provide the basis for an examination of the theology of these letters according to each letter's own pattern (structure) rather than the preconceived pattern of the examiner.

---

3.   Marshall 1996: 139.

4.   Cf. Stanislav Segert who writes, 'The author or authors of the Pastoral epistles followed Paul not only in content but also in form. Their poetic devices correspond in type and frequency to those in Paul's own episltes' ('Semitic Poetic Structures in the New Testament,' *ANRW* II, 25.2, 1458).

5.   Cf. Towner 1989; Lau 1996; Couser 2000: 262–83. The detriment caused by inattention to structure was illustrated by *some* of the (unpublished) papers presented to the SBL discussion of the theology of the Pastorals where 'doctrinal' passages are lifted out and treated in isolation from the rest of the letter as if the theology was something that could be neatly extracted.

6.   Young 1994: 48.

APPENDIX:
COHESION SHIFT ANALYSIS OF THE PASTORAL EPISTLES

A vital element of the analysis discussed in this thesis was the cohesion shift analysis of 1 Timothy, 2 Timothy, and Titus. Tables recording the basic data of these analyses are included here in Appendix one, though the electronic copy cannot reproduce all the observations scribbled in the hard copy during the analysis. Such conclusions and observations are found in the discussion in the chapters.

Each verb of the letters is listed along with the verb's tense, voice, mood, person and number (as applicable), along with the participants, genre, and topic. The size of the tables limits what can be recorded in participants, genre, and topic but the general movement can be seen. Space limitations also require some abbreviations unique to this appendix which are listed below.

Abbreviations:

Dox	Doxology
Exhort	Exhortation
Exp	Exposition
Opp	Opponents, opposition
Qualif	Qualifications
Remind	Reminder
State	Statement
Thanks	Thanksgiving
Tim	Timothy
Warn	Warning

Cohesion Shift Analysis of 1 Timothy

Verse	Verb	Tense	Voice	Mood	Pers/#	Participants	Genre	Topic
1.3	Παρακαλέω	Aor	A	Ind	1s	Paul, Tim	Reminder	Opp
1.3	προσμένω	Aor	A	Inf	-	Tim		
1.3	πορεύομαι	Pres	M	Ptcp	mns	Paul		
1.3	παραγγέλλω	Aor	A	Subj	2s	Tim		
1.3	ἑτεροδιδασκαλέω	Pres	A	Inf	-	Opp		
1.4	προσέχω	Pf	P	Ptcp	-			
1.4	παρέχω	Pres	A	Ind	3p	Myths, genealogies		
1.5	εἰμί	Pres	-	Ind	3s	Goal		
1.6	ἀστοχέω	Aor	A	Ptcp	mnp	Opp		
1.6	ἐκτρέπω	Aor	P	Ind	3p	Opp		
1.7	θέλω	Pres	A	Ptcp	map	Opp		
1.7	εἰμί	Pres	-	Inf	-	Opp		
1.7	νοέω	Pres	A	Ptcp	map	Opp		
1.7	λέγω	Pres	A	Ind	3p	Opp		
1.7	διαβεβαιόομαι	Pres	M	Ind	3p	Opp		
1.8	οἶδα	Perf	A	Ind	1p	We		
1.8	χράομαι	Pres	M	Subj	3s	Law	State	Use of Law
1.9	οἶδα	Perf	A	Ptc	mns	Law		
1.9	κεῖμαι	Perf	M	Ind	3s	Law		
1.10	ὑγιαίνω	Pres	A	Ptcp	fds	Law	Vice list	
1.10	ἀντίκειμαι	Pres	M	Ind	3s	Things contra law		
1.11	πιστεύω	Aor	P	Ind	1s	Paul, gospel, God		

Verse	Verb	Tense	Voice	Mood	Pers/#	Participants	Genre	Topic
1.12	ἔχω	Pres	A	Ind	1s	Jesus, Paul	Thanks	Conversion/Call of Paul
1.12	ἐνδυναμόω	Aor	A	Ptcp	mds	Jesus, Paul		
1.12	ἡγέομαι	Aor	M	Ind	3s	Jesus, Paul		
1.12	τίθημι	Aor	M	Ptcp	mns	Jesus, Paul		
1.13	εἰμί	Pres	-	Ptcp	mas	Paul		
1.13	ἐλεέω	Aor	P	Ind	1s	Jesus, Paul		
1.13	ἀγνοέω	Pres	A	Ptcp	mns	Jesus, Paul		
1.13	ποιέω	Aor	A	Ind	1s	Paul		
1.14	ὑπερπλεονάζω	Aor	A	Ind	3s	Jesus, Paul		
1.15	(εἰμί)	Pres	-	Ind	3s			
1.15	ἔρχομαι	Aor	A	Ind	3s	Jesus		
1.15	σῴζω	Aor	A	Inf	-	Jesus, sinners		
1.15	εἰμί	Pres	-	Ind	1s	Paul		
1.16	ἐλεέω	Aor	P	Ind	1s	Jesus, Paul		
1.16	ἐνδείκνυμι	Aor	M	Subj	3s	Jesus, Paul		
1.16	μέλλω	Pres	A	Ptcp	mgp	Jesus, Paul, all believers		
1.16	πιστεύω	Pres	A	Inf	-			
1.17	(εἰμί)	Pres	-	Subj	3s		Dox	
1.18	παρατίθημι	Pres	M	Ind	1s	Paul, Tim	Exhort	Tim & Opp
1.18	προάγω	Pres	A	Ptcp	fap			
1.18	στρατεύω	Pres	M	Subj	2s	Tim		
1.19	ἔχω	Pres	A	Ptcp	mns	Tim		
1.19	ἀπωθέω	Aor	M	Ptcp	mnp	Opp		

Verse	Verb	Tense	Voice	Mood	Pers/#	Participants	Genre	Topic
1.19	ναυαγέω	Aor	A	Ind	3p	Opp		
1.20	εἰμί	Pres	-	Ind	3s	Opp		
1.20	παραδίδωμι	Aor	A	Ind	1s	Paul, Opp, Satan		
1.20	παιδεύω	Aor	P	Subj	3p	Opp, Hym/Alex		
1.20	βλασφημέω	Pres	A	Inf	-	Opp, Hym/Alex		
2.1	παρακαλέω	Pres	A	Ind	1s	Paul, church?		Prayer
2.1	ποιέω	Pres	P	Inf	-	Church		
2.2	διάγω	Pres	A	Subj	1p	Believers (Paul and church)		
2.3	(εἰμί)	Pres	-	Ind	3s	People, God		
2.4	θέλω	Pres	A	Ind	3s	God, all people		Salvation
2.4	σῴζω	Aor	P	Inf	-	God, all people		
2.4	ἔρχομαι	Aor	A	Inf	-	God, all people		
2.5	(εἰμί)	Pres	-	Ind	3s			
2.6	δίδωμι	Aor	A	Ptcp	mns	Jesus, all people	Exp	
2.7	τίθημι	Aor	P	Ind	1s	Paul, God		
2.7	λέγω	Pres	A	Ind	1s	Paul		
2.7	ψεύδομαι	Pres	M	Ind	1s	Paul		
2.8	βούλομαι	Pres	M	Ind	1s	Paul, men	Exhort	Prayer/men
2.8	προσεύχομαι	Pres	M	Inf	-	Men		
2.8	ἐπαίρω	Pres	A	Ptcp	map	Men		
2.9	(βούλομαι)	Pres	M	Ind	1s	Paul, women		
2.9	κοσμέω	Pres	A	Inf	-	Women		Women/dress
2.10	πρέπω	Pres	A	Ind	3s	Women		
2.10	ἐπαγγέλλομαι	Pres	M	Ptcp	fdp	Women		

Verse	Verb	Tense	Voice	Mood	Pers/#	Participants	Genre	Topic
2.11	μανθάνω	Pres	A	Imp	3s	Woman		Teaching
2.12	διδάσκειν	Pres	A	Inf	-	Woman		
2.12	ἐπιτρέπω	Pres	A	Ind	1s	Paul, woman		
2.12	αὐθεντέω	Pres	A	Inf	-	Woman, man		
2.12	εἰμί	Pres	A	Inf	-	Woman		
2.13	πλάσσω	Aor	P	Ind	3s	Adam, God, Eve	Exp	
2.14	ἀπατάω	Aor	A	Ind	3s	Adam		
2.14	ἐξαπατάω	Aor	P	Ptcp	fns	Eve		
2.14	γίνομαι	Perf	A	Ind	3s	Eve		
2.15	σῴζω	Fut	P	Ind	3s	Women (general)		
2.15	μένω	Aor	A	Subj	3p	Women		
3.1	ὀρέγω	Pres	M	Ind	3s	Someone in general	List	Qualif bishop
3.1	ἐπιθυμέω	Pres	A	Ind	3s	Someone in general		
3.2	δεῖ ... εἶναι	Pres	A	Ind	3s	Bishop		
3.4	προΐστημι	Pres	M	Ptcp	mas	Bishop, family		
3.4	ἔχω	Pres	A	Ptcp	mas	Bishop, children		
3.5	οἶδα	Perf	A	Ind	3s	Bishop, children		
3.5	προΐστημι	Aor	A	Inf	-	Bishop, children		
3.5	ἐπιμελέω	Fut	P	Ind	3s	Bishop, home, church		
3.6	τυφόομαι	Aor	P	Ptcp	mms	Bishop		
3.6	ἐμπίπτω	Aor	A	Subj	3s	Bishop, devil		
3.7	δεῖ ... ἔχειν	Pres	A	Ind	3s	Bishop, outsiders		
3.7	ἐμπίπτω	Aor	A	Subj	3s	Bishop, devil		
3.8	(δεῖ ... εἶναι)	Pres	A	Ind	3s	Deacons		Qualif deacons

Verse	Verb	Tense	Voice	Mood	Pers/#	Participants	Genre	Topic
3.8	προσέχω	Pres	A	Ptcp	map	Deacons		
3.9	ἔχω	Pres	A	Ptcp	map	Deacons		
3.10	δοκιμάζω	Pres	P	Imp	3p	Deacons/church?		
3.10	διακονέω	Pres	A	Imp	3p	Deacons		
3.10	εἰμί	Pres	-	Ptcp	mnp	Deacons		
3.11	(δεῖ ... εἶναι)	Pres	A	Ind	3s	Wives		
3.12	εἰμί	Pres	-	Imp	3p	Deacons		
3.12	προΐστημι	Pres	M	Ptcp	mnp	Deacons		
3.13	διακονέω	Aor	A	Ptcp	mnp	Deacons		
3.13	περιποιέω	Pres	M	Ind	3p	Deacons		
3.14	γράφω	Pres	A	Ind	1s	Paul, Tim	Exhort	Purpose
3.14	ἐλπίζω	Pres	A	Ptcp	mns	Paul		
3.14	ἔρχομαι	Aor	A	Inf	-	Paul, Tim		
3.15	βραδύνω	Pres	A	Ind	1s	Paul		
3.15	οἶδα	Pf	A	Subj	2s	Tim		
3.15	δεῖ ... ἀναστρέφεσθαι	Pres	A	Ind	3s	Tim		
3.15	εἰμί	Pres	-	Ind	3s	House of God, Church		
3.15	ζάω	Pres	A	Ptcp	mgs	House of God, Church		
3.16	εἰμί	Pres	-	Ind	3s	Mystery		
3.16	φανερόω	Aor	P	Ind	3s	Jesus	Exp	Work of Christ
3.16	δικαιόω	Aor	P	Ind	3s	Jesus		
3.16	ὁράω	Aor	P	Ind	3s	Jesus		
3.16	κηρύσσω	Aor	P	Ind	3s	Jesus		

Verse	Verb	Tense	Voice	Mood	Pers/#	Participants	Genre	Topic
3.16	πιστεύω	Aor	P	Ind	3s	Jesus		
3.16	ἀναλαμβάνω	Aor	P	Ind	3s	Jesus		
4.1	λέγω	Pres	A	Ind	3s	Holy Spirit, opp	Warm	Opp
4.1	ἀφίστημι	Fut	M	Ind	3p	Opp		
4.1	προσέχω	Pres	A	Ptcp	nmp	Opp		
4.2	καυστηριάζω	Perf	P	Ptcp	mgp	Opp		
4.3	κωλύω	Pres	A	Ptcpc	mgp	Opp		
4.3	γαμέω	Pres	A	Inf	-	Opp, others		
4.3	ἀπέχω	Pres	M	Inf	-	Opp, others		
4.3	κτίζω	Aor	A	Ind	3s	God		
4.3	ἐπιγινώσκω	Pf	A	Ptcp	mdp	God, believers		
4.4	(εἰμί)	Pres	-	Ind	3s	God, created things		
4.4	λαμβάνω	Pres	P	Ptcp	nas	Created things, people		
4.5	ἁγιάζω	Pres	P	Ind	3s	Created things, Word of God, prayer		
4.6	ὑποτίθημι	Pres	M	Ptcp	mns	Tim, church, ταῦτα	Exhort	Tim's work/personal
4.6	εἰμί	Fut	M	Ind	2s	Tim		
4.6	ἐντρέφω	Pres	P	Ptcp	mns	Tim, word, doctrine		
4.6	παρακολουθέω	Perf	A	Ind	2s	Tim, word, doctrine		
4.7	παραιτέομαι	Pres	M	Imp	2s	Tim		
4.7	γυμνάζω	Pres	A	Imp	2s	Tim		
4.8	εἰμί	Pres	-	Ind	3s			
4.8	εἰμί	Pres	-	Ind	3s			

Verse	Verb	Tense	Voice	Mood	Pers/#	Participants	Genre	Topic
4.8	ἔχω	Pres	A	Ptcp	fns			
4.8	μέλλω	Pres	M	Ptcp	fgs			
4.9	(εἰμί)	Pres	-	Ind	3s	Church, λόγος		
4.10	κοπιάω	Pres	A	Ind	1p			
4.10	ἀγωνίζομαι	Pres	M	Ind	1p			
4.10	ἐλπίζω	Perf	A	Ind	1p			
4.10	ζάω	Pres	A	Ptcp	mds	God		
4.10	εἰμί	Pres	-	Ind	3s	God		
4.11	παραγγέλλω	Pres	A	Imp	2s	Tim, Paul		Tim's work/ teaching
4.11	διδάσκω	Pres	A	Imp	2s	Tim, Paul		
4.12	καταφρονέω	Pres	A	Imp	3s	No one, Tim, Paul		
4.12	γίνομαι	Pres	A	Imp	2s	Tim, Paul, church		
4.13	ἔρχομαι	Pres	D	Ind	1s	Paul		
4.13	προσέχω	Pres	A	Imp	2s	Tim, Paul		
4.14	ἀμελέω	Pres	A	Imp	2s	Tim, Paul		
4.14	δίδωμι	Aor	P	Ind	3s	Gift, prophecy, elders		
4.15	μελετάω	Pres	A	Imp	2s	Tim, Paul		
4.15	εἰμί	Pres		Subj	3s	church, Tim's progress		
4.16	ἐπέχω	Pres	A	Imp	2s	Tim, Paul		
4.16	ἐπιμένω	Pres	A	Imp	2s	Tim, Paul		
4.16	ποιέω	Pres	A	Ptcp	mns	Tim		
4.16	σῴζω	Fut	A	Ind	2s	Tim, church		
5.1	ἐπιπλήσσω	Aor	A	Subj	2s	Tim, Paul, elders		Age groups
5.1	παρακαλέω	Pres	A	Imp	2s	Tim, Paul, elders		

Verse	Verb	Tense	Voice	Mood	Pers/#	Participants	Genre	Topic
5.2	(παρακαλέω)	Pres	A	Imp	2s	Tim, Paul, women		
5.3	τιμάω	Pres	A	Imp	2s	Tim, Paul, widows		Widows
5.4	ἔχω	Pres	A	Ind	3s	Widow, children		
5.4	μανθάνω	Pres	A	Imp	3p	Children		
5.4	εὐσεβέω	Pres	A	Inf	-	Children		
5.4	ἀποδίδωμι	Pres	A	Inf	-	Children		
5.4	εἰμί	Pres	-	Ind	3s	Children, action, God		
5.5	μονόω	Perf	P	Ptcp	fns	Widow, (children)		
5.5	ἐλπίζω	Perf	A	Ind	3s	Widow, God		
5.5	προσμένω	Pres	A	Ind	3s	Widow		
5.6	σπαταλάω	Pres	A	Ptcp	fns	Widow		
5.6	ζάω	Pres	A	Ptcp	fns	Widow		
5.6	τίθημι	Perf	A	Ind	3s	Widow		
5.7	παραγγέλλω	Pres	A	Imp	2s	Paul, Tim		
5.7	εἰμί	Pres	-	Subj	3p			
5.8	προνοέω	Pres	A	Ind	3s	Someone, his own family		
5.8	ἀρνέομαι	Perf	M	Ind	3s	Someone, faith		
5.8	εἰμί	Pres	-	Ind	3s	Someone, unbeliever		
5.9	καταλέγω	Pres	P	Imp	3s	Widows, Tim, Paul		
5.9	γίνομαι	Perf	A	Ptcp	fns	Widow		
5.10	μαρτυρέω	Pres	P	Ptcp	fns	Widow		
5.10	τεκνοτροφέω	Aor	A	Ind	3s	Widow		
5.10	χενοδοχέω	Aor	A	Ind	3s	Widow		
5.10	νίπτω	Aor	A	Ind	3s	Widow		

Verse	Verb	Tense	Voice	Mood	Pers/#	Participants	Genre	Topic
5.10	θλίβω	Pres	P	Ptcp	mdp	Widow		
5.10	ἐπαρκέω	Aor	A	Ind	3s	Widow		
5.10	ἐπακολουθέω	Aor	A	Ind	3s	Tim, Paul		
5.11	παραιτέομαι	Pres	M	Imp	2s	Young widows		
5.11	καταστρηνιάω	Aor	A	Subj	3p	Young widows		
5.11	γαμεῖν θέλουσιν	Pres	A	Ind	3p	Young widows		
5.12	ἔχω	Pres	A	Ptcp	fnp	Young widows		
5.12	ἀθετέω	Aor	A	Ind	3p	Young widows		
5.13	μανθάνω	Pres	A	Ind	3p	Young widows		
5.13	περιέρχομαι	Pres	M	Ptcp	fnp	Young widows		
5.13	λαλέω	Pres	A	Ptcp	fnp	Young widows		
5.13	δεῖ	Pres	A	Ptcp	nap	Things, young widows		
5.14	βούλομαι	Pres	M	Ind	1s	Paul, young widows		
5.14	γαμέω	Pres	A	Inf	-	Young widows		
5.14	τεκνογονέω	Pres	A	Inf	-	Young widows		
5.14	οἰκοδεσποτέω	Pres	A	Inf	-	Young widows		
5.14	δίδωμι	Perf	A	Inf	-	Young widows		
5.14	ἀντίκειμαι	Pres	D	Ptcp	mds	Young widows		
5.15	ἐκτρέπω	Aor	P	Ind	3p	Certain widows		
5.16	ἔχω	Pres	A	Ind	3s	Believer/widow		
5.16	ἐπαρκέω	Pres	A	Imp	3s	Believer/widow		
5.16	βαρέω	Pres	P	Imp	3s	Believer/widow		
5.16	ἐπαρκέω	Aor	A	Subj	3s	Church		
5.17	προΐστημι	Perf	A	Ptcp	mmp	Elders, church		Elders

Verse	Verb	Tense	Voice	Mood	Pers/#	Participants	Genre	Topic
5.17	ἀξιόω	Pres	P	Imp	3p	Elders, church, Paul, Tim		
5.17	κοπιάω	Pres	A	Ptcp	mmp	Elders		
5.18	λέγω	Pres	A	Ind	3s	Scripture		
5.18	ἀλοάω	Pres	A	Ptcp	mas	Ox		
5.18	φιμόω	Fut	A	Ind	2s	Ox		
5.18	(εἰμί)	Pres	-	Ind	3s	Worker		
5.19	παραδέχομαι	Pres	M	Imp	2s	Tim/Paul, elders		
5.20	ἁμαρτάνω	Pres	A	Ptcp	map			
5.20	ἔχω	Pres	A	Subj	3p	Other elders		
5.20	ἐλέγχω	Pres	A	Imp	2s	Tim/Paul, elders		
5.21	διαμαρτύρομαι	Pres	M	Ind	1s	Paul, Tim		
5.21	φυλάσσω	Aoe	A	Subj	2s	Tim, (Paul)		
5.21	ποιέω	Pres	A	Ptcp	mns	Tim, (Paul)		
5.22	ἐπιτίθημι	Pres	A	Imp	2s	Tim, (Paul)		
5.22	κοινωνέω	Pres	A	Imp	2s	Tim, (Paul)		
5.22	τηρέω	Pres	A	Imp	2s	Tim, (Paul)		
5.23	ὑδροποτέω	Pres	A	Imp	2s	Tim, (Paul)		
5.23	χράομαι	Pres	A	Imp	2s	Tim, (Paul)		
5.24	εἰμί	Pres	-	Ind	3p	Sins		
5.24	προάγω	Pres	A	Ptcp	fnp	Sins		
5.24	ἐπακολουθέω	Pres	A	Ind	3p	Sins		
5.25	(εἰμί)	Pres	-	Ind	3p	Good works		
5.25	ἔχω	Pres	A	Ptcp	nnp			
5.25	κρύπτω	Aor	P	Inf	-	Those with evil deeds		

Verse	Verb	Tense	Voice	Mood	Pers/#	Participants	Genre	Topic
5.25	δύναμαι	Pres	M	Ind	3p	Those with evil deeds		Slaves/Masters
6.1	εἰμί	Pres	-	Ind	3p	Slaves, masters		
6.1	ἡγέομαι	Pres	M	Imp	3p	Slaves, masters		
6.1	βλασφημέω	Pres	P	Subj	3s	Name of God, the teaching		
6.2	καταφρονέω	Pres	A	Imp	3p	Slaves, masters		
6.2	εἰμί	Pres	-	Ind	3p	Masters		
6.2	δουλεύω	Pres	A	Imp	3p	Slaves		
6.2	εἰμί	Pres	-	Ind	3p	Masters		
6.2	ἀντιλαμβάνομαι	Pres	M	Ptcp	mnp	Masters		
6.2	διδάσκω	Pres	A	Imp	2s	Tim/Paul		Tim's work
6.2	παρακαλέω	Pres	A	Imp	2s	Tim/Paul		
6.3	ἑτεροδιδασκαλέω	Pres	A	Imp	3s	Opp		Opp
6.3	προσέρχομαι	Pres	M	Ind	3s	Opp		
6.3	ὑγιαίνω	Pres	A	Ptcp	mdp	Opp		
6.4	τυφόω	Pres	P	Ind	3s	Opp	Warn	
6.4	ἐπίσταμαι	Pres	P	Ptcp	mns	Opp		
6.4	νοσέω	Pres	P	Ptcp	mns	Opp		
6.4	γίνομαι	Pres	M	Ind	3s	Disputes, strife, etc.		
6.5	διαφθείρω	Perf	P	Ptcp	mgp			
6.5	νομίζω	Perf	A	Ptcp	mgp	Opp		
6.5	εἰμί	Pres	-	Inf	-			
6.6	εἰμί	Pres	-	Ind	3s			
6.7	εἰσφέρω	Aor	A	Ind	1p	Believers in general		
6.7	ἐκφέρω	Aor	A	Inf	-	Believers in general		

Verse	Verb	Tense	Voice	Mood	Pers/#	Participants	Genre	Topic
6.7	δύναμαι	Pres	P	Ind	1p	Believers in general		
6.8	ἔχω	Pres	A	Ptcp	mmp	Believers in general		
6.8	ἀρκέω	Fut	P	Ind	1p	Believers in general		
6.9	βούλομαι	Pres	M	Ptcp	mmp	Those who desire to be rich		
6.9	πλουτέω	Pres	A	Inf	-	Those who desire to be rich		
6.9	ἐμπίπτω	Pres	A	Ind	3p	Those who desire to be rich		
6.9	βυθίζω	Pres	A	Ind	3p	Those who desire to be rich		
6.10	εἰμί	Pres	-	Ind	3s	Love of money		
6.10	ὀρέγω	Pres	M	Ptcp	mnp	Certain ones, love of money		
6.10	ἀποπλανάω	Aor	P	Ind	3p	Certain ones, love of money		
6.10	περιπείρω	Aor	A	Ind	3p	Certain ones, love of money		
6.11	φεύγω	Pres	A	Imp	2s	Tim/Paul, desire for money	Exhort	Tim's response
6.11	διώκω	Pres	A	Imp	2s	Tim/Paul, virtues		
6.12	ἀγωνίζομαι	Pres	M	Imp	2s	Tim/Paul		
6.12	ἐπιλαμβάνω	Aor	M	Imp	2s	Tim/Paul		
6.12	καλέω	Aor	P	Ind	2s	Tim (God)		
6.12	ὁμολογέω	Aor	A	Ind	2s	Tim, church		
6.13	παραγγέλλω	Pres	A	Imp	2s	Tim/Paul, the rich		
6.13	ζῳογονέω	Pres	A	Ptcp	mgs	God, all things		

Verse	Verb	Tense	Voice	Mood	Pers/#	Participants	Genre	Topic
6.13	μαρτυρέω	Aor	A	Ptcp	mgs	Jesus		
6.14	τηρέω	Aor	A	Inf	-	Tim/Paul		
6.15	δείκνυμι	Fut	A	Ind	3s	God/Jesus	Dox	
6.15	βασιλεύω	Pres	A	Ptcp	mgp			
6.15	κυριεύω	Pres	A	Ptcp	mgp			
6.16	ἔχω	Pres	A	Ptcp	mns	God		
6.16	οἰκέω	Pres	A	Ptcp	mns	God		
6.16	ὁράω	Aor	A	Ind	3s	No one/God		
6.16	ὁράω	Aor	A	Inf	-	No one/God		
6.16	δύναμαι	Pres	M	Ind	3s	No one/God		
6.17	παραγγέλλω	Pres	A	Imp	2s	Tim/Paul, the rich	Exhort	The rich
6.17	ὑψηλοφρονέω	Pres	A	Inf	-	The rich		
6.17	ἐλπίζω	Perf	A	Inf	-	The rich, God		
6.17	παρέχω	Pres	A	Ptcp	mds	God		
6.18	ἀγαθοεργέω	Pres	A	Inf	-	The rich		
6.18	πλουτέω	Pres	A	Inf	-	The rich		
6.18	εἰμί	Pres	-	Inf	-	The rich		
6.19	ἀποθησαυρίζω	Pres	A	Ptcp	map	The rich		
6.19	μέλλω	Pres	A	Ptcp	nas	The rich		
6.19	ἐπιλαμβάνω	Aor	M	Subj	3p	The rich		
6.20	φυλάσσω	Aor	A	Imp	2s	Tim/Paul	Warn	Tim vs. Opp
6.20	ἐκτρέπω	Pres	M	Ptcp	mns	Tim/Paul		
6.21	ἐπαγγέλλομαι	Pres	M	Ptcp	mnp	Opp		
6.21	ἀστοχέω	Aor	A	Ind	3p	Opp		

Cohesion Shift Analysis of 2 Timothy

Verse	Verb	Tense	Voice	Mood	Pers/#	Participants	Genre	Topic
1.3	ἔχω	Pres	A	Ind	1s	Paul/God	Thanks	Thoughts of Tim
1.3	λατρεύω	Pres	A	Ind	1s	Paul/God		
1.3	ἔχω	Pres	A	Ind	1s	Paul/Tim		
1.4	ἐπιποθέω	Pres	A	ptc	nms	Paul		
1.4	ὁράω	Aor	A	inf	-			
1.4	μιμνῄσκομαι	Pf	P	ptc	nms	Paul/Tim		
1.4	πληρόω	Aor	P	Subj	1s	Paul/Tim		
1.5	λαμβάνω	Aor	A	ptc	nms	Paul		
1.5	ἐνοικέω	Aor	A	Ind	3s	Faith (Tim/family)		
1.5	πείθω	Pf	P	Ind	1s	Paul/Tim		
1.6	ἀναμιμνῄσκω	Pres	A	Ind	1s	Paul/Tim		
1.6	ἀναζωπυρέω	Pres	A	inf	-	Tim	Exhort	Tim's work
1.6	εἰμί	Pres		Ind	3s	Gift/Tim & Paul		
1.7	δίδωμι	Aor	A	Ind	3s	God/us		
1.8	ἐπαισχύνομαι	Aor	D	Subj	2s	Tim/Jesus & Paul		
1.8	συγκακοπαθέω	Aor	A	Imptv	2s	Tim/Paul		
1.9	σῴζω	Aor	A	ptc	gms	God/us	Exp	Salvation
1.9	καλέω	Aor	A	ptc	gms	God/us		
1.9	δίδωμι	Aor	P	ptc	afs	God/us		
1.10	φανερόω	Aor	P	ptc	afs	God's grace & plan		
1.10	καταργέω	Aor	A	ptc	gms	Christ Jesus		
1.10	φωτίζω	Aor	A	ptc	gms	Christ Jesus		

Verse	Verb	Tense	Voice	Mood	Pers/#	Participants	Genre	Topic
1.11	τίθημι	Aor	P	Ind	1s	Paul/God	Test	Paul's example
1.12	πάσχω	Pres	A	Ind	1s	Paul		
1.12	ἐπαισχύνομαι	Pres	D	Ind	1s	Paul		
1.12	οἶδα	Pf	A	Ind	1s	Paul/God		
1.12	πιστεύω	Pf	A	Ind	1s	Paul/God		
1.12	πείθω	Pf	P	Ind	1s	Paul		
1.12	εἰμί	Pres		Ind	3s	God		
1.12	φυλάσσω	Aor	A	inf	-	God		
1.13	ἔχω	Pres	A	Imptv	2s	Tim		Tim's work
1.13	ἀκούω	Aor	A	Ind	2s	Tim/Paul		
1.14	φυλάσσω	Aor	A	Imptv	2s	Tim		
1.14	ἐνοικέω	Pres	A	ptc	gns	HS/Tim		
1.15	οἶδα	Pf	A	Ind	2s	Tim		
1.15	ἀποστρέφω	Aor	P	Ind	3p	All/Paul		
1.15	εἰμί	Pres		Ind	3s	Phygelus & Hermogenes	Report	Paul's situation
1.16	δίδωμι	Aor	A	Opt	3s	Lord/Onesiphorus		
1.16	ἀναψύχω	Aor	A	Ind	3s	Onesiphorus/Paul		
1.16	ἐπαισχύνομαι	Aor	D	Ind	3s	Onesiphorus/Paul		
1.17	γίνομαι	Aor	M	ptc	nms	Onesiphorus		
1.17	ζητέω	Aor	A	Ind	3s	Onesiphorus/Paul		
1.17	εὑρίσκω	Aor	A	Ind	3s	Onesiphorus/Paul		
1.18	δίδωμι	Aor	A	Opt	3s	Lord/Onesiphorus		
1.18	εὑρίσκω	Aor	A	inf	-	Onesiphorus		

Verse	Verb	Tense	Voice	Mood	Pers/#	Participants	Genre	Topic
1.18	διακονέω	Aor	A	Ind	3s	Onesiphorus		
1.18	γινώσκω	Pres	A	Ind	2s	Tim		
2.1	ἐνδυναμόω	Pres	P	Imptv	2s	Tim/Paul	Exhort	Tim's work
2.2	ἀκούω	Aor	A	Ind	2s	Tim/Paul		
2.2	παρατίθημι	Aor	M	Imptv	2s	Tim/Paul		
2.2	εἰμί	Fut		Ind	3p	Men		
2.2	διδάσκω	Aor	A	inf	-	Men		
2.3	συγκακοπαθέω	Aor	A	Imptv	2s	Tim/Paul		
2.4	στρατεύω	Pres	M	ptc	nms	Soldier	Proverbial	
2.4	ἐμπλέκω	Pres	P	Ind	3s	Soldier		
2.4	στρατολογέω	Aor	A	ptc	dms	Officer		
2.4	ἀρέσκω	Aor	A	Subj	3s	Soldier		
2.5	ἀθλέω	Pres	A	Subj	3s	Athlete		
2.5	στεφανόω	Pres	P	Ind	3s	Athlete		
2.5	ἀθλέω	Aor	A	Subj	3s	Athlete		
2.6	κοπιάω	Pres	A	ptc	ams	Farmer		
2.6	δεῖ	Pres	A	Ind	3s	Farmer		
2.6	μεταλαμβάνω	Pres	A	inf	-	Farmer		
2.7	νοέω	Pres	A	Imptv	2s	Tim/Paul		
2.7	λέγω	Pres	A	Ind	1s	Paul		
2.7	δίδωμι	Fut	A	Ind	3s	Lord		
2.8	μνημονεύω	Pres	A	Imptv	2s	Tim/Paul		
2.8	ἐγείρω	Pf	P	ptc	ams	Jesus Christ		
2.9	κακοπαθέω	Pres	A	Ind	1s	Paul		

Verse	Verb	Tense	Voice	Mood	Pers/#	Participants	Genre	Topic
2.9	δέω	Pf	P	Ind	3s	Word of God		
2.10	ὑπομένω	Pres	A	Ind	1s	Paul		
2.10	τυγχάνω	Aor	A	Subj	3p	Elect		
2.11	συναποθνῄσκω	Aor	A	Ind	1p	We	Statement	
2.11	συζάω	Fut	A	Ind	1p	We		
2.12	ὑπομένω	Pres	A	Ind	1p	We		
2.12	συμβασιλεύω	Fut	A	Ind	1p	We		
2.12	ἀρνέομαι	Fut	M	Ind	1p	We		
2.12	ἀρνέομαι	Fut	M	Ind	3s	Jesus		
2.13	ἀπιστέω	Pres	A	Ind	1p	We		
2.13	μένω	Pres	A	Ind	3s	Jesus		
2.13	ἀρνέομαι	Aor	M	inf	-	Jesus		
2.13	δύναμαι	Pres	D	Ind	3s	Jesus		Tim & Opp
2.14	ὑπομιμνῄσκω	Pres	A	Imptv	2s	Tim/Paul		
2.14	διαμαρτύρομαι	Pres	M	ptc	nms	Tim		
2.14	λογομαχέω	Pres	A	inf	-	'them'		
2.14	ἀκούω	Pres	A	ptc	gmp	Hearers		
2.15	σπουδάζω	Aor	A	Imptv	2s	Tim/Paul		
2.15	παρίστημι	Aor	A	inf	-	Tim/God		
2.15	ὀρθοτομέω	Pres	A	ptc	ams	Tim		
2.16	περιίστημι	Pres	M	Imptv	2s	Tim		
2.16	προκόπτω	Fut	A	Ind	3p	Errors; or people		
2.17	ἔχω	Fut	A	Ind	3s	Teaching		
2.17	εἰμί	Pres	-	Ind	3s	Opp		
2.18	ἀστοχέω	Aor	A	Ind	3p	Opp		

Verse	Verb	Tense	Voice	Mood	Pers/#	Participants	Genre	Topic
2.18	λέγω	Pres	A	ptc	nmp	Opp		
2.18	γίνομαι	Pf	A	inf	-	Resurrection		
2.18	ἀνατρέπω	Pres	A	Ind	3p	Opp		
2.19	ἵστημι	Pf	A	Ind	3s	Foundation		
2.19	ἔχω	Pres	A	ptc	nms	Foundation		
2.19	γινώσκω	Aor	A	Ind	3s	Lord		
2.19	εἰμί	Pres		ptc	amp			
2.19	ἀφίστημι	Aor	A	Imptv	3s	'Those who …'		
2.19	ὀνομάζω	Pres	A	ptc	nms			
2.20	εἰμί	Pres		Ind	3s	Vessels	Proverbial	
2.21	ἐκκαθαίρω	Aor	A	Subj	3s	τις		
2.21	εἰμί	Fut		Ind	3s	τις		
2.21	ἁγιάζω	Pf	P	ptc	nns	τις		
2.21	ἑτοιμάζω	Pf	P	ptc	nns	τις		
2.22	φεύγω	Pres	A	Imptv	2s	Tim		
2.22	διώκω	Pres	A	Imptv	2s	Tim		
2.22	ἐπικαλέω	Pres	M	ptc	gmp			
2.23	παραιτέομαι	Pres	M	Imptv	2s	Tim		
2.23	οἶδα	Pf	A	ptc	nms	Tim		
2.23	γεννάω	Pres	A	Ind	3p	Speculations		
2.24	δεῖ	Pres	A	Ind	3s	Servant (Tim)		
2.24	μάχομαι	Pres	M	inf	-	Servant (Tim)		
2.24	εἰμί	Pres		inf	-	Servant (Tim)		
2.25	παιδεύω	Pres	A	ptc	ams	Servant (Tim)		

Verse	Verb	Tense	Voice	Mood	Pers/#	Participants	Genre	Topic
2.25	ἀντιδιατίθημι	Pres	M	ptc	amp	Opp		
2.25	δίδωμι	Aor	A	Subj	3s	God		
2.26	ἀνανήφω	Aor	A	Subj	3p	Opp		
2.26	ζωγρέω	Pf	P	ptc	nmp	Opp		
3.1	γινώσκω	Pres	A	Imptv	2s	Tim/Paul	Warning	Opp
3.1	ἐνίστημι	Fut	M	Ind	3p	Times		
3.2	εἰμί	Fut		Ind	3p	Men		
3.4	τυφόω	Pf	P	ptc	nmp	Men		
3.5	ἔχω	Pres	A	ptc	nmp	Men		
3.5	ἀρνέομαι	Pf	M	ptc	nmp	Men		
3.5	ἀποτρέπω	Pres	M	Imptv	2s	Tim		
3.6	εἰμί	Pres		Ind	3s	Opp		
3.6	ἐδύνω	Pres	A	ptc	nmp	Opp		
3.6	αἰχμαλωτίζω	Pres	A	ptc	nmp	Opp		
3.6	σωρεύω	Pf	P	ptc	anp	Women		
3.6	ἄγω	Pres	P	ptc	anp	Women		
3.7	μανθάνω	Pres	A	ptc	anp	Women		
3.7	ἔρχομαι	Aor	A	inf	-	Women		
3.7	δύναμαι	Pres	P	ptc	anp	Women		
3.8	ἀνθίστημι	Aor	A	Ind	3p	Jannes/Jambres		
3.8	ἀνθίστημι	Pres	M	Ind	3p	Opp		
3.8	καταφθείρω	Pf	P	ptc	nmp	Opp		
3.9	προκόπτω	Fut	A	Ind	3p	Opp		
3.9	εἰμί	Fut	M	Ind	3s	Opp's folly		

Verse	Verb	Tense	Voice	Mood	Pers/#	Participants	Genre	Topic
3.9	γίνομαι	Aor	M	Ind	3s	Jannes'/Jambres' folly		
3.10	παρακολουθέω	Aor	A	Ind	2s	Tim	Exhort	Tim's work
3.11	γίνομαι	Aor	M	Ind	3s	Suffering/Paul		
3.11	ὑποφέρω	Aor	A	Ind	1s	Paul		
3.11	ῥύομαι	Aor	M	Ind	3s	Lord/Paul		
3.12	θέλω	Pres	A	ptc	Nmp	Those desiring		
3.12	ζάω	Pres	A	inf	-	Those desiring		
3.12	διώκω	Fut	P	Ind	3p			
3.13	προκόπτω	Fut	A	Ind	3p	Evil men		
3.13	πλανάω	Pres	A	ptc	nmp	Evil men		
3.13	πλανάω	Pres	P	ptc	nmp	Evil men		
3.14	μένω	Pres	A	Imptv	2s	Tim		
3.14	μανθάνω	Aor	A	Ind	2s	Tim		
3.14	πιστόω	Aor	P	Ind	2s	Tim		
3.14	οἶδα	Pf	A	ptc	nms	Tim		
3.14	μανθάνω	Aor	A	Ind	2s	Tim		
3.15	οἶδα	Pf	A	Ind	2s	Tim		
3.15	δύναμαι	Pres	P	ptc	anp	Scripture		
3.15	σοφίζω	Aor	A	inf	-	"/Tim		
3.17	εἰμί	Pres	A	Subj	3s	Tim		
3.17	ἐξαρτίζω	Pf	P	ptc	nms	Tim		
4.1	διαμαρτύρομαι	Pres	D	Ind	1s	Paul		
4.1	μέλλω	Pres	P	ptc	gms	God/Christ Jesus		
4.1	κρίνω	Pres	A	inf	-	God/Christ Jesus		

Verse	Verb	Tense	Voice	Mood	Pers/#	Participants	Genre	Topic
4.1	ζάω	Pres	A	ptc	amp			
4.2	κηρύσσω	Aor	A	Imptv	2s	Tim/Paul		
4.2	ἐφίστημι	Aor	A	Imptv	2s	Tim/Paul		
4.2	ἐλέγχω	Aor	A	Imptv	2s	Tim/Paul		
4.2	ἐπιτιμάω	Aor	A	Imptv	2s	Tim/Paul		
4.2	παρακαλέω	Aor	A	Imptv	2s	Tim/Paul		Opp
4.3	εἰμί	Fut	M	Ind	3s	Time	Warning	
4.3	ἀνέχομαι	Fut	M	Ind	3p	Opp		
4.3	ἐπισωρεύω	Fut	A	Ind	3p	Opp		
4.3	ὑγιαίνω	Pres	A	ptc	gfs			
4.3	κνήθω	Pres	P	ptc	nmp	Opp		
4.4	ἀποστρέφω	Fut	A	Ind	3p	Opp		
4.4	ἐκτρέπω	Fut	P	Ind	3p	Opp		
4.5	νήφω	Pres	A	Imptv	2s	Tim	Exhort	
4.5	κακοπαθέω	Aor	A	Imptv	2s	Tim		
4.5	ποιέω	Aor	A	Imptv	2s	Tim		
4.5	πληροφορέω	Aor	A	Imptv	2s	Tim		
4.6	σπένδω	Pres	P	Ind	1s	Paul	Test	Paul
4.6	ἐφίστημι	Pf	A	Ind	3s	Paul's departure		
4.7	ἀγωνίζομαι	Pf	D	Ind	1s	Paul		
4.7	τελέω	Pf	A	Ind	1s	Paul		
4.7	τηρέω	Pf	A	Ind	1s	Paul		
4.8	ἀπόκειμαι	Pres	D	Ind	3s	Crown/Paul		
4.8	ἀποδίδωμι	Fut	A	Ind	3s	Lord/Paul		

Verse	Verb	Tense	Voice	Mood	Pers/#	Participants	Genre	Topic
4.8	ἀγαπάω	Pf	A	ptc	dmp		Exhort	Travel/News
4.9	σπουδάζω	Aor	A	Imptv	2s	Tim		
4.9	ἔρχομαι	Aor	A	inf	-	Tim		
4.10	ἐγκαταλείπω	Aor	A	Ind	3s	Demas		
4.10	ἀγαπάω	Aor	A	ptc	nms	Demas		
4.10	πορεύομαι	Aor	P	Ind	3s	Demas		
4.11	εἰμί	Pres		Ind	3s	Luke		
4.11	ἀναλαμβάνω	Aor	A	ptc	nms	Tim/Mark		
4.11	ἄγω	Pres	A	Imptv	2s	Tim/Mark		
4.11	εἰμί	Pres		Ind	3s	Tim		
4.12	ἀποστέλλω	Aor	A	Ind	1s	Paul/Tychicus		
4.13	ἀπολείπω	Aor	A	Ind	1s	Paul		
4.13	ἔρχομαι	Pres	M	ptc	nms	Tim		
4.13	φέρω	Pres	A	Imptv	2s	Tim	(or warning)	
4.14	ἐνδείκνυμι	Aor	D	Ind	3s	Alex		
4.14	ἀποδίδωμι	Fut	A	Ind	3s	Lord		
4.15	φυλάσσω	Pres	M	Imptv	2s	Tim/Alex		
4.15	ἀνθίστημι	Aor	A	Ind	3s	Alex		
4.16	παραγίνομαι	Aor	M	Ind	3s	No one/Paul	Test.	Paul
4.16	ἐγκαταλείπω	Aor	A	Ind	3p	All/Paul		
4.16	λογίζομαι	Aor	P	Opt	3s	Their desertion		
4.17	παρίστημι	Aor	A	Ind	3s	Lord/Paul		
4.17	ἐνδυναμόω	Aor	A	Ind	3s	Lord/Paul		
4.17	πληροφορέω	Aor	P	Subj	3s	Preaching		

Verse	Verb	Tense	Voice	Mood	Pers/#	Participants	Genre	Topic
4.17	ἀκούω	Aor	A	Subj	3p	ἔθνή		
4.17	ῥύομαι	Aor	P	Ind	1s	Paul/Lord		
4.18	ῥύομαι	Fut	M	Ind	3s	Lord/Paul		
4.18	σῴζω	Fut	A	Ind	3s	Lord		
4.19	ἀσπάζομαι	Aor	M	Imptv	2s	Tim		Greetings
4.20	μένω	Aor	A	Ind	3s	Erastus		
4.20	ἀπολείπω	Aor	A	Ind	1s	Paul/Trophimus		
4.20	ἀσθενέω	Pres	A	ptc	Ams	Trophimus	Greeting/Travel	
4.21	σπουδάζω	Aor	A	Imptv	2s	Tim		
4.21	ἔρχομαι	Aor	A	inf	-	Tim		
4.21	ἀσπάζομαι	Pres	D	Ind	3s	group		

Cohesion Shift Analysis of Titus

Verse	Verb	Tense	Voice	Mood	Pers/#	Participants	Genre	Topic
1.2	ἐπαγγέλλομαι	Aor	M	Ind	3s	God, message	Exp	Salvation
1.3	φανερόω	Aor	A	Ind	3s	God, message		
1.3	πιστεύω	Aor	P	Ind	1s	Paul, Mesage		
1.5	ἀπολείπω	Aor	A	Ind	1s	Paul, Titus	Remind	Elders
1.5	ἐπιδιορθόω	Aor	M	Subj	2s	Titus, Paul		
1.5	καθίστημι	Aor	A	Subj	2s	Titus, Paul, elders		
1.5	διατάσσω	Aor	M	Ind	1s	Paul		
1.6	εἰμί	Pres	-	Ind	3s	Elders, someone	Virtue list	Qualif of elders
1.6	εἰμί	Pres	-	Ind	3s	Elders, someone		
1.6	ἔχων	Pres	A	Ptcp	mns	Elders, someone		
1.6	εἰμί	Pres	-	Ind	3s	Elders, someone		
1.7	δεῖ	Pres	A	Ind	3s	Bishop		
1.7	εἰμί	Pres	-	Ind	3s	Bishop		
1.9	ἀντεχόμενον	Pres	M	Ptcp	ams	Bishop		
1.9	εἰμί	Pres	-	Subj	3s	Bishop		
1.9	παρακαλέω	Pres	A	Inf	-	Bishop, opp		
1.9	ἐλέγχω	Pres	A	Inf	-	Bishop, opp		
1.10	εἰμί	Pres	-	Ind	3p	Opp	Exhort/Warn	Opp
1.11	δεῖ	Pres	A	Ind	3s	Titus		
1.11	ἐπιστομίζω	Pres	A	Inf	-	Titus		
1.11	ἀνατρέπω	Pres	A	Ind	3p	Opp		
1.11	διδάσκω	Pres	A	Ptcp	mmp	Opp		

Verse	Verb	Tense	Voice	Mood	Pers/#	Participants	Genre	Topic
1.12	λέγω	Aor	A	Ind	3s	Cretan prophet		
1.12	εἰμί	Pres	-	Ind	3s			
1.13	εἰμί	Pres	-	Ind	3s	Previous quote		
1.13	ἐλέγχω	Pres	A	Imptv	2s	Titus		
1.13	ὑγιαίνω	Pres	A	Subj	3p	Cretans		
1.14	προσέχω	Pres	A	Ptcp	mnp	Cretans		
1.14	ἀποστρέφω	Pres	M	Ptcp	mgp	Cretans		
1.15	εἰμί	Pres	-	Ind	3s			
1.15	εἰμί	Pres	-	Ind	3s			
1.15	εἰμί	Pres	-	Ind	3s	Opp		
1.16	ὁμολογέω	Pres	A	Ind	3p	Opp		
1.16	οἶδα	Perf	A	Inf	-	Opp		
1.16	ἀρνέομαι	Pres	M	Ind	3p	Opp		
1.16	εἰμί	Pres	A	Ptcp	mnp	Opp		
2.1	λαλέω	Pres	A	Imptv	2s	Titus	Exhort	Titus' teaching
2.1	πρέπω	Pres	A	Ind	3s	Titus		
2.2	εἰμί	Pres	-	Inf	-			
2.3	εἰμί	Pres	-	Inf	-			
2.4	σωφρονίζω	Pres	A	Subj	3p			Conduct of groups
2.4	εἰμί	Pres	-	Inf	-			
2.5	βλασφημέω	Pres	P	Subj	3s			
2.6	παρακαλέω	Pres	A	Imptv	2s	Titus		
2.6	σωφρονέω	Pres	A	Inf	-			
2.7	παρέχω	Pres	M	Ptcp	mms	Titus		

Verse	Verb	Tense	Voice	Mood	Pers/#	Participants	Genre	Topic
2.8	ἐντρέπω	Aor	P	Subj	3s	Opp		
2.9	ὑποτάσσω	Pres	P	Inf	-	Slaves		
2.9	εἰμί	Pres	-	Inf	3s	Slaves		
2.9	ἀντιλέγω	Pres	A	Ptcp	map	Slaves		
2.10	νοσφίζω	Pres	M	Ptcp	map	Slaves		
2.10	ἐνδείκνυμι	Pres	M	Ptcp	map	Slaves		
2.10	κοσμέω	Pres	A	Subj	3p	Slaves		
2.11	ἐπιφαίνω	Aor	P	Ind	3s	God's grace	Exp	Salvation
2.12	παιδεύω	Pres	A	Ptcp	fns	God's grace		
2.12	ἀρνέομαι	Aor	M	Ptcp	mmp	Us		
2.12	ζάω	Pres	A	Subj	1p	Us		
2.13	προσδέχομαι	Pres	M	Ptcp	mmp	Us		
2.14	δίδωμι	Aor	A	Ind	3s	Jesus		
2.14	λυτρόω	Aor	M	Subj	3s	Jesus		
2.14	καθαρίζω	Aor	A	Subj	3s	Jesus		
2.15	λαλέω	Pres	A	Imptv	2s	Titus	Exhort	Titus' teaching
2.15	παρακαλέω	Pres	A	Imptv	2s	Titus		
2.15	ἐλέγχω	Pres	A	Imptv	2s	Titus		
2.15	περιφρονέω	Pres	A	Imptv	3s	Titus		
3.1	ὑπομιμνῄσκω	Pres	A	Imptv	2s	Titus		
3.1	ὑποτάσσω	Pres	P	Inf	-	Cretan church		
3.1	πειθαρχέω	Pres	A	Inf	-	Cretan church		
3.1	εἰμί	Pres	-	Inf	-	Cretan church		Conduct
3.2	βλασφημέω	Pres	A	Inf	-	Cretan church		

Verse	Verb	Tense	Voice	Mood	Pers/#	Participants	Genre	Topic
3.2	εἰμί	Pres	-	Inf	-	Cretan church	Exp	Salvation
3.2	ἐνδείκνυμι	Pres	M	Ptcp	map	Cretan church		
3.3	εἰμί	Impf	-	Ind	1p	We		
3.4	ἐπιφαίνω	Aor	P	Ind	3s	God's mercy		
3.5	ποιέω	Aor	A	Ind	1p	We		
3.5	σῴζω	Aor	A	Ind	3s	God		
3.6	ἐκχέω	Aor	A	Ind	3s	God		
3.7	δικαιόω	Aor	P	Ptcp	mnp	God		
3.7	γίνομαι	Aor	P	Subj	1p			
3.8	βούλομαι	Pres	M	Ind	1s	Paul	Exhort	Titus' teaching
3.8	διαβεβαιόομαι	Pres	M	Inf	-			
3.8	φροντίζω	Pres	A	Subj	3p	Believers		
3.8	εἰμί	Pres	-	Ind	3s			
3.9	περιΐστημι	Pres	M	Imptv	2s	Titus		
3.9	εἰμί	Pres	-	Ind	3p			Opp
3.10	παραιτέομαι	Pres	M	Imptv	2s	Titus		
3.11	οἶδα	Perf	A	Ptcp	mns	Titus		
3.11	ἐκστρέφω	Perf	P	Ind	3s	Opp		
3.11	ἁμαρτάνω	Pres	A	Ind	3s	Opp		
3.12	πέμπω	Aor	A	Subj	1s	Paul	Travel	Travel
3.12	σπουδάζω	Aor	A	Imp	2s	Titus		
3.12	ἔρχομαι	Aor	A	Inf	-	Titus		
3.12	κρίνω	Perf	A	Ind	1s	Paul		
3.12	παραχειμάζω	Aor	A	Inf	-	Paul		

Verse	Verb	Tense	Voice	Mood	Pers/#	Participants	Genre	Topic
3.13	προπέμπω	Aor	A	Imptv	2s	Titus	Also Exhort	Also conduct
3.14	μανθάνω	Pres	A	Imptv	3p	Cretan church		
3.14	προΐστημι	Pres	M	Inf	-	Cretan church		
3.14	εἰμί	Pres	A	Subj	3p	Cretan church		
3.15	ἀσπάζομαι	Pres	M	Ind	3p		Greeting	Greeting
3.15	ἀσπάζομαι	Aor	M	Imptv	2s		Greeting	Greeting

BIBLIOGRAPHY

Primary Sources

Boeckhius, A. (ed.)
    1843   *Corpus Inscriptionum Graecarum* (vol. 2; Berolini: Officina Acade-
            mica).
Brooke, D.
    1930   *Private Letters Pagan and Christian* (New York: E.P. Dutton and
            co., inc.).
Brown, G.M. (ed.)
    1970   *Documentary Papyri from the Michigan Collection* (American
            Studies in Papyrology, vol. 6; Toronto: A.M. Hakkert, Ltd.).
Constable, G.
    1976   *Letters and Letter Collections* (Turnhout, Belgium: Brepols).
Dittenberger, W.
    1942   *Sylloge Inscriptionum Graecarum* (Lipsiae: S. Hirzelium).
Hercher, R. (ed.)
    1873   *Epistolographi Graeci* (Paris: Didot).
Hunt, A.S., and C.C. Edgar (eds.)
    1932–34   *Select Papyrii* (LCL; 2 vols.; London: Heinemann).
Kim, C.H., and J.L. White.
    1974   *Letters from the Papyri: A Study Collection for Consultation on
            Ancient Epistolography* (Missoula, MT: Scholars Press).
Lucian
    1968   *How to Write History*, in *Lucian in Eight Volumes* (vol. 6, trans. by
            K. Kilburn; LCL 430; London/Cambridge, MA: Heinemann/
            Harvard University Press).

    1905   *How to Write History*, in *The Works of Lucian* (vol. 2, trans. H.W.
            Fowler and F.G. Fowler, Oxford: Clarendon).
Malherbe, A.J.
    1977   *The Cynic Epistles: A Study Edition* (SBLSBS 12; Missoula:
            Scholars Press, repr. 1986).
Milligan, G.
    1910   *Selections from the Greek Papyri* (Cambridge: University Press).

Milne, H.J.M. (ed.)
1927   *Catalogue of the Literary Papyri in the British Museum* (London: Trustees of the British Museum).

Sherk, R.
1969   *Roman Documents from the Greek East: Senatus consulta and Epistulae to the Age of Augustus* (Baltimore: Johns Hopkins University Press).

Sherwin-White, A.N.
1966   *The Letters of Pliny: A Historical and Social Commentary* (Oxford: Clarendon Press).

Smallwood, E.M.
1967   *Documents Illustrating the Principates of Gaius Claudius and Nero* (Cambridge: Cambridge University Press).

Tcherikover, U.A., A. Fuks, and M. Stern (eds.)
1957–64   *Corpus Papyrorum Judaicorum* (3 vols.; Cambridge, MA: Harvard University Press).

Welles, C.B.
1934   *Royal Correspondence in the Hellenistic Period: A Study in Greek Epigraphy* (New Haven: Yale University Press).

Winter, J.G.
1927   'In the Service of Rome: Letters from the Michigan Collection of Papyri', *Classical Philology* 22: 237–56.

1936   *Papyri in the University of Michigan Collection: Miscellaneous Papyri, Michigan Papyri* (vol. 3; Ann Arbor: University of Michigan Press).

General Bibliography

Achtemeier, P.J.
1990   '*Omne Verbum Sonat*: The New Testament and the Oral Environment of Late Western Antiquity', *JBL* 109: 3–27.

Aletti, J.-N.
1992   'La *dispositio* rhetorique dans les epitres pauliniennes: proposition de methode', *NTS* 38: 385–401.

Alexander, L.
1989   'Hellenistic Letter-Forms and the Structure of Philippians', *JSNT* 37: 87–101.

Anderson, R.D., Jr.
1996   *Ancient Rhetorical Theory and Paul* (Contributions to Biblical Exegesis & Theology, 18; Kampen: Kok Pharos).

Archer, R.L.
1951–52   'The Epistolary Form in the New Testament', *ExpTim* 63: 296–98.

Arzt, P.
1994   'The "Epistolary Introductory Thanksgiving" in the Papyri and in Paul', *NovT* 36: 29–46.

Audet, J.P.
  1958   'Esquisse historique du genre littéraire de la "Bénédiction" Juive et de l' "Eucharistie" Chrétienne', *Revue Biblique* 65: 371–99.
Aune, D.E.
  1987   *The New Testament in its Literary Environment* (Philadelphia: Westminster).

  1988   (ed.) *Greco-Roman Literature and The New Testament: Selected Forms and Genres* (Atlanta: Scholars Press).
Bahr, G.J.
  1966   'Paul and Letter Writing in the First Century', *CBQ* 28 (1966): 465–77.

  1968   'The Subscriptions in the Pauline Letters', *JBL* 87: 27–41.
Bailey, K.E.
  1996   '"Inverted Parallelisms" and "Encased Parables" in Isaiah and Their Significance for OT and NT Translation and Interpretation', in *Literary Structure and Rhetorical Strategies in the Hebrew Bible* L.J. Regt, J. de Waard, and J.P. Fokkelman (eds.) (Assen, Netherlands: Van Gorcum & Comp.): 14–30.
Bakker, E.J.
  1993   'Boundaries, Topics and the Structuring of Discourse, an Investigation of the Ancient Greek Particle DÉ', *Studies in Language* 17: 275–311.
Balch, D.L.
  1989   'Review of *Pseudepigraphy and Ethical Argument in the Pastoral Epistles*, by L.R. Donelson', in *JR* 69: 235–37.
Banker, John
  1987   *Semantic Structure Analysis of Titus* (Dallas: Summer Institute of Linguistics).
Barclay, J.M.G.
  1987   'Mirror Reading a Polemical Letter: Galatians as a Test Case', *JSNT* 31: 73–93.
Bar-Efrat, S.
  1980   'Some Observations on the Analysis of Structure in Biblical Narrative', *Vetus Testamentum* 30: 154–73.
Barnett, P.W.
  1963   'Wives and Women's Ministry (1 Timothy 2:11–15)', *EvQ* 61: 225–38.
Barrett, C.K.
  1963   *The Pastoral Epistles* (Oxford: Clarendon Press).

  2001   'Review of *A Critical and Exegetical Commentary on the Pastoral Epistles*, by I.H. Marshall', in *JTS* 52.2: 827–29.
Bassler, J.
  1984   'The Widow's Tale: A Fresh Look at 1 Tim 5:3–16', *JBL* 103: 23–41.

  1988   'Adam, Eve, and the Pastor', in G.A. Robbins (ed.), *Genesis 1–3 in the History of Exegesis: Intrigue in the Garden* (Lewiston, NY: The Edwin Mellen Press): 43–65.

1996   *1 Timothy, 2 Timothy, Titus* (Nashville: Abingdon Press).

Bauer, D.R.

1988   *The Structure of Matthew's Gospel, A Study in Literary Design* (JSNTSup, 31; Sheffield: Almond Press).

Bauer, W.

1979   *A Greek-English Lexicon of the New Testament and Other Early Christian Literature* (trans. W.F. Arndt and F.W. Gingrich; rev. Gingrich and F.W. Danker, 2nd edn; Chicago: University of Chicago Press).

Beardslee, W.A.

1970   *Literary Criticism of the New Testament* (Philadelphia: Fortress Press).

1989   'Recent Literary Criticism', in E.J. Epp and G.W. MacRae (eds.), *The New Testament and Its Modern Interpreters* (Atlanta: Scholars Press), 175–98.

Beekman, J. and J. Callow.

1974   *Translating the Word of God* (Grand Rapids: Zondervan).

Beekman, J., J. Callow, and M.F. Kopesec.

1981   *The Semantic Structure of Written Communication* (5th revision; Dallas: Summer Institute of Linguistics).

Belleville, L.L.

1987   'Continuity or Discontinuity: A Fresh Look at 1 Corinthians in the Light of First-Century Epistolary Forms and Conventions', *EvQ* 59: 15–37.

Berger, K.

1974   'Apostelbreif apostolische Rede/Zum Formular fruhchristlicher Briefe', *ZNW* 65: 190–231.

1977   *Exegese des Neuen Testaments* (Heidelberg: Quelle & Meyer).

1984   'Hellenistiche Gattungen im Neuen Testament', *ANRW* 25.2 (ed. Hildegaard Temporini and Wolfgang Haase; Berlin: Walter de Gruyter): 1031–1432.

Bernard, J.H.

1906   *The Pastoral Epistles* (Cambridge: Cambridge University Press).

Bertram, G.   'στρέφω', *TDNT*, vol. 7.

Betz, H.D.

1979   'The Literary Composition and Function of Galatians', in *Galatians: A Commentary on Paul's Letter to the Churches in Galatia* (Philadelphia: Fortress): 14–25.

Black, C.C.

1989   'Keeping Up with Recent Studies XVI: Rhetorical Criticism and Biblical Interpretation', *Exp Tim* 100: 252–58.

1990   'Rhetorical Questions: The New Testament, Classical Rhetoric, and
            Current Interpretation', *Dialog* (Minnesota) 29: 62–70.

1995   'Rhetorical Criticism', in J.B. Green (ed.), *Hearing the New
            Testament: Strategies for Interpretation* (Grand Rapids: Eerdmans):
            256–78.

Black, D.A.
1988   *Linguistics for Students of New Testament Greek* (Grand Rapids:
            Baker).

1992   ed. *Linguistics and New Testament Interpretation, Essays on
            Discourse Analysis* (Nashville: Broadman).

Blass, F. and A. Debrunner.
1961   *A Greek Grammar of the New Testament and Other Early Christian
            Literature* (trans. and ed. R.W. Funk; Chicago: University of
            Chicago Press).

Blight, R.C.
1977   *A Literary-Semantic Analysis of Paul's First Discourse to Timothy*
            (Dallas: Summer Institute of Linguistics).

Blomberg, C.L.
1989   'The Structure of 2 Corinthians 1–7' *CTR* 4: 3–20.

Bockmuehl, M.N.A.
1990   *Revelation and Mystery in Ancient Judaism and Pauline Christianity*
            (WUNT 2.36; Tübingen: Mohr).

Bodner, K.D.
1996   'Illuminating Personality: The Dynamics of Characterization in
            Biblical Hebrew' (unpublished PhD thesis, University of Aber-
            deen).

Boers, H.
1975   'The Form-Critical Study of Paul's Letters: 1 Thessalonians as a
            Case Study', *NTS* 22: 140–58.

Bornkamm, G. 'μυστήριον', *TDNT*, vol. 4.
            'πρέσβυς', *TDNT*, vol. 6.

Botha, Pieter J.J.
1993   'The Verbal Art of the Pauline Letters: Rhetoric, Performance and
            Presence', in S.E. Porter and T.H. Olbricht (eds.), *Rhetoric and the
            New Testament, Essays from the 1992 Heidelberg Conference*
            (JSNTSup 90; Sheffield: JSOT Press): 409–28.

Bowman, A.L.
1992   'Women in Ministry: An Exegetical Study of 1 Timothy 2:11–15',
            BSac 149: 193–213.

Bradley, D.G.
1953   'The Topos as a Form in the Pauline Parenesis', *JBL* 72: 238–46.

Breck, J.
1987   'Biblical Chiasmus: Exploring Structure for Meaning', *BTB* 17: 70–
            74.

Brett, M.

1990 'Four or Five Things to do with Texts: A Taxonomy of Interpretive Interests', in D.J.A. Clines, S.E. Fowl, and S.E. Porter (eds.), *The Bible in Three Dimensions: Essays in Celebration of Forty Years of Biblical Studies in the University of Sheffield* (JSOTSup 87; Sheffield: JSOT Press): 359–73.

Brown, G. and G. Yule.

1983 *Discourse Analysis* (Cambridge: Cambridge University Press).

Brown, L.A.

1992 'Asceticism and Ideology: The Language of Power in the Pastoral Epistles', *Semeia* 57: 77–94.

Brox, N.

1969a *Die Pastoralbriefe* (Regensburg: Verlag Friedrich Pustet).

1969b 'Zu den personlichen Notizen der Pastoralbriefe', *BZ* 13: 76–94.

Bush, P.G.

1990 'A Note on the Structure of 1 Timothy', *NTS* 36: 152–56.

Byrskog, S.

1997 'Epistolography, Rhetoric and Letter Prescript: Romans 1.1–7 as a Test Case', *JSNT* 65: 27–46.

Callow, K.

1974 *Discourse Considerations in Translating the Word of God* (Grand Rapids: Zondervan).

Calvin, J.

1861 *Commentaries on the Epistles to Timothy, Titus, and Philemon* (trans. from Latin by W. Pringle; Edinburgh: Calvin Translation Society).

Campbell, A.

1992 'Do the Work of an Evangelist', *EQ* 64: 117–29.

Campbell, R.A.

1994 'Identifying the Faithful Sayings in the Pastoral Epistles', *JSNT* 54: 73–86.

Caragounis, C.

2000 'Dionysius Halikamasseus, the Art of Composition and the Apostle Paul', *Journal of Greco-Roman Christianity and Judaism* 1: 25–54.

Carcipino, J.

1951 *Cicero: The Secrets of His Correspondence I* (London: Routledge and Kegan Paul; reprint Westport, CT: Greenwoood, 1969; French original, 1947).

Champion, L.G.

1934 *Benedictions and Doxologies in the Epistles of Paul* (Oxford: Kemp Hall Press).

Clark, D.J.

1975 'Criteria for Identifying Chiasm', *Linguistica Biblica* 35: 63–72.

Classen, C.J.

1993 'St. Paul's Epistles and Ancient Greek and Roman Rhetoric', in S.E. Porter and T.H. Olbricht (eds.), *Rhetoric and the New*

Testament, Essays from the 1992 Heidelberg Conference (JSNTSup 90; Sheffield: JSOT Press): 265–91.

1997   'A Rhetorical Reading of the Epistle to Titus', in S.E. Porter and T.H. Olbricht (eds.), *The Rhetorical Analysis of Scripture, Essays from the 1995 London Conference* (JSNTSup 146; Sheffield: Sheffield Academic Press): 427–44.

2000   *Rhetorical Criticism of the New Testament* (WUNT 128; Tübingen: Mohr Siebeck).

Coggins, R.
1984   'Keeping up with Recent Studies; X. The Literary Approach to the Bible', *ExpTim* 96: 9–14.

Collins, J.J.
1961   'Chiasmus, the ABA Pattern and the Text of Paul' in *Studiorum Paulinorum Congressus Internationalis Catholicus* (vol. 2; Rome: Editrice Pontifico Istituto Biblico): 575–83.

Collins, R.F.
1975   'The Image of Paul in the Pastorals', *LTP* 31: 147–73

1998   'The Theology of the Epistle to Titus', unpublished paper presented to the Disputed Paulines Group, SBL Annual Meeting.

Cook, D.
1982   '2 Timothy 4:6–8 and the Epistle to the Philippians', *JTS* ns 33: 168–71.

1984   'The Pastoral Fragments Reconsidered', *JTS* ns 35: 120–31.

Cotterell, P.
1997   'Linguistics, Meaning, Semantics, and Discourse Analysis', in W.A. VanGemeren (ed.), *The New International Dictionary of Old Testament Theology and Exegesis* (vol. 1, Carlisle: Paternoster): 134–60.

Cotterell, P., and M. Turner.
1989   *Linguistics and Biblical Interpretation* (Downers Grove, IL: IVP).

Couser, G.A.
1992   'God and Christian Existence in 1 and 2 Timothy and Titus' (unpublished PhD Thesis, Aberdeen).

2000   'God and Christian Existence in the Pastoral Epistles: Toward Theological Method and Meaning', *NovT* 42: 262–83.

Cranfield, C.E.B.
1982   'Changes of Person and Number in Paul's Epistles', in M.D. Hooker and S.G. Wilson (eds.), *Paul and Paulinism* (London: SPCK): 280–89.

Culpepper, R.A.
1983   *Anatomy of the Fourth Gospel: A Study in Literary Design* (Philadelphia: Fortress).

Dahl, N.
1977   'The Missionary Theology in the Epistle to the Romans', in *Studies in Paul* (Minneapolis: Augsburg): 70–94.
Dalton, W.J.
1989   *Christ's Proclamation to the Spirits: A Study of 1 Peter 3:18–4:6* (An Bib 23 Rome: Pontifical Biblical Institute; 2nd edn).
Dana, H.E. and J.R. Mantey.
1957   *A Manual Grammar of the Greek New Testament* (New York: Macmillan Publishing Co.).
Davies, M.
1996   *The Pastoral Epistles* (Sheffield: Sheffield Academic Press).
Davis, C.W.
1999   *Oral Biblical Criticism: The Influence of the Principles of Orality on the Literary Structure of Paul's Epistle to the Philippians* (JSNTSup 172; Sheffield: Sheffield Academic Press).
De Beaugrande, R.
1980   *Text, Discourse and Process: Toward a Multidisciplinary Science of Texts* (Norwood, NJ: Ablex).
Deissmann, A.
1901   *Bible Studies. Contributions Chiefly from Papyri and Inscriptions to the History of the Language, the Literature, and the Religion of Hellenistic Judaism and Primitive Christianity* (Edinburgh: T&T Clark).

1927   *Light from the Ancient East* (transl. L.R.M. Strachan; New York: Geoge H. Doran Co.; reprint, Peabody, MA: Hendrickson, 1995).
Delling, G.   'γοής', *TDNT* vol. 1: 737–38.
Denniston, J.D.
1952   *Greek Prose Style* (Oxford: Clarendon Press).

1953   *The Greek Particles* (Oxford: Clarendon Press; 2nd edn).
Dibelius, M. and H. Conzelmann.
1972   *The Pastoral Epistles* (Philadelphia: Fortress).
DiMarco, A.
1975   'Der Chiasmus in der Bibel 1. Teil: Beitrage zur strukturellen stilistik', *Linguistica Biblica* 36: 21–97.

1976a   'Der Chiasmus in der Bibel 2. Teil: Ein Beitrage zur strukturellen stilistik', *Linguistica Biblica* 37: 49–68.

1976b   'Der Chiasmus in der Bibel 3. Teil', *Linguistica Biblica* 39: 37–85.

1979   'Der Chiasmus in der Bibel IV', *Linguistica Biblica* 44: 3–70.

1993   'Rhetoric and Hermeneutic – On a Rhetorical Pattern: Chiasmus and Circularity', in S.E. Porter and T.H. Olbricht (eds.), *Rhetoric and the New Testament, Essays from the 1992 Heidelberg Conference* (JSNTSup 90; Sheffield: JSOT Press): 479–91.

Donelson, L.R.
1986 *Pseudepigraphy and Ethical Argument in the Pastoral Epistles* (HUT 22; Tübingen: Mohr).

1988 'The Structure of Ethical Argument in the Pastorals', *BTB* 18: 108–13.

Dornier, P.
1969 *Les Epîtres Pastorales* (Paris: Gabalda).

Dorsey, D.
1999 *The Literary Structure of the Old Testament: A Commentary on Genesis–Malachi* (Grand Rapids: Baker).

Doty, W.G.
1969 'The Classification of Epistolary Literature', *CBQ* 31: 183–99.

1972 *Contemporary New Testament Interpretation* (Englewood Cliffs, NJ: Prentice Hall).

1973 *Letters in Primitive Christianity* (Philadelphia: Fortress).

Easton, B.S.
1932 'New Testament Ethical Lists', *JBL* 51: 1–12.

1947 *The Pastoral Epistles* (London: SCM Press).

Ellicott, C.J.
1856 *A Critical and Grammatical Commentary on the Pastoral Epistles* (London: John W. Parker and Son).

Ellingworth, P.
1980 'The "True Saying" in 1 Timothy 3,1', *BT* 31: 443–45.

Elliot, J.K.
1968 *The Greek Text of the Epistles to Timothy and Titus* (Studies and Documents XXXVI; Salt Lake City: University of Utah Press).

Ellis, E.E.
1993 'Pastoral Letters', in G.F. Hawthorne, R.P. Martin, and D.G. Reid (eds.), *Dictionary of Paul and His Letters* (Downers Grove, IL: InterVarsity Press): 658–66.

1999 *The Making of the New Testament Documents* (Leiden: Brill).

Endberg-Pedersen, T.
1998 'What is the "Theology" of ...?', unpublished paper presented to the Theology of the Disputed Paulines Group, SBL Annual Meeting.

Exler, F.X.J.
1923 *The Form of the Ancient Greek Letter* (Washington, DC: Catholic University of America).

Falconer, R.A.
1937 *The Pastoral Epistles* (Oxford: Oxford University Press).

| 1941 | '1 Timothy 2, 14.15. Interpretative Notes', *JBL* 60: 375–79. |

Fee, G.D.

| 1988 | *1 and 2 Timothy, Titus* (Peabody, MA: Hendrickson). |

| 1990 | 'Issues in Evangelical Hermeneutics, Part III: The Great Watershed – Intentionality and Particularity/Eternality: 1 Timothy 2:8–15 as a Test Case', *Crux* 26: 31–37. |

| 1994 | *God's Empowering Presence: The Holy Spirit in the Letters of Paul* (Peabody, MA: Hendrickson). |

Fiore, B.

| 1986 | *The Function of Personal Example in the Socratic and Pastoral Epistles* (An Bib 105; Rome: Biblical Institute Press). |

Fitzgerald, J.T.

| 1997 | 'The Catalogue in Ancient Greek Literature', in S.E. Porter and T.H. Olbricht (eds.), *The Rhetorical Analysis of Scripture, Essays from the 1995 London Conference* (JSNTSup 146; Sheffield: Sheffield Academic Press): 275–93. |

Fitzmeyer, J.A.

| 1974 | 'Some Notes on Aramaic Epistolography', *JBL* 93: 201–25. |

Francis, F.O.

| 1970 | 'The Form and Function of the Opening and Closing Paragraphs of James and 1 John', *ZNW* 61: 110–26. |

Francis, F.O. and J.P. Sampley (eds.)

| 1984 | *Pauline Parallels* (Philadelphia: Fortress; 2nd edn). |

Freedman, W.

| 1971 | 'The Literary Motif: A Definition and Evaluation', *Novel* 4: 123–31. |

Fuller, J.W.

| 1983 | 'Of Elders and Triads in 1 Timothy 5:19–25', *NTS* 29: 258–63. |

Fung, R.Y.K.

| 1987 | 'Ministry in the New Testament', in D.A. Carson (ed.), *The Church in the Bible and the World: An International Study* (Grand Rapids: Baker): 154–212. |

Funk, R.W.

| 1966 | 'The Letter: Form and Style', in *Language, Hermeneutic, and Word of God: The Problem of Language in the New Testament and Contemporary Theology* (NY: Harper and Row): 250–79. |

| 1967 | 'The Apostolic *Parousia*: Form and Significance', in W.R. Farmer, C.F.D. Moule, and R.R. Niebuhr (eds.), *Christian History and Interpretation: Essays Presented to John Knox* (Cambridge: Cambridge University Press): 249–68. |

| 1970 | 'The Form and Function of the Pauline Letter', in SBL Seminar Papers (Missoula, MT: Scholars Press). |

Furnish, V.P.
    1968   *Theology and Ethics in Paul* (Nashville: Abingdon).
Garland, D.E.
    1985   'The Composition and Unity of Philippians: Some Neglected Literary Factors', *NovT* 27: 141–73.
Gealy, F.D. and M.P. Noyes
    1955   *The First and Second Epistles to Timothy and the Epistle to Titus* (The Interpreter's Bible, vol. XI; Nashville: Abingdon Press).
Gibson, R.J.
    1995   'The Literary and Theological Coherence of 1 Timothy', (unpublished Masters thesis, Australian College of Theology, Kensington, NSW).

    1996   'The Literary Coherence of 1 Timothy', *RTR* 55: 53–66.
Givón, T.
    1983   *Topic Continuity in Discourse: A Quantitative Cross-Language Study* (Amsterdam: Benjamins).

    1987   'Beyond Foreground and Background', in R.S. Tomlin (ed.), *Coherence and Grounding in Discourse* (Philadelphia: John Benjamins Publishing Company): 175–88.
Goodwin, M.J.
    1996   'The Pauline Background of the Living God as Interpretive Context for 1 Timothy 4.10', *JSNT* 61: 65–85.
Green, J.B.
    1995   'Discourse Analysis and New Testament Interpretation', in J.B. Green (ed.), *Hearing the New Testament: Strategies for Interpretation* (Grand Rapids: Eerdmans): 175–96.
Grimes, J.E.
    1975a   'Signals of Discourse Structure in Koine', SBL Seminar Papers: 151–64.

    1975b   *The Thread of Discourse* (The Hague: Mouton).
Gruenler, R.G.
    1998   'The Mission-Lifestyle Setting of 1 Tim 2:8–15', *JETS* 41: 215–38.
Grundmann, W. 'ἀγαθός', *TDNT*, vol. 1.
Gundry, R.H.
    1970   'The Form, Meaning and Background of the Hymn Quoted in 1 Timothy 3:16', in W.W. Gasque and R.P. Martin (eds.), *Apostolic History and the Gospel* (Exeter: Paternoster): 203–22.
Guthrie, D.
    1990   *The Pastoral Epistles* (London: Tyndale; 2nd edn).
Guthrie, G.H.
    1994   *The Structure of Hebrews: A Text-Linguistic Analysis* (NovT Sup 73; Leiden: Brill).

    1995   'Cohesion Shifts and Stitches in Philippians', in S.E. Porter and

D.A. Carson (eds.), *Discourse Analysis and Other Topics in Biblical Greek* (JSNTSup 113; Sheffield: Sheffield Academic Press): 36–59.

1997 'New Testament Exegesis of Hebrews and the Catholic Epistles', in S.E. Porter (ed.), *Handbook to Exegesis of the New Testament* (NTTS 25; Leiden: Brill): 591–606.

1999 'Review of Jonas Holmstrand, *Markers and Meaning in Paul*', *Biblica* 80: 144–46.

Güting, E.W., and D.L. Mealand
1998 *Asyndeton in Paul: A Text-Critical and Statistical Enquiry into Pauline Style* (Lewiston, NY: The Edwin Mellen Press).

Hackforth, R., and B.R. Rees
1970 'Letters, Greek' *OCD* (Oxford: Oxford University Press; 2nd edn).

Hagner, D.A.
1998 'Titus as a Pauline Letter', paper presented to the Disputed Paulines Group, SBL.

Halliday, M.A.K.
1994 *Introduction to Functional Grammar* (London: Arnold; 2nd edn).

Halliday, M.A.K., and R. Hasan
1976 *Cohesion in English* (London: Longman).

1980 'Text and Context: Aspects of Language in a Social-Semiotic Perspective', *Sophia Linguistica* 6: 4–90.

1989 *Language, Context, and Text: Aspects of Language in a Social-Semiotic Perspective* (Oxford: Oxford University Press).

Hansen, G.W.
1989 *Abraham in Galatians: Epistolary and Rhetorical Contexts* (JSNTSup 29; Sheffield: JSOT Press).

1993 'Rhetorical Criticism', in G.F. Hawthorne, R.P. Martin, and D.G. Reid (eds.), *Dictionary of Paul and His Letters* (Downers Grove, IL: IVP).

Hanson, A.T.
1968 *Studies in the Pastoral Epistles* (London: SPCK).

1982 *The Pastoral Epistles* (Grand Rapids: Eerdmans).

Harding, M.
1998 *Tradition and Rhetoric in the Pastoral Epistles* (Frankfurt: Lang).

2001 *What Are They Saying About the Pastoral Epistles?* (Mahwah, NJ: Paulist Press).

Harrill, J.A.
1999 'The Vice of Slave Dealers in Greco-Roman Society: The Use of a Topos in 1 Timothy 1:10', *JBL* 118: 97–122.

Harris, J.R.
1926   'The Influence of Philo upon the New Testament', *ExpTim* 37: 565–
            66.
Harris, T.J.
1990   'Why Did Paul Mention Eve's Deception? A Critique of P.W.
            Barnett's Interpretation of 1 Timothy 2', *EvQ* 62: 335–52.
Harrison, P.N.
1921   *The Problem of the Pastoral Epistles* (London: Oxford University
            Press).

1955   'Important Hypotheses Reconsidered. III. The Authorship of the
            Pastoral Epistles', *ExpTim* 67: 77–81.

1964   *Paulines and Pastorals* (London: Villiers).
Harvey, J.D.
1998   *Listening to the Text: Oral Patterning in Paul's Letters* (Grand
            Rapids: Baker).
Hayes, J.H., and C.R. Holladay
1987   *Biblical Exegesis: A Beginner's Handbook* (London: SCM Press;
            2nd edn).
Heckert, J.K.
1996   *Discourse Function of Conjoiners in the Pastoral Epistles* (Dallas:
            Summer Institute of Linguistics).
Hijmans, B.L.
1976   *Inlaboratus et Facilis: Aspects of Structure in Some Letters of
            Seneca* (Leiden: E.J. Brill).
Ho, C.E.
2000   'Do the Work of an Evangelist: The Missionary Outlook of the
            Pastoral Epistles' (unpublished PhD thesis, University of Aberd-
            een).
Holmes, J.M.
2000   *Text in a Whirlwind: A Critique of Four Exegetical Devices at 1
            Timothy 2.9–15* (JSNTSup 196; SNTG 7; Sheffield: Sheffield
            Academic Press).
Holmstrand, J.
1997   *Markers and Meaning in Paul: An Analysis of 1 Thessalonians,
            Philippians, and Galatians* (ConBNT 28; Stockholm: Almqvist &
            Wiksell).
Holtz, G.
1972   *Die Pastoralbriefe* (Berlin: Evangelische Verlagsanstalt).
Holtzmann, H.J.
1880   *Die Pastoralbriefe, Kritisch und Exegetisch Behandelt* (Leipzig:
            Engelmann).
Hort, F.J.A.
1894   'The Pastoral Epistles', in *Judaistic Christianity: A Course of
            Lectures* (Cambridge and London: Macmillan): 130–46.

Houlden, J.L.
1976   *The Pastoral Epistles* (Harmondsworth: Penguin; reprint, London: SCM Press, 1989).

House, P.R.
1992   'The Rise and Current Status of Literary Criticism of the Old Testament', in P.R. House (ed.), *Beyond Form Criticism: Essays in Old Testament Literary Criticism* (Winona Lake, IN: Eisenbrauns): 3–22.

Jervis, L.A.
1991   *The Purpose of Romans: A Comparative Letter Structure Investigation* (JSNTSup 55; Sheffield: JSOT Press).

1999   'Paul the Poet in First Timothy 1:11–17; 2:3b-7; 3:14–16', *CBQ* 61: 695–712.

Jewett, R.
1969   'The Form and Function of the Homiletic Benediction', *ATR* 51: 18–34.

Johanson, B.C.
1987   *To All the Brethren: A Text-Linguistic and Rhetorical Approach to 1 Thessalonians* (ConBNT 16; Uppsala: Almqvist & Wiksell).

Johnson, L.T.
1978   'II Timothy and the Polemic against False Teachers: A Re-examination', *Ohio Journal of Religious Studies* 6: 1–26.

1988   'Review of *Pseudepigraphy and Ethical Argument in the Pastoral Epistles*, by L.R. Donelson', in *CBQ* 50: 131–33.

1996   *Letters to Paul's Delegates: 1 Timothy, 2 Timothy, Titus* (Valley Forge, PA: Trinity Press International).

2001   *The First and Second Letters to Timothy* (New York: Doubleday).

Karris, R.J.
1971   'The Function and Sitz im Leben of the Parenetic Elements in the Pastoral Epistles' (unpublished dissertation, Harvard University).

1973   'The Background and Significance of the Polemic of the Pastoral Epistles', *JBL* 92: 549–64.

1979   *The Pastoral Epistles* (Wilmington, DE: Michael Glazier).

Katsouris, A.G.
1975   *Linguistic and Stylistic Characterization: Tragedy and Menander* (Joannina: University Press).

Kelly, J.N.D.
1963   *A Commentary on the Pastoral Epistles* (London: A. and C. Black; reprint, Grand Rapids: Baker, 1981).

Kennedy, G.A.
    1984   *New Testament Interpretation through Rhetorical Criticism* (Chapel
                Hill: The University of North Carolina Press).
Kern, P.H.
    1998   *Rhetoric and Galatians, Assessing an Approach to Paul's Epistle*
                (SNTSMS 101; Cambridge: Cambridge University Press).
Keyes, C.W.
    1935   'The Greek Letter of Introduction', *American Journal of Philology*
                56: 28–44.
Kidd, R.M.
    1990   *Wealth and Beneficence in the Pastoral Epistles* (SBLDS 122;
                Atlanta: Scholars Press).

    1998   'Reflections on the Theology of Titus: A Response', paper
                presented to the Disputed Paulines Group, SBL.
Kim, C.-H.
    1972   *The Familiar Letter of Recommendation* (SBLDS 4; Missoula, MT:
                Scholars Press).

    1975   'The Papyrus Invitation', *JBL* 94: 391–402.
Kittel, G.   'αὐτάρκεια', *TDNT*, vol. 1.
Kittel, G., and G.F.
    1964–76   *Theological Dictionary of the New Testament* (ed, and trans. G.W.
                Bromiley; 10 vols; Grand Rapids: Eerdmans).
Knight, G.W. III.
    1992   *The Pastoral Epistles: A Commentary on the Greek Text* (Grand
                Rapids/Carlisle: Eerdmans/Paternoster).
Köstenberger, A.J.
    1995   'Syntactical Background Studies to 1 Timothy 2.12 in the New
                Testament and Extrabiblical Greek Literature', in S.E. Porter and
                D.A. Carson (eds.), *Discourse Analysis and Other Topics in Biblical
                Greek* (Sheffield: Sheffield Academic Press): 156–79.
Kraftchick, S.
    1998   'A Synthetic Overview of Issues Related to the Theology of the
                Disputed Paulines', unpublished paper presented to the Theology
                of the Disputed Paulines Group, SBL Annual Meeting.
Kramer, W.
    1966   *Christ, Lord, Son of God* (London: SCM Press).
Labov, W.
    1972   *Sociolinguistic Patterns* (Philadelphia: University of Pennsylvania
                Press).
Läger, K.
    1996   *Die Christologie der Pastoralbriefe* (Hamburger Theologische
                Studien 12; Munster: Lit).
Lambrecht, J.
    1989   'Rhetorical Criticism and the New Testament', *Bijdragen, Tijds-
                chrift voor Filosofie en Theolgie* 50: 239–53.

Lampe, G.W.H.
1961   *A Patristic Greek Lexicon* (Oxford: Clarendon Press).
Lau, A.
1996   *Manifest in the Flesh* (WUNT 2.86; Tübingen: J.C.B. Mohr [Paul Siebeck]).
Leaney, A.R.C.
1960   *The Epistles to Timothy, Titus, and Philemon* (London: SCM Press).
Levinsohn, S.H.
1989   'Phrase Order and the Article in Galatians: A Functional Sentence-Perspective Approach', *Occasional Papers in Translation and Textlinguistics* 3: 44–64.

1999   'Some Constraints on Discourse Development in the Pastoral Epistles', in S.E. Porter and J.T. Read (eds.), *Discourse Analysis and the New Testament* (JSNTSup 170; Sheffield: Sheffield Academic Press): 316–33.
Liddell, H.G., and R. Scott
1940   *A Greek-English Lexicon* (rev. H.S. Jones; Oxford: Clarendon Press).

Lock, W.
1924   *The Pastoral Epistles* (Edinburgh: T. & T. Clark).
Lohfink, G.
1981   'Paulinische Theologie in der Rezeption der Pastoralbriefe', in K. Kertlege (ed.), *Paulus in den neutestamentlichen Spätschriften: Zur Paulusrezeption im Neuen Testament* (Freiburg: Herder): 70–121.
Longacre, R.E.
1976   *An Anatomy of Speech Notions* (Lisse: Peter de Ridder).
Longenecker, B.W.
2001   '"Linked Like a Chain": Rev 22.6–9 in Light of an Ancient Transition Technique', *NTS* 47: 105–17.
Longenecker, R.N.
1990   *Galatians* (Dallas: Word).
Longman, T.
1996   'Literary Approaches to Biblical Interpretation', in M. Silva (ed.), *Foundations of Contemporary Interpretation* (Grand Rapids: Zondervan).
Louw, J.P.
1973   'Discourse Analysis and the Greek New Testament', *BT* 24: 101–18.

1982   *Semantics of New Testament Greek* (Philadelphia: Fortress).
Louw, J.P., and E.A. Nida, *et al.*
1989   *Greek–English Lexicon of the New Testament Based on Semantic Domains I* (2 vols; New York: United Bible Societies; 2nd edn).
Lund, N.
1942   *Chiasmus in the New Testament* (Chapel Hill: University of North Carolina).

McEleney, N.J.
  1974   'The Vice Lists of the Pastoral Epistles', *CBQ* 63: 203–219.
McGuire, M.R.P.
  1960   'Letters and Letter Carriers in Christian Antiquity', *Classical World*
                53: 150.
McKnight, E.V.
  1992   'Literary Criticism', in J.B. Green, S. McKnight, and I.H. Marshall
                (eds.), *Dictionary of Jesus and the Gospels* (Downers Grove, IL:
                InterVarsity Press).
Mack, B.L.
  1990   *Rhetoric and The New Testament* (Minneapolis: Fortress Press).
Malbon, E.S. and E.V. McKnight (eds.)
  1994   *The New Literary Criticism and the New Testament* (JSNTSup 109;
                Sheffield: Sheffield Academic Press).
Malherbe, A.J.
  1980   'Medical Imagery in the Pastoral Epistles', in W.E. March (ed.),
                *Texts and Testaments: Critical Essays on the Bible and Early
                Christian Fathers* (San Antonio: Trinity University Press): 19–35.

  1984   '"In Season and Out of Season": 2 Timothy 4:2', *JBL* 103: 235–43.

  1986   *Moral Exhortation, A Greco-Roman Sourcebook* (Philadelphia:
                Westminster Press).

  1988   *Ancient Epistolary Theorists* (Atlanta: Scholars Press).

  1998   'Response to Raymond Collins, Donald Hagner, Bonnie
                Thurston', paper presented to the Disputed Paulines Group, SBL.
Marrou, H.I.
  1956   *A History of Education in Antiquity* (trans. George Lamb; New
                York: Sheed and Ward).
Marshall, I.H.
  1984   'Faith and Works in the Pastoral Epistles', *SNT(SU)* 9: 203–18.

  1988   'The Christology of the Pastoral Epistles', *SNT(SU)* 13: 157–77.

  1993   '"Sometimes Only Orthodox" – Is there More to the Pastoral
                Epistles?', *Epworth Review* 20.3: 12–24.

  1994   'The Christology of Luke-Acts and the Pastoral Epistles', in S.E.
                Porter, P. Joyce, and D.E. Orton (eds.), *Crossing Boundaries:
                Essays in Biblical Interpretation in Honor of Michael D. Goulder*
                (Leiden: Brill): 167–82.

  1996   'Prospects for the Pastoral Epistles', in D. Lewis and A. McGrath
                (eds.), *Doing Theology for the People of God: Studies in Honor of
                J.I. Packer* (Downers Grove, IL: InterVarsity): 137–55.

1997   'Recent Study of the Pastoral Epistles', *Themelios* 23.1: 3–29.

1999   *A Critical and Exegetical Commentary on the Pastoral Epistles* (Edinburgh: T. & T. Clark).

2003   'The Pastoral Epistles in (very) Recent Study', *Midwestern Journal of Theology* 2.1: 3–37.

Martin, S.C.
1997   *Pauli Testamentum: 2 Timothy and the Last Words of Moses* (Rome: Gregorian University Press).

Martin, T.W.
1992   *Metaphor and Composition in 1 Peter* (SBLDS 131; Atlanta: Scholars Press).

Meier, J.P.
1973   '*Presbyteros* in the Pastoral Epistles', *CBQ* 35: 323–45.

Meecham, H.G.
1923   *Light from Ancient Letters* (NY: Macmillan).

Merkel, H.
1991   *Die Pastoralbriefe* (Göttingen: Vandenhoeck und Ruprecht).

Metzger, B.M.
1971   *A Textual Commentary on the Greek New Testament* (Stuttgart: United Bible Societies).

Meynet, R.
1998   *Rhetorical Analysis: An Introduction to Biblical Rhetoric* (JSOTSup 256; Sheffield: Sheffield Academic Press).

Michel, O.
1948   'Grundfragen der Pastoralbriefe', in M. Loeser (ed.), *Auf dem Grunde der Apostel und Propheten* (Stuttgart: Kohlhammer): 83–99.

Miller, J.D.
1997   *The Pastoral Letters as Composite Documents* (SNTSMS 93; Cambridge: Cambridge University Press).

Mitchell, M.M.
1992   'NT Envoys in the Context of Greco-Roman Diplomatic and Epistolary Conventions: The Example of Timothy and Titus', *JBL* 111: 641–62.

2001   'P. Tebt. 703 and the Genre of 1 Timothy', unpublished paper presented to the 'Papyrology and Early Christian Backgrounds Consultation' at SBL.

Moffat, J.
1918   *An Introduction to the Literature of the New Testament* (Edinburgh: T & T Clark; 3rd rev. edn).

Moo, D.J.
1980   '1 Timothy 2:11–15: Meaning and Significance', *TrinJ* 1 ns.: 62–83.

Moule, C.F.D.
    1953   *An Idiom Book of New Testament Greek* (Cambridge: Cambridge
                University Press).

    1965   'The Problem of the Pastoral Epistles: A Reappraisal', *BJRL* 47:
                430–52.
Moulton, J.H.
    1903   'Notes from the Papyri', *Expositor*, 6th series, 7: 104–21.
Moulton, J.H. and W. Milligan
    1914–29   *The Vocabulary of the Greek Testament Illustrated from the Papyri
                and Other Non-literary Sources* (London: Hodder and Stoughton).
Mounce, W.D.
    2000   *Pastoral Epistles* (Nashville: Thomas Nelson).
Muilenberg, J.
    1969   'Form Criticism and Beyond', *JBL* 88: 1–18; repr. in P.R. House
                (ed.), *Beyond Form Criticism: Essays in Old Testament Literary
                Criticism* (Winona Lake, IN: Eisenbrauns, 1992): 46–69.
Müller-Bardorff, J.
    1958   'Zur Exegese von 1 Tim 5,3–16', in G. Delling (ed.), *Gott und die
                Götter* (Berlin: Evangelische Verlagsanstalt): 113–33.
Mullins, T.Y.
    1962   'Petition as a Literary Form', *NovT* 5: 46–54.

    1964   'Disclosure: A Literary Form in the NT', *NovT* 7: 44–50.

    1968   'Greeting as a NT Form', *JBL* 87: 418–426.

    1972   'Formulas in NT Epistles', *JBL* 91: 380–90.

    1972–73   'Ascription as a Literary Form', *NTS* 19: 194–205.

    1973   'Visit Talk in New Testament Letters', *CBQ* 35: 350–58.

    1977   'Benediction as a New Testament Form', *AUSS* 15: 59–64.
Murphy-O'Connor, J.
    1995   *Paul the Letter-Writer, His World, His Options, His Skills*
                (Collegeville, MN: Michael Glazier).
Neumann, K.J.
    1993   'Major Variations in Pauline and Other Epistles in Light of Genre
                and the Pauline Letter From', in B.H. McLean (ed.), *Origins and
                Method: Towards a New Understanding of Judaism and Christianity*
                (JSNTSup 86; Sheffield: JSOT Press): 199–211.
Nida, E.A.
    1999   'The Role of Context in the Understanding of Discourse', in S.E.
                Porter and J.T. Reed (eds.), *Discourse Analysis and the New
                Testament* (JSNTSup 170; Sheffield: Sheffield Academic Press): 20–
                27.

Nida, E.A., J.P. Louw, A.H. Snyman, and J.v.W. Cronje
   1983   *Style and Discourse: With Special Reference to the Text of the Greek New Testament* (Cape Town, South Africa: Bible Society of South Africa).

Oberlinner, L.
   1980   'Die "Epiphaneia" des Heilswillens Gottes in Christus Jesus: Zur Grundstruktur der Christologie der Pastoralbriefe', *ZNW* 71: 192–213.

   1994   *Die Pastoralbriefe. Erste Folge. Kommentar zum Ersten Timotheusbrief* (Freiburg: Herder).

   1995   *Die Pastoralbriefe. Zweite Folge. Kommentar zum Zweiten Timotheusbrief* (Freiburg: Herder).

   1996   *Die Pastoralbriefe. Dritte Folge. Kommentar zum Titusbrief* (Freiburg: Herder).

O'Brien, P.T.
   1977   *Introductory Thanksgivings in the Letters of Paul* (NovTSup 49; Leiden: Brill).

   1993   'Letters, Letter Forms', in G.F. Hawthorne, R.P. Martin, and D.G. Reid (eds.), *Dictionary of Paul and His Letters* (Downers Grove, IL: InterVarsity Press).

Olbricht, T.H.
   1990   'An Aristotelian Rhetorical Analysis of 1 Thessalonians', in D. Balch, E. Ferguson, and W.A. Meeks (eds.), *Greeks, Romans, and Christians: Essays in Honor of Abraham J. Malherbe* (Minneapolis: Fortress): 216–31.

Olsson, B.
   1985   'A Decade of Text-Linguistic Analyses of Biblical Texts at Uppsala', *Studia Theologica* 39: 107–26.

Osborne, G.R.
   1993   'Hermeneutics/Interpreting Paul', in G.F. Hawthorne, R.P. Martin, and D.G. Reid (eds.), *Dictionary of Paul and His Letters* (Downers Grove, IL: InterVarsity Press).

Padgett, A.
   1987a   'The Pauline Rationale for Submission: Biblical Feminism and the *hina* Clauses of Titus 2:1–10', *EQ* 59: 39–52.

   1987b   'Wealthy Women at Ephesus: 1 Timothy 2:8–15 in Social Context', *Interpretation* 41: 19–31.

Palmer, M.W.
   1995   *Levels of Constituent Structure in New Testament Greek* (Studies in Biblical Greek 4; New York: Peter Lang).

Pardee, D.
   1978   'An Overview of Ancient Hebrew Epistolography', *JBL* 97: 321–46.

Parry, R.StJ.
 1920   *The Pastoral Epistles* (Cambridge: Cambridge University Press).
Parunak, H.V.D.
 1981   'Oral Typesetting: Some Uses of Biblical Structure', *Biblica* 62: 153–68.

 1983   'Transitional Techniques in the Bible', *JBL* 102: 525–48.

 1992   'Dimensions of Discourse Structure: A Multidimensional Analysis of the Components and Transitions of Paul's Epistle to the Galatians', in D.A. Black (ed.), *Linguistics and New Testament Interpretation: Essays on Discourse Analysis* (Nashville: Broadman): 207–39.
Pearson, B.W.R.
 1997   'New Testament Literary Criticism', in S.E. Porter (ed.), *Handbook to Exegesis of the New Testament* (NTTS 25; Leiden: Brill): 241–66.
Pearson, B.W.R. and S.E. Porter
 1997   'The Genres of the New Testament', in S.E. Porter (ed.), *Handbook to Exegesis of the New Testament* (NTTS 25; Leiden: Brill).
Pease, E.M.
 1902   'The Greetings in the Letters of Cicero', in *Studies in Honor of Basil L. Gildersleeve* (Baltimore: Johns Hopkins Press): 395–404.
Perriman, A.C.
 1993   'What Eve Did, What Women Shouldn't Do: The Meaning of ΑΥΘΕΝΤΕΩ in 1 Timothy 2:12', *TynBul* 44: 129–42.
Pervo, R.I.
 1994   'Romancing an Oft-Neglected Stone: The Pastoral Epistles and the Epistolary Novel', *Journal of Higher Criticism* 1: 25–48.
Petersen, N.R.
 1978   *Literary Criticism for New Testament Critics* (Philadelphia: Fortress).

 1980   'Literary Criticism in Biblical Studies', in *Orientation by Disorientation: Studies in Literary Criticism and Biblical Literary Criticism* (Pittsburgh: The Pickwick Press).
Peterson, E.
 1926   ΕΙΣ ΘΕΟΣ: *Epigraphische, formgeschichtliche Untersuchungen* (Göttingen: Vandenhoeck & Ruprecht).
Pfitzner, V.C.
 1967   *Paul and the Agon Motif: Traditional Athletic Imagery in the Pauline Literature* (Leiden: Brill).
Porter, S.E.
 1992   *Idioms of the Greek New Testament* (Sheffield: JSOT Press).

 1993a   'The Theoretical Justification for Application of Rhetorical Categories to Pauline Epistolary Literature', in S.E. Porter and T.H. Olbricht (eds.), *Rhetoric and the New Testament, Essays from the 1992 Heidelberg Conference* (JSNTSup 90, Sheffield: JSOT Press): 100–22.

1993b   'What does it mean to be "saved by Childbirth" (1 Timothy 2:15)?', *JSNT* 49: 87–102.

1995a   'Discourse Analysis and New Testament Studies: An Introductory Survey', in S.E. Porter and D.A. Carson (eds.), *Discourse Analysis and Other Topics in Biblical Greek* (JSNTSup 113; Sheffield: Sheffield Academic Press): 14–35.

1995b   'How Can Biblical Discourse Be Analyzed? A Response to Several Attempts', in S.E. Porter and D.A. Carson (eds.), *Discourse Analysis and Other Topics in Biblical Greek* (JSNTSup 113; Sheffield: Sheffield Academic Press): 107–16.

1995c   'Literary Approaches to the New Testament: From Formalism to Deconstruction and Back', in S.E. Porter and D. Tombs (eds.), *Approaches to New Testament Study* (JSNTSup 120; Sheffield: Sheffield Academic Press): 77–128.

1997a   'Ancient Rhetorical Analysis and Discourse Analysis of the Pauline Corpus', in S.E. Porter and T.H. Olbricht (eds.), *The Rhetorical Analysis of Scripture, Essays from the 1995 London Conference* (JSNTSup 146; Sheffield: Sheffield Academic Press): 249–74.

1997b   'Exegesis of the Pauline Letters, Including the Deutero-Pauline Letters', in S.E. Porter (ed.), *Handbook to Exegesis of the New Testament* (Leiden: Brill): 503–63.

1997c   'Introduction: The London Papers in Perspective', in S.E. Porter and T.H. Olbricht (eds.), *The Rhetorical Analysis of Scripture, Essays from the 1995 London Conference* (JSNTSup 146; Sheffield: Sheffield Academic Press): 17–21.

1997d   (ed.) *A Handbook on Classical Rhetoric in the Hellenistic Period (330 BC–AD 400)* (Leiden: Brill).

1997e   (ed.) *Handbook to Exegesis of the New Testament* (NTTS 25; Leiden: Brill).

1997f   'Paul of Tarsus and His Letters', in S.E. Porter (ed.), *A Handbook on Classical Rhetoric in the Hellenistic Period (330 BC-AD 400)* (Leiden: Brill): 533–85.

1999   (ed.) *Discourse Analysis and the New Testament* (JSNTSup 170; Sheffield: Sheffield Academic Press).

Porter, S.E., and D.A. Carson (eds.)
1995   *Discourse Analysis and Other Topics in Biblical Greek* (JSNTSup 113; Sheffield: Sheffield Academic Press).
Porter, S.E., and D.A. Carson (eds.)
1999   *Linguistics and the New Testament: Critical Junctions* (JSNTSup 168; SNTG 5; Sheffield: Sheffield Academic Press).
Porter, S.E., and L.M. McDonald.
1995   *New Testament Introduction* (Grand Rapids: Baker Books).
Porter, S.E., and T.H. Olbricht (eds.).
1993   *Rhetoric and the New Testament, Essays from the 1992 Heidelberg Conference* (JSNTSup 90; Sheffield: JSOT Press).
Porter, S.E., and T.H. Olbricht (eds.)
1997   *The Rhetorical Analysis of Scripture, Essays from the 1995 London Conference* (JSNTSup 146; Sheffield: Sheffield Academic Press).
Porter, S.E., and J.T. Reed.
1991   'Greek Grammar since BDF: A Retrospective and Prospective Analysis', *FN* 4.8: 143–64.
Porter, S.E., and J.T. Reed (eds.)
1999   *Discourse Analysis and the New Testament: Approaches and Results* (JSNTSup170; SNTG 4; Sheffield: Sheffield Academic Press).
Porter, S.E., and D.L. Stamps (eds.)
1999   *The Rhetorical Interpretation of Scripture: Essays from the 1996 Malibu Conference* (JSNTSup 180; Sheffield: Sheffield Academic Press).
Poythress, V.S.
1984   'The Use of Intersentence Conjunctions *De, Oun, Kai,* and Asyndeton in the Gospel of John', *NovT*: 312–37.
Prior, M.
1989   *Paul the Letter-Writer and the Second Letter to Timothy* (JSNTSup 23; Sheffield: JSOT Press).
Qimron, E., and J. Strugnell.
1985   'An Unpublished Halakhic Letter from Qumran', in *Biblical Archaeology Today: Proceedings of the International Congress on Biblical Archaeology, April 1984, Jerusalem* (Jerusalem: Israel Exploration Society).
Quinn, J.D.
1980   'Paul's Last Captivity', in E. Livingstone (ed.), *Studia Biblica 3* (JSNTSup 3; Sheffield: Sheffield Academic Press): 289–98.

1989   'Tertullian and 1 Timothy 5:22 on Imposing Hands: Paul Galtier Revisited', in E.A. Livingstone (ed.), *Studia Patristica XXI* (Leuven: Peeters): 268–70.

1990   *The Letter to Titus* (New York: Doubleday).
Quinn, J.D., and W.C. Wacker.
2000   *The First and Second Letters to Timothy* (Grand Rapids: Eerdmans).

Reed, J.T.

1992   'Cohesive Ties in 1 Timothy: In Defense of the Epistle's Unity', *Neotestamentica* 26/1: 192–213.

1993a   'Discourse Features in New Testament Letters, with Special Reference to the structure of 1 Timothy', *Journal of Translation and Textlinguistics* 6: 228–52.

1993b   'To Timothy or Not? A Discourse Analysis of 1 Timothy', in S.E. Porter and D.A. Carson (eds.), *Biblical Greek Language and Linguistics* (JSNTS 80; Sheffield: JSOT Press): 90–118.

1993c   'Using Ancient Rhetorical Categories to Interpret Paul's Letters: A Question of Genre', in S.E. Porter and T.H. Olbricht (eds.), *Rhetoric and the New Testament, Essays from the 1992 Heidelberg Conference* (JSNTSup 90; Sheffield: JSOT Press): 292–324.

1995a   'Identifying Theme in the New Testament: Insights from Discourse Analysis', in S.E. Porter and D.A. Carson (eds.), *Discourse Analysis and Other Topics in Biblical Greek* (JSNTSup 113; Sheffield: Sheffield Academic Press): 75–101.

1995b   'Modern Linguistics and the New Testament: A Basic Guide to Theory, Terminology, and Literature', in S.E. Porter and D. Tombs (eds.), *Approaches to New Testament Study* (JSNTSup20; Sheffield: Sheffield Academic Press): 222–65.

1996a   'Are Paul's Thanksgivings "Epistolary"?', *JSNT* 61: 87–99.

1996b   'Discourse Analysis as a New Testament Hermeneutic: A Retrospective and Prospective Appraisal', *JETS* 39: 223–40.

1997a   'Discourse Analysis', in S.E. Porter (ed.), *Handbook to Exegesis of the New Testament* (NTTS 25; Leiden: Brill): 189–217.

1997b   *A Discourse Analysis of Philippians, Method and Rhetoric in the Debate over Literary Integrity* (JSNTSup 136; Sheffield: Sheffield Academic Press).

1997c   'The Epistle', in S.E. Porter (ed.), *A Handbook on Classical Rhetoric in the Hellenistic Period (330 BC-AD 400)* (Leiden: Brill): 171–93.

1999a   'The Cohesiveness of Discourse: Towards a Model of Linguistic Criteria for Analyzing New Testament Discourse', in S.E. Porter and J.T. Reed (eds.), *Discourse Analysis and the New Testament* (JSNTSup 170; Sheffield: Sheffield Academic Press): 28–46.

1999b   'Modern Linguistics and Historical Criticism: Using the Former for Doing the Latter', in S.E. Porter and D.A. Carson (eds.), *Linguistics and the New Testament: Critical Junctions* (JSNTSup 168; SNTG 5; Sheffield: Sheffield Academic Press): 36–62.

Richards, E.R.
1991   *The Secretary in the Letters of Paul* (WUNT 24.2; Tübingen: J.C.B. Mohr).

Rigaux, B.
1968   *Letters of St. Paul: Modern Studies* (trans. S. Yonick; Chicago: Franciscan Herald Press).

Robbins, V.K.
1996   *Exploring the Texture of Texts: A Guide to Socio-Rhetorical Interpretation* (Valley Forge, PA: Trinity Press International).

Robbins, V.K., and J.H. Patton
1980   'Rhetoric and Biblical Criticism', *Quarterly Journal of Speech* 66: 327–50.

Roberts, J.H.
1986a   'Pauline Transitions to the Letter Body', in A. Vanhoye (ed.), *L'Apôtre Paul. Personnalité style et conception, du ministère* (BETL 73; Leuven: Peeters).

1986b   'Transitional Techniques to the Letter Body in the *Corpus Paulinum*', in J.H. Petzer and P.J. Hartin (eds.), *A South African Perspective on the New Testament: Essays by South African New Testament Scholars presented to Bruce Manning Metzger during his Visit to South Africa in 1985* (Leiden: Brill): 187–213.

Roetzel, C.
1969   'The Judgment From in Paul's Letters', *JBL* 88: 305–12.

Roller, O.
1993   *Das Formular der Paulinischen Briefe: Ein Beitrag zur Lehre vom antiken Briefe* (Stuttgart: Kohlhammer).

Roloff, J.
1988   *Der Erste Brief an Timotheus* (Zürich/Neukirchen-Vluyn: Benziger/ Neukirchener).

Rowe, Galen O.
1997   'Style', in S.E. Porter (ed.), *A Handbook on Classical Rhetoric in the Hellenistic Period (330 BC–AD 400)* (Leiden: Brill): 121–57.

Russell, R.
1982   'Pauline Letter Structure in Philippians', *JETS* 25: 295–306.

Sanders, J.T.
1962   'The Transition from Opening Epistolary Thanksgiving to Body in the Letters of the Pauline Corpus', *JBL* 81: 348–62.

Schiffrin, D.
1994   *Approaches to Discourse* (Oxford: Basil Blackwell).

Schlarb, E.
1990   *Die gesunde Lehre: Häresie und Wahrheit im Spiegel der Pastoral-briefe* (Marburg: Elwert).
Schleiermacher, F.
1836   'Ueber den sogenannten ersten Brief des Paulos an den Timotheos', in *Sämmtliche Werke*, vol. 1, part 2 (Berlin: G. Reimer).
Schmidt,
K.L.   'καλέω', *TDNT*, vol. 3.
Schnider, F., and W. Stenger.
1987   *Studien zum neutestamentlichen Briefformular* (NTTS 11; Leiden: Brill).
Schreiner, T.R.
1990   *Interpreting the Pauline Epistles* (Grand Rapids: Baker).

1995   'An Interpretation of 1 Timothy 2:9–15: A Dialogue with Scholarship', in A.J. Köstenberger, T.R. Schreiner, and H.S. Baldwin (eds.), *Women in the Church: A Fresh Analysis of 1 Timothy 2:9–15* (Grand Rapids: Baker): 105–54.
Schubert, P.
1939a   'The Form and Function of Pauline Letters', *JR* 19: 365–77.

1939b   *Form and Function of the Pauline Thanksgivings* (BZNW 20; Berlin: Alfed Töpelmann).
Scott, E.F.
1936   *The Pastoral Epistles* (New York/London: Harper and Brothers).
Segert, S.   'Semitic Poetic Structures in the New Testament', in *ANRW* II, 25.2, 1458.

Silk, M.S.
1974   *Interaction in Poetic Imagery, with Special Reference to Early Greek Poetry* (Cambridge: Cambridge University Press).
Silva, M.
1995   'Discourse Analysis and Philippians', in S.E. Porter and D.A. Carson (eds.), *Discourse Analysis and Other Topics in Biblical Greek* (JSNTSup 113 Sheffield: Sheffield Academic Press): 102–106.

1996   *Explorations in Exegetical Method: Galatians as a Test Case* (Grand Rapids: Baker Books).
Simpson, E.K.
1954   *The Pastoral Epistles* (London: Tyndale).
Skeat, T.C.
1979   '"Especially the Parchments": A Note on 2 Tim 4.13', *JTS* ns 30: 173–77.
Smith, R.E., and J.A. Beekman.
1981   *A Literary Semantic Analysis of Second Timothy* (Dallas: Summer Institute of Linguistics).
Snyman, A.H.
1991   '*Discourse Analysis*: A Semantic Discourse Analysis of the Letter to

Philemon', in P.J. Hartin and J.H. Petzer (eds.), *Text and Interpretation: New Approaches in the Criticism of the New Testament* (NTTS 15; Leiden: E.J. Brill).

Sophocles, E.A.
1914   *A Greek Lexicon of the Roman and Byzantine Periods (from B.C. 146 to A.D. 100)* (Cambridge: Harvard University Press).

Soulen, R.N.
1977   *Handbook of Biblical Criticism* (London: Lutterworth Press).

Spencer, A.B.
1990   'God's Order is Truth', *Brethren in Christ, History and Life* 13: 51–63.

1991   'Literary Criticism', in D.A. Black and D.S. Dockery (eds.), *New Testament Criticism and Interpretation* (Grand Rapids: Zondervan): 227–51.

Spicq, C.
1969   *Les Épîtres Pastorales* (Paris: J. Gabalda; 4th edn).
Stählin, G.   'αἰτέω', *TDNT*, vol. 1.
Stamps, D.L.
1995   'Rhetorical Criticism and the New Testament: Ancient and Modern Evaluations', in S.E. Porter and D. Tombs (eds.), *Approaches to New Testament Study* (JSNTSup 120; Sheffield: Sheffield Academic Press): 126–69.

1997   'Rhetorical and Narratological Criticism', in S.E. Porter (ed.), *Handbook to Exegesis of the New Testament* (NTTS 25; Leiden: Brill): 219–39.
Stauffer, E. 'ἀγών', *TDNT*, vol. 1.
Steele, R.B.
1902   'Chiasmus in the Epistles of Cicero, Seneca, Pliny and Fronto', in *Studies in Honor of Basil L. Gildersleeve* (Baltimore: Johns Hopkins Press): 339–52.

Sternberg, M.
1985   *The Poetics of Biblical Narrative: Ideological Literature and the Drama of Reading* (Bloomington: Indiana University Press).

Stettler, H.
1998   *Die Christologie der Pastoralbriefe* (WUNT 2.105; Tübingen: J.C.B. Mohr [Paul Siebeck]).

Stiefel, J.H.
1995   'Women Deacons in 1 Timothy: A Linguistic and Literary Look at "Women Likewise ..." (1 Tim 3.11)', *NTS* 41: 442–57.

Stirewalt, M.L.
1974   'Official Letter Writing and the Letter of Paul to the Churches of Galatia', unpublished paper presented to SBL Paul Seminar.

1977   'The Form and Function of the Greek Letter-Essay', in K.P.

Donfried (ed.), *The Romans Debate* (Minneapolis: Augsburg Publishing House): 175–206.

Stirewalt, M.L., Jr.

1993   *Studies in Ancient Greek Epistolography* (Atlanta: Scholars Press).

Stock, A.

1984   'Chiastic Awareness and Education in Antiquity', *BTB* 14: 23–27.

Stowers, S.K.

1986   *Letter Writing in Greco-Roman Antiquity* (Philadelphia: Westminster).

1988   'Social Typification and the Classification of Ancient Letters', in J. Neusner, *et al.* (eds.), *The Social World of Formative Christianity and Judaism* (Philadelphia: Fortress Press): 78–89.

Sumney, J.L.

2000   *'Servants of Satan', 'False Brothers' and Other Opponents of Paul* (JSNTSup 188; Sheffield: Sheffield Academic Press).

Synge, F.C.

1965   'Studies in Texts: 1 Timothy 5.13–16', *Theology* 68: 200–201.

Tate, W.R.

1997   *Biblical Interpretation, An Integrated Approach* (rev. edn; Peabody, MA: Hendrickson).

Thatcher, T.

1995   'The Relational Matrix of the Pastoral Epistles', *JETS* 38: 51–62.

Thiselton, A.C.

1980   *The Two Horizons: New Testament Hermeneutics and Philosophical Descriptions* (Grand Rapids: Eerdmans).

1995   'New Testament Interpretation in Historical Perspective', in J.B. Green (ed.), *Hearing the New Testament: Strategies for Interpretation* (Grand Rapids: Eerdmans): 10–36.

Thomson, I.H.

1995   *Chiasmus in the Pauline Letters* (JSNTSup 111; Sheffield: Sheffield Academic Press).

Thurén, J.

1970   'Die Struktur der Schlussparänese 1 Tim 6,3–21', *TZ* 26: 241–53.

Thuren, L.

1993   'On Studying Ethical Argumentation and Persuasion in the New Testament', in S.E. Porter and T.H. Olbricht (eds.), *Rhetoric and the New Testament, Essays from the 1992 Heidelberg Conference* (JSNTSup 90; Sheffield: JSOT Press): 464–78.

Trible, P.

1978   *God and the Rhetoric of Sexuality* (Philadelphia: Fortress).

Thurston, B.

1998   'The Theology of Titus', paper presented to the Disputed Paulines Group, SBL.

Towner, P.H.
1986   'The Present Age in the Eschatology of the Pastoral Epistles', *NTS* 32: 427–48.

1987   'Gnosis and Realized Eschatology in Ephesus (of the Pastoral Epistles) and the Corinthian Enthusiasm', *JSNT* 31: 95–124.

1989   *The Goal of Our Instruction: The Structure and Theology of Ethics in the Pastoral Epistles* (JSNTSup 34; Sheffield: Sheffield Academic Press).

1994   'Structure and Meaning in Titus' (unpublished paper).

1995   'Pauline Theology or Pauline Tradition in the Pastoral Epistles: The Question of Method', *TynBul* 46.2: 287–314.

1997   'Can Slaves Be Their Masters' Benefactors?', *Current Trends in Scripture Translation* 182/183: 39–52.

Turner, M.
1995   'Modern Linguistics and the New Testament', in J.B. Green (ed.), *Hearing the New Testament: Strategies for Interpretation* (Grand Rapids: Eerdmans): 146–74.

Turner, N.
1963   *Syntax* (Edinburgh: T. & T. Clark).

Vanhoye, A.
1976   *La Structure littéraire de l'Épître aux Hébreux* (Paris: Desclée de Brouwer; 2nd edn).

1989   *Structure and Message of the Epistle to the Hebrews* (Rome: Editrice Pontificio Istituto Biblico).

Van Neste, R.
2002   'Structure and Cohesion in Titus', *BT* 53.1: 118–33.

2003   'The Message of Titus: An Overview', *The Southern Baptist Journal of Theology* 7.3: 18–30.

Verner, D.C.
1983   *The Household of God: The Social World of the Pastoral Epistles* (SBLDS 71; Chico, CA: Scholars Press).

Vorster, J.N.
1990   'Toward an Interactional Model for the Analysis of Letters', *Neotestamentica* 24.2: 118–25.

Wagener, U.
1994   *Die Ordnung des 'Hauses Gottes': der Ort von Frauen in der Ekklesiologie und Ethik der Pastoralbriefe* (WUNT 2.65; Tübingen: J.C.B. Mohr [Paul Siebeck]).

Watson, D.F.
1992   'Rhetorical Criticism', in J.B. Green, S. McKnight, and I.H.

Marshall (eds.), *Dictionary of Jesus and the Gospels* (Downers Grove, IL: InterVarsity Press).

1997a   'The Integration of Epistolary and Rhetorical Analysis of Philippians', in S.E. Porter and T.H. Olbricht (eds.), *The Rhetorical Analysis of Scripture, Essays from the 1995 London Conference* (JSNTSup 146; Sheffield: Sheffield Academic Press): 398–426.

1997b   'Structuralism and Discourse Analysis', in R.P. Martin and P.H. Davids (eds.), *Dictionary of the Later New Testament and its Developments* (Downers Grove, IL: InterVarsity Press).

Weima, J.A.D.
1994   *Neglected Endings: The Significance of the Pauline Letter Closings* (JSNTSup 101; Sheffield: JSOT Press).

Weiser, A.
1989   'Titus 2 als Gemeindeparänese', in H. Merklein (ed.), *Neues Testament und Ethik* (Freiburg: Herder): 397–41.

Welch, J.W. (ed.)
1981   *Chiasmus in Antiquity* (Hildesheim: Gerstenberg).

Wendland, E.R.
1992   'Cohesion in Colossians: A Structural-Thematic Outline', *Notes on Translation* 6: 28–62.

1999   '"Let No One Disregard You!" (Titus 2:15): Church Discipline and the Construction of Discourse in a Personal, "Pastoral' Epistle"', in S.E. Porter and J.T. Reed (eds.), *Discourse Analysis and the New Testament* (JSNTSup 170; Sheffield: Sheffield Academic Press): 334–51.

Werner, J.R.
1982   'Discourse Analysis of the Greek New Testament', in J.H. Skilton and C.A. Ladley (eds.), *The New Testament Student and His Field* (Phillipsburg, NJ: Presbyterian and Reformed Publishing Company).

White, J.L.
1971a   'Introductory Formulae in the Body of the Pauline Letter', *JBL* 90: 91–97.

1971b   'The Structural Analysis of Philemon: A Point of Departure in the Formal Analysis of the Pauline Letter', in SBL Seminar Papers. 107th Annual Meeting (Missoula, MT: Scholars Press): 1–47.

1972a   *The Body of the Greek Letter* (SBLDS 2; Cambridge, MA: Scholars Press).

1972b   *The Form and Structure of the Official Petition: A Study in Greek Epistolography* (SBLDS 5; Missoula, MT: Scholars Press).

1983   'Saint Paul and the Apostolic Letter Tradition', *CBQ* 45: 433–44.

1984   'New Testament Epistolary Literature in the Framework of Ancient Epistolography', in *ANRW*, II: 25.2, H. Temporini and W. Hasse (eds.), 1730–1756 (Berlin: Walter de Gruyter).

1986   *Light from Ancient Letters* (Philadelphia: Fortress).

1988   'Ancient Greek Letters', in D.E. Aune (ed.), *Greco-Roman Literature and the New Testament* (Atlanta: Scholars Press): 96–99.

1993   'Apostolic Mission and Apostolic Message: Congruence in Paul's Epistolary Rhetoric, Structure and Imagery', in B.H. McLean (ed.), *Origins and Method: Towards a New Understanding of Judaism and Christianity, Essays in Honor of John C. Hurd* (JSNTSup 86; Sheffield: JSOT Press): 145–61.

White, J.L., and K.A. Kensinger.

1976   'Categories of Greek Papyrus Letters', in G. McRae (ed.), *SBL 1976 Seminar Papers* (Missoula: Scholars Press): 79–91.

Wilder, A.N.

1971   *Early Christian Rhetoric: The Language of the Gospel* (Cambridge: Harvard University Press).

Wilson, S.G.

1979   *Luke and the Pastoral Epistles* (London: SPCK).

Winter, B.W.

1988   'Providentia for Widows of 1 Timothy 5:3–16', *TynBul* 39: 83–99.

1993   'Rhetoric', in G.F. Hawthorne, R.P. Martin, and D.G. Reid (eds.), *Dictionary of Paul and His Letters* (Downers Grove, IL: IVP).

Wolter, M.

1988   *Die Pastoralbriefe als Paulustradition* (FRLANT 146; Göttingen: Vandenhoeck und Ruprecht).

Wuellner, W.

1979   'Greek Rhetoric and Pauline Argumentation', in W.R. Schoedel and R.L. Wilken (eds.), *Early Christian Literature and the Classical Intellectual Tradition* (Paris: Beauchsene): 177–88.

1987   'Where is Rhetorical Criticism Taking Us?', *CBQ* 49: 448–63.

1991   '*Rhetorical Criticism*: Rhetorical Criticism and its Theory in Culture Critical Perspective: The Narrative Rhetoric of John 11', in P.J. Hartin and J.H. Petzer (eds.), *Text and Interpretation: New Approaches in the Criticism of the New Testament* (NTTS 15; Leiden: E.J. Brill): 171–85.

Young, F.

1994   *The Theology of the Pastoral Epistles* (Cambridge: Cambridge University Press).

SCRIPTURE REFERENCE INDEX

AUTHOR INDEX